G000097493

FARM LABOR: 21ST CENTURY ISSUES AND CHALLENGES

FARM LABOR: 21ST CENTURY ISSUES AND CHALLENGES

ALVIN W. BURTON

AND

IRWIN B. TELPOV

EDITOR

Nova Science Publishers, Inc.

New York

For permission to use material from this book please contact us:
Telephone 631-231-7269; Fax 631-231-8175
Web Site: http://www.novapublishers.com

NOTICE TO THE READER

The Publisher has taken reasonable care in the preparation of this book, but makes no expressed or implied warranty of any kind and assumes no responsibility for any errors or omissions. No liability is assumed for incidental or consequential damages in connection with or arising out of information contained in this book. The Publisher shall not be liable for any special, consequential, or exemplary damages resulting, in whole or in part, from the readers' use of, or reliance upon, this material.

Independent verification should be sought for any data, advice or recommendations contained in this book. In addition, no responsibility is assumed by the publisher for any injury and/or damage to persons or property arising from any methods, products, instructions, ideas or otherwise contained in this publication.

This publication is designed to provide accurate and authoritative information with regard to the subject matter covered herein. It is sold with the clear understanding that the Publisher is not engaged in rendering legal or any other professional services. If legal or any other expert assistance is required, the services of a competent person should be sought. FROM A DECLARATION OF PARTICIPANTS JOINTLY ADOPTED BY A COMMITTEE OF THE AMERICAN BAR ASSOCIATION AND A COMMITTEE OF PUBLISHERS.

LIBRARY OF CONGRESS CATALOGING-IN-PUBLICATION DATA

Farm labor : 21st century issues and challenges / Alvin W. Burton and Irwin B. Telpov (editors).
    p. cm.
 ISBN 978-1-60456-005-3 (hardcover)
 1. Agricultural laborers--United States. 2. Agricultural laborers, Foreign--United States. I. Burton, Alvin W. II. Telpov, Irwin B.
 HD1525.F292 2007
 331.7'830973--dc22
                              2007041498

Published by Nova Science Publishers, Inc. ✤ New York

CONTENTS

Preface   **vii**

Chapter 1   Migrant and Seasonal Agricultural Workers:
                 Protective Statutes   **1**
                 William G. Whittaker

Chapter 2   Labor Practices in the Meat Packing and
                 Poultry Processing Industry: An Overview   **63**
                 William G. Whittaker

Chapter 3   Immigration: Policy Considerations Related to
                 Guest Worker Programs   **109**
                 Andorra Bruno

Chapter 4   The Comprehensive Immigration Reform Act
                 of 2006 (S. 2611): Potential Labor Market Effects
                 of the Guest Worker Program   **145**
                 Gerald Mayer

Chapter 5   Farm Labor Shortages and Immigration Policy   **173**
                 Linda Levine

Chapter 6   The Effects on U.S. Farm Workers of an
                 Agricultural Guest Worker Program   **189**
                 Linda Levine

Chapter 7   Farm Labor: The Adverse Effect Wage Rate (AEWR)   **195**
                 William G. Whittaker

Index   **201**

PREFACE

Farm labor was and remains an extremely controversial issue. This new book presents in-depth analyses relevant at the outset of the 21st century.

Chapter 1 - Workers in agriculture, generally, have experienced a different pattern of labor-management relations and labor standards than those in the industrial workforce. In part, such disparity was related to the nature of the work and the workforce. Some agricultural workers have tended to be migratory or seasonal — and they have tended to be employed, more or less casually, for short periods by any single employer who, perhaps not surprisingly, did not want to be burdened by a regular employer/employee relationship. Some agricultural workers are skilled; the majority are probably marginally skilled or unskilled — though they perform necessary services.

Two pieces of legislation, sequentially, have dealt in a significant manner with migrant or seasonal agricultural labor. *In 1964*, Congress passed the Farm Labor Contractor Registration Act (FLCRA). For a decade, little attention was paid to the statute, but then, in 1974, it was amended and suddenly, a storm of protest was heard. It was argued that the *wrong people* were being forced to register. Through the next nine years, various interests sought modification of the act to conform to their perceptions of the original intent of the Congress. *In 1983*, Congress repealed the FLCRA and replaced it with the Migrant and Seasonal Agricultural Workers' Protection Act (MSPA). With a very few exceptions, MSPA has operated without controversy. But, at the same time, some may ask, has the new enactment been effective?

The two statutes — FLCRA and MSPA — are intimately connected and have triggered similar reactions with respect to immigration policy, to the inability of agricultural workers to organize and to bargain collectively, and to more general labor standards. Some have suggested that practices under FLCRA and of MSPA have been unduly burdensome. Has the concept of *farm labor contractor* been defined with sufficient care? Have agricultural interests made effective use of their employees, providing them with training and with consistency of employment? Might better utilization of employees prove more productive and more profitable? And, might these changes, in turn, prove more attractive to domestic American workers?

This chapter is a summary and a survey, spelling out the considerations that Congress found were necessary to face. It begins in the 1960s with the advent of FLCRA, and proceeds through the enactment of MSPA and to the end of the century. But, it is also *a summary* of developments in the history of the two statutes, written from the perspective of a labor economist. It may, from time to time, be revised as new developments occur.

During the late 1950s, a general congressional interest had developed in the condition of migratory or seasonal farm workers in the United States. Several exploratory hearings had been held, but no new legislation had been adopted. Then, on a Friday evening, the day after Thanksgiving (1960), a television program aired—Harvest of Shame, with Edward R. Murrow.

"Harvest of Shame was a report on the plight of the migratory farm workers ... who as virtual peons kept the nation's larders stocked. The public reaction to it was one of surprised horror at the conditions portrayed. Farm organizations were horrified for other reasons, charging 'highly colored propaganda' and 'deceit.' Farmers' spokesmen demanded 'equal time'...."

The Murrow broadcast emphasized the risks and hazards associated with crew leaders and agricultural employment at large. Whatever the flaws of the film, it provided a context for various pieces of migrant and seasonal farmworker legislation that had been (and would continue to be) before the Congress.

Through the next several years, Congress would consider a number of pieces of remedial legislation focusing upon the farm environment. Two bills that became law are of special importance: the *Farm Labor Contractor Registration Act* (FLCRA: 1964-1983) and a successor statute, the *Migrant and Seasonal Agricultural Workers' Protection Act* (MSPA: 1983 ff.). The two statutes, sequentially, provide the basis for regulation of migrant agricultural and seasonal agricultural workers. A focal point of each of the statutes, however, has been the farm labor contractor.

Through nearly 50 years, intermittently, the Congress has debated the two statutes and their implications — for labor supply, for immigration, and for equity for the several parties involved. The issues have changed little through the years, though their focus may have altered. Initially (up to 1974), concern was voiced with respect to farm labor contractors and their alleged excesses. Then, after the 1974 amendments to FLCRA, concern moved away from contractors and toward those who used migrant and seasonal workers — essentially, the growers and their agents. In 1983, FLCRA was repealed and replaced with the Migrant and Seasonal Agricultural Workers Protection Act. The latter (MSPA), with few exceptions (notably, the case of *Adams Fruit*; see below), has remained as written. But there have been numerous hearings on the act — and, likely, more will follow. This article summarizes the debates over the acts and their evolution thus far.

Chapter 2 - During the early 1960s, segments of the meat packing industry began to move from large urban centers to small communities scattered throughout the Midwest. By century's end, this migration had effected major changes within the industry. The old packing firms that had established their dominance during the late 1800s had largely disappeared or been restructured as part of a new breed of packers. Joining with the poultry processors who had emerged in the wake of World War II, they quickly became a major force in American and, later, global industry.

The urban-to-rural migration, some suggest, had at least two major motivations. One was to locate packing facilities in areas where animals were raised rather than transporting the stock to urban packinghouses as had been the tradition: a more economical arrangement. The other was a quest for lower labor costs: to leave behind the urban unions and their collective bargaining agreements and to operate, as nearly as possible, in a union-free environment. This initiative involved a low-wage strategy, allowing for employment of lower skilled and low-wage workers.

The aftermath of this migration was complex. The urban unionized workforce, by and large, did not follow the migrating plants. Since most local communities could not provide an adequate supply of labor, the relocation process implied recruitment of workers from outside the area of production. In practice, packers and processors came increasingly to rely upon recent immigrants or, allegedly in some instances, upon workers not authorized for employment in the United States.

Gradually, the new breed packers (and their poultry counterparts) began to dominate the market — through various business arrangements consolidating the industry into a small number of large firms. This corporate *churning* impacted the trade union movement and its relations with the industry. The unions, too, were restructured. The labor-management relationship, largely set during the 1940s, was gradually replaced with new patterns of bargaining. Further, the demographics of the workforce changed with the introduction of a new racial/ethnic and gender mixture. Distances between the rural plants made union organization difficult, as did the new linguistic and cultural differences among workers. Gradually, the workforce was transformed from high-wage, stable, and union, to lower-wage and often non-union, and came to be characterized by a high turnover rate.

From time to time, the Congressional Research Service (CRS) has received requests for information on labor standards and labor-management relations in the meat packing industry. Often, these queries have been associated with the Fair Labor Standards Act and the National Labor Relations Act, but there has been concern with other legislation and issues as well. Some of these areas have been (and continue to be) the subject of litigation. This article is intended as an introduction to the meat packing/processing industry, the unions that have been active in that field, and labor-management practices among the packers and their employees. It will not likely be updated.

During the early 1960s, segments of the meat packing industry began to move from urban centers to rural communities scattered throughout the Midwest. By century's end, this migration had effected major changes within the industry. The old packing firms that had established their dominance during the late 1800s had largely disappeared or had been restructured as part of a *new breed* of packers. Joining with the poultry processors who had emerged in the wake of World War II, they became a major force in American (and, later, global) industry — and a major employer.

Business practices have affected the labor-management relationship, recruitment of workers, and the protective labor standards that apply to persons employed in the industry. The last half of the 20th century witnessed relocation of major firms, a move from predominantly urban to more heavily rural production, and a shift in the demographics of the industry's workforce. The dispersal of the industry, some argue, has also affected the manner in which employment-related law is enforced. Clearly, it has impacted the trade unionization of the workforce. At issue are a number of federal statutes and their administration: the Fair Labor Standards Act, the National Labor Relations Act, the Occupational Safety and Health Act and, potentially, the Migrant and Seasonal Agricultural Workers Protection Act. Similarly, both the industry and its workforce have been affected by federal immigration policy. These general areas have been a continuing focus of Department of Labor (DOL) action and of litigation.

This article provides an introduction to labor issues in meat packing and poultry processing. It sketches the evolution of the industry and of the related trade union movement, stressing development of corporate and trade union cultures and the shifting demographics of the workforce. It notes areas of tension and conflict within and between both labor and management. And, it points to considerations of public policy that affect the continuing labor-management relationship.

Chapter 3 - At present, the United States has two main programs for temporarily importing low-skilled workers, sometimes referred to as guest workers. Agricultural guest workers enter through the H-2A visa program, and other guest workers enter through the H-2B visa program. Employers interested in importing workers under either program must first apply to the U.S. Department of Labor for a certification that U.S. workers capable of performing the work are not available and that the employment of alien workers will not adversely affect the wages and working conditions of similarly employed U.S. workers. Other requirements of the programs differ.

The 109th Congress revised the H-2B program in the FY2005 Emergency Supplemental Appropriations Act (P.L. 109-13). Among the changes, a temporary provision was added to the Immigration and Nationality Act (INA) to exempt certain returning H-2B workers from the H-2B annual numerical cap. The FY2007 Department of Defense authorization act (P.L. 109-364) extended this exemption through FY2007. Other bills before the 109th Congress proposed to make changes to the H-2A program (S. 359/H.R. 884, H.R. 3857, S. 2087, Senate-passed S. 2611), the H-2B program (S. 278, H.R. 1587, S. 1438, S. 1918), and the "H" visa category generally (H.R. 3333), and to establish new temporary worker visas (S. 1033/H.R. 2330, S. 1438, S. 1918, H.R. 4065, Senate-passed S. 2611). S. 359/H.R. 884, S. 1033/H.R. 2330, S. 1918, and S. 2611 also would have established mechanisms for certain foreign workers to become U.S. legal permanent residents (LPRs). None of these bills were enacted. Various guest worker measures were also introduced in the 108th Congress, but they saw no action beyond committee referrals. President George W. Bush proposed a new, expanded temporary worker program in January 2004 when he announced his principles for immigration reform. In a May 2006 national address on comprehensive immigration reform, he reiterated his support for a temporary worker program.

The current discussion of guest worker programs takes place against a backdrop of historically high levels of unauthorized migration to the United States. Supporters of a large-scale temporary worker program argue that such a program would help reduce unauthorized immigration by providing a legal alternative for prospective foreign workers. Critics reject this reasoning and instead maintain that a new guest worker program would likely exacerbate the problem of illegal migration.

The consideration of any proposed guest worker program raises various issues, including the following: how new program requirements would compare with those of the H-2A and H-2B programs; how the eligible population would be defined; whether the program would include a mechanism for participants to obtain LPR status; how family members of eligible individuals would be treated; what labor market test, if any, the program would employ; whether the program would be numerically limited; how the rules and requirements of the program would be enforced; and what security-related provisions, if any, would be included.

Chapter 4 - In the 109th Congress, the Senate passed S. 2611, the Comprehensive Immigration Reform Act of 2006, which would have created a new H-2C guest worker program. The 110th Congress may consider similar legislation.

The guest worker program included in S. 2611 would allow up to 200,000 foreign workers into the United States annually. An employer would have to pay an H-2C worker the greater of the "actual" wage paid by the employer to other workers who do the same kind of work and have similar experience or the "prevailing" wage. Employers would be prevented from hiring H-2C workers if the area unemployment rate for unskilled workers averaged more than 9% for the previous six months. The language in S. 2611 would allow employers to hire skilled, semi-skilled, or unskilled workers, but not agricultural workers or certain types of skilled workers. The kinds of jobs filled under the H-2C program could be similar to the kinds of jobs filled under an existing (H-2B) program, which is used mainly to hire lower-skilled workers.

Initially, an increased supply of lower-skilled foreign workers could be expected to lower the relative wages of lower-skilled U.S. workers. If the H-2C program were enacted, an increased supply of lower-skilled foreign workers may have the greatest impact on young, native-born minority men and on foreign-born minority men in their early working years. In 2005, lower-skilled U.S. workers were mainly white, non-Hispanic males under the age of 45. But a disproportionate number of these workers were young (16 to 24), minority (black or Hispanic) men. The unemployment rate among young, native-born minority men tends to be higher than among similar nonminority men. In 2005, almost a fifth of lower-skilled workers were foreign born, and a disproportionate number of these were minority (nonwhite or Hispanic) men in their early working years (25 to 44). Foreign-born minority men in their early working years tend to earn less than similar native-born workers.

In response to an initial decline in the relative wages of lower-skilled workers employers may hire more lower-skilled workers and fewer skilled workers. Thus, the initial widening of the wage gap may narrow over time. Other factors — such as technological change, trade, saving and investment, education and training, demographic changes — may also affect the wages of U.S. workers.

The H-2C program could be used by employers to meet seasonal demand, to hire foreign workers at full employment, or to fill jobs when there is a mismatch in a geographic area between the skills demanded and the skills available. In each case, U.S. workers may not be available at the wages offered. They may or may not be available at higher wages.

If employers are not able to hire qualified U.S. workers in high unemployment areas (i.e., more than 9%), there may be a mismatch between the skills available and the skills employers need.

Chapter 5 - The connection between farm labor and immigration policies is a longstanding one, particularly with regard to U.S. employers' use of workers from Mexico. The Congress is revisiting the issue as it continues debate over initiation of a broad-based guest worker program, increased border enforcement, and employer sanctions to curb the flow of unauthorized workers into the United States.

Two decades ago, the Congress passed the Immigration Reform and Control Act (IRCA, P.L. 99-603) to reduce illegal entry into the United States by imposing sanctions on employers who knowingly hire individuals who lack permission to work in the country. In addition to a general legalization program, IRCA included legalization programs specific to the agricultural industry that were intended to compensate for the act's expected impact on the farm labor supply and encourage the development of a legal crop workforce. These provisions of the act, however, have not operated in the offsetting manner that was intended, as substantial numbers of unauthorized aliens have continued to join legal farmworkers in performing seasonal agricultural services (SAS).

Currently, a little more than one-half of the SAS workforce is not authorized to hold U.S. jobs. Perishable crop growers contend that their sizable presence implies a shortage of native-born workers willing to undertake seasonal farm jobs. (An increasing share of IRCA-legalized farmworkers have entered the ages of diminished participation in the SAS workforce, as well.) Grower advocates argue that farmers would rather not employ unauthorized workers because doing so puts them at risk of incurring penalties. Farmworker advocates counter that crop growers prefer unauthorized workers because they are in a weak bargaining position with regard to wages and working conditions. If the supply of unauthorized workers were curtailed, it is claimed, farmers could adjust to a smaller workforce by introducing labor-efficient technologies and management practices, and by raising wages, which, in turn, would entice more U.S. workers to seek farm employment. Farmers respond that further mechanization would be difficult for some crops, and that substantially higher wages would make the U.S. industry uncompetitive in the world marketplace — without expanding the legal farm labor force. These remain untested arguments because perishable crop growers have rarely, if ever, operated without unauthorized aliens in their workforces.

Trends in the agricultural labor market generally do not suggest the existence of a nationwide shortage of domestically available farmworkers, in part because the government's databases cover authorized *and* unauthorized employment. (This finding does not preclude the possibility of spot labor shortages, however.) Farm employment did not show the same upward trend of total U.S. employment during the 1990s expansion. The length of time hired farmworkers are employed has changed little or decreased over the years. Their unemployment rate has varied little and remains well above the U.S. average, and underemployment among farmworkers also remains substantial. These agricultural employees earn about 50 cents for every dollar paid to other employees in the private sector.

Chapter 6 - Guest worker programs are meant to assure employers (e.g., fruit, vegetable, and horticultural specialty growers) of an adequate supply of labor when and where it is needed while not adding permanent residents to the U.S. population. They include mechanisms, such as the H-2A program's labor certification process, intended to avoid adversely affecting the wages and working conditions of similarly employed U.S. workers. If amendment of the H-2A program or initiation of a new agricultural guest worker program led growers to employ many more aliens than is now the case, the effects of the Bracero program might be instructive: although the 1942-1964 Bracero program succeeded in expanding the farm labor supply, studies estimate that it also harmed domestic farm workers as measured by their reduced wages and employment. The magnitudes of these adverse effects might differ today depending upon how much the U.S. farm labor and product markets have changed over time, but their direction likely would be the same.

The nation has had a long history of guest worker programs targeted at the agricultural industry, which have enabled farmers to temporarily import foreign workers to perform seasonal jobs without adding permanent residents to the U.S. population. Unsuccessful attempts were made during the past few Congresses to amend the H-2A program, the only means currently available to employers who want to legally utilize aliens in temporary farm jobs. Recent interest among some Members of Congress in a broad-based guest worker program has renewed efforts to enact legislation that relates specifically to the agricultural sector (e.g., S. 359/H.R. 884, the Agricultural Job Opportunity, Benefits, and Security Act; H.R. 3857, the Temporary Agricultural Labor Reform Act; and S. 2087 (Agricultural Employment and Workforce Protection Act).

Chapter 7 - American agricultural employers have long utilized foreign workers on a temporary basis, regarding them as an important labor resource. At the same time, the relatively low wages and adverse working conditions of such workers have caused them to be viewed as a threat to domestic American workers.

Some have argued that foreign *guest workers* compete unfairly with U.S. workers in at least two respects. First, they are alleged to compete unfairly in terms of the compensation that they are willing to accept. Second, their presence is alleged to render it more difficult for domestic workers to organize and to bargain collectively with management.

To mitigate any "adverse effect"for the domestic workforce, a system of wage floors was developed that applies, variously, both to alien and citizen workers —i.e., the *adverse effect wage rate* (AEWR).

This article deals with one element of the immigration issue: the question of the use of H-2A workers. It introduces the *adverse effect wage rate*, it examines the concerns out of which it grew, and it explains at least some of the problems that have been encountered in giving it effect.

The article is based, statistically, upon the AEWR issued each spring by the Employment and Training Administration, U.S. Department of Labor. It will be updated periodically as new information becomes available.

The article is written *from the perspective of labor policy, not of immigration policy.* For discussion of immigration policy, see the Current Legislative Issues (CLIs) on the Congressional Research Service webpage.

In: Farm Labor: 21st Century Issues and Challenges   ISBN: 978-1-60456-005-3
Editors: A. W. Burton, I. B. Telpov, pp. 1-61   © 2007 Nova Science Publishers, Inc.

Chapter 1

MIGRANT AND SEASONAL AGRICULTURAL WORKERS: PROTECTIVE STATUTES[*]

William G. Whittaker

ABSTRACT

Workers in agriculture, generally, have experienced a different pattern of labor-management relations and labor standards than those in the industrial workforce. In part, such disparity was related to the nature of the work and the workforce. Some agricultural workers have tended to be migratory or seasonal — and they have tended to be employed, more or less casually, for short periods by any single employer who, perhaps not surprisingly, did not want to be burdened by a regular employer/employee relationship. Some agricultural workers are skilled; the majority are probably marginally skilled or unskilled — though they perform necessary services.

Two pieces of legislation, sequentially, have dealt in a significant manner with migrant or seasonal agricultural labor. *In 1964*, Congress passed the Farm Labor Contractor Registration Act (FLCRA). For a decade, little attention was paid to the statute, but then, in 1974, it was amended and suddenly, a storm of protest was heard. It was argued that the *wrong people* were being forced to register. Through the next nine years, various interests sought modification of the act to conform to their perceptions of the original intent of the Congress. *In 1983*, Congress repealed the FLCRA and replaced it with the Migrant and Seasonal Agricultural Workers' Protection Act (MSPA). With a very few exceptions, MSPA has operated without controversy. But, at the same time, some may ask, has the new enactment been effective?

The two statutes — FLCRA and MSPA — are intimately connected and have triggered similar reactions with respect to immigration policy, to the inability of agricultural workers to organize and to bargain collectively, and to more general labor standards. Some have suggested that practices under FLCRA and of MSPA have been unduly burdensome. Has the concept of *farm labor contractor* been defined with sufficient care? Have agricultural interests made effective use of their employees, providing them with training and with consistency of employment? Might better utilization of employees prove more productive and more profitable? And, might these changes, in turn, prove more attractive to domestic American workers?

---

[*] Excerpted from CRS Report 33372, dated May 24, 2006.

This article is a summary and a survey, spelling out the considerations that Congress found were necessary to face. It begins in the 1960s with the advent of FLCRA, and proceeds through the enactment of MSPA and to the end of the century. But, it is also *a summary* of developments in the history of the two statutes, written from the perspective of a labor economist. It may, from time to time, be revised as new developments occur.

During the late 1950s, a general congressional interest had developed in the condition of migratory or seasonal farm workers in the United States. Several exploratory hearings had been held, but no new legislation had been adopted. Then, on a Friday evening, the day after Thanksgiving (1960), a television program aired —Harvest of Shame, with Edward R. Murrow.

"Harvest of Shame was a report on the plight of the migratory farm workers ... who as virtual peons kept the nation's larders stocked. The public reaction to it was one of surprised horror at the conditions portrayed. Farm organizations were horrified for other reasons, charging 'highly colored propaganda' and 'deceit.' Farmers' spokesmen demanded 'equal time'...."[1]

The Murrow broadcast emphasized the risks and hazards associated with crew leaders and agricultural employment at large. Whatever the flaws of the film, it provided a context for various pieces of migrant and seasonal farmworker legislation that had been (and would continue to be) before the Congress.

Through the next several years, Congress would consider a number of pieces of remedial legislation focusing upon the farm environment. Two bills that became law are of special importance: the *Farm Labor Contractor Registration Act* (FLCRA: 1964-1983) and a successor statute, the *Migrant and Seasonal Agricultural Workers' Protection Act* (MSPA: 1983 ff.). The two statutes, sequentially, provide the basis for regulation of migrant agricultural and seasonal agricultural workers. A focal point of each of the statutes, however, has been the farm labor contractor.

Through nearly 50 years, intermittently, the Congress has debated the two statutes and their implications — for labor supply, for immigration, and for equity for the several parties involved. The issues have changed little through the years, though their focus may have altered. Initially (up to 1974), concern was voiced with respect to farm labor contractors and their alleged excesses. Then, after the 1974 amendments to FLCRA, concern moved away from contractors and toward those who used migrant and seasonal workers — essentially, the growers and their agents. In 1983, FLCRA was repealed and replaced with the Migrant and Seasonal Agricultural Workers Protection Act. The latter (MSPA), with few exceptions (notably, the case of *Adams Fruit*; see below), has remained as written. But there have been numerous hearings on the act — and, likely, more will follow. This article summarizes the debates over the acts and their evolution thus far.

PART I. THE FARM LABOR CONTRACTOR REGISTRATION ACT, ORIGINS, AND CONGRESSIONAL ENACTMENT (1964)

The farm labor contractor (or crew leader) "is the bridge between the farm operator and the migrant laborer." Farm operators would go south each year to "meet the crew leader" and arrange for migratory crews. A large majority of migrants belong to crews. In 1960, it was

---

1 Alexander Kendrick, Prime Time: The Life of Edward R. Murrow (Boston: Little, Brown and Company, 1969), p. 453.

reported, the largest crew numbered 185 workers, the smallest 13 — with the usual size between 45 and 74 members. The crews grew out of "the need of inarticulate people to have someone to speak for them" and the farmer's problem "of recruiting and handling labor."[2]

In 1959, Senator Harrison Williams (D-NJ) introduced legislation seeking, through federal registration, "to eliminate the relatively few migrant labor contractors who are dishonest and immoral, and who exploit migrant workers and growers." A slightly different bill was introduced by Senators Jacob Javits (R-NY) and Kenneth Keating (R-NY). In the House, Representative James Roosevelt (D-CA) was an early sponsor of such legislation.[3] Neither of these bills was approved. It would take hearings and subsequent refinement through three Congresses before adoption.

THE VARIOUS ROLES OF THE FARM LABOR CONTRACTOR

In theory, the crew leader is an "independent businessman" with varied tasks. Some crew leaders do little more than recruit for farm operators — but for a farmer several hundred (or several thousand) miles away from the areas of labor supply, that task is monumental. Others become more deeply involved in the management of the crew. The report to the Senate Subcommittee on Migratory Labor (1960) observed that

> "Some ... provide transportation for the migrant. Others oversee the work of the crew upon its arrival; manage the camps where the migrants are housed; provide the commissary and food facilities; pay the crew members; haul the produce from the fields to the packing sheds...."

The profit for the farm labor contractor "lies in the differential between what they are paid by the farmer and [what they] pay to the worker." Some crew leaders work on a commission basis, taking a few cents from each item produced by crew members.[4]

The list of alleged abuses associated with the farm labor contractor appears to have been as long and varied as those engaged in the field. As the 1961 hearings commenced, William Batt, Pennsylvania's Secretary of Labor and Industry, noted "The good ones [crew leaders] say to me, 'I preach to the men to save their money.'" Of the less desirable crew leaders, Batt noted the then standard complaints:

> "Changing wage rates without explanation." "Exploitation of child labor." "Illegal sale of alcoholic beverages." "Charging the workers a rental fee on housing provided free by the grower." "Importation of prostitutes, with sharing of the 'take.'" "Food profiteering in crew-leader-operated commissaries." "Hunting deer out of season." "Shooting and beating up other crew leaders." "Rigged crew-leader-operated gambling games." "Paying crew members in 'scrip' in lieu of cash." "Charging exorbitant transportation fees."

---

2 U.S. Congress, Senate, Subcommittee on Migratory Labor of the Committee on Labor and Public Welfare. 86th Cong., 2nd Sess. (1960). Committee Print, The Migrant Farm Worker in America, p. 34. Report by Daniel H. Pollitt, et al. Cited hereafter as Pollitt, The Migrant Farm Worker in America.

3 Pollitt, The Migrant Farm Worker in America, pp. 36-38.

4 Ibid., pp. 34-36.

Batt continued. "In the case of one crew leader who kept accurate wage records, the services of a prostitute were a payroll deductible item."[5]

Matt Triggs, speaking for the American Farm Bureau Federation and defending the contractors, suggested that stories of abuse were "told and retold" with a "misleading implication that there is more of this than there really is."[6] Another witness, with legislation in mind, argued that contractors "are educationally unequipped to perform the laborious clerical function this bill would impose."[7] A third stated that with their "limited education," the contractors would be "unable to fill out the necessary forms" that the act will require.[8] Yet another declared "They are not schooled.... Much recordkeeping, much bookkeeping is anathema to them. They are not trained for it."[9] Triggs asserted that "most leaders have previously been migratory workers. They are semi-literate."[10] And, Triggs affirmed, "You have got to realize that an awful lot of these crew leaders are very simple people...."[11]

Nonetheless, contractors may undertake relatively sophisticated responsibilities. Secretary of Labor Willard Wirtz pointed out that, in Oregon, it was "the general practice" of using the crew leader "as a paymaster."[12] The "crew leader acts as an intermediary between the grower and the workers," and in nearly "two thirds (63 percent) of the areas surveyed" nationally, the "workers were paid by the crew leaders...."[13] Similarly, "the crew leader is responsible in certain circumstances for making the necessary deductions and keeping payroll records" with respect to social security participation.[14] Sarah Newman, then of the National

---

5 U.S. Congress, Senate Committee on Labor and Public Welfare, Subcommittee on Migratory Labor. Migratory Labor. Hearings, 87th Cong., 1st Sess., Apr. 12-13, 1961, pp. 45-46. (Hereafter cited as Hearings, Senate, 1961.) See also U.S. Congress, Senate, Subcommittee on Migratory Labor, Committee on Labor and Public Welfare. Migratory Labor Bills. 88th Cong., 1st Sess., Apr. 10, 23, and 24, 1963, pp. 38-40. (Hereafter cited as Hearings, Senate, 1963.)

6 Hearings, Senate, 1961, p. 53.

7 James B. Moore, National Apple Institute, Hearings, Senate, 1961, p. 183.

8 Charles M. Creuziger, Vegetable Growers Association of America, Hearings, Senate, 1961, p. 82.

9 Carroll Miller, West Virginia State Horticultural Society, Hearings, Senate, 1961, p. 125.

10 Hearings, Senate, 1961, p. 54. See U.S. Congress. House, Committee on Education and Labor, Subcommittee on Labor. Migratory Labor. Hearings, 87 Cong., 1st Sess., May 9-10, 1961, and May 19-20, 1961, p. 238 (Hereafter cited as Hearings, House, 1961.)

11 Hearings, House, 1963, p. 15.

12 Hearings, Senate, 1963, pp. 39-40. It would appear that the most frequent cause of concern, where farm labor contractors are involved, were problems associated in some manner with transportation. In the U.S. Congress, Senate, Committee on Labor and Public Welfare, 87th Cong., 1st Sess., Senate Report No 695 to accompany S. 1162, Aug. 9, 1961, p. 5, it is noted that "These abuses include overcharging workers for transportation advances, collecting for transportation expenses from both employers and workers, accepting transportation advances from employers and failing to report to work or reporting with a smaller crew than contractored for, abandoning a crew without means of transportation, and failure to return workers to their homes." (Cited hereafter as Senate Report No. 695, 1961.)

13 Hearings, Senate, 1963, p. 39. The reference was to a brochure, "Summary of Farm Labor Crew Leader Practices," Nov. 1962, prepared by the Farm Labor Service, Bureau of Employment Security, Department of Labor.

14 Senate Report No. 695, 1961, p. 5. During Hearings, House, 1963, p. 97, there was a dialogue between Representative James Roosevelt and Edith E. Lowry, testifying on behalf of the National Advisory Committee on Farm Labor. "Mr. Roosevelt: ... We would also, for social security purposes, have a better way of seeing whether the proper deductions were being made and forwarded to the Federal Government rather than having, as we now suspect, but have very little way of proving, many of them pay social security to the crew leader and yet get no credit for it by the social security headquarters. "Would you consider this was too onerous a task for us to impose upon a crew leader? "Miss Lowry: I don't think so because it seems to me it is essential for anybody who carries the responsibility of handling the affairs for so many people that find difficulty in fitting into our society to be required to handle these things in an orderly way. "I do know there is a real problem in the social security matter."

Consumers League, observed, "Because crew leaders are under no regulated responsibility to anyone, their many abuses have been able to flourish."[15]

ISSUES IN THE EARLY DEBATE

During three Congresses (from 1959 to 1964), numerous bills (not always labor-related) were introduced to ameliorate the conditions of agricultural workers. As these bills evolved, it was difficult to keep their implications separate. The following section analyses, in a general way, deal with issues and concepts common to many of these proposals.

State Versus Federal

"We do not believe this bill would serve any useful purpose since most farm labor contractors are already registered with one or more State employment services," stated Charles Creuziger, spokesperson for the Vegetable Growers Association of America. "We believe, as a matter of principle, that regulation of the contractors can best be handled by the States."[16]

Industry and non-industry forces divided on the issue of federalism. J. Banks Young of the National Cotton Council urged that the issue was strictly local and that federal intervention "would adversely restrict the availability and mobility of such workers and unnecessarily increase farm costs."[17] Noting the alleged abuses under the current system, Richard O'Connell of the National Council of Farmer Cooperatives stressed the local character of the problem. Most states, he suggested, have "laws prohibiting gambling, prostitution, unlawful narcotics, and liquor sales." If so, "the crew leaders should be indicted under the appropriate laws" and, having "paid their debt," should not be harassed.[18] Triggs also thought local government could handle the issue. "Even if the 9 or 10 farm labor bills now before the Congress were to be enacted, we believe they would represent an ineffectual approach to the problem, and in some cases would be decidedly harmful to the interests of workers and farmers."[19]

Observing that the states already had regulations dealing with labor camps, Triggs stated that "... only a handful of these laws are really adequate." Crew leaders "can evade their regulations by ... going to other States with their crews that do not have licensing

---

15 U.S. Congress, House, Committee on Labor, House Committee on Education and Labor, 88th Cong., 1st Sess., Hearing, Registration of Farm Labor Contractors, Apr. 3, 5, and 10, 1963, p. 70. (Cited hereafter as Hearings, House, 1963.) Newman, p. 69, notes: "Because of their dependency on the crew leader, migrant workers are particularly vulnerable to exploitation and abuse by these contractors. Migrants," she explained, "are usually isolated from the community, sometimes never even meeting the grower whose crop they pick. They are dependent on the crew leader for the next job, and for their daily living arrangements."

16 Hearings, Senate, 1963, p. 150. References to "this bill" or to "the bill" are generic. In some cases, it is not clear to which bill a speaker is referring or to an abstract bill. Further, reference is to a series of hearings with different bills.

17 Hearings, House, 1963, pp. 141-142.

18 Hearings, House, 1963, p. 22.

19 Hearings, House, 1963, p. 8.

requirements." If the federal government were to act, it should focus on "the licensing of crew leaders or contractors of migratory labor."[20]

The problem "requires the leadership of the Federal Government," Secretary Wirtz advised, because of the movement of contractors across state lines. A person "... involved in malpractice in this area is simply likely not to be there when somebody charges him."[21] Others concurred. "A fellow who is fined or barred in one State will simply duck into another State and there perhaps commit the same practices," suggested Arnold Mayer of the Amalgamated Meat Cutters and Butcher Workmen of North America. "The migrant labor stream is an interstate stream and dealing with it needs interstate legislation."[22]

Authority for the Secretary

Industry spokespeople questioned the wisdom of granting new authority to the Secretary of Labor to manage agricultural labor supply. "Many of the terms used ... are not clearly defined," stated Young, of the Cotton Council. As it stands, the "... power to issue regulations under the authority of the bill is extremely broad."[23]

The authority granted to the Secretary, remarked James Moore of the National Apple Institute, would "inevitably result in control by the Secretary ... of the agricultural migratory labor market."[24] The requirement "as to their financial responsibility would impose burdens which few individuals recruiting labor could meet."[25] The proposed legislation would establish the Secretary "as judge, jury, and prosecutor," stated Delmer Robinson of the Frederick County (Virginia) Fruitgrowers Association. "We do not feel that a man's livelihood [the contractor's] should depend on the benevolence of the Secretary of Labor."[26] The Secretary, in accord with his own regulations, can put out of business any contractor who has "'failed without justification'" to comply with the regulations — but the proposal "is completely silent as to who would decide whether or not there was 'justification.' It is presumed the Secretary ... could arbitrarily decide this point."[27]

Defining Terms

Through the hearings, concepts to be used in the act were gradually defined. Still, numerous concerns were voiced by industry with respect to the several bills that came before the committees.

---

20 Hearings, Senate, 1961, pp. 23-24.
21 Hearings, House, 1961, p. 116.
22 Hearings, House, 1963, p. 139.
23 Hearings, Senate, 1963, pp. 302-303.
24 Hearings, Senate, 1961, pp. 182-183.
25 Statement from the National Cotton Council, Hearings, House, 1961, p. 216.
26 Hearings, Senate, 1961, p. 63.
27 Hearings, House, 1963, p. 141.

Defining a Contractor

The Farm Bureau favored a narrow definition of contractor with registration "limited to crew leaders proper, and not extended to all persons who may recruit or transport workers." But how might one distinguish between a labor contractor (to be registered) and persons who may recruit or transport workers?[28]

The National Cotton Council argued that contractor, thus far defined, "would require registration of fraternal, religious, social and other organizations which frequently provide temporary agricultural employment for their members" — and to processors "who provide workers to farmers."[29] Others argued that the term might include "charitable and religious organizations" and "4-H advisers."[30] The proposal, it was suggested, "seems to make a crew leader out of everyone who contacts more than nine people"[31] and could include groups such as "sugar companies, canneries, and cotton gins" that provide labor only as "incidental to the main services they offer farmers." These, some felt, should be excluded.[32]

Even true crew leaders often work through "responsible employees" who would not have to register. It was argued "... that employees of any registered entity should not be required to register" but, rather, have "a single certificate of registration for the overall recruitment activity...."[33] The definition of contractor, it was urged, "... should be changed to cover the individual ... who gathers a crew of workers in one State and transports them to another State and stays with them in a supervisory capacity ... and is the actual crew leader."[34] Again: "We would strongly recommend that you eliminate at least the resident concern, the canner who recruits workers for farmers in the territory, the sugar companies, the cotton gins, ... labor associations, and others that are responsible financially...."[35]

Duration of Registration?

"Registration should be permanent and continue in effect until revoked for cause," the Farm Bureau spokesman held. "We see no valid reason for the annual licensing of crew leaders."[36]

The Department of Labor (DOL), however, *did* recognize a need for annual licensing. "The common phrase, 'fly by night' applies, I suppose, more aptly to this economic situation than to almost any other which I can think of," observed Secretary Wirtz.[37] "All the evidence we have indicates that there is considerable turnover among the crew leader personnel," observed Robert Goodwin of DOL's Bureau of Employment Security, making it "necessary, really, to have an annual certification...." Goodwin took note of auto and other insurance.

---

28 Hearings, House, 1963, p. 10.
29 Hearings, House, 1961, p. 216.
30 Hearings, House, 1961, p. 206.
31 Hearings, Senate, 1961, p. 129.
32 Hearings, House, 1963, p. 143.
33 Hearings, House, 1961, p. 206.
34 Hearings, House, 1961, p. 176. (Italics added.)
35 Hearings, Senate, 1963, p. 161. On this issue, see Hearings, House, 1963, pp. 10-13, where there is a dialogue between Representative Roosevelt and Triggs of the Farm Bureau.
36 Hearings, House, 1963, p. 10.
37 Hearings, House, 1963, p. 120.

"This would be issued on an annual basis and would require a determination as to whether the insurance had been purchased and was adequate, and only after that determination was made could the certification be completed. This would require the annual certification."[38]

The International Apple Association raised the issue of fees for service. While the current Secretary may not anticipate a significant fee, a future Secretary "might wish to put the contractors out of business" and could set an unreasonable sum.[39]

Senator Williams tended to agree. "My feeling is if there were a fee," he said, "it should be limited to taking care of the administrative costs...."[40]

Rulemaking Authority of the Secretary

"Eliminate the rulemaking authority...." stated a Farm Bureau spokesman. "The statute is complete in itself and requires no supplemental rulemaking authority."[41]

The rulemaking authority may have posed something of a dilemma for critics. On the one hand, many of the concepts "used in the bill are not clearly defined and will be given meaning only by regulation by the Secretary...." Conversely, the terms of the bill "... would permit the Secretary to require almost any kind of information he might desire" and "... could lead to the control of a large segment of domestic migrant farmworkers." This "broad ... grant of authority ... should be deleted."[42]

"We feel," asserted Robert Rea of the Virginia State Horticultural Society, "that it should be mandatory" for the Secretary to issue a certificate of registration as a migrant labor contractor to any person who files the required information and carries a reasonable amount of insurance. "The mere threat of withholding a certificate," Rea stated, "... places the labor contractor under direct control of the Secretary of Labor. This allows the Secretary to, in effect, dictate wage rates, housing and working conditions that the crew leader must agree to or be threatened with loss of the right to earn a livelihood." The proposal, "as written," he said, could "make the cure worse than the disease."[43]

Crossing State Boundaries

Concerning interstate commerce, Delmer Robinson's ranch straddled the Virginia-West Virginia frontiers. "You can almost figure that an employee of mine operating a wagon with 10 people on it going from one side of the orchard to the other is a migrant labor contractor, according to this definition. I am sure," he stated, "that is not what is meant" in the context of the legislation.[44]

The definition of contractor is so broad, stated Joseph Dorsey, Frederick County, Virginia, that it would "include any growers who hire and transport workers across State

38 Hearings, Senate, 1963, p. 144.
39 Hearings, Senate, 1963, p. 227.
40 Hearings, Senate, 1963, pp. 227-228.
41 Hearings, House, 1963, p. 10.
42 Hearings, House, 1963, pp. 142-143.
43 Hearings, Senate, 1961, pp. 199-200.

lines, which many of our members have to do daily in making use of labor within their various locations. Our association," by virtue of its location, "draws on several States for both regular and seasonal labor."[45] These definitions, stated another grower, are so broad that even a Greyhound bus would require registration if "10 or more" migrants were aboard.[46]

Financial Responsibility

During hearings in the House, Richard O'Connell, the National Council of Farmer Cooperatives, was asked,

> "Is it not a fair and reasonable requirement to expect these crew leaders who transport families of workers from one State to another to be financially responsible to the migrant workers which they transport for personal injuries... and property damage?"

O'Connell thought the requirement was appropriate *if* the question were, in fact, that explicit. However, O'Connell found the term "Financial Responsibility" to be obtuse and questioned whether it meant bonding. "This is one of these vague terms that if you start writing regulations on it it can mean anything."[47]

BRACEROS VERSUS DOMESTIC WORKERS

During the hearings of 1961, C. H. Fields (of the Farm Bureau of New Jersey) was questioned by Representative Herbert Zelenko (D-NY).

> "Mr. FIELDS. ... New Jersey farmers do not use migrant labor because they want to. They would much prefer not to use it if there were any other labor available at a wage they could afford to pay....
> "Mr. ZELENKO. You said the New Jersey farmer would not engage migrant labor if he could help it, but that he could not get local labor at the price he wants to pay.
> "Mr. FIELDS. At the price that he can afford to pay, I said.
> "Mr. ZELENKO. Would you be good enough to give this Committee ... what the prevailing wage is in New Jersey for a farm laborer doing the type of work that a migrant would do ...?
> "Mr. FIELDS.... $1.10 an hour."[48]

In the early 1960s, Congress had under consideration not only legislation dealing with farm labor contractors but, as well, with the *braceros*.[49] As it has evolved, the *bracero* program (and later, the H-2A program) has been based upon two premises.

---

44 Hearings, Senate, 1961, pp. 62-63.
45 Hearings, Senate, 1961, p. 174.
46 Hearings, House, 1961, p. 176. See also: Hearings, Senate 1961, pp. 62-63.
47 Hearings, House, 1961, pp. 32-33.
48 Hearings, House, 1961, p. 235. Mr. Fields went on to state that, in South Jersey, the prevailing wage was then $1.00.
49 The term, bracero, has a number of translations; but, in general, it refers to Mexican workers brought into the United States under a guest worker program. The bracero is a documented worker and should not be confused

A) "there are not sufficient workers who are able, willing, and qualified, and who will be available at the time and place needed, to perform the labor or services involved ...

B) "the employment of the alien in such labor or services will not adversely affect the wages and working conditions of workers in the United States similarly employed."[50]

An *adverse effect wage rate* was devised that must be paid to both foreign and domestic workers (where an effort has been made to employ the former), and which was intended, nominally, to prevent a negative impact from employment of *braceros*.

Comparing *Braceros* with Domestic Workers

Gradually, domestic employment and utilization of *braceros* became intertwined. "The documentation is clear," stated Vera Mayer, National Consumers' League, "that the massive importation of cheap foreign labor has lowered wages to American farmworkers and taken away job opportunities from them."[51] Labor Secretary Arthur Goldberg seemed to agree. "There is increasing evidence of the correlation between this large-scale use of foreign workers in agriculture and the employment situation of our own farmworkers." He stressed that the central problems of migrant farmworkers were the "lack of reasonably attractive employment opportunities" and "low wages."[52]

Here, the Secretary and Ms. Mayer were not alone. The Rev. John Wagner, associated with the National Council for the Spanish Speaking (of San Antonio), suggested that the impact of the *bracero* program "is very great." Father Wagner opined, "... it throws another large number of unskilled workers into a pool that is already overloaded with unskilled workers, and there becomes a mad scramble for jobs."[53] Meanwhile, Father James Vizzard, then associated with the National Catholic Rural Life Conference, posed the question: "What other group of farmers or workers have to compete in the marketplace with ... workers brought into this country by an agency of the Government, partly at taxpayers' expense?"[54]

Triggs of the Farm Bureau explained that the "... domestic worker is often severely disabled, physically, mentally, or psychiatrically or by reason of age. In such cases," he stated, "the employer should not be required to pay the same wages as for an able bodied man. Whereas," he added, "the Mexican workers are carefully screened, they are mostly young, vigorous, able bodied."[55] Twiggs added, "If the farmer prepays transportation for Mexican nationals it is with the assurance that the worker will not leave the job after he arrives to work for somebody else." Further, he stated, the Mexican workers "are

---

with the undocumented worker who has entered the United States illegally and, if employed, is employed illegally. See Howard N. Dellon, "Foreign Agricultural Workers and the Prevention of Adverse Effect," Labor Law Journal, Dec. 1966, pp. 739-748; and CRS Report RL32044, Immigration: Policy Considerations Related to Guest Worker Programs, by Andorra Bruno.

50 8 U.S.C. 1188(a)(A) and (B). See also CRS Report RL32861, Farm Labor: The Adverse Effect Wage Rate (AEWR), by William G. Whittaker.

51 Hearings, House, 1961, p. 211.

52 Hearings, House, 1961, p. 4.

53 Hearings, Senate, 1963, pp. 125-126.

54 Hearings, House, 1961, p. 145.

55 Hearings, House, 1961, p. 101.

unaccompanied by their families" and, as a result, "they need barracks type housing." Finally, he stated, "... the hours of employment are generally uniform and standardized."[56]

Both labor and management witnesses seemed in agreement with respect to domestic and Mexican crews. Arnold Mayer, of the Amalgamated Meat Cutters and Butcher Workmen of North America (AFL-CIO), stated

> "In the first place, the bracero is very docile, more so than even the domestic migrants are. Over the bracero's head hangs the threat that he may be sent back to Mexico if he complains too much or if he kicks up too much of a fuss. He has left his family, he expects to come back with some money, so he does not want to be sent back without money."

Mayer agreed that the "bracero is carefully screened so that the workers that do come from Mexico are prime labor." As "single men," the braceros have an impact on housing. "The growers can erect barrack-type housing for them." American migrants "very often move with their families and housing and facilities for them are more expensive." Mayer stated, "... the growers know that this importation causes a surplus of labor and that this surplus is very, very useful in keeping wage rates down." And, rather than "compete for labor," the foreign workers are made available.[57]

Sorting out the Workers

"There is a clear interrelationship between the administration of the migratory labor program and the administration of Public Law 78 [the *bracero* program]," stated Secretary Wirtz. If we can put domestic labor on a sounder administrative basis, "which this bill would help us very much to do, it would mean a lesser need for the use of Mexican nationals...." He referred to the "floating group of American migratory workers" and observed, "I feel quite strongly that the proper use of the crew leader can be of real advantage to the employing farmer as well as to the employees."[58]

During hearings in 1963, Representative Thomas Gill (D-HI) entered into a dialogue with Richard Shipman of the National Farmers Union. Gill observed that undocumented farm workers were sometimes cheated out of their earnings. Shipman replied, "Of course, if a person is in this country illegally, he is at the mercy of anybody, they have no rights...." Gill concurred: "... they are fair game for a shoddy operator."[59] In some parts of Oregon, Gill speculated, undocumented labor makes up about 20% of the workforce. In that particular region of Oregon, Representative Roosevelt stated, "practically all of the recruiting was done for a sugar company."[60]

---

56 Hearings, House, 1961, p. 103.

57 Hearings, House, 1963, pp. 136-137. Father Vizzard urged against the use of immigrant workers. On page 149, he suggested "... I don't think the way to help the Mexican economy or the individual Mexican people is by using them as, in effect, strikebreakers against our own people, for undercutting the wages and working conditions of our own citizens." See also comments of Senator Williams, Hearings, House, 1961, p. 53.

58 Hearings, House, 1963, p. 124.

59 Hearings, House, 1963, pp. 50-51.

60 Hearings, House, 1963, p. 51. Reference was to prior comments that sugar companies would not need to be covered since they were not involved (or only marginally involved) in recruitment — and they are fixed site employers.

Shipman concurred that the "wetback problem is of long standing." He stated: "In the total Spanish-speaking migrant group, approximately 20 percent enter the United States on 'border crosser permits' ... on forged documents, or in the old-fashioned wetback manner." Licensing would help. Roosevelt suggested that, under the current proposal, suspension would follow if the contractor "has recruited, employed or utilized the service of a person with knowledge that such a person is violating the provisions of the immigration and nationality laws." Such a person can be refused a license, but is also "subject to penalty under the Act." He further pointed to a provision allowing the Secretary, *under authority to obtain information*, to conduct a more specific investigation.[61]

CONGRESSIONAL ACTION ON CONTRACTOR REGISTRATION

During the late 1950s and early 1960s, Senator Williams had sought controls on farm labor contractors, and, though the measures were not adopted, he kept trying. In 1963, legislation began to move. The contractor registration bill was called up for Senate consideration on June 11, 1963. Williams explained the nature of farm labor contracting, concluding that many contractors "perform their functions in [a] satisfactory and responsible manner," but others "have exploited both farmers and workers."[62]

At that point, Senator John Tower (R-TX) objected to passage of the bill. "I do not believe the measure is needed." Tower noted that there are "occasional instances of crew leaders who don't deal fairly with workers or farmers," but these cases "are disputable" and "exaggerated." Since many states already register farm labor contractors, the proposed legislation would be redundant, he stated.[63] No other Senator arose in opposition. The Senate moved on to other business. A few minutes later, the Senate switched back to the farm labor contractor legislation and, following a brief discussion, the measure was adopted. Passage was on a voice vote.[64]

It was more than a year before Representative Roosevelt called up the measure in the House. The bill, he declared, was "essentially noncontroversial."[65] Representative Gill, the author of the bill, agreed that the bill was "a very minimal piece of legislation" but "the need for this ... is very obvious." Gill stated that

> "These crew chiefs deal with a type of labor ... which is often undereducated or in many instances completely uneducated. The literacy level is generally low. Their ability to understand their rights is ... minimal.
> "Many of these migrant laborers have no voting residence. They have no Congressman ... nor do they have access to other officials who may help them with their problems. Therefore, they are easy to victimize."

---

61 Hearings, House, 1963, pp. 51-53.
62 Congressional Record, June 11, 1963, pp. 10619-10621.
63 Congressional Record, June 11, 1963, p. 10621.
64 Congressional Record, June 11, 1963, p. 10625.
65 Congressional Record, Aug. 17, 1964, pp. 19894-19895.

The bill "... would be of great assistance to the good crew leaders ... the vast majority. It will prevent them from being daubed with the same brush used on the bad."[66]

Indeed, the bill *was* noncontroversial. Representative Robert Griffin (R-MI) rose "in support of this legislation." Representative Charles Bennett (D-FL) similarly expressed his "strong support" of the bill. "The migrant laborer should no longer be neglected," stated Representative William Fitts Ryan (D-NY). "This bill is belated recognition of his plight."[67]

Thereupon, the House passed the farm labor contractor registration legislation by 343 yeas to 7 nays — though with several changes from the Senate-passed version.[68] As amended, the bill was taken up in the Senate, passed by voice vote, and sent to President Lyndon Johnson, becoming P.L. 88-582 on September 7, 1964.[69]

THE FARM LABOR CONTRACTOR REGISTRATION ACT OF 1964

Congress finds, the act began, that "certain irresponsible contractors," by their activities in the migrant labor field, have "impeded, obstructed, and restrained" the flow of interstate commerce. Thus, Congress mandates that "all persons engaged in the activity of contracting for the services of workers for interstate agricultural employment comply with the provisions of this act and all regulations prescribed hereunder by the Secretary of Labor."[70] In general, the act provided the following:

Definitions

-   "The term 'farm labor contractor' means any person, who, for a fee, either for himself or on behalf of another person, recruits, solicits, hires, furnishes, or transports ten or more migrant workers ... at any one time in any calendar year for interstate agricultural employment."
-   "Such term shall not include (1) any nonprofit charitable organization, public or nonprofit private education institution, or similar organization; (2) any farmer, processor, canner, ginner, packing shed operator, or nurseryman who engages in any such activity for the purpose of supplying migrant workers solely for his own operation; (3) any full-time or regular employee of any entity referred to in (1) or (2) above; or (4) any person who engages in any such activity for the purpose of obtaining migrant workers of any foreign nation for employment in the United States, if the employment of such workers is subject to (A) an agreement between the United States and such foreign nation, or (B) an arrangement with the government of any foreign nation under which written contracts for the employment of such workers are provided for and the enforcement thereof is provided for in the United States by an instrumentality of such foreign nation."

---

66 Congressional Record, Aug. 17, 1964, p. 19895.
67 Congressional Record, Aug. 17, 1964, pp. 19895-19896.
68 Congressional Record, Aug. 17, 1964, p. 19896.
69 Congressional Record, Aug. 21, 1964, pp. 20874-20877.
70 All quotations, here, are from P.L. 88-582. However, the reader is urged to consult the statute for more specific details.

- "... 'state' means any of the States of the United States, the District of Columbia, the Virgin Islands, the Commonwealth of Puerto Rico, and Guam."
- "... 'migrant worker' means an individual whose primary employment is in agriculture ... or who performs agricultural labor ... on a seasonal or other temporary basis."

Certificate of Registration Requirement

- "No person shall engage in activities as a farm labor contractor unless he first obtains a certificate of registration from the Secretary, and unless such certificate is in full force and effect and is in such person's immediate possession."
- The act observes of a "full-time or regular employee" holding a valid certificate of registration: "Any such employee shall be required to have in his immediate personal possession when engaging in such activities such identification as the Secretary may require showing such employee to be an employee of, and duly authorized to engage in activities as a farm labor contractor for, a person holding a valid certificate of registration under the provisions of this Act."
- "... any such [regular or full-time] employee shall be subject to the provisions of this Act and regulations prescribed hereunder to the same extent as if he were required to obtain a certificate or registration in his own name."

Issuance of Certificate of Registration

- The Secretary shall issue a certificate of registration to any person who "has executed and filed with the Secretary" whatever documents "the Secretary may require in order effectively to carry out the provisions of this Act;" has filed with the Secretary documentation "satisfactory to the Secretary of the financial responsibility of the applicant" with respect to motor vehicles; and "has filed ... a set of his fingerprints."
- "... the Secretary may refuse to issue, and may suspend, revoke, or refuse to renew a certificate of registration to any farm labor contractor if he finds that such contractor" (inter alia):

    "knowingly has given false or misleading information to migrant workers concerning the terms, conditions, or existence of agriculture employment"
    "has failed, without justification, to perform agreements entered into or arrangements with farm operators"
    "has failed, without justification, to comply with the terms of any working arrangement he has made with migrant workers"
    "has failed to show financial responsibility satisfactory to the Secretary ... or has failed to keep in effect a policy of insurance required by subsection (a)(2) of this section"
    "has recruited, employed, or utilized the services of a person with knowledge that such person is violating the provisions of the immigration and nationality laws of the United States"
    "has been convicted of any crime under State or Federal law"

"has failed to comply with any of the provisions of this Act or any regulations issued hereunder."

- "A certification of registration ... shall be effective for the remainder of the calendar year during which it is issued, unless suspended or revoked by the Secretary as provided in this Act. A certificate of registration may be renewed each calendar year upon approval by the Secretary of an application for its renewal."

Obligations and Prohibitions

- The contractor will "... ascertain and disclose to each worker at the time the worker is recruited the following information to the best of his knowledge and belief: (1) the area of employment, (2) the crops and operations on which he may be employed, (3) the transportation, housing, and insurance to be provided him, (4) the wage rates to be paid him, and (5) the charges to be made by the contractor for his services...."
- "... upon arrival at a given place of employment, post in a conspicuous place a written statement of the terms and conditions of that employment...."
- "... in the event he manages, supervises, or otherwise controls the housing facilities, post in a conspicuous place the terms and conditions of occupancy...."
- In the event he pays migrant workers, to keep close and careful records of all transactions and to make them generally available.

Authority to Obtain Information

- "The Secretary or his designated representative may investigate and gather data with respect to matters which may aid in carrying out the provisions of this Act." He "... may investigate and gather data respecting such case, and may, in connection therewith, enter and inspect such places and such records (and make such transcriptions thereof), question such persons, and investigate such facts, conditions, practices, or matters as may be necessary or appropriate to determine whether a violation of this Act has been committed."

Agreements with Federal and State Agencies

- The secretary is allowed to enter into compacts with various state and federal agencies with respect to enforcement of the act and related activities.

Penalty Provisions

- A penalty of not more than $500 is prescribed for violations of the act.

Judicial Review

- A limited system of judicial review is prescribed under the act.

Rules and Regulations

- "The Secretary is authorized to issue such rules and regulations as he determines necessary for the purposes of carrying out" certain provisions of this act.

PART II. THE FIRST YEARS OF THE
FARM LABOR CONTRACTOR REGISTRATION ACT (1964-1974)

From 1964 until 1974, the FLCRA was given institutional life. Administration of the act was set in motion and patterns of interpretation were developed. There was, however, some criticism of the act and a sense that it had not lived up to the hope and expectations of its authors.

THE INAUGURAL PERIOD

FLCRA focused upon one aspect of the issue of migrant and seasonal worker protections: the farm labor contractor. In late December 1964, Secretary Wirtz issued regulations under the act, and the Manpower Administrator, Bureau of Employment Security, was given the responsibility as *the authorized designee* of the Secretary.[71]

There followed a series of directives published in the *Federal Register* dealing with insurance and financial responsibility.[72] However, some terms used in the legislation seem to have lent themselves to vague patterns of interpretation. For example, see the definition of farm labor contractor.

> "The term 'farm labor contractor' means any person ... [who] recruits, solicits, hires, furnishes, or transports ten or more migrant workers ... at any one time in any calendar year for interstate agricultural employment."

---

71 See Federal Register, Dec. 22, 1964, p. 18157, and Feb. 3, 1965, p. 1139. It was not until late 1972 that responsibility for FLCRA was shifted to the Wage/Hour Division which normally deals with labor standards issues. See Federal Register, Jan. 17, 1973, p. 1636.

72 See Federal Register, Oct. 12, 1966, pp. 13174-13176, Nov. 22, 1966, pp. 14772-14775, May 9, 1967, pp. 7025-7026, and July 20, 1967, p. 10649.

The official interpretation of the statute explores each of these concepts at some length but, seemingly, without resolution.[73]

In 1969, under Secretary George Shultz, DOL underwent administrative restructuring with FLCRA (and 28 other programs) assigned to the Assistant Secretary for Manpower.[74] Then, in 1972, under Secretary James Hodgson, a split was effected with the labor standards aspects of FLCRA assigned to the Wage/Hour Division in the Employment Standards Administration. For more general administration, authority was left with the Assistant Secretary for Manpower.[75] Under the act, the Secretary was permitted to enter into a cooperative agreement with state authorities where the states had roughly comparable laws. Where there might be a refusal to authorize (or re-authorize) issuance of a certificate of registration, a hearing would be scheduled before the Solicitor (after 1973, the Associate Solicitor) of DOL — or his designee.[76] For *a marginally educated* farm labor contractor (if that assessment were true), one might expect the total impact to have been a little confusing.[77]

A Certain Dissatisfaction

FLCRA had not been entirely successful. "Complaints have grown through the years," observed Senator Gaylord Nelson (D-WI), "that this first effort of the Congress was lacking in several areas...."[78]

During 1973 and 1974, further hearings were conducted on the issue. The current system, some suggested, "... has been the source of massive abuse and exploitation of agricultural workers." Though Congress had recognized the problem with adoption of FLCRA, the abuses have shown "no signs of moderating."[79] No matter "how strong the vote in the Congress, it

---

73 Federal Register, Mar. 6, 1965, pp. 2945-2950. For example, the rule states, "... if a person intends to recruit five (5) migrant workers one day for Farmer A and the next day is requested to recruit and does recruit eight (8) migrant workers for Farmer B, these are separate and independent acts and do not total up to thirteen (13) for purposes of the statutory requirement. However, if he has contracts to hire a total of eighteen (18) migrant workers for Farmers X, Y, and Z and he hires this number as a result of three days effort, the statutory amount of 'ten or more' would be present." But it concludes: "... the application of these principles to other situations will depend on all the facts."

74 Federal Register, Apr. 15, 1969, pp. 6502-6504.

75 Federal Register, Oct. 20, 1972, p. 22660.

76 See Federal Register, Jan. 17, 1973, pp. 1636-1637, and Aug. 24, 1973, p. 22778.

77 Father John Kelly, Our Lady of Lourdes Church, Seaford, Delaware, stated that there had been "a tremendous overlapping of intermeshing authorities...." He continued: "... we have federal regulations, we have state regulations and we have local county implementation." Kelly further observed, "When one has a problem you have to deal with the hour and wage [laws] and to deal with social security, you have to deal with health, education and welfare, you have to deal with the local labor office and no one in any of these departments is quite clear where" the migrant worker is located with respect to the several jurisdictions. "You can spend days trying to establish a relationship with any particular office and no one is sure at the end of the day whether he has a reason or not to handle your problem. Now for an illiterate perhaps non-English speaking person, the difficulty is multiplied 1,000 times. And the man who is supposed to solve all these problems is the crew leader." Representative William Ford (D-MI) would later concede, "We are painfully aware that it is very difficult to tie it all together because of the multitude of Federal agencies that have fragmented responsibilities in this area." See U.S. Congress, House, Subcommittee on Agricultural Labor, Committee on Education and Labor, Farm Labor Contractor Registration Act Amendments of 1973, pp. 179 and 183. (Cited hereafter as Hearings, House, 1973).

78 U.S. Congress, Senate, Subcommittee on Employment, Poverty, and Migratory Labor, Committee on Labor and Public Welfare. Farm Labor Contractor Registration Act Amendments, 1974. Fresno, Cal., Feb. 8, 1974, and Washington, D.C., Apr. 9, 1974, p. 2. (Cited hereafter as Hearings, Senate, 1974).

79 Hearings, Senate, 1974, p. 107.

[farmworker legislation] usually seems to be filed away in some cubbyhole without any appropriations, without any committee staff, and the result in almost all cases has been nonenforcement." In the "9 years of the existence of this bill," it was suggested, there "has been no enforcement. It has been totally ineffective. It has been a dud."[80]

Problems Associated with FLCRA

New legislation may take time to work through various impediments: FLCRA was no exception. From the testimony before the House and Senate Committees, it was clear that problems were numerous.

A Lack of Penalties

The Departments of Labor and Justice seemed to feel "that present penalties are insufficient to deter repeated violations," and this "deters them from pressing prosecutions," a witness stated, urging "greater penalties."[81]

Representative Augustus Hawkins (D-CA) posed the question to a group of DOL Administrators: Bernard DeLury, Assistant Secretary for Employment Standards; Warren Landis, Acting Administrator, Wage/Hour Division; and Eugene Bonfiglio, Chief, Branch of Farm Labor Contractor Registration.

"Mr. HAWKINS. What is the penalty at the present time for failure to register?

"Mr. LANDIS. There is no specific penalty in the present law, unless there is a willful violation, and then the present law provides a fine of up to $500.

"Mr. HAWKINS. Has anyone been fined, and if so, how many?

"Mr. LANDIS. I think one....

"Mr. BONFIGLIO. Since the act became operative in January 1965, we have had four cases that went to criminal court for prosecution. Of those four, two were thrown out by the Justice Department, and two were finally prosecuted and fined $100 in each case, and in one of the cases the fine was lifted.

"Mr. HAWKINS.... I assume that under the law those who commit violations can either have their registration revoked or other penalties imposed. Can you give us any idea how many registrations have been revoked.

"Mr. DeLURY. None, sir. "Mr. HAWKINS. None. "Mr. DeLURY. None this year. "What about last year?

"Mr. BONFIGLIO. Last year we revoked three certificates and suspended two, I believe. We had one employee who was denied based on a past criminal action."

A DOL spokesman stepped in to explain. The record "does not mean that crew leaders are not violating [the law] or that we are not attempting to enforce the law. Under the regulations ... the due process is required, we have to notify the crew leader that we intend to revoke this certificate and give him time to request a hearing." Then, there is the time factor. "If he requests a hearing ... the time element usually goes beyond his stay in one place, and by

---

80 Hearings, Senate, 1974, pp. 152-153. The speaker was Father James Vizzard, then of the United Farm Workers.
81 Hearings, Senate, 1974, pp. 115-116.

that time he is gone or the end of the season is on us." Landis then observed that unless the violation "is pretty bad we think it is better to get him into compliance and let him continue his work...." The dialogue continued.

> "Mr. HAWKINS. Well, the problem itself is not evaporating though; is it?
> "Mr. LANDIS. No sir. There still is a problem for the migrant workers, a big problem."[82]

Lack of Staff

In response to Representative Hawkins, it was noted that there were probably about 5,000 interstate crew leaders and another 3,000 intrastate crew leaders. The figures "are not accurate," Landis observed. "They are the best estimates that we could make." And, Landis continued, "... a little under 2,000" are registered.[83]

With more than eight years of experience under the act, Mr. Hawkins queried, "Are you making any effort to see that those who are not registered become registered? Who does the job of enforcing that?" Landis replied, "Well, that is our job, of course, to register them and to call them to account when they are not registered." DOL was trying to deal with that "through investigations" and "through public service announcements on radio and TV ... in both English and Spanish."[84]

We are not here "to be critical of you gentlemen," Representative William Ford (D-MI) stated, when introducing the Department witnesses, but "to determine whether ... we can find a way to make the law finally do what it was originally intended to do."[85] However, a certain amount of criticism emerged.

The 1963 Act "was never enforced because the bureaucrats who were given the responsibility to enforce it did not get out of the regional offices," argued Elijah Boone of the Community Action Migrant Program in Immokalee, Florida. He alleged that most of DOL's staff (where crew leaders were concerned) were recycled "from old rural manpower, which had already been shown to be ineffective."[86] Alcario Samudia, now with the Wisconsin Department of Labor, recalled that when the crew leader Act came into being in 1963, "... I registered ... but then we found out that the Government did not have anybody to enforce the new laws, so many of us did not even bother to register" after that.[87] "It is a law," explained Barbara Rhine, an attorney for the United Farm Workers, "that everyone here claims and knows is not enforced."[88]

Was the act fatally flawed? Or were enforcement officials jaded? Might the problem have more to do with appropriations? According to Luke Danielson, a former investigator for the Colorado Migrant Legal Services Agency, DOL officials had advised him that "they lack[ed] sufficient investigative staff to process complaints" — which resulted in this "abominable enforcement record."[89] Again:

---

82 Hearings, House, 1973, pp. 108-109.
83 Hearings, House, 1973, p. 107.
84 Hearings, House, 1973, pp. 107-108.
85 Hearings, House, 1973, p. 60.
86 Hearings, Senate, 1974, pp. 230-231.
87 Hearings, Senate, 1974, pp. 217-218.
88 Hearings, Senate, 1974, p. 36.
89 Hearings, Senate, 1974, p. 110.

"Mr. FORD. How many field enforcement people were actually involved in trying to check registrations ... of crew leaders prior to October 1972?

"Mr. BONFIGLIO. We had five field men in 1972. In 1965, we had 40. In 1966, that dropped to 17, and each year after that it declined down to 1972 when we had 5."[90]

Elsewhere, Representative Ford concluded, "It would appear that if we were operating with five people throughout the country to enforce this, knowing that we have in excess of 6,000 possible people to be policed, that we have not very aggressively ..." gone about enforcement of the statute.[91]

Other Issues

Clearly, other problems dogged enforcement of FLCRA during its first 10 years rendering the act either unenforceable or, perhaps, innocuous. Among allegations were the following:

The Language Question. Investigators were not always fluent in the language spoken by the workers: Spanish, particularly in the West. Though some announcements appear to have been made in Spanish, the cultural division was such that, often, they were inappropriately positioned. Even in terms of payment and Social Security, the pay stub may have been written in English, which "people don't understand."[92]

Crew Leader Versus Grower. There had been, through the decade, an intermittent conflict between the grower and the crew leader. If we could just "make the grower responsible," Landis stated for DOL, "... this would be the biggest boost to getting these crew leaders registered."[93] Conversely, Daniel Boone of the United Farm Workers charged that labor contractors "are used by the real employers, the growers, to maximize the insecurity of the worker" by adding yet another level of authority. The grower (farmer or company) "by the use of the contractor has insulated itself from any responsibility" for payment, insurance, and related costs associated with migratory employment.[94] Luke Danielson argued "If the crew leader is not in fact registered, make the farmer liable for the wrongdoings of the crew leader."[95]

Inflating Crew Levels. Guadalupe Murguia, a United Farm Worker rank-and-filer, testified that contractors exploit the growers by padding their payrolls with grandchildren and great-grandchildren. "As an example, we discovered that the contractors had people on their lists who had been dead for 4 or 5 years." Where there is contract work, the company "pays for the people that the contractor has on his payroll."[96] Pablo Espinosa, also a rank-and-filer, affirmed, "I used to work for a labor contractor where he used to come and tell me, put two or three more people on the books. Put so and so and so on. Well, so and so don't exist, I would say. Well, you put them on. Who pays for that? The grower."[97]

---

90 Hearings, House, 1974, p. 109.
91 Hearings, House, 1973, p. 55.
92 Hearings, Senate, 1974, p. 50. See also Hearings, Senate, 1974, p. 110, and Hearings, House, 1973, p. 108.
93 Hearings, House, 1973, p. 108.
94 Hearings, Senate, 1974, pp. 49-50.
95 Hearings, Senate, 1974, p. 105.
96 Hearings, Senate, 1974, p. 43.
97 Hearings, Senate, 1974, p. 45.

Inspector/Grower Collusion? There was a sense, among some workers, that inspectors had become an adjunct to the growers. They, the inspectors, were educated and, often, spoke a language different from the field workers. When abuses were complained of, the inspectors "let them know that they are coming" to inspect — which, from the workers' perspective, tended *to stack the deck* against honest inspection. "It doesn't do any good to report anybody," observed Jessie de la Cruz of the United Farm Workers. "Nothing is done about it."[98] It was only by contacting inspectors "on repeated occasions," Danielson noted, "that we were able to get them to take this complaint at all."[99] Again: "There is no incentive to understand the Act as contractors know that the Act is not being enforced."[100]

AMENDING THE STATUTE

In some respects, FLCRA appeared to have had little impact. Demands for its repeal (during the early years) seem to have been few.

"... I think it is appropriate for me to express a kind of personal 'mea culpa,'" suggested Father James Vizzard, an early backer of FLCRA. In the early 1960s, he stated that "under the leadership of Senator Harrison Williams and his Senate Migratory Labor Subcommittee, we were able to formulate and pass this legislation...." But, he added: "Hindsight tells us now that, despite a great deal of good will and technical competence, we really didn't do a very good job of it." Father Vizzard opined:

"First, at the time there was no organized grassroots body with sufficient knowledge and experience to advise us of the day-to-day realities of farm worker problems in all parts of our country. Despite extensive studies and hearings it still was principally a group of us here in Washington ... who did what we thought best, and as it turned out that wasn't good enough.

"Second, once a legislative battle had been won and a bill passed, our forces tended to disperse and forgot the second half of the battle, namely, appropriations. Almost every act we passed, therefore, was grossly underfunded and continues to be so even to this day.

"Third, and perhaps most important of all, we failed to build into the program adequate and continuous enforcement. Without any exception that I can recall, the agencies charged with enforcement have never done a satisfactory or, in very many cases, even an honest job of enforcing these laws passed by Congress."101

Amendments would bring forth a new phase (and, in some respects, a more turbulent phase) of the regulation of agricultural labor. As revision of the statute proceeded, a number of issues emerged: some old, others new.

---

98 Hearings, Senate, 1974, p. 41.
99 Hearings, Senate, 1974, p. 105.
100 Hearings, House, 1973, p. 165. The speaker, Joe Alexander, is a former farm labor contractor from Homestead, Florida.
101 Hearings, House, 1973, p. 63.

Changing Character of the Farm Labor Contractor

During hearings in the early 1960s, the farm labor contractor had been somewhat disparaged. A decade later, that view had mellowed. There were still tales of "short-counts" and beatings of workers who ran into "disfavor" with the crew chief — but these were issues with which DOL did not seem to become involved.[102]

"The great majority of these people," suggested C. H. Fields of the Farm Bureau, "are responsible businessmen who have made a significant investment in their businesses and who make every effort to abide by the law." Again:

> "... these people are small businessmen; they operate under extremely difficult circumstances; they do not have the services of accountants, bookkeepers, or legal advisors; and the more paperwork that is required the more apt they are to call it quits and go out of business."[103]

Definitional elements entered the picture as well. Elijah Boone of the Community Migrant Action Program (Immokalee, Florida) said that there were different kinds of crew leaders. "A contractor might be a very well to do, upper middle-class white businessman, who has money to invest in necessary machinery that a farm worker would know of." The contractor might be the person in charge of the contract and "... then he would hire the crew leader who would recruit the labor...."[104] Who might be charged with the payment of the workers (and with making deductions for Social Security and related matters) seems to have been unclear.

Defining a Labor Dispute or Strike

Immigration officials, argued Father Vizzard, appear "to be in the pocket of large-scale employers," while "notorious labor contractors have been allowed repeatedly to build up their strike-breaking crews with these known illegals recruited throughout the Southwest."[105] Dan Pollitt, now special counsel to the Subcommittee, questioned Vizzard. A contractor, Pollitt suggested, was required to explain to contract workers "where they are going, wages, housing conditions, and so on." Pollitt asked, "Do you think it would be helpful to add that you must also say whether or not there is a strike going on or whether a contract is at its last stages of negotiations." Father Vizzard responded: "Yes. I would."[106]

But again, there were problems. Guinn Sinclair, president, National Farm Labor Contractors Association, suggested an almost "complete lack of legislation" on labor-management relations in the agricultural field as to what "constitutes a labor dispute." Sinclair questioned: "Why should a contractor be the judge when our courts have issued conflicting decisions?" And: "Does a labor dispute exist when the United Farm Workers Union issues a

---

102 Hearings, House, 1973, p. 155. See also Hearings, House, p. 118. DOL did have grower complaints concerning funds forwarded to cover transportation costs of farmworkers.
103 Hearings, Senate, 1974, pp. 154-156.
104 Hearings, Senate, 1974, pp. 323-324.
105 Hearings, House, 1973, p. 64.
106 Hearings, House, 1973, p. 92.

boycott of lettuce and table grapes?" Or, again, when the Teamsters or the United Farm Workers, then in a contest for farmworker loyalties, "claim jurisdiction and yet no laws exist to determine the will of the workers themselves?" Sinclair protested, "... I don't think the contractor should be the one to decide that there is a dispute."[107]

The Farm Bureau argued that agriculture "is exempt from the National Labor Relations Act and farmers have no legal method to deal with labor disputes" and "unfair labor practices." Again, there were definitional issues: "... what constitutes a strike, slowdown or labor-management dispute," and when does "such a condition exist at a particular farm." Were a farmer to become engaged in such issues, the proposal "could have the effect of determining whether or not his crop would be harvested." The Bureau continued, "Fruits and vegetables tend to reach the harvest stage as determined by the inexorable laws of nature," and a farm "cannot wait around until someone," perhaps the state or the federal government, "decides whether there is a legally-constituted strike or labor dispute." The provision, it stated, "would seem to be an unworkable and unreasonable responsibility" to place upon contractors.[108]

DeLury of DOL took a cautious attitude, suggesting that the provision was "pretty broad" as written.[109] Later, Bruce Burkdoll, speaking for the Central California Farmers Association, charged that "a union or group of workers" could create "a labor dispute, even though the union does not represent" the workers involved. He concluded, "... just because a student or someone else that never saw you on your ranch stops in front and waves a flag, we just cannot live with that."[110]

The Day Haul and the Shape-Up

The *shape-up* exists in most regions from which growers or contractors recruit. "That is the place where the people gather to find out whether there will be work that day, sometimes as early as 2 a.m....." The *shape-up* varies from one locality to another. So does the nature of the work sought.[111]

"The contractor ... will have the pick of the lot," according to Barbara Rhine, United Farm Workers attorney. "He will choose the strong, the young, the healthy.... Or the attractive women who have to turn a pretty face and act at the driver's bidding ... Or the illegal alien, whom he can have taken back by the border patrol before he pays the day's wages." If the character of the work is marginal, "then the shape-up area will be filled with the local winos, the sad, stumbling men and women who are so abject that all it takes is the promise of wine to get them into the fields." Rhine stated

> "And so the people get on the buses and hard-seated trucks and try to sleep on their way to work. If they get miles into the fields and find that it's not the first picking that they have been promised, or that there are no toilets and drinking water, or that the gloves to protect their hands are torn, missing, or not provided at all, then their choice is to work anyhow or

---

107 Hearings, Senate, 1974, p. 32-33.
108 Hearings, Senate, 1974, p. 163.
109 Hearings, Senate, 1974, p. 142.
110 Hearings, Senate, 1974, p. 172.
111 Hearings, Senate, 1974, p. 35.

walk back to town and miss the whole day. If they complete the day's work, they frequently get paid less than the promise, and with deductions made for fees and transportation."

Further, she alleged that "If they get their slips showing the deductions for social security and disability, they find out later when they are old and sick that the money somehow never found its way to the proper State or Federal agency."[112]

Rhine's comments focused upon California, but, Theodore Dietz of the New Jersey Department of Community Affairs explained the conditions of *day-haul* workers in his part of the country — casual workers employed on a daily basis.

-   Both federal and state minimum wage laws are consistently broken.
-   "Many crew leaders go unregistered." They disguise their function as crew leaders by using a number of cars and "by carrying less than ten people per vehicle."
-   The crew leader provides "either insufficient information or misinformation" to the worker. "Because there is no written contract between the crew leader and worker, the worker may agree to pick one crop and end up picking another at a different piece rate."
-   "Social Security deductions are never made for day haul workers, eliminating many of them from eligibility when they reach 65."
-   No statement of earnings, deductions or hours worked is provided to the worker.
-   "Day haul workers rarely are provided toilet facilities in the field and occasionally no water...."
-   Children of a very young age are a part of the system.
-   "Arbitrary dismissals and blacklisting" are part of the day haul system.
-   "No protective clothing against weeds, rain or pesticides are ever provided...." ! "No health or first aid services are available to day haul workers."[113]

Proposed amendments tended to exclude day haul workers. Father Vizzard (now of the United Farm Workers) expressed concern. "Our experience," he stated, "tells us that some of the grossest abuses against both farm workers and employers are perpetrated by day haulers." The rationale for this exemption is "'because there are so few inspectors.' We think that the proper response to this fact is ... a notable increase in enforcement staff."[114] David Sweeney, Political and Legislative Director for the Teamsters, agreed. "We concur with the statement made by the United Farm Workers in their testimony ... 'We think that the proper response to this fact is, as stated above, a notable increase in the enforcement staff.'"[115] Further, Dietz observed that exclusion of day hauling left him "in a word, dumbfounded."[116]

Even DeLury affirmed DOL's opposition to eliminating day haulers from coverage. "This exclusion would deprive laborers working for a day-haul contractor of guaranteed insurance protection and basic information about the job. These guarantees," DeLury stated,

---

112 Hearings, Senate, 1974, p. 35. See also Hearings, Senate, 1974, p. 154, for an analysis by C. H. Fields of the Farm Bureau.
113 Hearings, House, 1973, p. 174.
114 Hearings, House, 1973, p. 63.
115 Hearings, House, 1973, p. 94. Sweeney proposed inclusion of day haulers in the bill.
116 Hearings, House, 1973, p. 174.

"are as important to the day worker as to the laborer who works for a contractor over an extended period."[117]

The Administration, however, was divided on the issue. Jack Donnachie, Rural Manpower Service, DOL, raised the issue of practicality. "We do have some points where we supervise day haul, as well as they can be supervised," Donnachie stated. But he cautioned that "... you are out on a public corner with a day haul" and you "cannot stop a man," he argued, when the recruitment takes place in a public space. "We received a lot of criticism ... for day haul operations and justifiably so," he stated, "... so we are getting out of the day haul business as fast as we can get out because we cannot control it."[118]

As the hearings progressed, Representative Ford noted a certain level of caution. If day haulers were included in the bill, "... it is obvious that we are going to be picking up ... a situation that for some period of time would require constant day-by-day monitoring." He continued:

"Mr. FORD. So we are talking about more manpower than we have heretofore been using. Do you have any idea about what your additional manpower needs would be, taking into account the additional enforcement power of the Act. Have you given that any thought.

"Mr. DeLURY. Yes, we have. Recently we went up before Mr. [Daniel] Flood's Appropriations Subcommittee and requested a supplemental budget for the Employment Standards Administration, and in the area of farm labor contractor registration work we earmarked ... 10 additional positions for the coming years."[119]

In an aside to Father Vizzard, Ford stated that "... there was not any intent on the part of the authors of this bill to diminish our capacity to deal with the problem" of day haulers: "... we are just trying to deal in priorities with the resources we have."[120]

Interstate Versus Intrastate

The original labor contractor legislation focused upon interstate transportation of migrant and seasonal workers. Ben Robertson of the Wage/Hour Division explained that Florida crew leaders, under current law, "would not need to be registered ... until they indicated or got ready to move North. They would then come under the coverage of the act because of the interstate character of the work."[121]

An amendment to the act proposed to cover interstate intrastate operations. Fr. Vizzard applauded the new section, noting that "many — and I would say perhaps most — of the contractors operate wholly within one state. It is long overdue that they be covered by the provisions of the law."[122] DeLury was equally supportive.[123] And Alcario Samudia, the

---

117 Hearings, House, 1973, p. 97. DeLury also stated: "In addition, some day-haul work is interstate; this activity is covered under the current act. We oppose a change which would exempt this interstate activity." See also DeLury, Hearings, Senate, 1974, pp. 117, 147-148.

118 Hearings, House, 1973, p. 23.

119 Hearings, House, 1973, p. 102.

120 Hearings, House, 1973, p. 86.

121 Hearings, House, 1973, p. 23.

122 Hearings, House, 1973, p. 63. David Sweeney and William Grami, both from the Teamsters, noted their support of intrastate coverage. See Hearings, House, 1973, p. 187.

123 Hearings, House, 1973, p. 97.

former crew leader from Wisconsin, urged that all crew leaders "who recruit interstate or intrastate[,] regardless of whether they only recruit for themselves or a combination of employers," be registered.[124]

Fields of the Farm Bureau argued against this expansion. "We strongly urge that it be made clear ... that it is not the intent of Congress to cover the intrastate activities of farm labor contractors," he stated.[125] George Sorn, of the Florida Fruit and Vegetable Association, urged that FLCRA continue to apply "only to crew leaders who cross state lines." Sorn stated that registration of other workers would be a "needless expenditure of taxpayers' money." He continued: "We believe leaders who operate only on an intrastate basis should not become subject to the Federal Act in those states which have adequate crew leader laws of their own."[126]

Establishing Responsibility: Growers Versus Farm Labor Contractors

In FLCRA, as originally adopted, a "farmer, processor, canner, ginner, packing shed operator, or nurseryman who engaged in" farm labor recruitment "solely for his own operations," shall not be included within the concept of a *farm labor contractor*.[127] Under the proposed amendments, the issue was raised anew.

There was a sense, among advocates of a stronger FLCRA, that growers had, by use of the contractor, "insulated" themselves from responsibility for a diverse range of employer-associated responsibilities.[128] At the same time, it was argued that the farm labor contractor does not set policy but, rather, merely follows orders laid down by growers. In south Texas, it was explained, the contractor does not set the rate of pay or determine the hours of work. He merely follows established policy and is nothing more, in effect, "than a crew foreman."[129] Barbara Rhine of the United Farm Workers explained that "whoever recruits labor for the grower is nothing more or less than his employee...."[130]

Some were willing to assign the contractor the role of an employee of the grower. DeLury of Labor, however, supported a provision in the draft bill making "growers liable for damages resulting from acts or omissions of *unregistered* farm labor contractors with whom they have contracted for services." He also recommended "a provision to prohibit outright the use of *unregistered* crew leaders by growers."[131] Joseph McAuliffe of the Wage/Hour Division noted an absence of responsibility. Someone, "we don't care which," has to assume responsibility.[132]

This issue, grower versus contractor, would remain central to the debate on FLCRA through the next decade. Much agricultural work seems to have been conducted on a quasi-cash basis. Or, where there were more formal processes, it may have been unrealistic to

---

124 Hearings, Senate, 1974, p. 220. Under the 1964 legislation, growers who recruited "solely for his own operation," were not covered.
125 Hearings, Senate, 1974, p. 156.
126 Hearings, House, 1973, pp. 190-191.
127 See Section 3(b)(2) of P.L. 88-582.
128 Hearings, Senate, 1974, p. 49.
129 Hearings, Senate, 1974, p. 249.
130 Hearings, Senate, 1974, p. 37.
131 Hearings, Senate, 1974, p. 116. (Italics added.)
132 Hearings, House, 1973, p. 104.

expect a worker, thirty years hence, to attempt to prove that he or she actually worked, for what period, and what was (or was not) taken out of his pay. Pay stubs may be written in English and may be basically unintelligible for non-English speaking workers. Given the migratory character of such workers, compensation information may well have been lost with the passage of time.[133]

Immigration and *Adverse Effect*

Section 5(b)(6) of FLCRA provided that the Secretary might "refuse to issue" or "suspend, revoke, or refuse to renew a certificate of registration" if the farm labor contractor had "with knowledge" hired workers in violation of the immigration and nationality laws of the United States.

As the 1974 amendment moved through the legislative process, there was an effort to restructure this provision. Everyone, it seems, knew that undocumented aliens were employed in American agriculture but, beyond that awareness, there seemed little agreement as to a course to follow. Father Vizzard concluded: "It is too easy for the crew leader or labor contractor to escape the impact of that section of the law by simply claiming innocence, and who can prove to the contrary?"[134]

Much of the discussion focused upon *knowledge*. Rudy Juarez, a former farm worker experienced with crew leading operations, suggested that "contractors and the farmers [they represent] are heavily recruiting illegals from Mexico. Many times we have reported this to the border patrol," Juarez stated, "but they do not seem to be interested until the harvest is over." Senator Nelson inquired of Juarez: "I understand you to say that the employers frequently pay transportation of the illegals." Juarez replied, "Yes, sir. For many years I was a contractor myself."[135]

With one witness after another, though from different perspectives, the issue of use of undocumented workers was raised. Identity papers, it was alleged, were easy to acquire; but, once armed with fraudulent documents, who was to judge? "Since the Border Patrol cannot determine who is an illegal in the United States," opined Guinn Sinclair, "we do not feel you should impose upon the contractor the absolute law that he should know." Sinclair and Nelson discussed the problem of identification. "You know," Sinclair suggested to Nelson, "that the magnitude of Mexicans working in the United States is much greater than I think is conceived here." Part of the problem, the farm labor contractor suggested, rests with the governments of the United States and of Mexico. But, notwithstanding the source of the problem, "the contractor has no way of knowing who should be here and who should not be here."[136]

Mabel Mascarenas, wife of a farm labor contractor, questioned the "should know" proposal. "Are people going to wear a sign that says *I am an alien*, or are we expected to act as Immigration Officers and know all the details of immigration papers?" Much of the work on the farms deals with perishable commodities. "When we need people, and people come to

---

133 Hearings, Senate, 1974, pp. 49-50.
134 Hearings, House, 1973, pp. 87-88. See also Hearings, Senate, 1961, p. 130.
135 Hearings, Senate, 1974, pp. 226-227.
136 Hearings, Senate, 1974, pp. 183-184. See also, ibid, pp. 170-172.

us seeking work,"she said, "we hire them. We are the most integrated business in America."[137]

"It is our view," suggested Joseph Phelan, National Council of Agricultural Employers, "that the imposition of the provision prohibiting the employment of illegal aliens would be tantamount to transferring to the employer a responsibility which correctly lies with the Immigration and Nationalization Service."[138] The Farm Bureau took a similar position. "On the surface," it noted, the premise, "'know or should know' to be in violation of the immigration laws," some may find appealing. But, "the question arises as to how a labor contractor is expected to know or determine whether a given worker is in this country illegally." The bill "is silent with regard to any procedure a contractor would be expected to follow." We urge "that this subsection be deleted." And it further stated: "The Immigration Service itself has not been too successful in stopping illegal entries or discovering those who enter illegally."[139]

Father Vizzard seemed unimpressed with arguments for use of illegals. He suggested that if one were "to raise the wages and improve the working conditions" under which aliens worked, American workers would be found. "When that happens traditionally in any part of American economic life, there are American workers to do the jobs." The system, he stated, "... is simply a fraud and the disguise has to be stripped back again and again and again."[140]

A New Statute Through Amendment

Although the issues raised during hearings on revision of FLCRA were of substance, they seem to have attracted relatively little attention. With hearings concluded, the Congress moved on to enactment of the farm labor amendments of 1974.

Bipartisanship Emerges in the House

In March 1974, Representative Ford introduced a nonpartisan bill incorporating the findings of the hearings — at least as they were understood.[141] Ford thanked Earl Landgrebe (R-IN), especially, for helping to invoke "a spirit of bipartisanship" that has resulted in a "unanimous vote" in committee. The bill is "cosponsored by every member of the Subcommittee on Agricultural Labor" and by other members on each side of the aisle.[142]

Bipartisan support was evident. "H.R. 13342 provides," explained James O'Hara (D-MI), "for stiffer penalties ... A civil remedy is made available in Federal court for those aggrieved

---

137 Hearings, Senate, 1974, pp. 245-246. (Italics added).
138 Hearings, Senate, 1974, p. 260. Phelan added: "Moreover, this provision poses the question of whether you are crossing jurisdictional lines with the Committee on the Judiciary. You will recall that this language was included in the proposed amendment to the Fair Labor Standards Act last year and was subsequently dropped for that reason."
139 Hearings, Senate, 1974, p. 163.
140 Hearings, House, 1973, pp. 89-90.
141 Congressional Record, Mar. 7, 1974, p. 5694. Original sponsors were: Earl Landgrebe (R-IN), Ella Grasso (D-CN), Frank Thompson (D-NJ), Gus Hawkins (D-CA), William Lehman (D-FL), James O'Hara (D-MI), Lloyd Meeds (D-WA), Albert Quie (R-MN), David Towell (R-NV), William Steiger (R-WI), John Erlenborn (R-IL), and Orval Hansen (R-ID).

under the act."[143] Frank Thompson (D-NJ), with others, emphasized that day haul workers would now be under the act.[144] The bill "broadens the definition of those covered," stated William Lehman (D-FL), "to include crew leaders recruiting for work done in the same State...."[145] Landgrebe affirmed that the Secretary will now "have an affirmative duty to monitor and investigate violations of the law." Both he and Albert Quie (R-MN) stressed that the grower will need to "observe a certificate of registration in the possession." At present, Representative Quie stated, "the crew leader is required to display it, but no one is required to observe it." Quie reassured the growers: "We are not attempting to make the growers joint employers with the crew leaders, nor are we attempting to make them responsible for the crew leader's unlawful actions."[146]

At the end of the colloquy, the rules were suspended and the bill was passed on a voice vote.[147] The following day, the bill was dispatched to the Senate where it was assigned to the Committee on Labor and Public Welfare.[148]

The Senate Concurs

It was October, six months later, before the bill reached the Senate floor. Then, the Senate moved to strike everything after the enacting clause and to insert its own language. Only two speakers addressed the issue, each expressing disenchantment with the original FLCRA. Recent testimony, observed Senator Williams, "... indicates that the act of 1963 has failed to achieve some of its original objectives."[149] Similarly, Senator Javits noted: "After 10 years of experience, ... we find that this act has largely been ignored and cannot be effectively enforced."[150]

While the provisions of the bill were briefly discussed, Senator Williams took note of "one new provision which I deem to be of such importance, that I wish to discuss it in some detail." Williams explained that farm labor contractors

"... will be subject to a criminal penalty of up to a $10,000 fine or a prison sentence of up to 3 years (or both), if such contractor has knowingly engaged the services of an illegal alien. Illegal alien has been defined to mean any person who is an alien not lawfully admitted for permanent residence, or who has not been authorized by the Attorney General to accept employment. (...)

"Illegal aliens have become an increasingly large source of farm labor in this country, and the services of a contractor are often utilized to procure this clandestine workforce. The existing act generally prohibits such activities by making it grounds for revoking or suspending the contractor's registration. However, if this tide of illegal immigration is to be stemmed, stricter enforcement and stronger penalties must be applied against those who violate the act. *These additional steps are necessary in light of the adverse effect such*

---

142 Congressional Record, May 7, 1974, pp. 13402-13405.
143 Congressional Record, May 7, 1974, p. 13405.
144 Congressional Record, May 7, 1974, p. 13406.
145 Congressional Record, May 7, 1974, p. 13406.
146 Congressional Record, May 7, 1974, pp. 13408-13409.
147 Congressional Record, May 7, 1974, p. 13409.
148 Congressional Record, May 8, 1974, p. 13619.
149 Congressional Record, Oct. 3, 1974, pp. 33745-33746.
150 Congressional Record, Oct. 3, 1974, p. 33746.

importation of illegal aliens has had on the wages and job security of our citizens, especially in times such as these of high unemployment." (Italics added.)

Williams quoted Leonard Chapman of the Immigration and Naturalization Service. "'There are probably from six to 10 million illegal aliens in the country today. They are occupying jobs that unemployed Americans ought to have.'" No doubt, Williams asserted, "illegal farm labor would account for a sizable share."[151]

No one else spoke. Apparently regarded as routine, the bill was read a third time and passed on a voice vote — but in a form different from that of the House.[152]

Compromise is Reached

The Senate-passed bill was sent back to the House where Representative Ford reported it. "Certain provisions in the Senate amendment," explained Mr. Landgrebe, "were very broad, would probably discourage registration, and possibly make the act more difficult to enforce." Landgrebe stated: "Since this is a 'crew leader' bill, *and not a bill covering farmers or growers,*" certain adjustments seemed in order. (Italics added.) Representative Quie defended the growers. "The Senate version implicitly imposed upon growers and processors — all those with whom a labor contractor provided migrant workers — the obligation to enforce the act. In other words," Quie stated, "the Senate version held them responsible for the crew leaders' abuses and failures. We did not believe that it was necessary to hold a farmer criminally liable for the acts and omissions of another." He concluded: "... the responsibility for enforcing the act is where it belongs — on the Secretary of Labor and not on the farmer."153 The new version retained the provisions concerning undocumented aliens.

Once again, the House voted to approve the measure on a voice vote — and, sent the new bill back to the Senate.154 To this point, the two bodies had worked separately. No conference had been requested: none was deemed necessary. However, there now developed within the Senate a colloquy among Senators from the Pacific Northwest and from Florida.

Senator Mark Hatfield (R-OR) commenced. Out in the Pacific Northwest, "... we have a number of row crops and berries which lean heavily upon the use of student labor.... This is usually under the leadership of school teachers or other public education employees who take the responsibility of acting as crew leaders for these students" or are under the supervision of parents who, collectively, act "as crew leaders." Hatfield asked a question: Does the bill "include or does it exempt such cases as I have indicated — namely, teachers and public education employees and parents who act as crew leaders?" Second, does the bill as, currently drawn, include (or exclude) the permanent employee of the farmer (or, perhaps, the farmer himself) who hired these people? Senator Nelson, for the subcommittee, concurred with Senator Hatfield — and with Senator Warren Magnuson (D-WA) — in affirming that the Department of Labor was "not to consider this type of activity" when enforcing the act.155

---

151 Congressional Record, Oct. 3, 1974, p. 33746.
152 Congressional Record, Oct. 3, 1974, p. 33747.
153 Congressional Record, Oct. 11, 1974, pp. 35468-35471.
154 Congressional Record, Oct. 11, 1974, p. 35471.
155 Congressional Record, Oct. 16, 1974, pp. 35901-35902. Both Senators Hatfield and Magnuson specifically endorsed the day haul provisions of the bill. However, for the next several Congresses, that provision (in the context of youth labor under the Fair Labor Standards Act) would remain very controversial.

A second colloquy occurred with Senator Lawton Chiles (D-FL). In the bill, the contractor *could* be exempt if his "recruitment activity is solely for his employer on no more than an incidental basis." Chiles agreed that "registration should be required of the individual whose sole job is to hire and recruit migrant labor" but he had concerns about the term "incidental." He stated: "I do not feel that the committee intended that regular employees who may perform some duties for their employer relative to securing migrant labor are to be required to register. It is my understanding," he stated, "that the bill aims at those who on a full-time basis hire or recruit migrant labor." Senator Nelson noted that "the purpose of this provision is to prevent farm labor contractors from avoiding registration by becoming the employee of each and every grower for whom they recruit and hire migrant workers...." But, *it was not the intent* of the act to include the "regular employee" of the grower. Chiles was not yet entirely clear. "Even though this duty might be considered to be an important aspect of his job responsibility by his employer ... , if he were a permanent employee and continued to have other duties, he would not be considered to have to register," Chiles inquired. "The Senator is absolutely correct in the manner in which he has stated it," Nelson replied.156

Following a summary statement by Senator Williams, the Senate concurred in the House-passed version of the bill. The vote was a voice vote.157

On October 19, President Gerald Ford returned the bill with a veto message. "This bill contains provisions designed to strengthen the protections of migrant farm workers ... which I support." But he noted that the Senate has added certain extraneous materials to the bill dealing with the federal personnel system. He directed that Congress remove them and promised to "approve" the bill as amended.158 Senator Nelson had introduced S. 3202 in March 1974.159 That bill was now resurrected, modified, and reported to the Senate on November 21160 — and was adopted by a voice vote on November 22.161 The House concurred (by a voice vote) on November 26.162 On December 7, 1974, the bill was signed into law (P.L. 93-518).163

The 1974 Flcra Amendments

The 1974 amendments represented a tightening up of the initial Farm Labor Contractor Registration Act. The focus was still primarily on the contractor. *Inter alia*, it provided:

-   The concept of "interstate" was stricken, affirming by implication that the new act would apply as well to those persons operating within a state —but having an impact upon interstate commerce.
-   The phrases "ten or more" and "at any one time in any calendar year" were deleted.
-   It exempted from coverage any farmer or processor "who personally engages in any such activity."

156 Congressional Record, Oct. 16, 1974, p. 35902.
157 Congressional Record, Oct. 16, 1974, p. 35903.
158 Congressional Record, Nov. 18, 1974, pp. 36246-36247.
159 Congressional Record, Mar. 20, 1974, p. 7383.
160 Congressional Record, Nov. 21, 1974, p. 36822.
161 Congressional Record, Nov. 22, 1974, pp. 37040-37042.
162 Congressional Record, Nov. 26, 1974, pp. 37372-37376.
163 Congressional Record, Dec. 11, 1974, p. 39005.

- Similarly exempt was any full-time or regular employee "who engages in such activity solely for his employer *on no more than an incidental basis....*" (Italics added.)

- In order to deal with students and their elders (but to include day haul operators), there was added: "any person who engaged in any such activity (A) solely within a twenty-five-mile intrastate radius of his permanent place of residence and (B) for not more than thirteen weeks per year...."

- Added to the concept of agricultural employment was "the handling, planting, drying, packing, packaging, processing, freezing, or grading prior to delivery for storage of any agricultural or horticultural commodity in its unmanufactured state."

- "No person shall engage the services of any farm labor contractor ... unless he first determines that the farm labor contractor possesses a certificate from the Secretary that is in full force and effect at the time he contracts with the farm labor contractor."

- The applicant (contractor) must file a statement affirming that "each vehicle" and the "housing" to be used by migrants "conform to all applicable Federal and State safety and health standards" — to the extent that they are under "the applicant's ownership or control...."

- The applicant (contractor) shall designate the Secretary as his agent to accept "service summons" where he has departed from his original address/ jurisdiction or "has become unavailable to accept service...."

- The contractor must make known to the farm workers "the existence of a strike or other concerted stoppage, slowdown, or interruption of operations by employees at a place of contracted employment...."

- The contractor must "refrain from recruiting, employing, or utilizing, with knowledge, the services of any person, who is an alien not lawfully admitted for permanent residence or who has not been authorized by the Attorney General to accept employment...."

- Any agreement by an employee "to waive or to modify his rights" under the statute "shall be void as contrary to public policy" — except that a waiver to the Secretary for enforcement purposes is valid.

The rights and obligations of the several parties were spelled out in some detail.[164] Though certain segments of agriculture had reservations, the new amendments did not seem to represent a threat — and, indeed, they had been approved, repeatedly, with little debate and by voice vote.

PART III. IMPLEMENTING A REVISED STATUTE (1974-1983)

By nearly all assessments, FLCRA had not been entirely successful in alleviating problems associated with migratory labor.[165] Revisions crafted during the 1973-1974 hearings

---

164 See P.L. 93-518 for precise wording of the amendments.
165 U.S. Congress, House, Committee on Education and Labor, Subcommittee on Agricultural Labor, Oversight Hearings on the Farm Labor Contractor Registration Act, Hearings, 94th Cong., 1st Sess., Oct. 1 and Oct. 11, 1975, pp. 113-136. (Hereafter cited as Hearings, House, 1975).

brought some refinement of the statute. Few voices in Congress had been raised against the statute. Still, the act was not perceived as threatening to users of migrant workers.

PRESSURES BEGIN TO MOUNT

In October 1975, the House Subcommittee on Agricultural Labor conducted hearings on FLCRA. "As you may know," commenced Representative John McFall (D-CA), "my District in California includes the central part of the San Joaquin Valley. This is one of the most productive agricultural areas in the country, and as a result, agricultural labor is a vital part of the economic foundation of the area."[166]

McFall explained that DOL had failed "to adhere to ... clearly expressed Congressional intent" but had also failed "to provide its field personnel clear directions on the implementation of these [1974] amendments." It (DOL) had required "a farm or ranch foreman" to register as a farm labor contractor though he performed "many other duties" beyond worker recruitment. McFall had written to Labor Secretary John Dunlop but had not yet received a response. While he was "not opposed" to FLCRA or to the 1974 amendments ("I believe there is a need to ensure that farm labor is not exploited by labor contractors," he said.), his concern was over the DOL's failure "to provide an equitable and clearly defined implementation of the Act."[167]

Prior to the 1974 amendments, the focus had been on the plight of agricultural workers. Now, it shifted to employers and to the structure of the industry. The *wrong people*, it was argued, were being caught up in the Department's net.

GENERAL PROBLEMS OF ADMINISTRATION

We have had "statements of concern" (and "some compliments") that DOL was "too vigorous in its administration of the act" — and, conversely, that it "is not vigorous enough," stated Chairman Ford of the House Agricultural Labor Subcommittee. The Congress has "used every device possible," he noted, "... to prod, criticize, and sometimes castigate the Labor Department to push for vigorous enforcement of laws." Still, the Committee does not want to "make compliance with the law so unpalatable" that we end up "litigating while farmworkers receive no real factual benefits from the enactment of the legislation."[168] Regulations had not yet been proposed, Ford reminded DOL: "We are, in fact, developing a considerable body of controversy in administration of this law because of the absence of these regulations."[169]

---

166 Hearings, House, 1975, p. 10.
167 Hearings, House, 1975, pp. 10-11. On Congressional opinion, see pp.85 and 93-94.
168 Hearings, House, 1975, p. 15.
169 Hearings, House, 1975, p. 16. DOL's failure to publish regulations for the 1974 amendments seemed to permeate the entire proceedings. Robert Mills, Salinas Valley Independent Growers' Association (p. 284), stated: "I think the whole effort of the testimony here today is, please, may we have some definitive regulations from the Department of Labor and not try to define what we believe the intent of Congress is...." Similarly, Donald Dressler, Western Growers' Association (p. 273), taking note of litigation then before the courts, stated, "We would wish ... that the court would have required the Department to first draft regulations before they ran off in all these different directions."

DOL intends to continue our "enforcement efforts and our multi-media information campaign," DeLury stated, "and will get as many farm labor contractors registered as possible so that the benefits of the law will be available" to the crews.[170] Then, he turned to administration. We have "a total of 19 man-years assigned to the activities under this Act" to cover the entire country.[171] As one of the later witnesses explained, "[m]ost of our [farm] workers are Spanish-speaking people."[172] As things then stood, "... we do not have a Spanish-speaking compliance officer."[173]

MORE SPECIALIZED CONCERNS WITH FLCRA

Older questions — whether dormant or never having been formally raised —assumed a sharper focus. Since the regulations had not been released at that time, there was a good bit of speculation about almost all aspects of FLCRA.

Internal Definitions

Representative Ford, speaking at the 1975 hearings on FLCRA, suggested that "that the lack of definitions and uniform regulations" seems to be the heart of complaints. He urged that the target date for release of the regulations (then, by the end of November) be moved up "so that we can start solving these problems before everybody ends up in court?"[174] Robert Chase, Deputy Assistant Secretary of Labor, assured Ford that regulations have received "priority attention" but that it was impossible, just then, to provide "an earlier date."[175]

For ten years under the act, it was assumed that everyone understood what was meant by *a crew leader* or *farm labor contractor* or *a migrant worker*. After 1974, however, definitions became more problematic. Some witnesses asserted that they "had no objections" to the act[176] and that FLCRA was "appropriate and reasonable"[177] — so long as it was not *their clients* who were affected. "In our wildest dreams we did not consider that the people which we represent," stated industry spokesman R. V. Thornton, "would be covered" under FLCRA.[178]

Who is a Farm Labor Contractor?

Representative McFall stated that he had received numerous inquiries concerning DOL's efforts to register a farm or ranch foreman as a farm labor contractor. Under the 1974

---

170 Hearings, House, 1975, p. 13. As of Sept 20, 1975, DeLury testified, "we had issued 3,718 certificates" — more than in prior years but less than expected with "approximately 10,000 or more" contractors that should be subject to coverage under the act.
171 Hearings, House, 1975, p. 14.
172 Hearings, House, 1975, p. 106.
173 Hearings, House, 1975, p. 53.
174 Hearings, House, 1975, p. 15.
175 Hearings, House, 1975, p. 16. Regulations were proposed, Dec. 8, 1975, Federal Register, pp. 57332-5733.
176 Hearings, House, 1975, pp. 258-259.
177 Hearings, House, 1975, p. 270.
178 Hearings, House, 1975, p. 252.

compromise, a foreman might be FLCRA-exempt if, in his regular work, he performs duties other than assisting his employer in acquiring migrant workers. But, how might one distinguish between primary and secondary duties? "Clearly," DeLury objected, "this language does not provide an exemption from the application of the law to all full-time employees."[179]

The relationship of the contractor to the grower was critical — and, it would seem, difficult to define. Does the contractor provide services (employees) to one employer or to several? What services does he provide to the employees? What records does the contractor keep? Guinn Sinclair observed of California:

> "We have examples of where a contractor has been successfully prosecuted, his license has been revoked by the State, and the next day he is still with the same crews working the same ranches, only now he is an employee of the ranch. Clearly he is still a farm labor contractor...."[180]

Conversely, *if a grower* provides farm hands to a series of farmers, when does he cross the line from grower to contractor? Suddenly, such questions become relevant — and, ultimately, perhaps, a subject of litigation.

And who is a Migrant?

How long might a migrant remain in one location before he or she ceased to be migratory? Some workers are engaged by a firm (or firms) in an area for two, three — ten months out of the year. Can a migrant also be seasonal? "They come back every year. You see ... we have county housing." "They come there and they live in those houses until the crops are over." "They are really not migrant because they only come from Texas to Patterson [California]"[181]

Another witness stated, "To my way of thinking, a migrant worker is one who travels away from his regular place of residence. A great many of these migrant workers who move throughout the United States in agricultural labor, live and make their homes in our immediate area ... ," he stated. "They come back to that area about this time of year and stay there, generally, until about May again."[182]

Representative Ford asked about the responsibility for transportation while recruiting. "The only time we ever go out and recruit anybody, we don't recruit them really, we just go down ... to Calexico. We have 23 foremen this year in cantaloups and those 23 foremen will go out."[183] This would seem to recall the initial question implied by Representative McFall: When is a foreman a regular employee and when is he really a farm labor contractor? Conversely, does it really matter so long as he or she is engaged *in the work of* a farm labor contractor?

---

179 Hearings, House, 1975, p. 14. DeLury continued: "Certainly an employee of a grower, whether full-time or not, who devotes all of his time or the majority of his time to farm labor contractor activities is not within the exemption and such an employee should register under the law." (Italics added).
180 Hearings, House, 1975, p. 261.
181 Hearings, House, 1975, p. 280.
182 Hearings, House, 1975, p. 68.
183 Hearings, House, 1975, p. 280.

Interpreting the Word "Personally"

In 1974, the concept of personally was added to the list of exemptions. "While this language is clear with respect to sole proprietors," DeLury stated, "interpretative problems do arise with respect to partnerships, associations, joint stock companies, trusts and corporations." DeLury explained how it might apply to an individual with the responsibility of "a sole proprietor" if he "acts personally with respect only to farm labor contracting activities at the operation involved." But, he concluded, such an interpretation may raise problems of proof to be resolved on a "case-by-case basis."[184]

Ford responded that he was "loath to suggest that his committee would ever write anything that is ambiguous," stating: "What we are really trying to do is find the point at which we should ascribe responsibility for the employer/employee relationship." Again: "The farm labor contractor that we are trying to reach is the body broker."[185]

Reaching the body broker, however, proved difficult. Some in agriculture objected to DOL's interpretation of personally: i.e., "... a farmer who operates as an individual and performs all the activity ... without the assistance of any employee, agent or contractor...."[186] But firms have "a variety of arrangements" with the grower.

A small grower may produce a crop to the point of harvest, then through one of several arrangements, have that crop harvested by a shipper. The shipper will harvest, pack and sell the crop, based on financial arrangements with the grower. We also have large cooperatives which provide harvesting, packing, and sales facilities for its [sic] grower members.

It was asserted that, in a large company, there could be "between 10 and 30 small growers for whom some agricultural work is done by the company's employees." Obviously, it was explained, "the owner does not personally engage in such activity" but allows the duties to be "delegated."[187]

In other cases, ownership itself becomes a factor. Where crops are harvested in the field by a client (non-grower) making use of migratory labor (but, with the crops still owned by a separate entity, the grower), who is the responsible party? If ownership changes hands while the crop is in the field, does responsibility follow the crops? There seemed, suddenly, a host of issues that may not have been considered when FLCRA was largely unenforced — but, after the 1974 amendments, became critical.

On an Incidental Basis

"A full time or regular employee of a farmer is exempt," wrote Dante Nomellini, a Stockton-based attorney for the growers, if he is engaged in farm labor contracting activity for his employer "on no more than an incidental basis." The term, "'incidental' is not defined," he declared, but the "plain meaning" would seem to render him exempt if his "labor contracting function was not his primary function or primary responsibility."[188]

---

184 Hearings, House, 1975, p. 14.
185 Hearings, House, 1975, pp. 16-18.
186 Hearings, House, 1975, p. 97.
187 Hearings, House, 1975, pp. 258-259.
188 Hearings, House, 1975, p. 100.

What was plain to Nomellini was less so to DOL. DeLury, with other Departmental witnesses, objected that the agency had received virtually no guidance from Congress. "Unfortunately," said Bobbye Spears, Associate Solicitor and charged with preparation of the regulations, "the act does not think in terms of the primary duty, nor does it tell us to look behind the subjective interest of the employer in hiring a particular person."[189]

Arguably, a case-by-case approach might have resolved the problem; but, in practice, such discretion may have been ill-advised. For example, "a farmer's or processor's operations manager, his personnel director, his foreman, or all of them, may find that they must, for a temporary period, devote an unusual amount of their time to soliciting, recruiting, or hiring workers." In the process (for a brief period), the amount of time expended might "substantially exceed" the time taken by a farm labor contractor for roughly similar tasks.[190]

'Who For A Fee ...'

Another aspect of FLCRA administration that caused concern was interpretation of "who, for a fee...." Perry Ellsworth (National Council of Agricultural Employers) argued that the term, as used under the act, had several potential meanings. A "fee" would seem to mean "a payment asked or given for a specific service." But DOL would argue that if a full-time employee "has any dealings with agricultural labor, a portion of the salary that employee receives is a 'fee.'"[191] On this matter, Representative Ford wrote to Secretary Dunlop: "... I would assume that the words 'for a fee' would not be construed to include any part of the salary of a full-time or regular employee who, as part of his job, is required to transport workers between a meeting place in the city and his employer's farm."[192]

As with many areas of labor policy, an answer may have been complex. For example, the Benita Packing Company, one of the firms in contention, "goes into the field with its own employees, harvests the crop, brings it to the packing shed, packs it for market and sells the commodity on behalf of the grower," stated attorney Donald Dressler. *"The grower pays a fee which covers the labor expense...."* Benita Packing "is in control of the workers at all times" and the *"grower has no control or involvement with them at all."* (Italics added.) In this case, to whom would FLCRA apply — if, indeed, it would apply at all?[193]

Leon Gordon, counsel for the Agricultural Producers Labor Committee (a *labor* co-op serving Arizona and California), also addressed the issue of fees. The Committee is non-profit, but operates a series of worker-related activities.[194] "Its books are zeroed out at the end of the year, and each grower defrays his exact proportionate share of the cost of the labor and overhead expenses of the association determined on a volume basis." However, DOL "... has adamantly taken the position that *a fee is involved* even in the case of a cooperative labor

---

189 Hearings, House, 1975, pp. 19-20.
190 Comments of Perry Ellsworth for management, Hearings, House, 1975, pp. 89-93.
191 Hearings, House, 1975, p. 82.
192 Hearings, House, 1975, p. 94.
193 Hearings, House, 1975, p. 270.
194 Gordon testified, Hearings, House, 1975, p. 285: "They operate dining facilities, and in some cases provide hot meals in the orchards. These camps provide recreation facilities, television rooms, chapels, and in some cases they provide counseling for the workers. This housing and attendant facilities are provided on a cost or below cost basis to the workers."

association...." (Italics added.) The result was litigation — with Gordon drawn into court to protect the grower/co-ops.[195]

Insurance

Under FLCRA, insurance was to have been roughly on a par with common carriers used to transport passengers in interstate commerce. Several concerns were voiced here — some focusing upon the character of the farm labor contractor.[196]

The farm labor contractor "... is a small businessman. He has just one little truck that he is trying to make a living with.... If he owns two or three trucks, it is just that much more," one witness stated. "It is the recordkeeping, the details. He does not have a bookkeeper. *In most instances, he cannot read and write himself very well.*

He is being required to keep all these records that he just does not have any way of doing." "In the first place, many of them cannot afford the insurance requirements even if they can find a company that will write the insurance." Finally, he concluded, "We do not quite understand why we should be required to furnish all of these buses and all these high insurance requirements to transport people 5 or 6 miles. Many of our workers are not transported more than just 10 or 15 or 20 miles."[197]

Bobbye Spears, with the Solicitor's Office, addressed the same issue — but with a somewhat different twist. She recalled a recent case in which a farmer said that "I have to have peas picked tomorrow and a neighbor farmer saying, I will be glad to round up a crew of people and transport them down to your farm and pick your peas tomorrow." Ms. Spears noted: "The helpful farmer took his truck, which, in this case, was an open truck, transported them down to the neighbor's farm, they picked the peas, and on the way back there was a wreck. There were several children under the age of 12. I believe that three were killed."[198]

EMPLOYMENT OF ALIENS

"Quite obviously, we anticipated that a central problem in dealing with this law would be the problem of illegal aliens," stated Representative Ford, "because it was one of the purposes we had in mind in amended the law."[199] There were several factors at issue: the bureaucracy, employer-employee relations, and the local reaction.

---

195 Hearings, House, 1975, pp. 285-287.
196 See Section 5(a)(2) of the act. The Secretary had some measure of discretion in this matter.
197 Statement of Scott Toothaker, Texas Citrus and Vegetable Growers and Shippers, Hearings, House 1975, pp. 67-69. Italics added.
198 Hearings, House, 1975, p. 20. See also section on Adams Fruit litigation, below.
199 Hearings, House, 1975, p. 52.

Dealing with the Bureaucracy

Warren Landis of the Wage/Hour Division affirmed that DOL had "worked very closely with ... Immigration and Naturalization" but suggested the issue was "quite thorny." Landis speculated

> "What, in fact, constitutes *knowing employment* of illegal aliens and what are the bona-fide efforts that a contractor would make so that he would be absolved of knowing employment of illegal aliens? (Italics added.)
> "I wish we had a full answer this morning, but we do not. This is another situation that we are addressing on a case-by-case basis."

Landis stated that he had "one case where we denied a certificate ... because of a history of employment of illegal aliens" and we have "some other — perhaps similar — cases that are pending." John Silver of the Wage/Hour Division from Fresno noted that "... the Border Patrol indicates to us that they believe that 30 percent of the farm-workers who are harvesting crops in California are illegal aliens. So," he stated, "... you can see that our problems are great." Part of the problem may have been linguistic. "There are groups where very few of them speak English. They cannot communicate," observed Joe Fernandez, with the Wage/Hour Division from Raleigh, North Carolina, and "we have had difficulty locating a crew leader."[200]

Ford turned to Bobbye Spears of the Solicitor's Office. Do the contemplated regulations have "any specific requirements" to show that a grower or farm labor contractor actually "tried to know" the worker's status? Spears replied, "We have been working very closely with the INS lawyers and with the Attorney General's staff to see what would be reasonable within constitutional restraints." She added, "What could we require within the constraints of the Constitution? What sort of affirmative duty could we place on the grower?" Spears stated, "We think we have a reasonable set of requirements which we do intend to propose when the regulations come out." But, she added: "It is very tricky."[201]

Reaction from the Industry

"The burden placed ... on the employer," stated Dante Nomellini, attorney for the growers, "to be able to identify an illegal alien" is "unfair and in most cases the labor contractor or the farmer or any employer is not in a position to accomplish an adequate interrogation of the individual involved."[202]

Nomellini acknowledged that the statute says "knowingly," but that the act still placed an unfair burden upon the employer. An illegal, picked up and deported, may end up back on the same farm — without the employer/grower being aware.

---

200 Hearings, House, 1975, pp. 52-54.
201 Hearings, House, 1975, p. 54. This conversation took place some twenty years after the end of the bracero program.
202 Hearings, House, 1975, p. 106.

"You have to recognize that the farmer himself is not just one individual working on the farm and he is not the one who goes out and supervises the worker and he is not the one generally who has the contact. We have a language differential here ... most of the farmers are not fluent in Spanish nor are they capable, or their agents, of interrogating that man to find out if he is legal or illegal without violating that man's rights."

He suggested, after analysis, that it can be asked "if he is a lawful resident of the United States" and for "his name and social security number." "We don't have this capability to interrogate. The Border Patrol, a very sophisticated group of people who have been trained, even they have problems. The burden shouldn't be placed on industry."[203]

Nomellini's solution was direct. The State Department "ought to be asked to cooperate with Congress in coming up with a situation where the individual who is an illegal, once apprehended, is punished in a significant way so that ... he won't come back across the border." The problem, he stated, "has to be attacked at its roots and that is right at the border. If anything significant is going to be done to keep aliens out — *and I don't know whether we want to*, that's a matter of policy...." (Italics added.) It's a matter for the Congress and for those directly involved: "... not the farmers and not the labor contractors and not the general employers in industry."[204]

The Local Reaction

Scott Toothaker, a management attorney from Texas, lives right up against the Mexican border. And, that creates another dimension to the problem. Some Spanish-speakers may be illegal — but others may be local.

"How is this truck driver [picking up job applicants] with nothing more than a second, third, fourth, or fifth grade education, to pass on whether that guy is an illegal alien or not? They all have some kind of a card.... But I defy anyone in this [hearing] room to tell me whether he is an illegal alien."

Ford responded that regulations — which "have not yet been written" — provide ways through which to render an analysis. The presumption of *knowingly* employing an alien "would have to be overcome by proving actual knowledge, and while it is less than perfect, we do know that there are ... people who habitually rehire people."[205]

Guinn Sinclair, representative of the farm labor contractors, voiced similar concerns, suggesting that "the Department of State should be the one" to determine who is in the country illegally. "Trying to get the businessman to enforce the laws of the United States just is not good."[206]

---

203 Hearings, House, 1975, pp. 106-107.
204 Hearings, House, 1975, p. 107. Nomellini questioned, p. 98, the ability of the "foreman and supervisors who are not sophisticated interrogators" to screen for illegal immigration. "If it is your desire to keep illegal aliens out of the country then cooperation from the State Department will be required and still penalties will have to be imposed upon the apprehended illegal alien himself." He added: "The slap on the hand and free transportation to Mexico is not an adequate deterrent." See also pp. 146-148.
205 Hearings, House, 1975, p. 77.
206 Hearings, House, 1975, p. 262.

Zora Arredondo was equally direct. A self-described "hillbilly from Kentucky talking before all these lawyers," queried: "Do you know what it is to need to have your crops thinned, or weeded before you can irrigate and you have 1 or 2 days before you get the water? Have you ever seen fruit that was falling on the ground ready to be picked?" Moving on to policy implications:

> "If you need people and some come to the field wanting to work, you are going to put them to work. The crop is the important thing, not who the man is or where he comes from. Besides, the place to stop the illegal aliens isn't there in the fields, it is at the port of entry. (...) Do we have the right to ask people if they are citizens? The Department of Labor doesn't know the answer."

Ms. Arredondo turned to the Members: "Do you? When we do ask people for papers, they tell you, 'I don't have to show you my papers.' How many of us have anything to prove we are U.S. citizens? I don't."[207]

NEW REGULATIONS RELEASED

On June 29, 1976, final regulations were published. Of 61 substantive comments, items of principal concern were (a) the increased amounts of insurance coverage, (b) the applicability of the amended act to include intrastate, as well as interstate, farm labor activities, and (c) the proposed regulations relating to illegal aliens.[208]

On insurance coverage, DOL "concluded that the increased amounts ... were necessary to protect workers." Coverage of intrastate farm workers was, of course, part of the 1974 Act and could not be changed without legislation.[209] Concerning employment of aliens, the farm labor contractor was to give evidence of "an affirmative showing of a *bona fide* inquiry of each prospective employee's status as a United States citizen or as a person lawfully authorized to work in the United States." The regulation provides a series of acceptable routes — birth certificate, certificate of naturalization, passport, certain INS forms — through which a determination might be made.[210]

COVERAGE AND CONTROVERSY

With the passage of time, some Members of Congress, with others, began to reassess the impact of FLCRA and to urge modification of coverage. At least three areas stand out: custom combining, poultry harvesting, and detasseling of corn.

---

207 Hearings, House, 1957, pp. 277-279.
208 Federal Register, June 1976, p. 26820. See also Federal Register, Dec. 8, 1975, pp. 57332-57339, for the proposed regulations.
209 Federal Register, June 29, 1976, p. 26820.
210 Federal Register, June 29, 1976, pp. 26825-26826.

Custom Combining, Hay Harvesting, and Sheep Shearing

On March 4, 1976, Representative Larry Pressler (R-SD) introduced legislation to exempt from FLCRA "contractors of workers engaged in custom cutting or combine operations" and "contractors of workers engaged in the shearing of sheep."[211] Roughly comparable legislation was introduced on March 9 with two more bills on March 11.[212]

"In Nebraska, the major part of our extensive wheat acreage is harvested by 'custom cutters,'" stated Representative Virginia Smith (R-NE). "These operations do not involve migrant labor in the accepted sense of the definition," she stated, "... so all of the added precaution against abuses is not necessary." Smith suggested that these contractors and crew leaders "... should not be required to be registered, or to be certified, or to meet the other requirements for insurance, transportation, and housing." Seeking exemption, she stated: "Otherwise, we have placed a hardship on the agricultural equivalent of the small businessman and ... have subjected him to more of that over-regulation which strangles and can eventually destroy."[213]

Members from other grain growing states also suggested change. James Abourezk (D-SD) introduced a new bill (March 18), observing that the 1974 FLCRA amendments had "inadvertently expanded the scope of the law to cover sheep shearers and custom combine crews." Senators Lloyd Bentsen (D-TX) and Abourezk had met with Department officials on the issue; Senator Nelson and Representative Ford had written to DOL. These informal efforts, however, were of no avail.[214]

Senator Robert Dole (R-KS) explained the purposes of the exemption. FLCRA was intended "to end abuses against migrant workers and farmers" by farm labor contractors. While custom combining workers are migratory (starting in Texas and moving on to the far north), they were *really not migratory* in the sense that farm laborers might be. There was "no record of exploiting or abusing" of such employees. As for safety and health requirements, "custom operators are already meeting the standards necessary to protect their employees." Thus, Senator Dole saw "no need for the additional safety and health requirements" of FLCRA. He objected to "time-consuming paperwork" and to requirements for "higher insurance. FLCRA was intended for farmworkers "from a poverty-stricken environment," who have "little or no knowledge of the English language," and are moved in "unsafe transportation."

Dole concluded, "There is no similarity in any respect between farm labor contractors and custom combine operators"[215] — or sheep shearing crews, for that matter.

On March 23, Representative Pressler introduced yet another version of his FLCRA-exemption bill — as did Representative Berkeley Bedell (D-IA).[216] Bedell had written to the Department on February 23, 1976, and, his request for exemption having been denied, he called DOL and spoke with Herbert Cohen of Wage/Hour. Cohen acknowledged receiving communications from Members involved in drafting the act.

---

211 Congressional Record, Mar. 4, 1976, p. 5571.
212 Congressional Record, Mar. 9, 1976, pp. 5955, 5956-5957, and Mar. 11, 1976, p. 6192.
213 Congressional Record, Mar. 17, 1976, pp. 6802-6803.
214 Congressional Record, Mar. 18, 1976, p. 7108. See letter of Representative Ford and Senator Nelson to William Usery, Secretary of Labor, Feb. 23, 2976, reprinted in Congressional Record, Mar. 23, 1976, p. 7611.
215 Congressional Record, Mar. 18, 1976, pp. 7108-7110.
216 Congressional Record, Mar. 23, 1976, pp. 7719 and 7720.

"He [Cohen] then related that, despite this testimony, the Department decided to proceed with the implementation of the new requirements because its lawyers felt that the legislative history of the 1974 amendments did not specifically call for the exemption of such crews."[217]

Bedell called the incident "a classic example of the executive branch using its rulemaking authority to usurp the legislative function of the Congress" and of "attempting to legislate by fiat." Finally, he called upon the Congress "to thwart executive excesses in the rulemaking area" by enacting corrective legislation.[218]

On March 23, as the Senate considered the Rural Development Act of 1972, Senator Dole proposed FLCRA exemption of custom combine, hay harvesting, and sheep shearing workers. Senators Abourezk, Bentsen, and Nelson were supportive; without dissent, the amendment was adopted.[219] The following day, Representative Tom Foley, a Democrat from Washington state, called up the Rural Development Act with the Dole amendment. Mr. Foley explained that the problem was "technical" —that the issues were neither "labor contractors [n]or migrant laborers" but, rather, "independent contractors who until now have not been subjected" to the FLCRA.[220] The only other speaker was Representative Ford — who announced that, although the subject matter of the bill should have been directed to a subcommittee of the Committee on Education and Labor, he would not object.[221]

On April 5, 1976, the Rural Development Act (with the Dole amendment) was signed into law (P.L. 94-259).[222]

POULTRY SERVICES

During the spring of 1976, a seemingly uncontroversial bill was introduced dealing with internal Department of Agriculture administration. The measure was passed by the House[223] and was forwarded to the Senate. There, it was reported on September 30, 1976, considered later that same day, and passed with an amendment.[224]

Referred back to the House, Representative Tom Foley presented the measure and the clerk read the title of the bill and the Senate amendments. At the conclusion, a paragraph had been added amending FLCRA.

"(9) any custom poultry harvesting, breeding, debeaking, sexing, or health service operation, providing the employees of the operation are not regularly required to be away from their domicile other than during their normal working hours."

---

217 Congressional Record, Mar. 23, 1976, p. 7689.
218 Ibid. Representative Bedell explained: "The original act exempted crews employing less than 10 people from its registration requirements. However, in 1974, the statute was amended to include any group which 'recruits or transports' more than one employee. This numerical change technically brought small custom combiners and sheep shearers under the law despite the fact that there is no specific reference to these groups in the legislative history of the act."
219 Congressional Record, Mar. 23, 1976, pp. 7608-7612.
220 Congressional Record, Mar. 24, 1976, pp. 7785-7786.
221 Congressional Record, Mar. 24, 1976, p. 7786.
222 Congressional Record, Apr. 6, 1976, p. 9554.
223 Congressional Record, July 26, 1976, pp. 23735-23741. See H.R. 10133 (94th Congress).
224 Congressional Record, Sept. 30, 1976, pp. 33815-33816, 33866-33867.

Representative Edward Madigan (R-IL) queried: "I wonder if the gentleman ... could explain the one amendment the Senate has placed on the bill." Foley responded: "...the Senate has placed on the bill a provision relating to the Farm Labor Contractor Registration Act." William Wampler (R-VA) added that the FLCRA amendment was the only change in the House-passed bill.[225]

The bill was approved, sent to the White House and signed into law on October 1976 (P.L. 94-561).

To Detassel and Rogue Hybrid Seed Corn

During hearings early in 1978, Representative Virginia Smith complained about the "narrowminded and ridiculous interpretations" of the "over-zealous bureaucrats at the Department of Labor who don't have anything better to do than harass our businessmen." Smith went on to discuss actions that "endanger yet another of the fragile freedoms that still exist for individuals in this country."[226] She observed that "thousands of farmers" have "come to Washington during the past few weeks in search of help to raise farm prices." To raise farm income, she seemed to suggest, farmers should be permitted to pay less to the "several thousand high school students" who are hired each year "to detassel seed corn, thin out test plots or rogue sorghum." She stated,

"... in no way can the salary from this job be considered as their primary means of support. In many cases, it is more of a social event than a job. It also provides a good opportunity for a coach, high school teacher, or college student to pick up some extra money and for the students to keep in touch during part of the summer."

Ms. Smith stated, "I believe that unless this law is changed to stop the action proposed by the Department of Labor, we face a serious challenge to our freedom."[227]

On April 11, Representative James Leach (R-IA) introduced H.Res. 1124 expressing the sense of the House "that certain individuals employed in the detasseling of hybrid seed corn should not be considered to be migrant workers" for purposes of FLCRA.[228] Shortly thereafter, a bill was introduced by Leach that would have amended FLCRA to deal with the same issue.[229] No hearings were held: in legislative terms, the issue seemed to disappear. Momentum, however, was building.

---

225 Congressional Record, Oct. 1, 1976, pp. 35170-35171.

226 U.S. Congress, House, Committee on Education and Labor, Subcommittee on Economic Opportunity. Farm Labor Contractor Registration Act, Hearings, 95th Cong., 2nd Sess., Feb. 22-23, 1978, pp. 35-36. (Cited hereafter as Hearings, House, 1978).

227 earings, House, 1978, pp. 36-37. Rep. Charles Grassley (R-IA), p. 49, questioned the "loss of an important source of youth employment." Rep. Charles Thone (R-NE), p. 43, argued that "such stupid regulations" might force companies to turn "to mechanical methods of detasseling and then what would this do to our employment problems?" In a letter, Feb. 28, 1978, pp. 40-41, later submitted for the record, Smith wrote to Secretary Marshall and explained: "We have thousands and thousands of workers who will be affected by this matter and are waiting to see if their government has the capacity to exercise some restraint in its authority, and some common sense in its actions." See testimony of Representative David Stockman (R-MI), ibid, pp. 45-48, and comments of Richard O'Connell, National Council of Farmer Cooperatives, Hearings, Senate, Apr. 1963, pp. 199-200.

228 Congressional Record, Apr. 11, 1978, p. 9697.

229 Congressional Record, Apr. 25, 1978, p. 11363.

In September, the "Perishable Agricultural Commodities Act" (PACA) was under consideration. Senator Richard Clark (D-IA) proposed an amendment to FLCRA to correct "an example of government out of control." The amendment would exempt "a portion of the seed industry" from FLCRA registration. "These are young people [with about 280,000 young persons who work seasonally] ranging in age from 14 to 16 years old who work for an average of 10 days to 2 weeks each summer," Clark stated, and who "detassel seed corn, eliminate 'rogue' plants, and perform other functions, related to seed production." The employees are from the local area, residing within a 30 to 40 mile radius, and who return to their home each evening, he suggested. These people are "clearly not migrants by any reasonable definition."[230] His constituents "are very much up in arms about this," he stated, "and ... I do not blame them."[231]

It had only been through the past year, it was stated, that DOL had sought to enforce FLCRA against the seed corn industry.[232] On February 23, 1978, Senator Clark had addressed a letter to Secretary Marshall in which the issue was discussed — and followed that up with a phone call to Marshall and a personal visit with Assistant Secretary Daniel Elisburg, but DOL "refused to change its position."[233] Senator Richard Lugar (R-IN) similarly wrote to Marshall in late July, but without apparent impact.[234] Now, with no objection having been heard, an amendment was added to PACA and a quarter-plus million workers were exempted from FLCRA.

The Clark amendment was accepted and approved by the Congress.[235] On November 1, 1978, the root bill was signed into law (P.L. 95-562).

THE LESSENING COVERAGE OF FLCRA

Various segments of the agricultural industry had been eliminated from FLCRA coverage as, it was argued, the wrong people were brought under the act's purview. Senator David Boren (D-OK) would later observe: "We could go through the entire food and fiber industry, sector by sector, adopting amendments to clarify the act." He suggested that a wiser course would be to "enact legislation to clarify the act completely once and for all."[236]

HEARINGS IN THE HOUSE: 1978

In mid-1977, Representative McFall wrote once more to Secretary Marshall concerning registration under FLCRA. McFall stated that farmers in his district (part of the San Joaquin

---

230 Congressional Record, Sept. 8, 1978, pp. 28565-28566. Senator Richard Lugar (R-IN) stated, p. 28568: "Activities exempted include detasseling but also include activities such as roguing and hand pollenation which are typically performed by young people."
231 Congressional Record, Sept. 8, 1978, p. 28566.
232 See comments of Senator Williams (D-NJ), Sept. 8, 1978, Congressional Record, pp. 28568-28569, about the seed corn industry.
233 Congressional Record, Sept. 8, 1978, p. 28566.
234 Congressional Record, Sept. 8, 1978, p. 28568.
235 Congressional Record, Oct. 13, 1978, pp. 36707-36709, 37113-37114.
236 Congressional Record, June 25, 1978, p. 16748.

Valley) would be forced to register as farm labor contractors under the definition of *personally*.[237] Marshall's response was less than some Members had hoped — providing the context for the 1978 hearings.[238]

Starting from the McFall/Marshall correspondence, the hearings explored a variety of FLCRA definitions. Most critics followed the lead of Perry Ellsworth (National Council of Agricultural Employers). He did not seek to diminish worker protections, but, that having been said, he continued to argue against the "untold harassment" of farmers and others — who were "by no stretch of the imagination crew leaders."[239] Many argued for *the original intent* of the Congress.[240]

Day haul workers raised broader questions. Representative William Hefner (D-NC) acknowledged that such workers had not been "inadvertently included under the law." Still, he urged the Members to "reexamine those intentions" and to exempt workers living within a 75-mile radius of agricultural operations. "In North Carolina," he stated, "day haul workers are almost always, local, permanent residents of the area in which they work." They do not necessarily go through a labor contractor and, when they do, "... it is more a matter of convenience rather than economic necessity." He stated: "Day haul workers *are not migrant workers, as the term is commonly understood*.... And day haul operators, who transport these workers ... are not crew leaders in the usual sense of this term."[241] (Italics added.)

But, if not migratory, such workers may still have been subject to transportation provided by growers or contractors. "The gist of this problem seems to be in the insurance coverage required of anyone defined by the law as a farm labor contractor, whether he transports local day labor or true migrant labor," Hefner stated. No one suggests that day haul workers go unprotected, he stated, but they still have under state insurance laws requirements similar to "all other workers in the State."[242]

The issue was taken up by Representative B. F. Sisk (D-CA) in a letter to DOL. Elisburg replied that state coverage varied "in accordance with the mandate of the particular state legislation." Such laws are work-related and apply only where "the passengers are clearly 'employees' of the insured employer." Dependents of migrant workers are not covered, Elisburg continued. "In addition, liability under State workers compensation plans would not extend to the times migrant workers are being transported from one employer to a prospective employer."[243]

These several issues were joined with respect to *shared worker* arrangements. Representative David Stockman (R-MI) proposed that FLCRA should not apply to farmers who shared the services of agricultural workers and who receive "no monetary consideration" other than actual expenses. "The potential for abuse," Representative Stockman stated, "is in

---

237 See John McFall to Ray Marshall, June 30, 1977, reprinted in U.S. Congress, House, Committee on Education and Labor, Subcommittee on Economic Opportunity, Farm Labor Contractor Act, Hearings, 95th Cong., 2nd Sess., Feb. 22-23, 1978, pp. 13-14. (Cited hereafter as Hearings, House, 1978.) Others joining McFall in his inquiry to Marshall were Robert Leggett, John Moss, B. F. Sisk, and Harold Johnson, all Democrats from California.

238 Hearings, House, 1978, pp. 14-16.

239 Hearings, House, 1978, p. 78.

240 Hearings, House, 1978, pp. 13, 42-43, and 48.

241 Hearings, House, 1978, pp. 21-28. Current radius was 25 miles.

242 Hearings, House, 1978, p. 23.

243 Hearings, House, 1978, p. 8. The correspondence between Rep. Sisk and Elisburg appears on pages 7-12. See also comments by Rep. McFall on this issue, pp. 18-19.

my view almost nil."[244] Elisburg responded that, "as an enforcement policy," DOL "would prefer to put our resources elsewhere" rather than come after small farmers who, on a local basis, share workers.[245] The response did not satisfy Stockman, and Representative William Goodling (R-PA) suggested: "He [Elisburg] is saying if we had more resources we would get after them, too...." But Elisburg stated, "... large or small, if we found abuses of the work force we would go wherever they are."[246]

Some urged that legislation exempt "nonprofit charitable organizations," "public or nonprofit private educational institutions," and "bona fide nonprofit agricultural cooperatives engaged in labor contracting for their own members." Elisburg suggested that such proposals were something of a ruse — and one that DOL would oppose — that they would "substantially narrow the act's coverage and would deny its protection to large numbers of agricultural workers." Elisburg stated,

"We have been told by those who support this exemption that such organizations are fixed and have assets which would be reachable in a law suit by their employees. I think that we all have to recognize, generally, agricultural workers do not have the financial resources to independently assert their rights against such organizations, and we question why this economically disadvantaged group should be placed in this position."

Further, Elisburg stated that "... employment by a nonprofit organization has nothing to do with a need to protect agricultural workers under FLCRA, particularly if the nonprofit venture consists of profit-making organizations."[247]

CONCERNS GROW

"These individuals," registered under FLCRA, are "not farmers; they were 'agents' who arranged to provide migrant labor to farmers," Representative Stockman affirmed. Many of them have "long criminal records. They stole from the workers, they stole from the farmers, and they needlessly endangered the health and safety of migrant workers."[248]

Yet, it was with these same, perhaps unscrupulous, middlemen that farmers dealt. The contractors, some alleged, provided the services of low-wage and, often low-skilled workers: some Native Americans, some foreign-born — and some ineligible to work in the United States. They broke strikes, some said, and prevented domestic workers from organizing. Further, critics suggested that they provided *cover* for their farmer/business partners.

DOL, some urged, had "consistently misinterpreted" the rules governing such contractors. Though he believed "that agricultural workers must be protected from abuse by unethical crew leaders" (a consistent sub-theme of FLCRA critics), Representative Leon Panetta (D-CA) protested that "family farmers" were "forced to comply with complicated registration forms, maintain detailed records, and are subject to a variety of investigations and

---

244 Hearings, House, 1978, pp. 45-47. When introducing FLCRA legislation, Stockman referred to "predatory bureaucrats" that have turned the law into "a weapon against the farmer." He explained (Congressional Record, June 20, 1977, p. 19982): "In the Department of Labor's eyes, the expectation that the laborers would return to his farm became 'valuable consideration' to the farmer entering into a casual agreement with his neighbor. This play upon words turned the farmers, he said, into 'farm labor contractors.'"
245 Hearings, House, 1978, p. 52.
246 Hearings, House, 1978, p. 52.
247 Hearings, House, 1978, pp. 54-55.

inspections." Faced with "growing anger" from the farming community, Representative Panetta proposed a substantial restructuring of FLCRA.[249]

Relations with the Department of Labor

Under date of October 24, 1979, fifty-two Senators [led by J. Bennett Johnston (D-LA)] wrote to Secretary Marshall expressing "our increasing concern" over DOL's management of FLCRA.

The Johnston letter explained the purposes of the act (as the signers perceived them) and observed that "farmers and certain other agricultural employers" are being required to register — "a requirement we believe goes beyond any reasonable interpretation of the law." DOL's actions, "apparently based on its own extremely narrow interpretation" of the act, are "completely contrary to Congressional intent," and impose "an undue penalty and economic burden on those specifically exempted" by Congress. "... these actions have resulted in a misdirection of the Department's limited resources at the expense of those the law was intended to protect."[250]

Marshall's response, dated November 26, 1979, offered few accommodations. He agreed that enforcement of the act "be targeted on repeat and serious violations which jeopardize labor standards...." Marshall observed that the first ten years "under the Act" have not ended abuse. Thus, the 1974 amendments were enacted "to extend coverage and improve enforcement."

The Secretary acknowledged that a farmer (or other agriculturally-related person) would be exempt if he or she "'personally' recruited migrant labor for their own operation" and that "any full-time or regular employees of any incorporated farm or agricultural business" might also be exempt if the employee "only performed farm labor contractor-type activities on an 'incidental' basis." On both issues, DOL had been consistent.

> "We believe ... that FLCRA applies where there is a crewleader hiring or transporting workers or where there are company employees substantially engaged in activities generally performed by crewleaders. We also believe that it is critical to enforce the Act in a way which discourages evasion of its provisions — *to deter farm labor contractors from being placed on payrolls and appearing to assume the status of full-time or regular employees.* This enforcement approach is consistent with both the letter and spirit of the Act." (Italics added.)

The Secretary conceded that "the term 'incidental'" may not have been defined "as specifically as possible." He therefore stated that, for the future, such a person would be one "who does not spend more than 20 percent of his time in farm labor contracting activities and performs that activity solely for his employer." These changes will provide "clarity [to] our

---

248 Congressional Record, June 20, 1977, p. 19982.

249 Congressional Record, May 21, 1979, p. 11996. The Panetta proposal was only one of a number of FLCRA-related bills that surfaced during the late 1970s and early 1980s.

250 See J. Bennett Johnston, with 51 other Members of the Senate, to F. Ray Marshall, Oct. 24, 1979, reprinted in the Congressional Record, Nov. 14, 1979, pp. 32322-32323.

enforcement position while at the same time preserving important protections for farm workers under the Act."[251]

The Senators were not entirely pleased with Marshall's letter. On December 5, 1979, Senator Johnston [with Russell Long (D-LA)] concurred with Marshall's emphasis on "'traditional farm labor contractors'" — and requested "a copy of instructions being prepared for enforcement officers." But, they disagreed on the impact of such changes.

> "First, in order to know if an employee is engaged on more than an incidental basis, he must be engaged less than 20 percent of some time period. Logically, the time period should be his total manhours of employment. The failure of your letter to specify a time period leaves open the possibility that '20 percent of his time' means 20 percent of any work week, any work day, or any pay period. Any one of these possible meanings would render the 20 percent standard ineffective as far as strengthening the exemption provided by Congress.
>
> "Second, your letter is not specific about the meaning of farm labor contracting activities. As we understand the Department's interpretation of the Act, supervision is considered to be a farm labor contracting activity. Since your letter does not clarify this, the new definition of 'incidental' again becomes less significant.
>
> "Third, your letter does not indicate what regulatory standing the new definition of 'incidental' would have. The Department's intent should have been set forth in formal regulations, subject to public comment. Similarly, the interpretative regulations for the Act itself are long overdue."[252]

Through the last year and a half that Marshall was in office, such correspondence took on a regular pattern as first one and then another Member of Congress became distressed with the provisions of FLCRA.

The Boren Amendment and the Panetta Bill (1980)

During consideration of the Child Nutrition Amendments of 1980, Senator Boren proposed an amendment "to clarify the provisions" of FLCRA. "All of us," he commenced, "... want to see an end to any abuse of migrant farm workers. But, at the same time," he affirmed, "We very strongly want to assure that an additional regulatory burden is not placed upon the farmers, the farm co-ops, and others involving agriculture across the country."[253]

Senator Boren was critical of DOL administration of FLCRA. It had moved, he stated, "far from the intent of the Congress" and of those who spoke on the 1963 legislation. The Department has been "subjecting farmers and other agricultural employers, including their employees, to civil and criminal penalties for failing to comply with" the requirements of the act. Senator Boren listed organizations that had "joined in support" of his amendment. He called upon DOL "to quit harassing the farmers" and "to curb ... unnecessary abuse of authority by the bureaucracy.[254]

---

251 Labor Secretary Marshall to J. Bennett Johnston (with others), Congressional Record, Dec. 18, 1979, pp. 36850-36851.

252 Senators J. Bennett Johnston and Russell B. Long to Labor Secretary Marshall , reprinted in Congressional Record, July 24, 1980, p. 19561.

253 Congressional Record, July 24, 1980, p. 19557.

254 Congressional Record, July 24, 1980, pp. 19557-19558. Among groups backing his amendment, Senator Boren listed: "The American Soybean Association; the American Farm Bureau Federation, with some 3 million

The Senate was split. Senator Gaylord Nelson noted that the bill was essentially similar to S. 2875, introduced with 39 cosponsors a month earlier. Nelson urged that Boren, having made his point, would "be willing to withdraw his amendment" and to wait for hearings that had already been scheduled by his (Nelson's) Committee. "As the Senator knows, this law is within the exclusive jurisdiction of the Labor and Human Resources Committee." There was yet another option: i.e., S. 2789, introduced by Senator Javits. Senator Nelson agreed that there have been "serious problems" since enactment of the 1974 amendments. "Numerous lawsuits have been filed, and both agricultural employers as well as farm workers have expressed dissatisfaction" with DOL's administration of this law — "and justifiably so, in my opinion." Senator Nelson noted that he had personally written to the Secretary "expressing my concern." But, he also affirmed that the proper place for consideration of "corrective legislation" was the Labor and Human Resources Committee.[255]

The Boren amendment, however, was not withdrawn and, on a vote of 57 yeas to 37 nays, the measure was passed.[256]

The House was similarly divided on the issue. Representative Panetta, who had earlier introduced general reform of FLCRA, was now joined by Representatives Foley (of Washington State, chair of the Agriculture Committee) and William Goodling of the Committee on Education and Labor, with numerous others.[257][2]Panetta affirmed:

> "The Farm Labor Contractor Registration Act was passed in 1963 to protect migrant farmworkers from abuse by unscrupulous crew leaders. This act was also intended to protect farmers and other agricultural employers from the irresponsible action of some crew leaders. I firmly believe that the act should continue to serve that purpose."[258]

But — it may need a few changes. "Unfortunately, in spite of the request of a majority of the Senate, the problem has not been resolved," Representative Panetta observed, noting "misinterpretations by the Department," "ambiguities in the act," and "a particular interpretation of its statutory authority."[259] Representative Goodling (with John Ashbrook (R-OH), ranking Member on the Committee on Education and Labor) offered an amendment "to clarify the act." DOL, Goodling stated, has engaged in "unnecessary and unproductive harassment" of many Pennsylvania farmers.[260]

In early September, Representative Goodling again addressed the House. His amendments, he said, "except for technical improvements," basically parallels the Panetta and

---

farmers as members; the American Frozen Food Institute; the American Mushroom Institute; the American Seed Trade Association; the American Sod Producers Association; the American Sugar Beet Growers Association; the Florida Citrus Processors Association; the Florida Sugar Cane League; the International Apple Institute; the National Broiler Council; the National Institute of Wheat Growers; the National Cattleman's Association; the National Cotton Council; the National Council of Agricultural Employers; the National Council of Farmer Cooperatives; the National Food Processors Association; the National Grange, with more than 500,000 members, made up of farmers; the National Meat Association; the National Peach Council; the Pennsylvania Food Processors Association; the Rio Grande Valley Sugar Growers Cooperative; the Society of American Florists; the United Fresh Fruit and Vegetable Association; and the Western Growers Association."

255 Congressional Record, July 24, 1980, pp. 19558-19564.
256 Congressional Record, July 24, 1980, p. 19574.
257 Congressional Record, Dec. 18, 1979, p. 36851.
258 Congressional Record, July 24, 1980, p. 19456.
259 Congressional Record, July 24, 1980, p. 19457.
260 Congressional Record, Aug. 26, 1980, pp. 23411-23413.

Boren proposals — which he urged his colleagues to support.[261] Goodling was not alone: "over 100 Members of the House" (including Panetta) endorsed the Boren option.[262] Representative Ford did not. "I strongly oppose the Boren amendment," he stated. "... it would effectively repeal the FLCRA, the only Federal legislation that protects migrant farmworkers against the most common abuses they endure in their hiring, transportation, housing, and employment in agricultural labor." Ford placed in the *Record* a letter from Ray Marshall in which he, too, expressed "my deep concern and strong opposition" to the Boren amendment."[263]

The Boren amendment, however, was caught up in parliamentary procedures and migrated to a series of proposals. In a report for 1980, the *CQ Almanac* noted: "An amendment restricting coverage of a 1963 law aimed at preventing exploitation of migrant farm workers was added to a continuing resolution (H.J.Res. 637) but later dropped."[264] For the present, FLCRA remained unchanged.

The Boren Bill and the Panetta Bill (1981)

In the 97th Congress, critics of the Farm Labor Contractor Registration Act returned to the fray. On April 8, 1981, Senator Boren introduced S. 922, a measure designed "to provide for the proper administration and enforcement of" FLCRA. Conceding that one problem has been the "somewhat vague and ambiguous" language that had "resulted in gross misinterpretation," Boren's proposal sought "to clarify" the meaning of the act.[265]

Senator Chiles, co-sponsor of the Boren bill, having "stressed my support" for the purposes of the act, stated that FLCRA's "vague language and convoluted format" allows DOL to "subvert ... the intent of Congress" and to take advantage "of these procedural defects in its unrelenting efforts to envelop farmers, packers, processors, and their employees within the regulatory scheme of the act." The result has been "widespread harassment" of agricultural interests with "little discernable effect" with respect to crew leaders. Farmers "face enough problems in today's economy without this one."[266]

On May 20, 1981, Representative Panetta introduced H.R. 3636, similar in some respects to his bill from the 96th Congress.[267] FLCRA remains, he stated, "a significant problem of unnecessary and burdensome regulation" which has "grown as more and more farmers and other fixed-base agricultural employers" have found that they are required to comply with its terms.[268]

In the interim between introduction of the Boren bill and Panetta bill, however, there had been a discernible change. The Education and Labor Committee, Representative Panetta announced, "is contemplating hearings" on the issue this year, and there is "no doubt in my

---

261 Congressional Record, Sept. 9, 1980, pp. 28405-28406.

262 Congressional Record, Sept. 9, 1980, pp. 24805-24807.

263 Congressional Record, Sept. 10, 1980, pp. 25102-25103.

264 Congressional Quarterly Almanac (1980), Washington: Congressional Quarterly Inc., 1981, p. 453.

265 Congressional Record, Apr. 8, 1981, p. 6941. As a result of the 1980 election, Ray Marshall was replaced as Labor Secretary by Raymond J. Donovan.

266 Congressional Record, Apr. 8, 1981, p. 6943.

267 In the 96th Congress, the Panetta bill carried the names of 160 Members. See Congressional Record, May 20, 1981, p. 10353.

268 Congressional Record, May 20, 1991, p. 10353.

mind that we can work out the problems that exist with the act." Panetta wrote into his bill several proposals which may have been viewed as the start of compromise. *First*: He proposed to eliminate the "distinction between 'full-time or regular'" and to make clear the distinction between "a bona fide employee and an independent contractor." *Second*: He proposed to allow the Secretary some discretion in causing "a cooperative to register" — depending upon the purposes of the co-operative arrangement. *Third*: He proposed a modification in the definition of "day-haul worker" with the stated intention of securing their protection.[269]

"It is in this constructive spirit," Panetta affirmed, "that I look forward to working with my colleagues on the Committee on Education and Labor, and particularly with my good friend from California (Mr. Miller), who is chairman of the Subcommittee on Labor Standards."[270] But, negotiations would be long and intense.

THE MILLER HEARINGS AND THEIR AFTERMATH (1982)

From the spring of 1981 and into the fall of 1982, the several parties at interest met and reviewed proposals for revision of FLCRA. From all sides, there were serious concerns "with the existing law that they felt needed to be addressed," according to Representative George Miller. Negotiations, he stated, "were long and, at times, frustrating."[271] Finally, on September 1, 1982, Secretary of Labor Raymond Donovan sent to Congress a bill entitled the "Migrant and Seasonal Agricultural Worker Protection Act which was referred to the Committee on Education and Labor."[272]

The Hearing

On September 14, 1982, Miller called together for a single hearing the Subcommittee on Labor Standards. The bill at issue was H.R. 7102, an Administration proposal but with more generalized backing. Robert B. Collyer, Deputy Under Secretary of Labor, was the first witness. Reviewing the recent history of the Administration's bill, Collyer affirmed

> "This cooperative effort has now resulted in a consensus bill, endorsed by the AFL-CIO, the migrant legal action program, and by major agricultural employer organizations, such as the American Farm Bureau Federation, the National Food Processors Association, and the National Council of Agricultural Employers.

---

269 Congressional Record, May 20, 1981, pp. 10353-10354.
270 Congressional Record, May 20, 2981, p. 10354. Both the Boren and Panetta bills were superceded by the Administration's bill, introduced by request by Representative Miller.
271 U.S. Congress. House. Subcommittee on Labor Standards, Committee on Education and Labor, Hearings on the Migrant and Seasonal Agricultural Worker Protection Act, Sept. 14, 1982, p. 1. (Cited hereafter as Hearings, House, 1982).
272 U.S. Congress, House, Committee on Education and Labor, Migrant and Seasonal Agricultural Worker Protection Act, H.Rept. 97-885, Sept. 28, 1982, p. 4. (Cited hereafter as House, Committee Report 97-885, Sept. 28, 1982).

"While none of these groups believes the bill to be ideal from its individual standpoint, there is important agreement that the bill materially improves the law."[273]

The 1974 FLCRA amendments, Collyer explained, had resulted in "a great deal of litigation."[274] The essence of the new bill was compromise.

Representatives from industry and the AFL-CIO endorsed the changes in policy included within the new bill.[275] Representatives of farmworkers were more skeptical, but acquiesced.[276] As the hearing closed, Representative Miller thanked the witnesses for their support. "I take a great deal of pride in seeing that I am not the victim of testimony 5 years down the road, that it didn't work." Miller stated: "... I do recognize that a good number of your associates and clients are very skeptical about entering into this agreement." Again: "I don't know if this law is perfect or not. I think it's an improvement, and I gather from your testimony that you believe it is an improvement."[277]

Consideration and Floor Action

"The failure of current law to achieve its goal of fairness and equity for migrant workers," the House Report stated, "combined with employer objections as to their treatment under the Act" gave the negotiations momentum and "made the attainment of legislative change obligatory."[278] FLCRA as amended, had "failed to reverse the historical pattern of abuse and exploitation of migrant and seasonal farm workers" and, as a result, argued for a "new approach."[279] The Committee on Education and Labor reported the bill on September 28, 1982.[280]

On September 29, Representative Miller urged that the rules be suspended and H.R. 7102 be passed. Recounting the "months of negotiations and compromise," he noted the certainty that the legislation might bring.[281] John Erlenborn (R-IL), a cosponsor, recalled that "for over 18 months the interested parties, including staff from the House and Senate majority and minority, have been engaged in negotiations" to work out a successor to FLCRA. Representative Panetta affirmed that the bill "eliminates undue red-tape and harassment for farmers ... while at the same time provides real protection to migrant and seasonal agricultural workers." Representative Goodling, for his part, cited the "unwarranted and overzealous tactics of the wage and hour division"but, at the same time, he acknowledged that the "long

---

273 Hearings, House, 1982, p. 43.
274 Hearings, House, 1982, p. 44. Collyer, p.50, proceeded to thank "all those persons and organizations who participated in the cooperative effort over the past 18 months to develop this legislation."
275 See testimony of Jay Power, Legislative Representative, AFL-CIO, and of Perry Ellsworth, National Council of Agricultural Employers, Hearings, House, 1982, pp. 54-60.
276 See testimony of William Beardall, staff attorney, Texas Rural Legal Aid, Marh Schacht of the Farmworker Justice Fund, and Garry B. Bryant, an attorney from Tucson with several years representing agricultural employees, Hearings, House, 1982, pp. 60-173.
277 Hearings, House, 1982, p. 174. See also Representative Panetta's statement, Sept. 14, 1982, p. 23441. Panetta was a co-sponsor of the legislation.
278 House, Committee Report 97-885, Sept. 28, 1982, p. 1.
279 House, Committee Report 97-885, Sept. 28, 1982, p. 3.
280 Congressional Record, Sept. 28, 1982, p. 25609.
281 Congressional Record, Sept. 29, 1982, p. 25609.

negotiations between all parties" had made the new bill possible. Finally, the debate closed. The rules were suspended: the bill was passed — on a voice vote.[282]

In the Senate, the bill was held at the desk (not referred to a committee)[283] until on December 19, 1982, Senator Howard Baker (R-TN) called up the measure for floor action. Senator Orrin Hatch (R-UH) remarked that the measure, now passed by the House, was "identical to the measure" that he had introduced in the Senate (S. 2930) — with Senators Boren and Edward Kennedy (D-Ma), among others, as co-sponsors. Senator Hatch reviewed the history of FLCRA and presented an analysis of H.R. 7102. As in the House, the bill was adopted by a voice vote.[284]

On January 14, 1983, H.R. 7102 was signed into law by President Ronald Reagan (P.L. 97-470). The new law "will result in substantially improved protection for migrant and seasonal agricultural workers," he said, "many of whom are disadvantaged minorities." Conversely: "We will continue our efforts to both reduce unnecessary regulatory burdens and at the same time, protect essential employment standards in America's workplaces."[285]

PART IV. A NEW STATUTE EMERGES (1983 FF.)

With enactment of P.L. 97-470, FLCRA disappeared. In its place was a new statute: the *Migrant and Seasonal Agricultural Workers Protection Act* (MSPA). For more than twenty years, MSPA has been generally (though not entirely) free from controversy.

THE STRUCTURE AND PROVISIONS OF THE NEW LAW

MSPA has remained largely unchanged since its enactment.[286] Although its terms are spelled out in detail adapted to specific farmworker employment situations, its structure is relatively simple.

The introduction states the purposes of the act: i.e., to require that farm labor contractors register with the Secretary of Labor and to assure "necessary protections for migrant and seasonal agricultural workers, agricultural associations, and agricultural employers." It then proceeds to a list of definitions used: *inter alia*, "agricultural association," "agricultural employer," "agricultural employment," "day-haul operation," "employ," "farm labor contracting activity," "farm labor contractor," "migrant agricultural worker," "person," and "seasonal agricultural worker."[287]

The act includes exemptions — i.e., some family farms and related agricultural industries. Also exempt are labor organizations, any "nonprofit charitable organization or public or private nonprofit educational institution," and any person "engaged in any farm

---

282 Congressional Record, Sept. 29, 1982, pp. 26008-26010.
283 Congressional Record, Sept. 29, 1982, p. 25866.
284 Congressional Record, Dec. 19, 1982, pp. 32458-32466.
285 Public Papers of the President of the United States. Ronald Reagan, 1983. Book 1, January 1 to July 1, 1983. Washington, U.S. Government Printing Office, 1984, p. 47.
286 See the Adams Fruit case, discussed below.

labor contracting activity solely within a twenty-five mile interstate radius of such person's permanent place of residence and for not more than thirteen weeks per year." Custom combining, hay harvesting, or sheep shearing operations are exempt — as are persons engaged in custom poultry harvesting, breeding, debeaking, etc., where workers are not required to be away from their permanent place of residence overnight. Persons are exempt when their "principal occupation ... is not agricultural employment" and who provide "full-time students" to detassel corn, etc., when such students are not required to be away from their permanent place of residence overnight. Any "common carrier" who would be a farm labor contractor solely because the carrier is engaged in transporting migrant or seasonal agricultural workers is exempt.

Title 1 explains the *conditions under which farm labor contractors are required to register* and the process of registration. The registrant must be of good character (specified in the act), with right to appeal if he or she is denied registration. A certificate of registration may not be transferred or assigned and will normally cover a twelve-month period. Any change of address (or other material variation in registration) must be made known to the Secretary. Finally, the farm labor contractor is restricted from hiring aliens not authorized to work in the United States.

(a) "No farm labor contractor shall recruit, hire, employ, or use, with knowledge, the services of any individual who is an alien not lawfully admitted for permanent residence or who has not been authorized by the Attorney General to accept employment.

(b) " A farm labor contractor shall be considered to have complied with subsection (a) if the farm labor contractor demonstrates that the farm labor contractor relied in good faith on documentation prescribed by the Secretary, and the farm labor contractor had no reason to believe the individual was an alien referred to in subsection (a)."[288]

Title II deals with *migrant agricultural workers.*[289] Each "farm labor contractor, agricultural employer, and agricultural association" who employs a migrant agricultural worker shall disclose to the worker at the time of his or her recruitment: the place of employment, the wage rates to be paid, the crops and kinds of activities on which the worker may be employed, the period of employment, matters with respect to housing, transportation, and "any other employee benefit to be provided, if any," and "any costs to be charged for each of them." The existence "of any strike or other concerted work stoppage, slowdown, or interruption of operations by employees at the place of employment" must be disclosed. Any commission arrangements must also be disclosed. At each place of employment, in a conspicuous place, a form from the Secretary "setting forth the rights and protections

---

287 All language, where in quotation marks, in this section is taken from P.L. 97-470. However, some variation may result from codification and from subsequent amendments that impinge upon the act. This is a summary. The reader may want to consult the current text of MSPA.

288 This section was subsequently repealed and its substance was moved to Title VIII, Aliens and Nationality, as part of the general restructuring under the Immigration Reform and Control Act of 1986.

289 In the section on definitions, discussed above, it is stated: "(8)(A) Except as provided in subparagraph (B), the term 'migrant agricultural worker' means an individual who is employed in agricultural employment of a seasonal or other temporary nature, and who is required to be absent overnight from his permanent place of residence. (B) The term "migrant agricultural worker" does not include — (i) any immediate family member of an agricultural employer or a farm labor contractor; or (ii) any temporary nonimmigrant alien who is authorized to work in agricultural employment in the United States under sections 101(a)(15)(H)(ii) and 214(c) of the Immigration and Nationality Act."

afforded" to such migrant workers must be posted. Where housing is provided, the terms and conditions under which such housing is made available shall be provided to the migrant worker.

Each "farm labor contractor, agricultural employer, and agricultural association" who employs migrant workers shall keep specified records of his or her employment — and shall provide a copy to the migrant. The basic information (terms and conditions of employment) shall be provided in English "or, as necessary and reasonable, in Spanish or other language common to migrant agricultural workers who are not fluent or literate in English."[290] No *company store* arrangement is permissible.

Title III deals with *seasonal agricultural worker* protections.[291] Each "farm labor contractor, agricultural employer, and agricultural association" who recruits seasonal agricultural workers shall ascertain "and, upon request, disclose in writing," the following: the place of employment, the wage rates to be paid, the crops and kinds of activities on which the worker may be employed, the period of employment, and the costs and terms of transportation. If there is a "strike or other concerted work stoppage, slowdown, or interruption of operations," such information shall be made known. Any commission arrangement or day-haul operation shall also be made known. The various protections shall be posted in a conspicuous place.

Records will be kept with respect to an individual worker and a copy will be provided to such worker. Information to be provided will be in English or, as reasonable, "in Spanish or other language common to seasonal agricultural workers who are not fluent or literate in English."[292] Wages are to be paid "when due." There will be *no company store* arrangement.

Title IV deals with *further protections for migrant and seasonal agricultural workers.* The title deals primarily with insurance.[293] It begins by specifying the type/mode of transportation in question.

> "This section *does not apply* [italics added] to the transportation of any migrant or seasonal agricultural worker on a tractor, combine, harvester, picker, or other similar machinery and equipment while such worker is actually engaged in the planting, cultivating, or harvesting of any agricultural commodity or the care of livestock or poultry."

However, where this section does apply (to normal and/or regular vehicle usage), the "agricultural employer, agricultural association, and farm labor contractor" shall "ensure that the vehicle does comply" with "Federal and State safety standards," and ensure that "each driver has a valid and appropriate license." Such employer shall have in effect "an insurance

---

290 DOL will make available the necessary linguistic forms.
291 In the section on definitions, it is stated, "(10)(A) Except as provided in subparagraph (B), the term 'seasonal agricultural worker' means an individual who is employed in agricultural employment of a seasonal or other temporary nature and is not required to be absent overnight from his permanent place of residence — (i) when employed on a farm or ranch performing field work related to planting, cultivating, or harvesting operations; or (ii) when employed in canning, packing, ginning, seed conditioning or related research, or processing operations, and transported, or caused to be transported, to or from the place of employment by means of a day-haul operation. (B) The term 'seasonal agricultural worker' does not include — (i) any migrant agricultural worker; (ii) any immediate family member of an agricultural employer or a farm labor contractor; or (iii) any temporary nonimmigrant alien who is authorized to work in agricultural employment in the United States under sections 101(a)(15)(H)(ii) and 214(c) of the Immigration and National Act."
292 DOL will make available the necessary linguistic forms.

policy or a liability bond" that insures the employer "against liability for damage to persons or property arising from the ownership, operation, or the causing to be operated, of any vehicle used to transport any migrant or seasonal agricultural worker." The provision goes on to explain the various terms and conditions under which insurance may be applicable.

How might the individual employer confirm that the individual farm labor contractor has, indeed, complied with the terms of his or her craft?

> "No person shall utilize the services of any farm labor contractor to supply any migrant or seasonal agricultural worker unless the person first takes reasonable steps to determine that the farm labor contractor possesses a certificate of registration which is valid and which authorizes the activity for which the contractor is utilized. In making that determination, the person may rely upon either possession of a certificate or registration, or confirmation of such registration by the Department of Labor. The Secretary shall maintain a central public registry of all persons issued a certificate of registration."

At the close of the act, *Title V* provides for *general provisions*. These are divided into three sections and, appear, in part, as follows.

Enforcement Provisions. Any person "who willfully and knowingly" violates the act (or regulations under this act) shall be fined "not more than $1,000 or sentenced to prison for a term not to exceed one year, or both." However, any "subsequent violation of this act (or regulation) carries with it, potentially, a fine of "not more than $10,000" or a sentence of "not to exceed three years, or both." A special provision applies for farm labor contractors who violate section 106: the provision against the employment "with knowledge" of aliens. Hearings are permitted and the rights of the defendant are specified.

There is a private right of action. Any person "... may file suit in any district court of the United States having jurisdiction of the parties ... without regard to the citizenship of the parties and without regard to exhaustion of any alternative administrative remedies provided herein." Limitations on damages and equitable relief are spelled out.

No person shall be discriminated against for having, "with just cause, filed any complaint or instituted, or caused to be instituted, any proceeding under or related to this Act...." Appeal can be made to the Secretary of Labor. Any waiver of rights (except to the Secretary of Labor for enforcement purposes) "shall be void as contrary to public policy...."

Administrative Provisions. The Secretary of Labor "may issue such rules and regulations as are necessary to carry out this Act," consistent with the U.S. Code.

As may be appropriate, the Secretary may "investigate, and in connection wherewith, enter and inspect such places (including housing and vehicles) and such records (and make transcriptions thereof), question such persons and gather such information to determine compliance with this Act...." The Secretary "may issue subpoenas requiring the attendance and testimony of witnesses or the production of any evidence in connection with such investigations."

The Secretary may "enter into agreements with Federal and State agencies" in carrying out the program under MSPA.

Miscellaneous Provisions. "This Act is intended to supplement State law, and compliance with this Act shall not excuse any person from compliance with appropriate state law and regulation."

---

293 See discussion, below, under Adams Fruit.

ADAMS FRUIT CO., INC. V. BARRETT

Perhaps only a consensus bill (such as that creating MSPA) could have been enacted under the circumstances. Yet, that would not end complaints, both pro and con. Migrant farmworkers, observed Representative Mickey Leland (D-TX) in 1985, just two years after MSPA was adopted, "are among the most vulnerable workers in our Nation." The conditions under which they live and work has resulted in "... an infant mortality rate that is two and one-half times the national average."[294] During the late 1980s, several Members protested about the alleged tendency of some Legal Services offices "to represent, or, I suggest, misrepresent, some of these migrant workers" in bringing complaints against farmers.[295] And, in 1993, Representative Miller argued that "Working and living conditions for migrant agricultural workers remain deplorable and in some cases have deteriorated" — and he introduced a comprehensive revision of MSPA.[296] The most serious complaint (one that would result in amendment of MSPA) grew out of the *Adams Fruit* case.[297]

A Ruling from the Court

In 1990, the U.S. Supreme Court ruled in *Adams Fruit Co.* v. *Barrett* that migrant farmworkers, employed by Adams Fruit Company, Inc., having "suffered severe injuries in an automobile accident" in an Adams Fruit van while traveling to work, had two options available for redress. They could file a claim under the Florida workmen's compensation law *and* they could avail themselves under the private right of action provision of MSPA.[298]

At issue before the Court was the question of exclusivity (or dual coverage) under the state and federal acts: i.e., worker's compensation *and* MSPA. The Court ruled that although Congress "may choose to establish state remedies as adequate alternatives to federal relief, it cannot be assumed that private federal rights of action are conditioned on the unavailability of state remedies absent some indication to that effect."[299]

In the view of the Court, no such alternative remedy was apparent. Adams Fruit argued that "in the absence of any explicit congressional statement regarding the preemptive scope" of MSPA, the Court should defer to the Department's position: i.e., a single remedy. The Court, however, rejected that view. It found that a "'gap' is not created in a statutory scheme merely because a statute does not restate the truism that States may not pre-empt federal law."[300] In summary, the Court held, "[o]ur review of the language and structure of AWPA [MSPA] leads us to conclude that AWPA does not establish workers' compensation benefits as an exclusive remedy...."[301]

---

294 Congressional Record, Sept. 1985, p. 22927.
295 Congressional Record, Sept. 30, 1986, pp. 27399-27401, Mar. 6, 1987, pp. 5048-5049, and July 17, 1989, p. 14919.
296 Congressional Record, Mar. 2, 1993, pp. 3953 and 3937. See also H.R. 1173 of the 103rd Congress.
297 Congressional Record, Oct. 27, 1990, p. 37188.
298 494 U.S. 638, 640 (1989).
299 494 U.S. 638, 639 (1989).
300 494 U.S. 638, 649 (1989).
301 494 U.S. 638, 650 (1989).

Hearings on Workmen's Compensation

Representative Goodling branded the decision as "bad for employers" and "bad for workers" — allowing the worker "the ability to both recover workers' compensation *and* sue for compensatory and punitive damages." Goodling asserted: "As one who worked many long and hard hours in 1981 and 1982 to achieve the MSAWPA [MSPA] consensus[,] I intend to preserve it by pressing for early action next year ... to overturn the Adams Fruit decision."[302]

On September 15, 1993, Representative Austin Murphy (D-PA) called together at Fresno, California, a hearing by the Labor Standards Subcommittee. Two bills were on the table: H.R. 1173 (Miller) and H.R. 1999 by Victor Fazio (D-CA). The Miller bill was a comprehensive measure which, among other provisions, would have codified the *Adams Fruit* decision. The Fazio bill had for its sole purpose the overturning of that decision.[303] They had evolved, though from different perspectives, through "many months of unsuccessful negotiations aimed at producing consensus legislation to resolve the difficulties and concerns voiced by farmworker advocates and growers."[304]

As the Fresno hearings opened, several Members of Congress spoke. Richard Lehman (D-CA) and Calvin Dooley (D-CA) commenced with opposition to any new restrictions upon agricultural interests. They were followed by Howard Berman (D-CA) and by Miller, generally supportive of worker interests. The several Members emphasized the dichotomy existing over the prospective legislation. They were followed by representatives of organized labor, civil rights attorneys, and spokespersons for industry.[305]

On May 25, 1995, with a change in control in the House, Goodling became chair of the full Committee on Economic and Educational Opportunities. Cass Ballenger (R-NC) now chaired the Subcommittee on Workforce Protections with jurisdiction over agricultural labor. New hearings addressed the issues similarly. The Court, Ballenger stated, had interpreted MSPA "to provide for a private right of action for certain job related injuries, even if the individual was covered by workers' compensation at the time of the injury" leaving employers "exposed to potentially enormous liability for damages in spite of the fact that they have contributed into the workers' compensation system."[306] Conversely, Representative Major Owens (D-NY) suggested that "Instead of insuring work place protections, this committee is preoccupied with eliminating all inconveniences for the rich and privileged, at the expense of the working poor...."[307]

Bruce Wood, Senior Counsel for the American Insurance Association, argued that the Court's opinion was "not grounded on public policy" and that the Court had acted "narrowly

---

302 Congressional Record, Oct. 27, 1990, p. 37188. At the close of the 102nd Congress, an amendment was added to the Legislative Branch Appropriations Act (H.R. 5427), suspending for a brief period the impact of the Adams Fruit decision. See Congressional Record, Oct. 3, 1992, p. 31243, and Oct. 5, 1992, p. 31598.

303 See also S. 1450 (Feinstein) to overturn Adams Fruit. None of the bills was enacted.

304 U.S. Congress, House, Subcommittee on Labor Standards, Occupational Health and Safety, Committee on Education and Labor, Hearing on H.R. 1173 and H.R. 1999. Sept. 15, 1993, p. 1. (Cited hereafter as Hearings, House, 1993.) See also for general reaction to the MSPA, U.S. Congress, Subcommittee on Labor Standards, Committee on Education and Labor, Oversight Hearings on the Migrant and Seasonal Agricultural Worker Protection Act, July 13, 1987. The 1987 hearing was conducted in Biglerville, Pa.

305 Hearings, House, 1993, p. 48.

306 U.S. Congress, House, Subcommittee on Workforce Protections, Committee on Economic and Educational Opportunities,. Hearings on Adams Fruit Co., Inc. V. Barrett.May 25, 1995, pp. 1-2. (Cited hereafter as Hearings, House, 1995.)

307 Hearings, House, 1995, p. 2.

and mechanically."[308] The "doctrine of exclusivity" was emphasized by Walter Kates, an industry representative. MSPA was "a consensus bill," he declared, with all parties in agreement that "the doctrine of workers' compensation exclusivity was a part" of the bill. The failure "to reverse the Adams Fruit decision," Kates stated, "could have adverse and unintentional consequences for both the farmer and the farmworker."[309] Steve Kenfield, a farm labor contractor from California, suggested that *Adams Fruit* "has complicated an already complex compliance situation." It "created frustration" in that payment of premiums for workers' compensation (mandatory in California) "is virtually meaningless." And, it suggested that "we could also face open-ended" liability. With others from industry, Kenfield called upon Congress to "reverse" the *Adams Fruit* decision.[310] Finally, David Moody, a former farmworker and the victim of an accident in Florida, testified about the problems and complexities of securing redress solely under the worker's compensation system.[311]

The Goodling Bill (1995)

On May 25, 1995, Representative Goodling introduced H.R. 1715, a bill dealing with workers' compensation benefits and MSPA. The bill was referred to the Committee on Economic and Educational Opportunities and passed.[312] Through the summer, discussions were conducted informally on the legislation and, in mid-October, Goodling was able to announce that a substitute would be offered for H.R. 1715 (with the same designation) that would carry with it the endorsement of Representatives Ballenger, Owens and William Clay (D-MO). [313]

The substitute version of H.R. 1715 provided that "where a State workers' compensation law is applicable and coverage is provided ... the workers' compensation benefits shall be the exclusive remedy for loss of such worker under this Act in the case of bodily injury or death...." In effect, *Adams Fruit* was overturned. The bill went on to discuss the expansion of statutory damages, the tolling of the statute of limitations under state workmen's compensation laws, disclosure of coverage (and processes) to the workers involved, and other matters. Mr. Goodling explained that H.R. 1715 "clarifies the relationship between workers compensation benefits and the private right of action" available under MSPA.[314]

Mr. Owens rose in support of the bill and expressed his appreciation to Representatives Goodling, Clay, and Ballenger — and to others: Representatives Miller, Berman and Fazio. "The efforts of all three gentlemen have been instrumental in the development of the

---

308 Hearings, House, 1995, p. 5.
309 Hearings, House, 1995, pp. 12-14. Kates is identified as representing the National Council of Agricultural Employers (as chairman of their Migrant and Seasonal Agricultural Worker Protection Act Committee), the Florida Fruit and Vegetable Association (as director of their Labor Relations Division), and the Workers' Compensatory Integrity, Stability, and Equity Coalition.
310 Hearings, House, 1995, pp. 16-19.
311 Hearings, House, 1995, pp. 21-22.
312 Congressional Record, May 25, 1995, pp. 14444 and 14641.
313 Congressional Record, Oct. 13, 1995, pp. 28027-28028. On Oct. 17, 1995, p. 28126, Mr. Goodling explained that the original bill had been reported from the Committee on Economic and Educational Opportunities but, after several weeks of negotiations, he was now able to offer a consensus bill.
314 Congressional Record, Oct. 17, 1995, pp. 28125-28127.

amendment before us" — which he regarded as a "compromise."[315] Mr. Fazio argued that the bill "... is the result of 5 years of discussions, but it is a bill that needed to be enacted...."[316]

At this juncture, the House suspended the rules and passed the compromise version of H.R. 1715.[317] The bill was promptly dispatched to the Senate where, under unanimous consent, it was adopted.[318] On November 15, 1995, the measure was signed into law (P.L. 104-49) by President William Clinton.

PART V. AGRICULTURAL WORKERS IN THE NEW CENTURY

For the most part, since the 1983 amendments (with the emergence of the Migrant and Seasonal Agricultural Workers Protection Act), the statute has remained largely unchanged — with the exception of the *Adams Fruit* legislation.[319319]

The history of FLCRA (and, now, MSPA) has been long and tedious. For almost ten years (1964 to 1974), legislation remained in place but was, largely, unenforced — or, perhaps, unenforceable. Revised in 1974, there were serious attempts to enforce the statute but these seem to have required that many of the *wrong people* register (i.e., fixed site farmers, growers, and a variety of other agricultural interests) — and, generally to comply with the act's restrictions. In 1983, FLCRA was repealed, and Congress started over with a new statute: the Migrant and Seasonal Agricultural Worker's Protection Act. The latter remains in place.

Debate over FLCRA and, to a lesser extent, MSPA, seems to have been exhausting. It could well be that some may now be disinclined to revisit the statute and to raise new questions. However, the need for oversight would seem to remain a priority where agricultural policy is concerned.

---

315 Congressional Record, Oct. 17, 1995, p. 28127.
316 Congressional Record, Oct. 17, 1995, p. 28128.
317 Congressional Record, Oct. 17, 1995, p. 28129.
318 Congressional Record, Oct. 31, 1995, p. 30907.
319 See U.S. Congress. House. Subcommittee on Workforce Protections, Committee on Education and the Workforce. Field Hearing on Issues Relating to Migrant and Seasonal Agricultural Workers and Their Employers (Newland, N.C.), 105th Cong., 1st Sess., Sept. 12, 1997, 164 pp.; and U.S. Congress. House. Subcommittee on Workforce Protections, Committee on Education and the Workforce. 105th Cong., 2nd Sess., The Effect of the Fair Labor Standards Act on Amish Families and H.R. 2028, The MSPA Clarification Act. Apr. 21, 1998, 167 pp.

In: Farm Labor: 21st Century Issues and Challenges
Editors: A. W. Burton, I. B. Telpov, pp. 63-108

ISBN: 978-1-60456-005-3
© 2007 Nova Science Publishers, Inc.

Chapter 2

LABOR PRACTICES IN THE MEAT PACKING AND POULTRY PROCESSING INDUSTRY: AN OVERVIEW[*]

William G. Whittaker

ABSTRACT

During the early 1960s, segments of the meat packing industry began to move from large urban centers to small communities scattered throughout the Midwest. By century's end, this migration had effected major changes within the industry. The old packing firms that had established their dominance during the late 1800s had largely disappeared or been restructured as part of a new breed of packers. Joining with the poultry processors who had emerged in the wake of World War II, they quickly became a major force in American and, later, global industry.

The urban-to-rural migration, some suggest, had at least two major motivations. One was to locate packing facilities in areas where animals were raised rather than transporting the stock to urban packinghouses as had been the tradition: a more economical arrangement. The other was a quest for lower labor costs: to leave behind the urban unions and their collective bargaining agreements and to operate, as nearly as possible, in a union-free environment. This initiative involved a low-wage strategy, allowing for employment of lower skilled and low-wage workers.

The aftermath of this migration was complex. The urban unionized workforce, by and large, did not follow the migrating plants. Since most local communities could not provide an adequate supply of labor, the relocation process implied recruitment of workers from outside the area of production. In practice, packers and processors came increasingly to rely upon recent immigrants or, allegedly in some instances, upon workers not authorized for employment in the United States.

Gradually, the new breed packers (and their poultry counterparts) began to dominate the market — through various business arrangements consolidating the industry into a small number of large firms. This corporate *churning* impacted the trade union movement and its relations with the industry. The unions, too, were restructured. The labor-management relationship, largely set during the 1940s, was gradually replaced with new patterns of bargaining. Further, the demographics of the workforce changed with the introduction of a new racial/ethnic and gender mixture. Distances between the rural

---

[*] Excerpted from CRS Report 33002, dated October 27, 2006.

plants made union organization difficult, as did the new linguistic and cultural differences among workers. Gradually, the workforce was transformed from high-wage, stable, and union, to lower-wage and often non-union, and came to be characterized by a high turnover rate.

From time to time, the Congressional Research Service (CRS) has received requests for information on labor standards and labor-management relations in the meat packing industry. Often, these queries have been associated with the Fair Labor Standards Act and the National Labor Relations Act, but there has been concern with other legislation and issues as well. Some of these areas have been (and continue to be) the subject of litigation. This article is intended as an introduction to the meat packing/processing industry, the unions that have been active in that field, and labor-management practices among the packers and their employees. It will not likely be updated.

During the early 1960s, segments of the meat packing industry began to move from urban centers to rural communities scattered throughout the Midwest. By century's end, this migration had effected major changes within the industry. The old packing firms that had established their dominance during the late 1800s had largely disappeared or had been restructured as part of a *new breed* of packers. Joining with the poultry processors who had emerged in the wake of World War II, they became a major force in American (and, later, global) industry — and a major employer.[1]

Business practices have affected the labor-management relationship, recruitment of workers, and the protective labor standards that apply to persons employed in the industry. The last half of the 20th century witnessed relocation of major firms, a move from predominantly urban to more heavily rural production, and a shift in the demographics of the industry's workforce. The dispersal of the industry, some argue, has also affected the manner in which employment-related law is enforced. Clearly, it has impacted the trade unionization of the workforce. At issue are a number of federal statutes and their administration: the Fair Labor Standards Act, the National Labor Relations Act, the Occupational Safety and Health Act and, potentially, the Migrant and Seasonal Agricultural Workers Protection Act. Similarly, both the industry and its workforce have been affected by federal immigration policy. These general areas have been a continuing focus of Department of Labor (DOL) action and of litigation.[2]

This article provides an introduction to labor issues in meat packing and poultry processing. It sketches the evolution of the industry and of the related trade union movement, stressing development of corporate and trade union cultures and the shifting demographics of the workforce. It notes areas of tension and conflict within and between both labor and management. And, it points to considerations of public policy that affect the continuing labor-management relationship.[3]

---

1 Seafood production, now largely absorbed into the meat and poultry industry, is not dealt with here. In general, see the essays from *Southern Exposure*, fall 1991: Richard Schweid, "Down on the Farm," pp. 14-21; Eric Bates, "The Kill Line," pp. 22-29; and Eric Bates, "Parting the Waters," pp. 34-36. See also David Griffith, *Jones's Minimal: Low-Wage Labor in the United States* (Albany: State University of New York Press, 1993), which deals with meat, poultry, and shellfish. (Hereafter cited as Griffith, *Jones's Minimal.*).

2 In general, see U.S. Department of Agriculture, Economic Research Service, Agricultural Economic Report No. 785, Feb. 2000, Consolidation in U.S. Meatpacking, by James M. MacDonald, Michael E. Ollinger, Kenneth E. Nelson, and Charles R. Handy, 42 pp.

3 The meat packing and poultry processing industries are complex structures. This report presents an overview of the industry and of labor policy and practice in that sector. It has been developed from published sources: synthesizing the academic literature, selectively examining industry journals and related materials. But, it is a sketch — an introduction. Occupational Safety and Health, a highly specialized and technical field, is discussed in other CRS reports and documents and is not dealt with in any substantial manner here.

ABBREVIATIONS

AFL	= American Federation of Labor (1881-1955)
AFL-CIO	= American Federation of Labor and Congress of Industrial Organizations (1955 ff.)
AMCBW	= Amalgamated Meat Cutters and Butcher Workmen (1897-1979)
CIO	= Committee for Industrial Organization (1935-1938)
CIO	= Congress of Industrial Organizations (1938-1955)
EWIC	= Essential Worker Immigration Coalition
FLSA	= Fair Labor Standards Act (1938)
IBP	= Iowa Beef Packers (later, Iowa Beef Processors and IBP)
IUAW	= Independent Union of All Workers (1933-1936)
IWW	= Industrial Workers of the World (1905 ff.)
NICWJ	= National Interfaith Committee for Worker Justice
NIRA	= National Industrial Recovery Act (1933-1935)
NLRA	= National Labor Relations Act (1935)
NLRB	= National Labor Relations Board (1935 ff.)
PWOC	= Packinghouse Workers Organizing Committee (1937-1943)
RCIU	= Retail Clerks International Union (1890-1979)
UFCW	= United Food and Commercial Workers (1979 ff.)
UPWA	= United Packinghouse Workers of America (1943-1968)

A SKETCH OF THE MEAT PACKING INDUSTRY

"Up to the 1860s," writes Lewis Corey, "meat packing was a small-scale enterprise, not yet industrial," dominated by merchants.[4] Livestock were slaughtered for local consumption where they were raised or, if transported to market, were shipped or driven live to rail yards and, then, to urban packinghouses. Butchers, both in small community packing houses and retail markets, were skilled craftsmen, often self-employed or engaged in a facility with only a few other similarly skilled workers.

Consolidation: Round One

Late in the 19th century, larger plants began to develop. Live animals, collected from throughout the Great Plains, were shipped to facilities normally located in major rail centers such as Chicago, Kansas City, or Omaha. Dressed beef was then shipped to branch houses for final processing and sale. Pork was treated somewhat differently, some being cured or, later, canned. The packing plants were enormous multistory facilities. Animals entered at an upper level and the carcass moved along *a disassembly line* until dressed meat and by-products emerged at ground level.

---

4 Lewis Corey, Meat and Man: A Study of Monopoly, Unionism, and Food Policy (New York: The Viking Press, 1950), p. 37. (Hereafter cited as Corey, Meat and Man.).

Refrigerated rail cars appeared in the 1870s and 1880s. While this made shipment of dressed meat less difficult, it appears not to have diminished the dominance of the great midwestern packing companies. Early in the 20th century, five firms became dominant: Swift, Armour, Morris, Wilson, and Cudahy. By 1916, the "Big Five" slaughtered the great bulk of cattle, calves, hogs and sheep moving in interstate commerce.[5]

The stock yards were "capital intensive" but with a rapidly expanding workforce. The workers (and cattlemen/farmers) found themselves at a disadvantage when dealing with the packers who were highly organized with an eye for efficiency and profitability. With the introduction of labor-saving equipment and careful structuring of the work process, the packers were increasingly able to employ largely low-wage workers with few skills.[6] Such work came to be associated with the most recent round of immigrant labor. "Immigrants flooded the labor market and ... accepted the common-labor earnings" offered by industry. "Simultaneously," notes David Brody, "an increasing number of women found a place in the packing houses at wages well below the unskilled male rate."[7] Gradually, if sporadically, the workforce became unionized: wages increased, worker protections were introduced, and work processes became institutionalized.

Consolidation: Round Two

In the late 1950s, two veteran packinghouse executives, Currier Holman and Andy Anderson, reassessed conditions in the beef packing industry. "Why should meat companies," they queried, "remain wage-locked in heavily unionized cities when unorganized workers could be hired at far lower wages out in the country?"[8] In March 1960, having accepted their own challenge, Holman and Anderson set up a new company: Iowa Beef Packers, Inc. — later, just IBP.

Though the old firms were still economically viable, the huge urban plants had become dated and, in some measure, inefficient. Further, the continuing "supply of cheap, unskilled labor" had begun to dry up[9] and, since the late 1930s, the industry had become increasingly unionized.

Led by IBP (among others), packers migrated to rural areas where land was cheaper and local communities, pressed for economic development, were willing to provide tax and other incentives to relocating firms.[10] But, there were other elements as well. Growers found it

---

5 Richard J. Arnould, "Changing Patterns of Concentration in American Meat Packing, 1880-1963," *Business History Review*, spring 1971, pp. 20-22. In 1923, Armour acquired Morris.

6 Corey, *Meat and Man*, p. 45.

7 David Brody, *The Butcher Workmen: A Study of Unionization* (Cambridge: Harvard University Press, 1964), p. 6. (Hereafter cited as Brody, *The Butcher Workmen*.).

8 Steve Bjerklie, "On the Horns of a Dilemma: The U.S. Meat and Poultry Industry," in Donald D. Stull, et al., *Any Way You Cut It: Meat Processing and Small-Town America* (Lawrence: University Press of Kansas, 1995), p. 53. (Hereafter cited as Bjerklie, *On the Horns of a Dilemma*.) That Anderson and Holman were concerned with efficiency and cost-cutting — and were anxious to operate with a minimal union presence — is stressed in Jeffrey Rodengen's corporate study, *The Legend of IBP* (Fort Lauderdale, Write Stuff Enterprises, Inc., 2000), pp. 22-25, and 47. (Hereafter cited as Rodengen, *The Legend of IBP*.).

9 Bjerklie, On the Horns of a Dilemma, pp. 56-57.

10 See Charles Craypo, "Strike and Relocation in Meatpacking," in Craypo and Bruce Nissen, eds., Grand Designs: The Impact of Corporate Strategies on Workers, Unions, and Communities (Ithaca: Cornell University Press, 1993), pp. 201-202. (Hereafter cited as Craypo, Strike and *Relocation*.) Concerning industrial migration and

more economical to move livestock to a local/regional center rather than shipping animals to Omaha or Chicago. The new (1950s) interstate highway system provided easy access to national markets. Rather than ship sides of beef to markets for on-site cutting, the packers introduced a system of *boxed beef* in which meat, deboned and trimmed, was sealed in vacuum bags and shipped directly to supermarkets. Easier to handle, boxed beef was quickly accepted by retailers —and had the added advantage of largely eliminating the need for retail butchers.[11]

Reduced labor costs were a significant aspect of the move. Relocation "altered the wage structure within which the industry operated."[12] The new workers were said to have been accustomed to low wages and to a "country-style" non-union work environment.[13] Further, automated facilities allowed the *new breed*[14] of packers to organize line operations in a manner that diminished the need for skilled workers, permitting employment of inexperienced and low-wage personnel.[15] Finally, formation of new corporate entities (with new plants in new locations) permitted a change from established labor-management relationships.[16]

This migration involved fierce competition between firms for market share. Some older established firms went out of business or were taken over by new breed packers (sometimes associated with conglomerates). Others adjusted to the new strategies but, in the process, changed their corporate culture — adopting a more contentious labor-management relationship. By 1990, a new "Big Three" had emerged: IBP, Excel (a subsidiary of Cargill) and ConAgra.

The Poultry Processing Industry

Poultry processing had early been a distinct sub-segment of the meat industry. With the restructuring of the 1960s, such distinctions came increasingly to be blurred. A single corporation might have interests in each line — and in other areas as well.

Until the early 1940s, poultry raising was largely a small farm type operation. Its transformation began with wartime demand. Initially, large numbers of relatively small growers entered the field; but, at least by the 1950s, some consolidation had begun. By the

local governmental policy, see, for example, James C. Cobb, The Selling of the South: The Southern Crusade for Industrial Development, 1936-1990 (Urbana: University of Illinois Press, 1993).

11 Bjerklie, On the Horns of a Dilemma, p. 54; Craypo, Strike and Relocation, p. 185; and Jimmy M. Skaggs, Prime Cut: Livestock Raising and Meatpacking in the United States,1607-1983 (College Station: Texas A and M University Press, 1986), pp. 190-196. On Sept. 15, 2003, p. C15, the Bureau of National Affairs' Daily Labor Report stated: "According to UFCW [United Food and Commercial Workers, AFL-CIO] data, approximately 100,000 of its 1.4 million members are retail meatcutters, compared with about 400,000 meatcutter-members 30 years ago."

12 Roger Horowitz, "The Decline of Unionism in America's Meatpacking Industry," Social Policy, spring 2002, p. 33. (Hereafter cited as Horowitz, The Decline of Unionism.)

13 Bjerklie, On the Horns of a Dilemma, p. 53.

14 The term, new breed, is widely used in the literature to differentiate the post-1950s packers from the more-traditional firms. It is suggestive more of a business approach, however, than of the age of the firm.

15 Wilson Warren, Struggling with "Iowa's Pride": Labor Relations, Unionism, and Politics in the Rural Midwest Since 1877 (Iowa City: University of Iowa Press, 2000), pp. 120-121. (Hereafter cited as Warren, Struggling with "Iowa's Pride".).

16 Carol Andreas, Meatpackers and Beef Barons: Company Town in a Global Economy (Niwot, Colorado: University Press of Colorado, 1994), pp. 59-82. (Hereafter cited as Andreas, Meatpackers and Beef Barons.)

late 20th century, five or six major concerns had come to dominate poultry production — with about 250,000 persons employed in the industry.[17]

"Before the 1960s," suggests Bob Hall of the Institute for Southern Studies, "nearly all birds were shipped whole from the slaughterhouse to the grocery store, where butchers cut them up or packaged them whole — sometimes with the store label. Today [1989]," he states, "poultry giants ... have replaced the neighborhood butcher with huge processing units attached to their slaughterhouses." By 1990, the industry expected to produce 5.5 billion broilers a year.[18] More recently, there has been a transition to *value-added* products such as chicken fajitas and nuggets.

Several patterns quickly developed. The industry, increasingly, came to be centered in the Delmarva region and the South. In structure, with growth, it became vertically integrated with corporate control of the birds from egg to market. Sequentially, two groups of workers are involved: grow-out farmers and hourly workers on the disassembly line. For the latter, work is unpleasant, hazardous, and reportedly requires only low levels of education or skill — but may be attractive to a rural population with few economic options.[19]

Grow-out Farmers

Typically, the corporate processor will contract-out the actual growth of the birds to local *grow-out* farmers. Usually, the processor (or *integrator*) provides the chicks, feed, any necessary medication, etc., to the grower. The grower provides the buildings in which the birds are raised and the labor involved in caring for them — receiving four or five batches of chicks each year. When the boilers are ready for slaughter, the integrator dispatches a crew of *chicken catchers* to retrieve the birds and haul them to the processing plant. Ordinarily, the farmer does not actually own the chickens that are raised for the processor.

For the grow-out farmer, several patterns have developed. *First.* Starting from a marginal agricultural operation, the farmer may take out a loan to construct his growing facilities. In the 1990s, a reasonable structure may well have cost about $100,000 — perhaps more. Several such chicken houses were often needed to sustain the farmer.[20] Speaking generally, the chicken houses were specialized structures with little value for other purposes. *Second.* The grower may begin operation with a substantial debt and, essentially, with a single market:

---

17 Industrial Safety and Hygiene News, July 2002, p. 14. See also The News and Observer (Raleigh, NC), June 6, 2001, p. A17.
18 Bob Hall, "Chicken Empires," Southern Exposure, summer 1989, pp. 12-17.
19 David Griffith, "Hay Trabajo: Poultry Processing, Rural Industrialization, and the Latinization of Low-Wage Labor," in Donald D. Stull, et al., Any Way You Cut It: Meat Processing and Small-Town America (Lawrence: University Press of Kansas, 1995), pp. 129-130. (Hereafter cited as Griffith, Hay Trabajo.)
20 Cost estimates vary. Of the early 1980s, Hope Shand, "Billions of Chickens: The Business of the South," Southern Exposure, Nov./Dec. 1983, p. 78, states: "A new fully automated chicken house costs from $60,000 to $80,000." (Hereafter cited as Shand, Billions of Chickens.) Steve Bjerklie, writing a decade later, "Dark Passage: Is Contract Poultry Growing a Return to Servitude?," Meat and Poultry, Aug. 1994, p. 25, states: "One integrator's figures show the cost of building a chicken grow-out house to company specifications to be about $125,000. A turkey house runs $190,000." By the late 1990s, grow-out chicken houses seem to have averaged about 40 feet in width and 400 feet long, covering 16,000 square feet and accommodating about 20,000 birds. See Stephen F. Strausberg, From Hills and Hollers: Rise of the Poultry Industry in Arkansas (Fayetteville: Arkansas Agricultural Experiment Station, 1995), p. 180. (Hereafter cited as Strausberg, From Hills and Hollers.) Donald D. Stull and Michael J. Broadway, in Slaughterhouse Blues: The Meat and Poultry Industry in North America (Belmont, CA: Thomson/Wadsworth, 2004), p. 46, state: "A broiler house costs between $125,000 and $140,000 and must be built to company specifications. Breeder and pullet houses can cost even more." (Hereafter cited as Stull and Broadway, Slaughterhouse Blues.).

i.e., the corporate processor. Grower/processor contracts have tended to be short-term, renewed with each new batch of chickens.[21]

The grow-out farmer normally "relinquishes all major decision-making responsibilities" when the contract is signed.[22] Though the farmer "pretty much works like a wage-earning worker," he is actually an *independent contractor* and, as such, lacks options a laborer might enjoy. Tied to his mortgage and chicken houses, he "can't change jobs" easily. The grower is not covered by wage/hour and related laws nor does he receive "retirement benefits, health insurance, or paid vacations."[23] In spite of intermittent attempts by growers to organize to enhance their bargaining power, they seem to have been unable to do so.[24]

Aside from profit motivation, brand name marketing may require that the processor retain quality control — including the manner in which birds are raised, fed and cared for. "Vertical integration allows us to control the quality of the birds from conception to consumption," John Lea, a Tyson vice president, reportedly stated.[25]

Given market constraints and fluctuations in demand, it may be unrealistic for a farmer to assume that the supply of chicks will be constant.[26]

Plant Workers

The poultry industry early developed in the rural South where land was relatively cheap and water, a prime requirement for meat packing and poultry processing, was relatively plentiful. As with beef packing, low-wage labor with a union-free environment seems to have been an important consideration.

In the 1960s, many rural workers lacked marketable skills. More traditional family farming, for many, no longer offered significant employment and, thus, the "superfluous labor" of farming communities became available for processing plants and for "part-time labor on the grow-out farms."[27] Some suggest that the industry had concentrated in *right-to-work* states in an effort to minimize labor costs and had systematically developed a *low-wage*

21 Stull and Broadway, in Slaughterhouse Blues, p. 41, state: "For growers, contracts offered a guaranteed income from their flocks and took the risks out of raising chickens, save one — the company did not have to renew the grower's contract." They observe, however, that the income of grow-out farmers can be relatively meager (pp. 41-51). See also Strausberg, From Hills and Hollers, p. 136; and Fred A. Lasley, et al., The U.S. Broiler Industry (Washington: U.S. Department of Agriculture, Nov. 1988), Economic Research Service, Agricultural Economic Report Number 591, p. 20.

22 William D. Heffernan, "Constraints in the U.S. Poultry Industry," in Harry K. Schwarzweller, ed., Research in Rural Sociology and Development: Focus on Agriculture (Greenwich, CT: JAI Press, Inc., 1984), p. 238.

23 Barry Yeoman, "Don't Count Your Chickens," Southern Exposure, summer 1989, pp. 22-23. See also Bob Hall, "The Kill Line: Facts of Life, Proposals for Change," in Donald Stull, et al., Any way You Cut It, p. 221. (Hereafter cited as Hall, The Kill Line.).

24 U.S. Department of Agriculture, The Broiler Industry: An Economic Study of Structure, Practices and Problems, 1967, p. 45. See also John Strange, "'One-Sided' Contracts Make Farming Risky," National Catholic Reporter, Nov. 15, 2002, p. 12; Richard Behar, "Arkansas Pecking Order," Time, Oct. 26, 1992, p. 53; Shand, Billions of Chickens, pp. 78 and 79; Strausberg, From Hills and Hollers, pp. 80, 91, 104, 122, and 136; Keith Nunes, "Developing a Common Voice," Meat and Poultry, Dec. 1992, pp. 16 and 18; and Chao Xiong, "Taking Wing: Hmong Are Moving Again, This Time to Poultry Farms," The Wall Street Journal, Jan. 26, 2004, pp. A1 and A6.

25 Scott Kilman, "Moving On Up," The Wall Street Journal, Oct. 25, 2004, pp. R6 and R10.

26 On the grower/integrator relationship, see three articles by Steve Bjerklie collectively titled "Dark Passage," which appeared in the industry journal, Meat and Poultry, Aug. 1994, pp. 24-26, and 55; Oct. 1994, pp. 32-35; and Dec. 1994, pp. 20, 22, 24, 26, and 28.

27 Griffith, Hay Trabajo, p. 130.

strategy.[28] Plants are described as operating on a two-tier labor system. On top are *core workers*: trained, stable, with strong labor market attachment, who keep the plants operating. They are supplemented by a body of unskilled low-wage workers with a high turnover rate. The latter, it appears, have low expectations, both with respect to living and working conditions, and may view their employment as short-term. They are unlikely to complain or to join a union, especially if they are not *authorized* residents. The two-tier system reportedly allows integration of new *line workers* with little disruption.[29]

The new breed packers and processors appear to have developed a workforce the demographics of which are somewhat different from that of the older urban packers. There are fewer African-American males and more Hispanic and Southeast Asian workers: often (but not always) transient, low-skilled but hard-working, less assertive of their workplace rights than experienced workers, and willing to work for low wages under conditions that may be adverse. But, conditions vary from plant-to-plant and from one location to another.[30]

UNIONIZATION OF THE MEAT AND POULTRY WORKFORCE

In the 19th century, most butchering was conducted at the local retail level. With the rise of the packing plants, a distinction was made between butchers, *per se*, and packinghouse workers; but trade unionization focused on the butchers (*craft workers*) rather than packinghouse workers (*industrial workers*).

The Early Years under the Amalgamated

The late 19th century witnessed a number of attempts by workers in the packing industries to organize. Generally, their efforts were without success. In 1894, during the Pullman (American Railway Union) strike, packinghouse workers engaged in a sympathetic walkout.[31] When the rail strike was broken, the packinghouse workers were replaced "from among the thousands of unemployed workers who crowded the yards, anxious to take any job they could get."[32] Other strikes would follow.

---

28 Lourdes Gouveia and Donald D. Stull, "Dances with Cows: Beefpacking's Impact on Garden City, Kansas, and Lexington, Nebraska," in Donald D. Stull, et al., Any Way You Cut It: Meat Processing and Small-Town America (Lawrence: University Press of Kansas, 1995), p. 103. See also Greig Guthey, "Mexican Places in Southern Spaces: Globalization, Work and Daily Life in and around the North Georgia Poultry Industry," in Arthur D. Murphy, et al., eds., Latino Workers in the Contemporary South (Athens: University of Georgia Press, 2001), p. 63.

29 Griffith, Hay Trabajo, p. 146; and Donald D. Stull, et al., Any Way You Cut It: Meat Processing and Small-Town America (Lawrence: University Press of Kansas, 1995), p. 8. (Hereafter cited as Stull, et al., Any Way You Cut It.).

30 In general, see Griffith, Jones's Minimal. Leon Fink, The Maya of Morganton: Work and Community in the Neuvo New South (Chapel Hill: University of North Carolina Press, 2003), provides a case study of labor supply and labor-management relations in a small North Carolina town. (Hereafter cited as Fink, The Maya of Morganton).

31 Brody, The Butcher Workmen, p. 13. See also Ken Fones-Wolf, "Eight-Hour and Haymarket Strikes of 1886," in Ronald Filippelli, editor, Labor Conflict in the United States (New York: Garland Publishing, Inc., 1990), pp. 164-169.

32 Walter A. Fogel, The Negro in the Meat Industry (Philadelphia: University of Pennsylvania Press, 1970), p. 19. (Hereafter cited as Fogel, The Negro in the Meat Industry.).

At first, the packers had hired "recent immigrants from eastern Europe" — but, then, they began to use African-Americans — at first as strikebreakers and, less often, as regular workers.[33] In so doing, explains Alma Herbst, the packers "tapped an almost inexhaustible supply of cheap labor" and secured a workforce more resistant to unionization than were the European immigrants.[34] While the "majority of the strikebreakers were white," the "Negro, because of his color, attracted more than his share of hostility and was associated by many packinghouse workers with the collapse of the strike[s]."[35]

The labor force was divided, roughly, into two groups: retail butchers and packinghouse workers. Among the latter was a hierarchy of sub-crafts. Workers in the packing houses, where unions were formed, had "invariably unionized along narrow craft lines" in the 1880s and 1890s.[36] But skill was coming to count for "less and less" and "[s]pecialization was making the employment of cheaper labor possible."[37] Recalcitrant workers could quickly be replaced — and both management and the workers knew it.[38]

Developing a Stable Union

In 1896, American Federation of Labor (AFL) president Samuel Gompers called a national convention of butchers. On January 26, 1897, a charter was issued to the Amalgamated Meat Cutters and Butcher Workmen of North America. Michael Donnelly of Omaha was elected president.[39]

The Amalgamated moved into Chicago in 1900 and began organization of packinghouse workers still demoralized from the strikes of the 1890s. The union faced a number of challenges. The companies had adopted a systematic approach of *de-skilling* packing jobs: segmenting the work process so that less expensive workers could be hired, given partial training, and engaged (when needed) as replacement workers for those with somewhat greater skills. Though a rational policy from the perspective of industry, it complicated the efforts of the union to recruit and hold members.[40] At the same time, by careful recruitment, the packers were able to shift dominance from one racial/ethnic faction to another — and to stir tensions between male and female workers.[41]

---

33 Ibid., p. 19.
34 Alma Herbst, The Negro in the Slaughtering and Meat-Packing Industry in Chicago
(Boston: Houghton Mifflin Company, 1932), pp. 19-20. (Hereafter cited as erbst, The Negro in the Slaughtering and Meat-Packing Industry.).
35 Fogel, The Negro in the Meat Industry, p. 19-20. Interpretation varies. See Sterling Spero and Abram Harris, The Black Worker: The Negro and the Labor Movement (New York: Columbia University Press, 1931), pp. 264 ff. (Hereafter cited as Spero and Harris, The Black Worker.); Horace R. Cayton and George S. Mitchell, Black Workers and the New Unions (Chapel Hill: The University of North Carolina Press, 1939), pp. 228 ff.; and William M. Tuttle, Jr., "Labor Conflict and Racial Violence: The Black Worker in Chicago, 1894-1919," in Milton Cantor, ed., Black Labor In America (Westport, CT: Negro Universities Press, 1969), pp. 88-89. (Hereafter cited as Tuttle, Labor Conflict and Racial Violence).
36 Brody, The Butcher Workmen, p. 15.
37 Spero and Harris, The Black Worker, p. 264.
38 Brody, The Butcher Workmen, p. 15.
39 Ibid., pp. 17-33; Gary M. Fink (ed.), Labor Unions (Westport, CT: Greenwood Press, 1977), p. 216 (Hereafter cited as Fink, Labor Unions); and Carl W. Thompson, "Labor in the Packing Industry," The Journal of Political Economy, Feb. 1907, pp. 96-97.
40 Tuttle, Labor Conflict and Racial Violence, p. 90. See also Stull and Broadway,Slaughterhouse Blues, pp. 34-35.
41 See, inter alia, Selig Perlman and Philip Taft, History of Labor in the United States, 1896-1932 (New York: Augustus M. Kelley, Publishers, 1966), vol. IV, p. 118; Fogel, The Negro in the Meat Industry, p. 18; Edith Abbott, and S. P. Breckinridge, "Women in Industry: The Chicago Stockyards," The Journal of Political Economy, Oct. 1911, pp. 649-651, and 639; and Rick Halpern and Roger Horowitz, Meatpackers: An Oral

These management-enhanced divisions within the workforce convinced some workers of the need for industrial (cross-craft) organization. All workers would have to be organized if the Amalgamated were to succeed; but, even so, solidarity —across racial, ethnic, gender and skill lines — would be difficult to achieve.[42]

A Time of Trial and Upheaval

Organizationally, the "great prize," according to Brody, was the packinghouse where large numbers could be organized "in one swift stroke." At the turn of the century, a little over 25,000 workers were employed in Chicago's stock yards, about a third of those employed in the industry nationally. Donnelly set out to organize the workers and to instruct them in trade union strategy. The skilled craft workers were the first organized and remained the core of the union. The union sought out the immigrant worker and actively courted African-American workers (about 500 then employed in the yards) — and the latter "hesitantly joined" the ranks of organized labor.[43]

Organization, alone, did not erase the workers' grievances. Increasing line speed was a concern — as it would continue to be through the rest of the 20th century. Jurisdictional issues arose. Hours of work, often irregular, and seasonal disparities in employment continued as a source of discontent. Wage considerations were always an issue. "Under any circumstances, it would have been difficult to control the untutored and excited mass of packinghouse men," Brody notes, but "... discontent was stirred by Donnelly's cautious negotiating policy ... benefits came too slowly and unevenly."[44]

On July 12, 1904, over Donnelly's reservations, the union struck. The weakness of the Amalgamated — internal dissension and lack of discipline — was quickly exposed. Again, industry imported black strikebreakers; and, as might have been anticipated, violence broke out — with the strikebreakers frequently the object of attack. With the union financially strapped, Donnelly sought accommodation — and was rebuffed. Intervention by Jane Addams (a Chicago social worker) and her associates brought an end to the strike, but the men were granted no concessions from the packers.[45] The union was largely fragmented and, in 1907, Donnelly resigned and left the movement.[46] For a decade, few victories appear to have been achieved by the Amalgamated.

History of Black Packinghouse Workers and Their Struggle for Racial and Economic Equality (New York: Twayne Publishers, 1996), p. 6. (Hereafter cited as Halpern and Horowitz, An Oral History.).

42 See James R. Barrett, "Immigrant Workers in Early Mass Production Industry: Work Rationalization and Job Control Conflicts in Chicago's Packinghouses, 1900-1904," in Hartmut Keill and John B. Jents, eds., German Workers in Industrial Chicago, 1850-1910: A Comparative Perspective (DeKalb: Northern Illinois University Press, 1983), pp. 104-124.

43 Brody, The Butcher Workmen, p. 34 and 41. For an overview of race and unionization, see Walter Fogel, "Blacks in Meatpacking: Another View of The Jungle," Industrial Relations, Oct. 1971, pp. 338-353.

44 Brody, The Butcher Workmen, pp. 47-48.

45 Ibid., p. 58. See John R. Commons, "Labor Conditions in Meat Packing and the Recent Strike," The Quarterly Journal of Economics, Nov. 1904, pp. 1-32. (Hereafter cited as Commons, Labor Conditions.) Black strikebreakers had also been used by the packers against the Packing House Teamsters in 1902. See Howard B. Myers, "The Policing of Labor Disputes in Chicago: A Case Study," Ph.D. dissertation, University of Chicago, 1929, pp. 347-366 (Hereafter cited as Myers, Labor Disputes); James R. Barrett, Work and Community in the Jungle: Chicago's Packinghouse Workers, 1894-1922 (Urbana: University of Illinois Press, 1987), pp. 118-187, (Hereafter cited as Barrett, Work and Community); Barrett, "Unity and Fragmentation: Class, Race, and Ethnicity on Chicago's South Side, 1900-1922," Journal of Social History, fall 1984, p. 50, (Hereafter cited as Barrett, Unity and Fragmentation); and David Witwer, "Race Relations in the Early Teamsters Union," Labor History, Nov. 2002, pp. 505-532.

46 Myers, Labor Disputes, pp. 532-533; and Brody, The Butcher Workmen, pp. 59-74.

In 1917, the United States entered the European war. Immigration, the traditional source of packinghouse labor, declined. The draft further reduced manpower availability. Labor shortages were accompanied by a heightened demand for meat — and the Amalgamated rebounded — but under federal wartime regulation. The war years also sparked a northward migration of southern blacks who, in significantly increased numbers, took jobs in the packing plants. Brody states that, by some estimates, "90 percent *of the northern Negroes* in the Chicago yards carried union cards." (Italics added.) But the newcomers, like immigrant groups before them, proved difficult to organize and, once in the union, to retain. By the end of the war, late in 1918, some 10,000 black workers were employed in the yards — "over 20 percent of the labor force."[47]

The post-war period, however, did not bode well for unions. The Chicago race riots (1919) added to tensions between black and white workers.[48] Then, internal union discord broke out. By 1921, the treasury of the Amalgamated was depleted. Wartime restraints vanished. Unemployment became widespread. Union membership shrank. So, in the dead of winter, in an effort to rebuild and regain its strength, the Amalgamated called a nation-wide strike.[49] Within weeks, on February 1, 1922, the strike was called off: again, a failed effort. The Amalgamated reverted largely to representation of local retail butchers.[50]

THE CIO AND THE PACKINGHOUSE WORKERS

By the 1930s, workers in meat packing had suffered defeats in a series of strikes: in 1894, 1904 and 1921-1922. The conflicts had been demoralizing and had left the packinghouse side of the union in shambles.

The Depression of 1929 hit the packinghouse industry hard and "... opened a period of social ferment in which radical ideas received a wide and sympathetic hearing."[51] "With hundreds at the gate begging for jobs, managers could select whom to employ as their whims or prejudices dictated." And, some managers, it appears, exacted retribution against workers who had been engaged in strike activity or now attempted to organize.[52]

---

47 Brody, The Butcher Workmen, p. 85. See also William C. Pratt, "Advancing Packinghouse Unionism in South Omaha, 1917-1920," Journal of the West, Apr. 1996, pp. 42-49.

48 Barrett, Unity and Fragmentation, p. 43, states: "While white butcher workmen had little to do with the attacks on Blacks, the riot ended any prospect of creating an interracial labor movement in the Yards for more than a generation."

49 Barrett, Work and Community, pp. 257-259.

50 Ibid., pp. 258-259; Roger Horowitz, "'It Wasn't a Time to Compromise': The Unionization of Sioux City's Packinghouses," The Annals of Iowa, fall 1989/winter 1990, p. 253 (Hereafter cited as Horowitz, 'It Wasn't a Time to Compromise'); and Rick Halpern, Down on the Killing Floor: Black and White Workers in Chicago's Packinghouses, 1904-1954 (Urbana: University of Illinois Press, 1997), p.71. (Hereafter cited as Halpern, Down on the Killing Floor.) William C. Pratt, in "Divided Workers, Divided Communities: The 1921-22 Packinghouse Strike in Omaha and Nebraska City," Labor's Heritage, winter 1994, p. 56, reports that Nebraska employers used "many African Americans as replacements during the strike" and attempted to secure Mexican-American strikebreakers as well. (Hereafter cited as Pratt, Divided Workers.).

51 oger Horowitz, "Negro and White, Unite and Fight!" — A Social History of Industrial Unionism in Meatpacking, 1930-1990 (Urbana: University of Illinois Press, 1997), p. 67. (Hereafter cited as Horowitz, Negro and White.).

52 Rick Halpern, "The Iron Fist and the Velvet Glove: Welfare Capitalism in Chicago's Packinghouses, 1921-1933," Journal of American Studies, Aug. 1992, pp. 161, 164-165. (Hereafter cited as Halpern, The Iron Fist.) On labor-management during the 1930s, see Irving Bernstein, The New Deal Collective Bargaining Policy

Ethnic/racial diversity still prevailed in the plants; but, now, these were often workers of a second generation. (See Table 1.) In their continuing search "for cheap labor," the packers looked "to Chicago's expanding Afro-American community";[53] but, these were people who had migrated north during World War I, had become acculturated to the industrial workplace, and were more supportive of unionization.[54] By the 1930s, they had become "a permanent component of the labor force" and, some argued, "provided the [union] organizing drive with its backbone ...[,] dynamism" and "key leadership."[55]

Table 1. Racial and Nationality Trends Among Slaughtering and Meat-Packing Workers in Chicago, 1909 and 1928

	1909		1928	
Race	Number	Percent	Number	Percent
Native-born				
White	2,031	18.9	3,604	27.3
Black	459	3.0	3,894	29.5
Foreign-born				
Polish	4,293	27.7	1,570	11.9
Lithuanian	1,860	12.0	1,033	7.8
Mexican	1	N.A.	746	5.7

Source: Paul S. Taylor, Mexican Labor in the United States: Chicago, and the Calumet Region
(Berkeley: University of California Press, Mar. 31, 1932), p. 40. By 1928, the Poles, Lithuanians, and
Mexicans were the three most numerous nationality groups — with a wide scattering of other
immigrants represented in smaller percentages.

Mexican workers began to appear in the meat packing industry of the Midwest during World War I. After 1920, Horowitz notes, "the Mexican presence increased sharply."[56] Most appear to have migrated from Mexico, rather than from other parts of the United States, having come north as agricultural or track laborers (railroad maintenance of way). After brief periods at such work (or in the steel mills), they migrated in the late 1920s "to other industries, particularly to meat-packing."[57]

(Los Angeles: University of California Press, 1950); and Jerold S. Auerbach, *Labor and Liberty: The La Follette Committee and the New Deal* (Indianapolis: The Bobbs-Merrill Company, Inc., 1966).

53 Halpern, *The Iron Fist*, p. 165. Halpern (pp. 166-167) notes an increased number of black workers in "the semi-skilled and skilled segment of the labour force."

54 Shelton Stromquist, Solidarity and Survival: An Oral History of Iowa Labor in the Twentieth Century (Iowa City: University of Iowa Press, 1993), p. 101. (Hereafter cited as Stromquist, Solidarity and Survival.).

55 Halpern, The Iron Fist, p. 162.

56 Horowitz, Negro and White, p. 62. Pratt, in Divided Workers, p. 52, notes that some 283 Mexicans were resident in the Omaha area at the time of the 1921-1922 strike and that, at least on that occasion, the union printed strike ballots in English, Polish, Lithuanian, Czech, and Spanish. Not all local residents of Mexican origin, of course, were employed in the packing plants. See T. Earl Sullenger, "The Mexican Population of Omaha," Journal of Applied Sociology, May-June 1924, pp. 289-293.

57 Paul S. Taylor, Mexican Labor in the United States: Chicago and the Calumet R egion (Los Angeles: University of California Press, Publications in Economics, 1932), vol. 7, no. 2, p. 41. There is some suggestion that Mexican workers were engaged as strikebreakers at various times — but, also, that some struck alongside non-Mexican workers (see p. 34 and 45). Taylor states on p. 68: "So far as I could ascertain, Mexican laborers were not imported to Chicago by packing plants." There was a perception, Taylor suggests, that Mexican workers were more adaptable and "that they would accept disagreeable work more readily than others, even than the Negroes." (See pp. 87-88.) See, also, Dionicio Nodin Valdes, Barios Nortenos: St. Paul and

Robert A. Slayton, in his study *Back of the Yards*, observed that "... Mexicans entered the packing plants gradually." He continues: "In 1920, Swift and Company employed 97 Mexicans; within a few years this figure rose to 217...." At Armour, during the period, 400 were employed — and 94 more were employed at Wilson and Company.[58]

Grass Roots Initiatives

In mid-1933, workers at Hormel (Austin, Minnesota) resolved to form a union. Under Frank Ellis, a "long-time member of the IWW" (the Industrial Workers of the World), organization began.[59] Soon, the Independent Union of All Workers (IUAW) emerged — and organization spread throughout Austin well beyond the packing plant.[60] In September 1933, with Ellis at its head, the IUAW won the right to bargain for the Hormel workers. After a brief lockout/strike, settlement was reached laying the foundation for labor-management cooperation at the Austin-based firm.

The IUAW then "organized a network of affiliated unions and supporters in the midwestern meatpacking industry" under the banner of industrial unionism. Gradually, its influence spread through the upper midwest.[61] But to sustain its position in Austin, the IUAW found that it would need to organize the entire industry — a task beyond its strength. Thus, it reached out to other independent unions such as the Cedar Rapids-based Midwest Union of All Packinghouse Workers. In early 1936, these groups combined to form the Committee for Industrial Organization in the Packing Industry (*still independent* but oriented toward the national CIO).[62]

Midwestern Mexican Communities in the Twentieth Century (Austin: University of Texas Press, 2000), p. 25. (Hereafter cited as Valdes, Barios Nortenos.) Here, Valdes divides early Mexican immigration to the Midwest into three periods: first, 1906-1910, "associated with railroad companies already employing Mexicans in the Southwest"; second, 1916-1919, "linked to railroad and industrial employer demands during the wartime economic boom and labor shortages that resulted from restricted immigration from Europe"; and, third, 1920-1921 and after. He states, perhaps in contrast to Taylor: "The colonia in the Stockyards district of Chicago appeared when employers seeking to break the packinghouse workers' strike in 1921-1922 hired a contingent of Mexicans." Valdes states (p. 29): "Smaller numbers of Mexicans also found work in the packing plants of Omaha, Kansas City, and Sioux City, Iowa. During the 1920s, packinghouses in South St. Paul offered the most important urban employment available to Mexicans in the Twin Cities." Immigrant attitudes toward organized labor, of course, varied among individuals, localities, and over time. See also Zaragosa Vargas, Proletarians of the North: A History of Mexican Industrial Workers in Detroit and the Midwest, 1917-1933 (Berkeley: University of California Press, 1993), pp. 80 and 90.

58 Robert A. Slayton, in Back of the Yards: The Making of a Local Democracy (Chicago: The University of Chicago Press, 1986), seems to suggest the same view as Valdes. He notes on pp. 179-180 that "... five hundred Mexicans arrived in 1921 and 1922" in the Back of the Yards neighborhood — though he does not specifically relate their arrival to strikebreaking. He does, however, suggest: "Most of these jobs were made available to Mexicans during the 1921 strike, when the packers hired anyone they could find."

59 Horowitz, Negro and White, p. 64. Founded in 1905 (and anti-AFL), the IWW was, by the 1930s, organizationally spent but still a strong intellectual force in portions of the labor movement. See, also, Peter Rachleff, "Organizing 'Wall-to-Wall,' The Independent Union of All Workers, 1933-1937," in Shelton Stromquist and Marvin Bergman, eds., Unionizing the Jungles: Labor and Community in the Twentieth-Century Meatpacking Industry (Iowa City: University of Iowa Press, 1997), pp. 51-74.

60 Larry D. Engelmann, "'We Were the Poor People' — The Hormel Strike of 1933," Labor History, fall 1974, p. 493. (Hereafter cited as Engelmann, The Hormel Strike of 1933.).

61 Horowitz, Negro and White, p. 45; and Engelmann, The Hormel Strike of 1933, p. 509.

62 The IUAW was not affiliated with the Amalgamated — and not yet affiliated with the CIO. For other upper-midwest organizing initiatives, see Farrell Dobbs, Teamster Rebellion (New York: Monad Press, 1972); and Philip A. Korth, The Minneapolis Teamsters Strike of 1934 (East Lansing: Michigan State University Press, 1995).

The Packinghouse Workers Organizing Committee (PWOC)

With passage of the National Industrial Recovery Act (NIRA, 1933), "[t]housands of American workers rushed to join the unions of their trade, and where unions did not already exist, they organized them." But much of industry remained unorganized and AFL efforts, some felt, were too tepid. In 1935, John L. Lewis of the United Mine Workers, with leaders of several other international unions, formed the Committee for Industrial Organization, an "extralegal committee organized to promote industrial unionism and to convert the AFL to that principle."[63]

The Amalgamated — half craft (retail butchers) and half-industrial — was the only AFL union active in the packinghouse field. It was presided over by Patrick Gorman who, though he understood the need for industrial organization, was also firmly rooted in the AFL. By late 1936, the CIO entered negotiations with the IUAW-Cedar Rapids group and, soon thereafter, IUAW-related entities began advertising themselves as affiliated with the CIO. Negotiations between Lewis and Gorman followed but, ultimately, Gorman opted to remain with the AFL. In October 1937, the PWOC was created with Van A. Bittner of the United Mine Workers (a Lewis associate) in charge.[64]

Industry raised strong opposition to the PWOC and organization was further complicated by hostilities between the PWOC and the Amalgamated. Only in February 1940 did the PWOC secure its first major contract. In 1943, in the context of World War II, the PWOC became the United Packinghouse Workers of America (UPWA).[65]

CIO organization of the packinghouse workers proved contentious. *First.* The emergence of the UPWA, out of the Amalgamated, was not entirely clearly drawn. Some packinghouse workers remained in the Amalgamated and, more broadly, there was the continuing clash (often bitter) between the AFL and the CIO. *Second.* The IUAW had been *of* the local rank-and-file. Joining the CIO jeopardized that tradition and entailed, Horowitz suggests, an alliance "with men and women who were sociologically very different."[66] The top leadership of the PWOC (appointed, not elected) was from outside the industry. While meat packers would come to play a leadership role, some still viewed the national PWOC/CIO as too far removed from *the line* — and, perhaps, too preoccupied with non-packinghouse matters.[67] *Third.* There was a cultural shift. Ellis, out of the IWW, "believed in union democracy, shop floor organization, direct action, an industrial structure, and solidarity among all workers," recalls Peter Rachleff.[68] He states: the IUAW had "demonstrated how to build a lively, democratic, militant labor movement, rooted in local control, committed to horizontal

---

63 Fink, Labor Unions, pp. 65-66. The Committee would become the Congress of Industrial Organizations or CIO only in May 1938. Here, keeping those dates in mind, both bodies will be referred to as the CIO.

64 Valdes, Barrios Nortenos, p. 167, states that Mexican packinghouse workers were "responsive" both to the Steel Workers Organizing Committee (SWOC) and to the PWOC.

65 Walter Galenson, The CIO Challenge to the AFL: A History of the American Labor Movement, 1935-1941 (Cambridge: Harvard University Press, 1960), pp. 349-374. (Hereafter cited as Galenson, The CIO Challenge.).

66 Horowitz, Negro and White, p. 52. See also Galenson, The CIO Challenge, p. 360.

67 Galenson, The CIO Challenge, pp. 362 and 374.

68 Peter Rachleff, Hard-Pressed in the Heartland: The Hormel Strike and the Future of the Labor Movement (Boston: South End Press, 1993) p. 28. (Hereafter cited as Rachleff,Hard-Pressed.).

solidarity. [But] ... had not found a way to keep this alive while building a strong national organization able to control conditions in any given industry."[69]

United Packinghouse Workers of America (UPWA)

The UPWA of 1943, Brody states, "failed to achieve the one-party rule characteristic of American trade unions" — a *failure* some might view as positive. Under Ralph Helstein (an attorney: first UPWA general counsel and, after 1946, president) and Ellis, the union would be politically liberal and protective of the rights of various racial/ethnic and political minorities.[70]

The new labor legislation of the 1930s and 1940s, some argue, tended to convert unions from bodies of militants to part of the regulatory structure: weakening the role of the rank-and-file and widening the gulf between workers and the union hierarchy. This thesis suggests that unions came to act "less as advocates for their members than as buffers, mediating between capital and labor." The UPWA, some argue, may have been an exception. *First.* Its origins were strongly of the rank-and-file. *Second.* There was a growing African-American component within the UPWA concerned with civil rights and social justice. *Third.* "... acceptance of racial diversity translated easily into tolerance of political diversity" (i.e., of a more left-of-center sort).[71]

Rank-and-file activism in the UPWA, Horowitz, states, resulted in an alliance of "black workers and white progressives" that allowed the union "to expand its program of social unionism" into "cooperation with the emerging civil rights movement."[72] As World War II commenced, many Afro-Americans urged a "Double V" campaign: "for victory over fascism abroad and Jim Crow at home."[73] Meanwhile, many white workers held that inter-racial solidarity was essential if wages and working conditions were to be improved.[74] The UPWA attacked discrimination both in the shop and in the community and "consciously worked with and influenced community-based organizations, especially local branches of the NAACP...."[75] After 1943, the UPWA negotiated anti-discriminatory provisions in its new national agreements.

During the war, controls had kept wage rates relatively stable even in the face of inflation. Since the UPWA was a party to a national no-strike pledge, there was little opportunity for more direct labor-management activity. With the end of the war, however,

---

69 Ibid., p. 42. Conversely, see Paul Street, "Breaking Up Old Hatreds and Breaking Through the Fear: The Emergence of the Packinghouse Workers Organizing Committee in Chicago, 1933-1940," Studies in History and Politics (1986), pp. 63-82.

70 Brody, The Butcher Workmen, pp. 226-227.

71 Halpern, Down on the Killing Floor, pp. 203-205.

72 Horowitz, Negro and White, p. 145.

73 Halpern, Down on the Killing Floor, p. 213.

74 Fogel, The Negro in the Meat Industry, pp. 68-69.

75 Halpern and Horowitz, An Oral History, p. 20. Ray Marshall, in The Negro and Organized Labor (New York: John Wiley and Sons, Inc., 1965), p. 179, observed: "No union operating in the South has followed a more militantly equalitarian racial position than the UPWA." Fogel, The Negro in Meat, p. 70, would add: "That same statement [Marshall's] applies equally well to the North." See Rick Halpern, "Interracial Unionism in the Southwest: Fort Worth's Packinghouse Workers, 1937-1954," in Robert H. Zieger, ed.,Organized Labor in the Twentieth-Century South (Knoxville: The University of Tennessee Press, 1991), pp.158-182. Halpern presents a somewhat more complicated picture. Bruce Fehn, "'The Only Hope We Had': United Packinghouse Workers Local 46 and the Struggle for Racial Equality in Waterloo, Iowa, 1948-1960," The Annals of Iowa, Summer 1995, pp. 185-216; discusses the campaign for civil rights undertaken by the Packinghouse Workers union.

pressure mounted. In late 1945, the UPWA began to map a strategy for a wage increase —
with some measure of cooperation from the Amalgamated. When, in January 1946, the
packers refused the union's wage demands, a strike was called that was immediately
effective.[76] Ten days into the strike, President Truman, still operating under wartime
emergency procedures, seized the plants and ordered work to resume. The union declined,
demanding that government guarantee enforcement of any settlement reached through a board
of inquiry. The Administration agreed and, while the locals were not wholly satisfied, the
settlement provided a wage increase.[77]

From across the industrial spectrum, management turned to Congress; and, in 1947, the
Taft-Hartley Act was passed. It imposed significant new restraints upon trade union activity
and, *inter alia*, required union officials to file non-communist affidavits if their unions were
to avail themselves of the services of the National Labor Relations Board. For some of the
CIO unions (like the UPWA) with a left-of-center leadership component, the requirement had
a serious impact.[78] *First.* In effect, it placed the government on the side of the more
conservative factions within the union. *Second.* It deprived these unions, it was argued, of
some of their most talented leaders. *Third.* Where the affidavit requirements were not
complied with (and the UPWA initially refused to do so), the NLRB refused to certify the
union for collective bargaining purposes. *Fourth.* Since the Amalgamated did comply, the
stage was set for renewed competition between the unions.[79]

At that juncture, the UPWA faced a new round of bargaining: this time, without the
cooperation of the Amalgamated. The union authorized a strike for February 1948 — that
some thought ill-timed and ill-advised. Although "hard-fought," it "lacked the unity and
purpose which could keep men out on the streets indefinitely."[80] In mid-May 1948, the union
capitulated. Financially weakened, its membership having dropped from about 100,000 to
about 60,000, it "faced dozens of legal cases arising out of picket line violence, as well as the
danger of losing NLRB certification at many plants because of election petitions" filed by
competing unions. The debate over non-compliance with Taft-Hartley had come to an end.[81]

THE MERGER: UPWA AND THE AMALGAMATED (1968)

Through the war years, the Amalgamated and the UPWA (like the AFL and the CIO —
to which they were respectively affiliated) had remained at odds. The unions were divided by

---

76 Brody, The Butcher Workmen, p. 228.
77 Horowitz, Negro and White, pp. 168-170.
78 Section 9(h) of the Taft-Hartley Act required, as a condition for utilization of the services of the Board, that there
    be on file with the Board "an affidavit ... by each officer of such labor organization and the officers of any
    national or international labor organization of which it is an affiliate or constituent unit that he is not a member
    of the Communist Party or...." The requirement was repealed by Section 201(d) of the Labor Management
    Reporting and Disclosure Act of 1959 (the Landrum-Griffin Act). See Charles O. Gregory, Labor and the Law
    (New York: W. W. Norton and Company, Inc., 1961), pp. 438-442 and 573-575.
79 Horowitz, Negro and White, pp. 182-183. See R. Alton Lee, Truman and Taft-Hartley: A Question of Mandate
    (Lexington: University of Kentucky Press, 1966); and Arthur F. McClure, The Truman Administration and the
    Problems of Postwar Labor, 1945-1948 (Rutherford: NJ: Fairleigh Dickinson University Press, 1969).
80 Brody, The Butcher Workmen, p. 233.
81 Horowitz, Negro and White, pp. 188-189. An accurate assessment of the strike appears clouded by rhetoric. See
    Halpern and Horowitz, An Oral History, p. 19; Brody, The Butcher Workmen, p. 235; and Bruce Fehn, "Ruin
    or Renewal: The United Packinghouse Workers of America and the 1948 Meatpacking Strike in Iowa,"
    Annals of Iowa, fall 1997, pp. 349-378.

philosophy: craft versus industrial unionism. They had different approaches to the new regulatory structure — notably, to alleged bias of the NLRB. There was disagreement concerning the political role of unions and where, along the political spectrum, the unions should stand. Most difficult, however, may have been conflicts rooted in personal hostilities dating from PWOC days.

While the UPWA was advancing the cause of social unionism, a new element was emerging on the scene: the decline of the old packing firms and emergence of the *new breed* of packers. Slowly, Brody states, it "became apparent to both unions," the UPWA and the Amalgamated, that cooperation would be mutually beneficial.[82] But, he suggests: "The past was ... not easy to exorcise."[83]

The new firms, emerging during the 1950s and 1960s, "took large chunks of the market away from the old dominant companies."[84] Technology changed as well and, with it, what the packinghouse workers actually did. Where employment once had been stable, the *new breed* firms accepted rapid employee turnover and structured to accommodate it. Urban-to-rural transition also meant that fewer African-American workers, a major segment of UPWA membership, would remain in the industry's workforce.[85] With its base shrinking, the UPWA changed its name to the United Packinghouse, Food and Allied Workers (1960) and reached out to new groups to organize. But, the "unrelenting drumbeat of plant closings placed a financial squeeze on the organization that made its rebuilding strategy impossible to sustain."[86] Mergers within the trade union movement had become a common response to shifts in industry and/or technology. In late 1967, UPWA leaders approached the Amalgamated; in 1968, a formal merger was effected.

The merger may not have been a perfect fit. The UPWA gave way to the Amalgamated nearly six times its size. Gorman remained at the helm: Helstein became "a titular vice president but without any responsibilities." Service units, regarded as vital within the UPWA, were disbanded. New units, subsumed into larger bodies, some suggested, were underfunded and unable to pursue normal/prior responsibilities. Some from the UPWA found it difficult to work within the new structure. Lines of communication were broken up. Much of the freedom and rank-and-file democracy, to which the UPWA locals had been accustomed, was said to have disappeared. Perhaps most important, the merger had occurred in the context of the restructuring of the industry. *New breed* packers were assembling a workforce quite different from that associated either with the UPWA or with the Amalgamated — and one increasingly devoid, perhaps by careful personnel selection, of trade union consciousness. The merged union had to reach out to a workforce neither accustomed to trade unionization nor predisposed toward organized labor.[87]

---

82 Brody, The Butcher Workmen, pp. 219-220. Through the period, the National Brotherhood of Packinghouse Workers (the Swift union) would maintain its independent status.

83 Brody, The Butcher Workmen, pp. 238-239.

84 Horowitz, Negro and White, p. 247.

85 Fogel, The Negro in the Meat Industry, pp. 1-2, 5, and 8; and Donald D. Stull, "'I Come to the Garden': Changing Ethnic Relations in Garden City, Kansas," Urban Anthropology, winter 1990, p. 314.

86 Horowitz, Negro and White, pp. 257-258.

THE UNITED FOOD AND COMMERCIAL WORKERS (UFCW)

In 1977, Patrick Gorman stepped down from leadership of the Amalgamated. Faced with a power vacuum and a general decline, the union sought yet another merger.[88] The Retail Clerks International Union (RCIU) seemed a likely candidate. In 1979, the two merged as the United Food and Commercial Workers (UFCW).

The Retail Clerks (RCIU) and the Amalgamated

The RCIU, a craft union chartered by the AFL in 1890, was neither activist nor especially successful. By 1933, it had a membership of about 5,000. "The RCIU was hampered by a timid, conservative leadership either unwilling or unable to take advantage of the organizing opportunities" of the New Deal era.[89] Then, in the mid-1940s, a new leadership assumed control and, largely based upon supermarket employment, the membership of the RCIU expanded rapidly making it one of the largest unions in the AFL.

There had been a long — not always harmonious — relationship between the RCIU and the Amalgamated. Their members often worked within the same firm and building: one union representing the sales staff; the other, meat cutters. Arguments were "almost endless."[90] But the conflicts involved the *retail butchers* — not packinghouse workers. At mid-century, however, conditions began to change as meat (with poultry and fish) came into the markets pre-packaged — largely eliminating the need for skilled butchers and replacing them with *food handlers*. Disputes continued as "the increasingly industrial structure of retailing" shifted work from butchers to clerks.[91]

A Merger is Consummated (1979)

When the Amalgamated and the RCIU merged in 1979 becoming the UFCW, the new union had an initial membership of 1.2 million: 525,345 members of the Amalgamated and 699,057 from the Clerks.[92]

The merger may have made sense for the old Amalgamated (pre-1968) and the RCIU. Whether it was similarly advantageous for the remnants of the UPWA remained an issue. The UPWA now "represented less than 10 percent of the UFCW membership." Institutionally, it was the retail clerks who would dominate the new union — and they had "even less experience with industrial unionism than the Amalgamated." If the UPWA rank-and-file had felt somewhat isolated within the post-1968 Amalgamated, that sense of distance may now

---

87 Ibid., pp. 258-261. See also Fink, Labor Unions, p. 218; and Rachleff, Hard-Pressed in the Heartland, pp. 56.

88 Horowitz, Negro and White, p. 264.

89 Fink, Labor Unions, p. 329.

90 Martin Estey, "The Retail Clerks," in Albert A. Blum, et al., White Collar Workers (New York: Random House, 1971), pp. 48 and 56.

91 Michael Harrington, The Retail Clerks (New York: John Wiley and Sons, Inc., 1962.) pp.70-73. (Hereafter cited as Harrington, The Retail Clerks.).

92 Bureau of National Affairs, Daily Labor Report, June 4, 1979, p. A7-A8. (Hereafter cited as DLR.) See also DLR, June 5, 1979, pp. A11-A12.

have been compounded. UFCW headquarters were in Washington, DC, far removed from the packing industry. William Wynn, UFCW president, had joined the RCIU while in high school and had moved up through the union hierarchy to become president in 1977.[93]

INDUSTRIAL RESTRUCTURING AND ITS IMPACT ON LABOR

"The 1980s," suggests historian Peter Rachleff, "was arguably the bleakest decade in the entire history of the U.S. labor movement."[94] *Bleakness* is clearly a relative concept: what is *bleak* for labor may well be *bright* for industry.

Conditions, assert economists Charles Perry and Delwyn Kegley, "were nothing short of chaos for the UFCW and for the industry." It was a time of "Chapter 11 filings and the scrapping of labor agreements, plant closings, strikes, lockouts, rebellious local unions, [and] corporate campaigns...." Master agreements, a fixture in the industry since World War II, "virtually disappeared, to be replaced almost entirely by individual plant bargaining." The once high wages in meat packing declined significantly. Old-line companies "were transformed and became virtually unrecognizable." Conglomerates that had acquired packing and processing companies during the 1960s and 1970s "became disenchanted with the meat business and began divesting themselves of those businesses in the 1980s."[95] Through it all, it was reported, there was "steadily declining union strength."[96]

The UFCW was sometimes viewed as a "labor conglomerate."[97] Within the UFCW, Horowitz notes, the packinghouse workers became "a dwindling minority in large, multi-unit locals covering entire states and headed by local union leaders who came from completely different trades."[98] Increasingly, its focus seems to have shifted away from the individual plant as UFCW leaders began "reorganizing locals into larger, amalgamated districts."[99] While consolidation, arguably, may have been appropriate, it may also have created a situation in which packinghouse workers felt divided from the UFCW's national leadership.

---

93 Horowitz, Negro and White, p. 265. Wynn continued as president of the UFCW until 1994, being succeeded by Douglas Dority (1994-2004), and by Joseph Hansen (2004 ff.). See, also, John Breuggemann and Cliff Brown, "The Decline of Industrial Unionism in the Meatpacking Industry ... 1946-1987," Work and Occupations, Aug. 2003, pp. 336 and 348. The May 1999 issue of Labor History presents a "Symposium on Halpern and Horowitz: Packinghouse Unionism." See, also, Joe W. Trotter, "The Continuing Transformation of Labor and Working-Class History: A Review Essay," The Annals of Iowa, Winter 1999, pp. 78-86.

94 Rachleff, Hard-Pressed, p. 3.

95 Charles R. Perry and Delwyn H. Kegley, Disintegration and Change: Labor Relations in the Meat Packing Industry (Philadelphia: University of Pennsylvania Press, 1989), pp. 165, 183, and 151. (Hereafter cited as Perry and Kegley, Disintegration and Change.).

96 Horowitz, Negro and White, p. 266.

97 Perry and Kegley, *Disintegration and Change*, p. 116.

98 Horowitz, Negro and White, p. 247.

99 Warren, Struggling with "Iowa's Pride", p. 125. The issue of size and consolidation, in a later context, is discussed by labor columnist Steven Greenhouse, New York Times, Nov. 10, 2004, p. A16, and Nov. 18, 2004, p. A24.

Managerial *Churning* and Collective Bargaining

In some measure, the climate of labor-management relations in America changed during the Reagan/Bush era, Horowitz suggests, with the President's "dismissal of striking air traffic controllers in 1982" which, he states, "encouraged employers to resist the demands of labor organizations." It was a time of concession bargaining, *give-backs*, and the hiring of permanent replacements for workers who struck. Coupled "with steadily declining union strength," the period, he argues, "would end in a catastrophe for American's packinghouse workers."[100]

By 1980, with IBP and other *new breed* packers in control of a significant segment of the industry, old firms argued "that production and employment at [their] plants would decline or cease altogether unless local unions agreed to various cost concessions to help firms deal with the low-cost competition."[101] Others hinted that work might be shifted to newer plants in remote areas — that happened to be nonunion. Clearly, future bargaining would be fierce: potentially involving strikes or lockouts — certainly loss of wages and possibly loss of employment.

Two options were *at least theoretically* available to the union: organize the nonunion firms and bring their labor standards up to the level of those under the old master agreements; or, grant concessions in terms of wages and/or work rules to the older union firms. Over the objections of many packinghouse workers, it appears, the UFCW began concession bargaining in the early 1980s.[102]

Closures and Concessions

The UFCW was confronted with demands for concessions.[103] Under pressure, the union entered upon a process of controlled retreat that "quickly disintegrated into a rout that not only lowered wage rates ... but also shredded the master agreements and de-unionized the core firms of the industry."[104]

The industry side, however, was even more complex. While the union may have tended to react, it was management that led. Some older family-owned and managed firms changed policy with generational shifts in management. Some sold out. Others merged or, retaining their corporate identity, were subsumed into larger entities. In some cases, corporate officers

---

100 Horowitz, Negro and White, p. 266. Concerning the air traffic controller issue and its impact, see Willis J. Nordlund, Silent Skies: The Air Traffic Controllers' Strike (Westport, CT: Praeger, 1998); and Herbert R. Northrup, "The Rise and Demise of PATCO," Industrial and Labor Relations Review, Jan. 1984, pp. 167-184.

101 Peter Cappelli, "Plant-Level Concession Bargaining," Industrial and Labor Relations Review, Oct. 1985, pp. 92-93. See also Audrey Freedman and William Fulmer, "Last Rites for Pattern Bargaining," Harvard Business Review, Mar./Apr. 1982, p. 31. (Hereafter cited as Freedman and Fulmer, Last Rites.).

102 Horowitz, Negro and White, p. 266. It was the firm view of the UFCW's packinghouse segment, state Perry and Kegley, Disintegration and Change, p. 182, that "wage concessions do not save plants but only buy a small amount of time before the closing....".

103 Freedman and Fulmer, Last Rites, pp. 42 and 44.

104 Horowitz, Negro and White, p. 267. See Patrick Houston and Aaron Bernstein, "The Pork Workers' Beef: Pay Cuts That Persist," Business Week, Apr. 15, 1985, p. 74 (Hereafter cited as Houston and Bernstein, The Pork Workers' Beef.); and Horowitz, The Decline of Unionism, p. 35. Charles Craypo, The Economics of Collective Bargaining: Case Studies in the Private Sector (Washington: The Bureau of National Affairs, Inc., 1986), p. 72, states: "By mid-1983 only one-third of the union's members in meatpacking were still working under the master agreement, down from 55 percent when the 1981 concessions were made."

promoted splits and spin-offs with new more focused firms emerging from older enterprises. Some, even very large firms, were acquired by conglomerates — only to be sold again or simply closed as conditions warranted. With each change of corporate control, there were usually changes in labor-management policy — often with demands for concessions and, in some cases, with closings and relocations of plants, consolidation of redundant facilities, and dismissal of superfluous workers.

Some observers believed this churning was purposeful beyond immediate profitability. Management was able to dispose of union agreements, restructure work processes, and hire less skilled (and cheaper) workers. It bargained with employment-desperate communities for concessions: tax reductions, subsidies, and exemptions from local ordinances.[105]

The Ascendance of the *New Breed*

Increasingly through the late 20th century, restructuring was seem as part of a business strategy. Both industry and the union had moved, in some measure, from the world of the *creators* to that of the *managers* — albeit in somewhat different contexts.

A certain mutual distrust persisted: perhaps a mixture of hostility or disdain and, more important, of indifference. Of industry, it was said, an "influx of executives who had never sliced a hog" had led to management "that was alienated from the product and the workers."[106] Of labor, one worker reportedly quipped: "Why do I need a union to negotiate a wage cut for me? I can do that just fine for myself."[107]

Lower Wages

The essential elements of conflict between labor and management remained the same. While the workers sought higher wages and improved conditions of work, industry was pursuing enhanced profitability through a lower wage strategy. Consolidation would be paramount.[108]

Contesting with Hormel. The Hormel case, perhaps, was the most dramatic of the packinghouse conflicts of the late 20th century. It was at Hormel that the Independent Union of All Workers (IUAW) had been organized. The IUAW had, in some respects, provided the philosophical core for the PWOC and, later, the UPWA. A strong labor tradition, it appears,

---

105 Corporate restructuring has been enormously complex. See, for example Warren, Struggling with "Iowa's Pride"; Harold B. Meyers, "For the Old Meatpackers, Things Are Tough All Over," Fortune, Feb. 1969, pp. 89-93, 134 and 136 (Hereafter cited as Meyers, Things are Tough All Over); Business Week, "The Slaughter of Meatpacking Wages," June 27, 1983, p. 71; Steve Bjerklie, "'A Classic Tragedy'," Meat and Poultry, Jan. 1995, pp. 44-45, 47-48, 51; Perry and Kegley, "The Rath Experiment," in Disintegration and Change, pp. 221-233; "Wilson Foods: Nine Days to Chapter 11," Business Week, May 30, 1982, pp. 68, 70, and 72; and Steve Kay, "Beef Woes Bedevil ConAgra," Meat and Poultry, June 1998, pp. 42, 45, 47-48. The literature is extensive.

106 McNaughton, "Like a Civil War Town," Meat and Poultry, Sept. 1995, p. 51.

107 Rachleff, *Hard-Pressed*, pp. 11-12.

108 Data on wage rates, profitability, and related elements in this section are drawn from the cited published sources. Further verification would require access to corporate records.

remained among the Hormel workers although relative labor-management peace seems to have prevailed after the initial confrontation of the early 1930s.

Jay Hormel, son of the company's founder, had negotiated the initial agreement with the IUAW. But, Hormel, who enjoyed a reputation for enlightened labor-management relations, died in 1954. Gradually, through attrition, new management had come to control the company which then encompassed a number of plants spread over several states. Similarly, a new leadership had emerged within the union.

By the mid-1970s, the original Austin, Minnesota, plant was old and in need of replacement; and, after negotiations between management and the union, it was agreed that a new facility would be built in Austin. The workers would make a number of concessions in order to assure its economic viability. Certain work rules and production standards would be altered and the union accepted a no-strike provision to last through three years from completion of the new plant.[109]

Various factors led to collapse of the agreement. Protracted negotiations between Hormel, the local union (Local P-9), and the UFCW, seem to have resulted in disagreement between Local P-9 and the international union (ultimately, with the AFL-CIO) — and in a contentious strike, the latter commencing in August 1985. In May 1986, the UFCW's Executive Committee imposed a trusteeship on Local P-9 and settled the strike. The provisions accepted by the national UFCW were, reportedly, "very close to the terms Hormel demanded" prior to the strike. It made no provision for re-employment of workers still out when the strike ended.[110]

With the end of the strike at Hormel (the mid-1980s), new officers took control of the local and the labor-management relationship was resumed. But, the tone of that relationship appears to have been quite different from that which preceded the strike and, some noticed, bitterness would linger.[111]

An Emerging Pattern. In 1960, the Monfort's opened a packing plant in Greeley, Colorado. It was a pioneering effort that originally operated on a union basis. Faced with increasing competition from other new breed firms, Monfort sought, in 1979, "a three-year wage freeze and operational changes." A strike followed. In March 1980, the plant was closed — but reopened two years later without a union contract. Some estimated that total labor costs would be reduced by 25%.[112] Monfort recovered, acquired ValAgri of Garden City, Kansas, and in 1987 merged into ConAgra: soon to become "the second largest food-processing firm in the United States and the fourth largest in the world."[113]

---

109 Perry and Kegley, Disintegration and Change, pp. 198-199. See also Marie McNaughton, "Like a Civil War," Meat and Poultry, Sept. 1995, p. 51; and Rachleff, Hard-Pressed, pp. 48-50.

110 DLR, May 12, 1986, pp. A2-A4. See also Rachleff, Hard-Pressed, pp. 52-60; Horowitz, Negro and White, pp. 271-273; Jeremy Main, "The Labor Rebel Leading the Hormel Strike," Fortune, June 9, 1986, pp. 105-106, 108-110; Houston and Bernstein, The Pork Workers' Beef, p. 76; and DLR, Dec. 24, 1984, pp. A1-A2; Feb. 2, 1986, A7-A9; Mar. 17, 1986, pp. A10-A12, E1-E5; May 12, 1986, pp. A12-A13; and July 22, 1987, p. A4.

111 On the Hormel strike at large, see Marie McNaughton, "'Like a Civil War Town': Austin Minnesota, 10 Years Later," Meat and Poultry, Aug. 1995, pp. 56-62, and Sept. 1995, pp. 50-64; Dave Hage and Paul Klauda, No Retreat, No Surrender: Labor's War at Hormel (New York; William Morrow and Company, Inc., 1989); and Hardy Green, On Strike at Hormel: The Struggle for a Democratic Labor Movement (Philadelphia: Temple University Press, 1990).

112 "Monfort: A Meatpacker Tries a Comeback by Trimming Labor Costs," Business Week, Mar. 15, 1982, pp. 52 and 54. Perry and Kegley, Disintegration and Change, p. 155, state that the reopened plant went from "a former base rate of $7.98 per hour to $5.00 per hour."

113 Andreas, Meatpackers and Beef Barons, pp. 42-43.

With the purchase of Singleton Seafood and Sea Alaska Products (1982), ConAgra had become the "largest U.S. shrimp processor."[114] In 1984, Greyhound, which had acquired Armour in 1970, sold the packing firm to ConAgra which reopened 17 plants that Greyhound/Armour had closed, reportedly hiring a nonunion workforce. ConAgra also acquired Beatrice Foods and Swift Independent Packing Company (SIPCO, spun off from Esmark, Inc., by a leveraged buy-out in 1981).[115] Merging the corporate cultures of the several firms (and dealing with various executives acquired in the process) proved to be a challenge. By the mid-1990s, ConAgra was itself in the process of reorganization.[116] The Omaha-based firm announced "plans to strengthen and improve profitability by significantly reconfiguring 29 production plants and exiting or restructuring nine smaller businesses." A report in Meat and Poultry observed: "Those most immediately affected are the 6,300 employees who will lose their jobs within the year."[117]

The process would be repeated by other firms. In 1979, Missouri Beef Packers (with IBP, one of the early new breed firms) was acquired by Cargill and, in 1982, renamed Excel.[118] Based in Wichita, Kansas, Excel would lease (1987) a plant in Ottumwa, Iowa, that Hormel had closed and, within "a few days of its closing," reopen it reportedly with a two-tier pay system: "$5.50 per hour for new workers and $6.50 for workers with Hormel experience."[119] Again, in 1982, Rodeo Meats, a Morrell subsidiary, closed its Arkansas City, Kansas, plant but reopened it nine months later "as Ark City Packing Company, offering wages at $5 an hour instead of the previous union wage of $11 an hour." During the same period, IBP bought an Oscar Mayer plant in Perry, Iowa, and reopened it reportedly at "a starting wage of $5.80 an hour ... nearly $4.00 less than Oscar Mayer's starting wage."[120]

The Case of Storm Lake Packing. In 1935, Storm Lake Packing opened in Storm Lake, Iowa. For nearly 20 years, it served the local community becoming Hygrade Food Products in 1953. In 1978, in the context of restructuring, Hygrade "announced the plant would close permanently" if the UFCW "did not accept contract concessions." The workers refused but the plant remained open.

Two years later, Hygrade again demanded concessions. Once more, plant management and the union worked out a compromise; but, this time, Hygrade's parent company, Hanson Industries, demurred. Negotiations continued with the city, heavily dependent on the packing plant, offering concessions. "In October [1981], Hygrade demanded a $3.00 per hour pay cut in all Hygrade plants as a prerequisite for keeping the Storm Lake plant open. The UFCW

[114] Michael J. Broadway, "From City to Countryside: Recent Changes in the Structure and Location of the Meat- and Fish-Packing Industries," in Stull, et al., Any Way You Cut It, p. 23. (Hereafter cited as Broadway, From City to Countryside.).

115 Craypo, Strike and Relocation, p. 189; "Meatpackers that Bounced Back," Business Week, Aug. 16, 1982, p. 103; "The Slaughter of Meatpacking Wages," Business Week, June 27, 1983, p. 71; Horowitz, The Decline of Unionism, p. 35; and Andreas, Meatpackers and Beef Barons, p. 43.

116 Steve Kay, "Beef Woes Bedevil ConAgra," Meat and Poultry, June 1998, pp. 42, 45, 47-49. See Mark Ivey, "How ConAgra Grew Big — and Now, Beefy," Business Week, May 18, 1987, pp. 87-88.

117 Valerie Freeman, "ConAgra Restructures," Meat and Poultry, June 1996, p. 12.

118 Based in Minneapolis, Cargill is "an international processor, marketer and distributor of agricultural, food, industrial and financial products." Excel is a "wholly owned subsidiary" of Cargill. See [http://www.excelmeats.com/about/history.htm] and [http://www.cargill.com].

119 Warren, Struggling with"Iowa's Pride," p. 128.

120 Broadway, From City to Countryside, p. 22-23. See also DLR, June 3, 1981, pp. A5-A8; Sept. 15, 1982, pp. A4-A5; July 27, 1983, pp. A1-A3; Feb. 17, 1984, pp. A9-A11; Oct., pp. A2-A3; George Ruben, "Problems Continue in Meat Processing Industry," Monthly Labor Review, Sept. 1983, p. 40; and Steve Kay, "Merger Madness," Meat and Poultry, Mar. 2002, p. 21, 24-26.

refused..." and the plant closed. As a result, "some 500 relatively high-wage unionized jobs that formed the backbone of a stable local workforce" were lost, along with 50 management jobs. In April 1982, IBP bought the Storm Lake facility, reopening it with what was, allegedly, a substantially reduced wage structure. The new IBP plant was said to have operated with about a 10% monthly turnover.[121]

Some Diverse Impacts. Relocation sites associated with restructuring varied. Most often, they were small towns where the economic impact of a plant closing would be severely felt. In 1992, for example, Morrell had closed its beef packing plant in Sioux Falls, South Dakota, eliminating 400 jobs. Thus, when it threatened to close its pork processing plant in Sioux City, Iowa, in fall 1993 (with 1,300 jobs at issue), the threat was taken seriously. As closure neared (December 1993), "Morrell received a combination of state and local incentives and a new five-year labor agreement with the union" — the plant remained open.[122]

Again, in the early 1980s, General Host (which had bought Cudahy packing a decade earlier) announced its decision to "get out of the meat processing business." Closure was averted (and, potentially, the loss of 1,500 jobs) when General Host sold four plants "to a management group." However, during an interim closure and reopening under a new name, "unionized production workers [were] terminated" and a new wage structure imposed.[123] The practice extended into other segments of the industry — and to other regions — as well.[124]

"If there was any remaining question over organized labor's influence in the beef industry," stated IBP historian Jeffrey Rodengen, "the issue was put to rest in the early 1980s when a wave of wage reduction swept through America's packing houses." He added: "This wage depression represented packers' efforts to bring wages down from among the highest in America to a level more in line with the rest of industry."[125]

Expansion as a Strategy

Plant closing, consolidation and/or restructuring inevitably affects workers. Similarly, however justified in terms of efficiency, it also affects the communities from which a facility moves and into which it relocates.

---

[121] Mark A. Grey, "Pork, Poultry, and Newcomers in Storm Lake, Iowa," in Stull, et al., *Any Way You Cut It*, pp. 109-113. (Hereafter cited as Grey, *Pork, Poultry, and Newcomers*.) See, also, Steve Bjerklie, "No Way Up? Pork, Poverty and IBP in Storm Lake, Iowa," *Meat and Poultry*, Sept. 1992, pp. 39-40, 42, 44, and 46; and Eric Hake and Martin King, "The Veblenian Credit Economy and the Corporatization of American Meatpacking," *Journal of Economic Issues*, June 2002, p. 497. (Hereafter cited as Hake and King, *The Veblenian Credit Economy*.) See, also, Grey's "Turning the Pork Industry Upside Down: Storm Lake's Hygrade Work Force and the Impact of the 1981 Plant Closure," *The Annals of Iowa*, Summer 1995, pp. 244-259.

122 Donald Stull "Of Meat and (Wo)Men: Meatpacking's Consequences for Communities," The Kansas Journal of Law and Public Policy, spring 1994, p. 116. (Hereafter sited as Stull, Of Meat and (Wo)Men.) Stull states that "the city's portion [of the settlement] alone is worth $1.3 million." See, also, Strausberg, From Hills and Hollers, pp. 76-78.

123 Perry and Kegley, Disintegration and Change, p. 90.

124 Bob Hall, "Chicken Empires," Southern Exposure, summer 1989, p. 17. (Hereafter cited as Hall, Chicken Empires.).

125 Rodengen, The Legend of IBP, p. 122. Roger Horowitz, in Putting Meat on the American Table: Taste, Technology, Transformation (Baltimore: The Johns Hopkins University Press, 2006), p. 151, states that by the 1990s, "... labor organizations had little power in the meat-processing industry." Further: "Without labor organizations to exert upward pressures on wages and to influence shop floor relations, workers had to accept companies' terms or go elsewhere."

The Emergence af IBP

Among the new breed packers, Iowa Beef Processors may have had the greatest impact upon the industry — and, thus, upon workers. From its beginnings in the early 1960s, IBP appears to have made clear that it intended to operate, as nearly as possible, in a non-union environment and it developed a low-wage strategy. "If we paid the base rate the union wants," an IBP official reportedly stated, "our whole program would fail."[126]

The first clash between IBP and the UPWA appears to have been at its Fort Dodge, Iowa, plant in 1965. The contest was relatively brief, ending with the intercession of Iowa's Governor.[127] More critical was a 1969 contest, soon after the UPWA/Amalgamated merger. The union had won certification to represent workers at the IBP flagship plant at Dakota City, Nebraska.[128] A contract would be more difficult to secure. With the plant structured to accommodate less-skilled workers, the company "claimed the union was trying to force skilled rates for relatively unskilled jobs."[129] A strike was called. IBP imported strikebreakers: some, it appears, "of Mexican descent recruited from the Southwestern United States." Violence erupted.[130] Ultimately, the Amalgamated secured a contract that "allowed IBP to keep its pay rates far beneath the master agreement levels."[131]

IBP may have been aware of philosophical and policy divisions within the union following the UPWA/Amalgamated merger and it may have utilized them to its advantage.[132] Then, in 1979, the second merger occurred, producing the UFCW. By the 1980s, IBP (then owned by Occidental Petroleum) "had become the pattern setter" in the industry both for operations in general and for "wages and working conditions." It still "operated union-free in ten of its thirteen plants."[133] Ever watchful of the union, IBP built new facilities at Amarillo, Texas, and Emporia, Kansas, with the expectation, some contented, that the facilities could be played off against each other to limit the strength of the union were further strikes to occur.[134]

On an expansion course, IBP moved gradually from beef to pork and on to "precooked pizza toppings, taco fillings" and "a range of deli meat products."

Reasonably, it developed a tannery processing leather goods.[135] With passage of NAFTA, American packers moved into the Canadian market. Cargill had bought Canada's largest beef packing plant. In late 1994, IBP bought Canada's second largest beef packing plant.[136]

---

126 The comment is attributed to Arden Walker, IBP vice president for industrial relations, quoted in Horowitz, Negro and White, p. 261.

127 Rodengen, *The Legend of IBP*, pp. 41-42.

128 Ibid., pp. 47, and 59-60.

129 Perry and Kegley, Disintegration and Change, p. 136. See also Rodengen, The Legend of IBP, p. 60.

130 Rodengen, The Legend of IBP, p. 61.

131 Horowitz, Negro and White, pp. 262-63.

132 Ibid., pp. 262-263.

133 Craypo, Strike and Relocation, p. 188-190. See also "Meatpackers that Bounced Back," Business Week, Aug. 16, 1982, p. 105; and DLR, Dec. 16, 1986, pp. A2-A3. IBP, acquired by Occidental Petroleum in 1981, was spun off in stages commencing in 1987 and concluding in 1991. See Rodengen, The Legend of IBP, pp. 118, 137, and 148-150; and Steve Kay, "Light at the End of the Tunnel?" Meat and Poultry, Jan. 1992, pp. 28-29, 31-32, 36, 38-40.

134 Horowitz, Negro and White, pp. 262-263. Freedman and Fulmer, Last Rites, p. 44, theorize that "fragmentation of pattern bargaining" would allow management "more easily [to] shift production from plants that are on strike to plants that are no longer part of a master agreement and therefore not on strike."

135 Steve Kay, "IBP Leader Dictates His Vision of the Future: $20 Billion by 2001," Meat and Poultry, July 1996, p. 18. (Hereafter cited as Kay, IBP Leader Dictates.)

136 Patrick Gallagher, "IBP Invades Alberta," Meat and Poultry, Jan. 1995, p. 12. The Canadian firm, Lakeside Farm Industries, Ltd., was said to have annual sales of $500 million. See Kay, IBP Leader Dictates, p. 20. The

Simultaneously, it reportedly was developing a joint venture with China "to raise, process and market hogs" to begin in 1997.[137] In spring 1997, IBP acquired Foodbrands America (Oklahoma City) for "$640 million and assumption of ... $348 million debt."[138]

The Growth and Development of Tyson Foods

Poultry had been largely a small farm operation until World War II with production oriented mainly to local markets. In the mid-1930s, John Tyson of Springdale, Arkansas, began trucking poultry to markets in Chicago and other midwestern cities. Initially, he hauled poultry and produce for local growers; but, gradually, he entered the business on his own. Tyson Feed and Hatchery was incorporated in 1947. By 1950, it "was processing about 96,000 broilers a week." The company went public in the early 1960s.[139]

Serious expansion had commenced in 1963 with the purchase of Garrett Poultry of Rogers, Arkansas. By 1977, Tyson had moved into pork production, acquiring facilities in North Carolina and handling 7,500 hogs a week. In 1983, it purchased a Mexican food company (Mexican Original) and moved into corn and flour tortilla products. In 1989, it acquired Holly Farms, then the nation's third largest poultry firm with interests in beef and pork: reportedly a $1.4 billion deal.[140] In 1992, Tyson's purchased Arctic Alaska Fisheries, Inc., and Louis Kemp Seafood;[141] in 1997, Mallard's Food Products (Modesto); in 1998, Arkansas-based Hudson Foods.

By the late 1990s, IBP was considering various restructuring initiatives: possibly going private, a leveraged buy-out, or another business arrangement. Instead, in 2001, Tyson acquired IBP reportedly for $4.7 billion and became "the largest meat and poultry company in the world."[142] By spring 2002, Tyson Foods had "proforma revenues of about $25 billion and more than 300 facilities and offices in 32 states and 22 countries."[143]

---

meat and poultry industry of Canada appears to have followed roughly the same pattern as that of the United States. See, for example, Ian MacLachlan, Kill and Chill: Restructuring Canada's Beef Commodity Chain(Toronto: University of Toronto Press, 2001), p. 245-288; Michael J. Broadway, "Bad to the Bone: The Social Costs of Beef Packing's Move to Rural Alberta," in Roger Epp and Dave Whitson (eds.), Writing Off the Rural West (Edmonton: The University of Alberta Press, 2001), pp. 39-51; Leo Quigley, "Canadian-style Case Ready," Meat and Poultry, Feb. 2002, pp. 30-36; and Quigley, "Retail Ready: Canada West Scores with Case-Ready Programs," Meat and Poultry, Feb. 2003, pp. 36-38.

137 Kay, IBP Leader Dictates, p. 24.

138 "IBP Acquires Foodbrands America; $20 Billion Vision Comes into Focus," Meat and Poultry, Apr. 1997, p. 3. Foodbrands, Meat and Poultry reported, "... processes pizza toppings, pizza crusts, burritos, stuffed pastas, breaded appetizers, soups, sauces and side dishes as well as deli meats and processed beef, poultry and pork."

139 For the history of Tyson Foods, see [http://www.tysonfoodsinc.com].

140 Stephanie A. Forest, "Tyson Is Winging its Way to the Top," Business Week, Feb. 25, 1991, pp. 57 and 60. See also Steve Bjerklie, "Tyson's New Speciality," Mean and Poultry, June 1995, pp. 22-23.

141 Keith Nunes, "Chicken of the Sea," Meat and Poultry," July 1992, p. 9; and Kris Freeman, "'Chicken and the Sea': What's Tyson up to with Arctic Alaska and Louis Kemp?" Meat and Poultry, Mar. 1993, p. 16-17, 20 and 22.

142 Negotiations are summarized in Steve Kay's, "We're More than Chicken," Meat and Poultry, Mar. 2001, pp. 48-51. Figures vary somewhat. See also "Tyson Foods Shells Out Billions to Acquire IBP, Inc.," Meat and Poultry, Jan. 2001, pp. 3-4.

143 "Tyson Plans 'Value-Added,'" Nation's Restaurant News, Apr. 1, 2002, p. 40. See also "Tyson Foods, Inc.," Meat and Poultry, Sept. 1998, p. 26; Nicholas Stein, "Son of a Chicken Man," Fortune, May 13, 2002, pp.136-138, 140, 142, 144, 146 (Hereafter cited as Stein, Son of a Chicken Man); and Steve Kay, "Bob Peterson: The End of the Line," Meat and Poultry, Oct. 2001, p. 32. (Hereafter cited as Kay, The End of the Line.).

The combined company, it was said, would "provide an estimated 23 percent of the U.S. meat and poultry supply while employing 120,000 people." But, it would also have a "total debt of approximately $5 billion" in 2002.[144] And, it would be necessary to integrate two very large companies and the component parts of each.

Labor Problems and Profit Margins

Despite sizeable expenditures by both IBP and Tyson Foods (and, perhaps, because of them), the firms would be concerned with savings. "Put simply," observed analyst Nicholas Stein, "Tyson is struggling to find enough cheap, unskilled labor to staff its processing plants." Stein pointed to employee turnover, "between 40% and 100% annually, meaning each of the company's 83 plants needs between 400 and 2,000 new workers every year."[145]IBP's Bob Peterson considered automation. "IBP will save more than $50 million because of automation this year [2001]," he stated. But, he conceded, "we will always have to have people."[146]

But, which people? The industry had been characterized as "difficult, dirty, and dangerous" with employees struggling "to keep up with the production line." The new breed restructuring had brought with it a workforce that was paid relatively low wages and was subject to high rates of turnover. "Increasingly," Stein states, "both Tyson and IBP came to rely on immigrants — mainly from Mexico and Central America." (Southeast Asia was another source of low-wage labor for the industry.) "By the late 1990s the Tyson work force was very heavily Hispanic — 40% according to Tyson, 60% or more according to union officials."[147]

AREAS OF ECONOMICS AND PUBLIC POLICY

"We did what we had to do," IBP's Peterson reflects. "We are not unreasonable, but we are not patient people, and we are not gentle." The meat processing industry is highly competitive and, like the economy at large, profit motivated. "We don't want to be tough and ornery, but if you want to be the best, and we are going to be the best, you need to have quality and consistency and be the low-cost producer."[148]

---

144 Steve Kay, "From IBP to 'TyBP': Will This Marriage Work?" Meat and Poultry, Dec. 2001, p. 26.

145 Stein, Son of a Chicken Man, p. 142.

146 Kay, The End of the Line, p. 36. Scott Kilman, "Moving On Up," The Wall Street Journal, Oct. 25, 2004, p. R10, reports: "Over the past three years, machines have replaced one-third of the jobs" at the Tyson chicken processing plant at Noel, Missouri. Kilman adds that the plant "... now has about 800 workers earning about $9 an hour on average. Some Tyson managers believe it will be possible to have a fully automated chicken plant within 15 years." See also Jane Kelly, "Perdue: New Processing Plant Is Strictly for the Foodservice Market," Meat and Poultry, Dec. 1992, pp. 14-15; Steve Kay, "Beef: The Next Generation," Meat and Poultry, Jan. 2002, pp. 40-44; and "Tyson Continues Focusing on Efficiencies," Meat and Poultry, Dec. 2003, p. 3.

147 Stein, Son of a Chicken Man, p. 144. For a general survey of consolidations, see Jon K. Lauck, "Competition in the Grain Belt Meatpacking Sector after World War II," The Annals of Iowa, Spring 1998, pp. 146-159.

148 Rodengen, The Legend of IBP, p. 193. The spring 1996 issue of Culture and Agriculture has a collection of essays by academic and public policy writers dealing with the varied impacts of the meatpacking and poultry processing industry.

Labor-management policy in the meat and poultry industry has not evolved by chance.[149] For the most part, it has been successful from industry's perspective —but success has not been without costs. Because of competition, firms have tended to seek the cheapest labor available that could meet their needs; often, racial/ethnic minorities. Early in the century, employers pitted workers against each other, separating them by nationality, religion, and culture in an apparent effort to keep the cost of labor low and to prevent trade unionization.[150] Through recent decades, waves of Hispanics, Vietnamese, Laotians, and refugees from the Balkans have taken jobs in packing and processing plants.[151] Because of their social, economic, and, in some cases, immigration status, they have willingly accepted hard, dirty, and sometimes dangerous work at low wages — at least in the short term — as had other racial/ethnic minorities and new immigrant groups before them.

ASSEMBLING A WORKFORCE

The movement of the packing industry to rural America (where the poultry industry was already sited) brought to it a new workforce. What would be the nature of the new workforce? And how would it be managed?

Recruitment and Characteristics

New breed packers, some have suggested, chose to relocate in rural areas and to recruit a workforce locally. And, some pledged to do so in exchange for concessions from communities eager for growth.[152] Andy Anderson, co-founder of IBP, explained his vision of the new workforce. "We've tried to take the skill out of every step," Anderson explained to a *Newsweek* reporter in early 1965. "We wanted to be able to take boys right off the farm and we've done it."[153] Relocation and recruitment of boys (and girls) "right off the farm," however, could have collateral benefits for companies: i.e., escape from unionized urban labor markets with collective bargaining, high wages, and existing work rules.

---

149 Rachleff, in Hard-Pressed, p.10, states that by the early 1980s, employers "were buttressed by the emergence of a veritable industry of 'management consultants' who preached the virtues of a 'union free' environment."

150 Stromquist, Solidarity and Survival, pp. 84-85. Concerning the general employment of racial/ethnic minorities and immigrant workers, in addition to sources cited elsewhere in this report, see The Work Experience: Labor, Class, and Immigrant Enterprise (New York: Garland Publishing, Inc., 1991) and Unions and Immigrants: Organization and Struggle (New York: Garland Publishing, Inc., 1991), both edited by George E. Pozzetta. As case studies in two very different settings, see also: Edward D. Beechert, Working in Hawaii: A Labor History (Honolulu: University of Hawaii Press, 1985), and Allan Kent Powell, The Next Time We Strike: Labor in Utah's Coal Fields, 1900-1933 (Logan: Utah State University Press, 1985). There were, of course, different realities (and reactions, both from labor and from employers) in every area and across time.

151 Stull and Broadway, "Killing Them Softly: Work in Meatpacking Plants and What it Does to Workers," in Donald D. Stull, et al., Any Way You Cut It, p. 62. (Hereafter cited as Stull and Broadway, Killing Them Softly.).

152 See, for example Mark A. Grey, "Pork, Poultry, and Newcomers in Storm Lake, Iowa," in Stull, et. al., Any Way You Cut It, pp. 113-115; Griffith, Hay Trabajo, pp. 132-133; Donald D. Stull and Michael J. Broadway, "The Effects of Restructuring on Beef-Packing in Kansas," Kansas Business Review, 14(1), 1990, p. 12; and David L. Ostendorf, "Packinghouse Communities: Exploiting Immigrant Workers," Christian Century, May 5, 1999, pp. 492-493. (Hereafter cited as Ostendorf, Packinghouse Communities.).

153 Newsweek, Mar. 8, 1965, p. 76.

But, local recruitment — even for firms disposed to recruit locally — proved difficult. A new plant, requiring hundreds of workers, could quickly exhaust the local labor supply. Thus, *outside recruitment* was almost inevitable.[154]

For an employer, hiring locally may not have been desirable. A successor firm, retaining a predecessor's workforce, could be inviting trouble — especially where the old firm had operated under a union contract. Since some *new breed* firms sought to operate non-union and to pay low-wages, a clash would be almost assured.

Experienced employees would likely resist change. *A workforce of newcomers* (new to the area and, perhaps, to the world of work) would allow greater flexibility.[155]

The demographics and character of the post-1960s meatpacking workforce seem to have differed from that of mid-century. With unionization, the old workforce (prior to the 1960s) had shifted from transient (largely immigrant) to greater stability: permanent residents with roots in the community. There was also a shift from a mainly white workforce to one more heavily African-American. Women had always worked in the packing industry; but, with new technology and systematic de-skilling, they would come to be more widely employed.[156]

Several changes in the relocated industry (poultry presents some exceptions) seem evident from the literature dealing with the post-1960s era. *First.* The packinghouse workforce seems to have become less black. There were few African-Americans in the rural midwestern communities to which the industry migrated: few urban workers — either whites or African-Americans — appear to have followed the migrating industry.[157] *Second.* Increasingly packers (and, later, poultry processors) began recruitment from outside the area of production: largely Southeast Asians and Hispanics — but other immigrants as well. These recruits, often unfamiliar with American labor law, lacked personal resources and community ties and, if unauthorized to be employed, were vulnerable to exploitation. *Third.* Where these newcomers were from *pre-industrial* societies, they tended to be unfamiliar with unions and may have been uncomfortable with trade unionization. Where they were transient, as many were, there was little incentive to think of long-term socioeconomic advancement through organization.[158] *Fourth.* Although African-Americans have continued to be employed (in poultry processing, *value added* work, and the seafood industry), they have tended to be working women. The urban-to-rural shift seems frequently to have been both of race and

154 See Warren, Struggling with "Iowa's Pride", pp. 128-129; and Robert A. Hackenberg, et al., "Creating a Disposable Labor Force," The Aspen Institute Quarterly, spring 1993, pp. 93-94. (Hereafter cited as Hackenberg, Creating a Disposable Labor Force.) See also Steve Bjerklie, "The Tip of the Iceberg," Meat and Poultry, Nov. 1992, p. 4.

155 See Craypo, Strike and Relocation, pp. 201-202; and Donald D. Stull and Lourdes Gouveia, "Dances with Cows: Beefpacking's Impact on Garden City, Kansas, and Lexington, Nebraska," in Donald D. Stull, et al., Any Way You Cut It, pp. 85-107. (Hereafter cited as Stull and Gouveia, Dances with Cows.).

156 Janet E. Benson, "The Effects of Packinghouse Work on Southeast Asian Refugee Families," in Louise Lamphere, et al., eds., Newcomers in the Workplace: New Immigrants and the Restructuring of the U.S. Economy (Philadelphia: Temple University Press, 1994), pp. 103-104. (Hereafter cited as Benson, The Effects of Packinghouse Work.) The value added product line (pre-cooked meals, case ready meats, etc.), though labor-intensive, requires less strength. See also Barrett, Unity and Fragmentation, pp. 38-39.

157 See Fogel, The Negro in the Meat Industry, pp. 8 and 124. In "'I Come to the Garden': Changing Ethnic Relations in Garden City, Kansas," Urban Sociology, 1990, pp. 310-311, Stull discusses the Garden City packing industry in terms of Anglos, Hispanics and Southeast Asians. He adds: "Blacks might be said to occupy a third rung on the social ladder, but their population remains too small to be accorded a separate group status." (Hereafter cited as Stull, I Come to the Garden.).

158 Benson states in "Households, Migration, and Community Context," Urban Anthropology, spring-summer 1990, p. 25, that given "the dead-end nature" of line work, "few Southeast Asians expect to spend more than five years or so in Garden City," Kansas.

gender: often from relatively highly paid black males to lower paid black females.[159] *Fifth.*
The post-1960s workforce (the lower tier) appears to have been heavily transient, whether in
industrial or geographical terms — and, perhaps, both.[160]

In general, the post-1960s lower tier workforce in packing and processing might be
characterized as unskilled, mobile, and sometimes lacking in strong labor-market attachment.
These were workers in whom employers had little invested, given the *churning* within the
industry and the nature of the drive for enhanced profitability.[161]

Turnover and Worker Retention

Nicholas Stein in *Fortune* suggests that it is "difficult" to find workers for processing
plants at $7 an hour "when they could earn the same or more at McDonald's."[162] But for
some, there may be few options: i.e., economic necessity or time to learn English and to
develop skills.

Rates and Costs

While the packing and processing industry is said to have a high rate of worker turnover,
it may not be entirely clear what is meant by turnover. Are seasonal workers, employed
regularly year after year, included in the concept? How about the part-time employee who
works when demand is sufficient — but who is not kept on the rolls through the intervening
periods? And, when does one become an employee for turnover calculation? When he or she
accepts employment? Shows up for work? Completes an orientation program?[163]

Estimates of turnover are difficult to assess.[164] Steve Kay of *Meat and Poultry* states: "No
major packer will disclose their current turnover rates" — which he estimates "may range

---

159 Fogel, The Negro in the Meat Industry, pp. 1-2, and 14. Broadway, From City to Countryside, pp. 36-37, states
     that most workers in catfish processing are black women.
160 See Broadway, From City to Countryside, pp. 36-37; Ken C. Erickson, "Guys in White Hats: Short-Term
     Participant Observation Among Beef-Processing Workers and Managers," in Louise Lamphere, et al.,
     Newcomers in the Workplace (Philadelphia: Temple University Press, 1994), p. 89 (Hereafter cited as
     Erickson, Guys in White Hats); David Griffith, "Consequences of Immigration Reform for Low-Wage
     Workers in the Southeastern U.S.: The Case of the Poultry Industry," in Urban Anthropology, spring-summer
     1990, pp. 165-173 (Hereafter cited as Griffith, Consequences of Immigration Reform); Ken Lawrence and
     Anne Braden, "The Long Struggle," Southern Exposure, Nov./Dec. 1983, p. 86; and Steve Striffler, "Inside a
     Poultry Processing Plant: An Ethnographic Portrait," Labor History, Aug. 2002. (Hereafter cited as Striffler,
     Inside a Poultry Processing Plant).
161 See Karen Olsson, "The Shame of Meatpacking," The Nation, Sept. 16, 2002, p. 12; (Hereafter cited as Olsson,
     The Shame of Meatpacking.); Griffith, Consequences of Immigration Reform, p. 156; Hackenberg, Creating a
     Disposable Labor Force, pp. 78-79; Fink, The Maya of Morganton, p. 180; and Edna Bonacich, "A Theory of
     Ethnic Antagonism: The Split Labor Market," American Sociological Review, Oct. 1972, pp. 547-559.
162 Stein, Son of a Chicken Man, pp. 142-144. Fogel, The Negro in the Meat Industry, p. 18, argues that workers
     with "skills and a moderate amount of formal education would not work in meat packing at common labor
     wages." See also Michael Broadway, "Meatpacking and Its Social and Economic Consequences for Garden
     City, Kansas, in the 1980s," Urban Anthropology, winter 1990, p. 323.
163 There seems to be a relative high attrition rate early in the employment process when recruits learn what the
     work involves. See Steve Kay, "The Nature of Turnover," Meat and Poultry, Sept. 1997, p. 32. (Hereafter
     cited as Kay, The Nature of Turnover.) See also Hackenberg, et al., Creating a Disposable Labor Force, p. 79.
164 See Jacqueline Nowell, "A Chicken in Every Pot: At What Price?" New Solutions, vol. 10(4), 2000, p. 329.
     (Hereafter cited as Nowell, A Chicken in Every Pot).

from 50 percent to 70 percent for most large packers."[165] Again, what is included within an estimate may not always be clear.

The impact of high turnover for employers varies from one observer to the next. Raoul Baxter, Smithfield International, Inc., argues that new cuts of beef and products for the international market "require the most skilled workers in the history of the meat industry." Such skills require, he states, "a three-month learning curve,"arguably making employee retention desirable.[166] There are also direct dollar costs associated with recruitment, training, and acclimation to the workplace and to the specific tasks. Documentation of such costs appears to be somewhat elusive, but they could be substantial.[167]

Some Implications

During field research, Stull and Broadway asked an interviewee with wide experience in the industry: "[D]o you think it pays the packer to turn over the workforce rapidly?" He replied: "It must or he wouldn't do it."[168]

Turnover rate is critical in assessing other aspects of the labor-management relationship. In a carefully structured and highly competitive industry, high turnover may not be accidental. Some would argue that worker retention may be neither desirable — nor profitable. "Ultimately, their concern is not about a stable work force," states Mark Grey of the University of Northern Iowa, "but maintaining a transient work force."[169]

Since both poultry and beef processing have become extremely competitive, it may not be surprising that firms would seek to cut costs wherever such economies are possible. A low wage and often non-union workforce would seem, some suggest, a likely context for such cost-cutting.

Some observers report that industry employers "aggressively recruit Mexicans and Southeast Asians" and supplement them with "growing numbers of single mothers from rural areas." Such practices, it is argued, have "impeded unionization" and promoted workforce instability.[170] Firms may "cut costs with low wages, minimum benefits, and, critics argue, ... high turnover." Some companies offer "yearly bonuses" but these are, often, "not paid until employees have worked for a full calendar year." The same can be said of paid vacations. With the reportedly high turnover rate, some workers "do not make it" long enough to qualify.[171]

---

165 Kay, The Nature of Turnover, pp. 31-32. Kay states: "There appears to be no published data on labor turnover or the cost to the industry as a whole." See also Stull and Broadway, Slaughterhouse Blues, p. 80, for a discussion of turnover rates in the industry.

166 Raoul Baxter, "Labor's Role in Exports," Meat and Poultry, Nov. 1997, p. 14.

167 See, for example, Kay, The Nature of Turnover, pp. 31-34; and Richard Alaniz, "Avoiding Rehiring Costs by Retaining Good Employees," Meat and Poultry, May 1999, p. 80.

168 Stull and Broadway, The Effects of Restructuring, p. 15. See also, Hackenberg, et al., Creating a Disposable Labor Force, p. 79; and Lourdes Gouveia and Stull, "Latino Immigrants, Meatpacking, and Rural Communities: A Case Study of Lexington, Nebraska" (East Lansing: Michigan State University, Julian Samora Research Institute, Aug. 1997), Research Report No. 26, p. 15.

169 Quoted in Christopher Cook, "Hog-Tied: Migrant Workers Find Themselves Trapped on the Pork Assembly Line," Progressive, Sept. 1999, p. 32. (Hereafter cited as Cook, Hog-Tied).

170 Horowitz, Black and White, p. 277. There may be other interpretations.

171 Stull and Broadway, The Effects of Restructuring, pp. 13-14. In "Introduction: Making Meat," Any Way You Cut It, p. 5, Donald D. Stull, et al., point to "workers from Mexico who migrate between different agricultural sectors: between agricultural harvest work, fruit, and vegetable packing, and meat and poultry processing...."

Healthcare may pose a similar problem. Some workers "cannot enroll until four to six months (depending on the plant) after they are employed." With high turnover, some may never qualify. "To avoid employee insurance claims, companies commonly find excuses to fire workers who show signs of debilitating injury," according to critic Janet Benson.[172] With high turnover, some assert, responsibility for work-related disability can be shifted "to the workers' home country" since the workers may have left the United States before serious conditions develop.[173] Some conditions may simply go unreported and untreated.[174]

Union avoidance may also result from high turnover. With a rotating workforce, many employers acquire no continuing obligation to their employees; but, workers, some suggest, may be similarly affected. They may view their work as temporary, not as a career. Their immediate concern is "economic survival and, if possible, capital accumulation."[175] Mexican workers, observes Arthur Campa, are not only "isolated from mainstream Anglo American life, but they are separate from the native Mexican American community as well." When they lose their jobs they move on, sometimes returning to Mexico.[176] Their awareness of their rights may be slight and contacts with trade union or social service workers lacking.[177] In this situation, workers may not "identify with traditional union concerns such as pension, medical care, and wage increases when they have no expectations of continued employment?"[178]

Arden Walker, former head of labor relations for IBP, summarized his perspective on the implications of worker turnover at an NLRB hearing in 1984:

> Counsel: With regard to turnover, since you are obviously experiencing it, does that bother you?
>
> Mr. Walker: Not really.
>
> Counsel: Why Not?
>
> Mr. WALKER: We found very little correlation between turnover and profitability. An employee leaves for whatever reason. Generally, we're able to have a replacement employee, and I might add that the way fringe benefits have been negotiated or installed, they favor long-term employees. For instance, insurance, as you know, is very costly. Insurance is not available to new employees until they've worked there for a

---

172 Janet E. Benson, The Effects of Packinghouse Work, pp.119-120. See also, Kay, The Nature of Turnover, p. 31; Warren, Struggling with "Iowa's Pride", p. 129-130; and Stephen J. Hedges, Dana Hawkins and Penny Loeb, "The New Jungle," U.S. News and World Report, Sept. 23, 1996, pp. 42-43. (Hereafter cited as Hedges, et al., The New Jungle.) Bob Hall, in The Kill Line, p. 220, suggests that some workers who do qualify for benefits may not utilize them through fear of losing their jobs.

173 Cook, Hog-Tied, p. 32.

174 Jenny Schulz, "Grappling with a Meaty Issue: IIRIRA's Effect on Immigrants in the Meatpacking Industry," The Journal of Gender, Race and Justice, fall 1998, p. 156. (Hereafter cited as Schulz, Grappling.) See also Stull and Broadway, Slaughterhouse Blues, p. 75; and Hackenberg, et al., Creating a Disposable Labor Force, p. 79. Mike Wilson, in an Associated Press article, Illegal Immigrants in Nebraska, Iowa[,]Complain of Abuses, Sept. 10, 2003, reported, citing Jose Luis Cuevas, Mexican consul in Omaha as his source, that "companies frequently fire workers when they're injured on the job." Cuevas reportedly stated: "They're using undocumented workers as disposable workers."

175 Janet E. Benson, "Households, Migration, and Community Context," Urban Anthropology, spring-summer 1990, p. 25.

176 Arthur Campa, "Immigrant Latinos and Resident Mexican Americans in Garden City, Kansas: Ethnicity and Ethnic Relations," Urban Anthropology, winter 1990, p. 351. (Hereafter cited as Campa, Immigrant Latinos).

177 See Janet E. Benson, "Good Neighbors: Ethnic Relations in Garden City Trailer Courts," Urban Anthropology, winter 1990, pp. 361-386.

178 Horowitz, Black and White, p. 277.

period of a year or, in some cases, six months. Vacations don't accrue until the second year. There are some economies, frankly, that result from hiring new employees.[179]

But some industry leaders deny that workers are transient. "We have no migrant workers at all," states Richard Lobb of the National Chicken Council. When people are given a job in a poultry plant, it is expected that it is a permanent full-time position.... They are not migrant, they are not seasonal."[180]

THE IMMIGRATION/ALIEN WORKER FACTOR

The workforce in the packing/processing industry has been characterized as *immigrant* (some, already citizens) and it has been observed that "the meat industry had always been a point of entry for immigrants joining American society."[1811] That may have been true up to World War I when industry had at its disposal "a ready supply of cheap labor."[182] Edna Bonacich recalls: "Europeans had also played a 'cheap labor' role."[183]

During mid-century, things changed. Unions demanded and secured better wages and working conditions: employment became more stable. Workers came to identify with their unions and their employers. They put down roots, bought homes, and raised families. Then, in the 1960s, things changed again. Newcomers, largely immigrant, were again actively recruited. Often with few marketable skills and/or otherwise disadvantaged, they were willing to work long hours at hard and disagreeable work for low wages — and, possibly, not join a union.[184]

"No one could have guessed," mused Steve Bjerklie, "that people from nations we had barely heard of in 1955 — Cambodia, Thailand, Vietnam — would one day comprise a significant percentage of our industry's workforce."[185]

179 The exchange is quoted in Stull and Broadway, Killing Them Softly, p. 70. Labor historian Dana Frank, in her study, "... The Detroit Woolworth's Strike of 1937," in Frank, Robin Kelley and Howard Zinn, Three Strikes: Miners, Musicians, Salesgirls, and the Fighting Spirit of Labor's Last Century (Boston, Beacon Press, 2001), p. 70, observed of 1930s retailing, "... if turnover rates are high, so much the better — managers can then pick and choose the pliant, the eager, and the charming."

180 Lobb is quoted in The Christian Science Monitor, Apr. 28, 1999, p. 3. See also Horowitz, The Decline of Unionism, pp. 35-36; and Richard Alaniz, "Multiple Factors Influence Declining Union Membership," Meat and Poultry, May 1998, p. 68.

181 Rodengen, The Legend of IBP, p. 181. The African-American experience must be viewed somewhat differently.

182 Ostendorf, Packinghouse Communities, p. 492.

183 Edna Bonacich, "Advanced Capitalism and Black/White Race Relations in the United States," American Sociological Review, Feb. 1976, p. 38. (Hereafter cited as Bonacich,

Advanced Capitalism.) See also Bjerklie, On the Horns of a Dilemma, p. 50.

184 Rodengen, The Legend of IBP, pp. 163-164, and 64; and Hake and King, "The Veblenian Credit Economy," p. 503.

185 Bjerklie, "Revelations: The Industry in the Year 2035," Meat and Poultry, Jan. 1955, p. 15.

A Shortage of Labor?

In the 1990s, University of Arkansas anthropologist Steve Striffler applied for work on the production line (poultry processing) at the Tyson plant in Springdale, Arkansas. He recalls, entering the personnel office:

The secretary and I are the only Americans, the only white folk, and the only English speakers in the room. Spanish predominates, but is not the only foreign language. Lao is heard from a couple in the corner, and a threesome from the Marshall Islands are speaking a Polynesian language.

Striffler would later observe: "... about three-quarters of plant labor force are Latin American, with Southeast Asians and Marshallese accounting for a large percentage of the remaining workers. U.S.-born workers," he adds, "are few and far between."[186]

When operating a labor-intensive facility in a sparsely populated area, labor scarcity might be anticipated.[187] If an employer has determined, in so far as possible, to work union-free (and to avoid hiring workers with trade union backgrounds), that might further reduce the pool from which a firm can recruit. The recruiting process may be further limited (and focused) by a policy of payment of low wages for work that is unpleasant, dirty, and dangerous. If recruitment for such jobs is directed toward persons of limited work experience, few marketable skills, and slight English language proficiency, then a demographic shift may not be unexpected. In pursuit of such a strategy, critics suggest, firms "deliberately recruit ... immigrants" who "almost universally lack any knowledge of U.S. working conditions, labor practices, or of their legal rights."[188] At the same time, some suggest that with active recruitment and serious retention efforts American workers could be found.[189]

The issue may have been one of definition: of distinguishing between shortages that are absolute and those that may be reflective of employer policies.[190]

Actively Seeking the Foreign Worker

Immigrant (or other alien) workers normally enter the United States with the intention of working.[191] Even adverse working conditions and low wages may be better than those offered in the immigrant's country of origin. As a result, new arrivals may have low expectations and

---

186 Striffler, Inside a Poultry Processing Plant, p. 305.
187 For example, Elzbieta M. Gozdziak and Micah N. Bump, "Poultry, Apples, and New Immigrants in the Rural Communities of the Shenandoah Valley: An Ethnographic Case Study," International Migration, vol. 42, no. 1, 2004, pp. 149-151, observe: "Processing companies, having relocated in small, rural communities with little local labour force, often actively recruit immigrant workers from traditional gateway states, as well as directly from Mexico and Central America."
188 Nowell, A Chicken in Every Pot, p. 329. Valdes, Barrios Nortenos, p. 225, states: "In Lexington [Nebraska], the Latino population rose from 3.3 percent of the total in 1990 to more than 30 percent by 1996 as a result of the opening of an IBP beef-packing plant, and an estimated 75 percent to 80 percent of the workers were from Texas and Mexico."
189 See Grey, Pork Poultry, and Newcomers, pp. 109-116.
190 Donald D. Stull, et al., "Introduction: Making Meat," in Any Way You Cut It, p. 3, suggest that the stability of the labor force in the meatpacking industry "... is largely dictated by corporate strategies." (Hereafter cited as Stull, et al., Introduction: Making Meat.) See also Hackenberg, et al., Creating a Disposable Labor Force, pp. 83-84; and Valdes, Barrios Nortenos, pp. 230-231.
191 Erickson, Guys in White Hats, p. 89.

be willing to endure conditions, both at work and of home life, that American workers would not willingly tolerate.[192]

The presence of Hispanics in the meat processing workforce, according to Griffith, "is correlated with lower wage rates" and lower numbers of African-American workers. While Asians "occupy a small place in most work forces," he observes, "they occupy a revered position, in many processor's minds, as embodying the quintessential work ethic." But, he states, Asians are "more upwardly mobile, taking advantage of refugee services to improve English skills and move into better paying jobs."[193]

From interviews with plant managers and personnel officers, Griffith found the "clearest theme" was "the belief that Hispanics and Asians have superior work habits" while those of blacks and whites have "been deteriorating." It may be that white and African-American workers, from experience in the industrial workforce, are less willing to adhere to managerial preferences. Conversely, those less familiar with American work practices (and labor law) may be less demanding. As immigrants become acclimated, they can be expected to move on to better jobs, creating a continuing demand for replacements. Some assert that this provides an incentive for employers to hire unauthorized immigrants who may more willingly cooperate with employers because they cannot legally work in the United States.[194]

Newcomers to the American workplace, Stull concurs, may be "more susceptible to labor-control mechanisms simply because they haven't had time to interpret the industry's behavior or to calculate the costs of resistance or militancy."[195]

Only Jobs that Americans Don't Want?

"American companies can't find enough workers in the United States to meet their needs," observed business spokesman Al Zapanta — reflecting what seems to be a widely held belief among employers: "We're [Americans] not willing to do these jobs anymore, but immigrants, like always, are willing to do it to provide for their families."[196]

The reality may be more complex. Some have argued that work involving "blood, unpleasant odors and repetitive tasks, is not attractive" to U.S. workers.[197] But other factors including low wages, high line speeds, little job security, rural-sited facilities, and diminished union protection may also make domestic recruitment difficult. "A decline in wage levels," together with other workplace considerations, Broadway says, "... has served to make meatpacking an unattractive employment option for many Americans."[198]

The issue may not be reluctance of Americans to work at these jobs (clearly, many are so employed); rather it may be the terms of employment. "If the job were 'decent,'" some critics

---

192 See Griffith, Consequences of Immigration Reform, pp. 164-165.
193 Ibid., pp. 165-168.
194 Ibid., pp. 168-173. See also Robert Lekachman, "The Specter of Full Employment," Harper's, Feb. 1977, pp. 36 and 38.
195 Stull, et al., Introduction: Making Meat, p. 7. See also Barrett, Unity and Fragmentation, p. 48.
196 Kirstin Downey Grimsley, "Tyson Foods Indicted in INS Probe," The Washington Post, Dec. 20, 2001, p. A13. Zapanta is identified as president of the U.S.-Mexico Chamber of Commerce.
197 Ibid.
198 Michael J. Broadway, "Beef Stew: Cattle, Immigrants and Established Residents in a Kansas Beefpacking Town," in Lamphere, Newcomers in the Workplace, p. 25. See also Benson, The Effects of Packinghouse Work, in Lamphere, pp. 103-104.

argue, "they would willingly do it."[199] Some employers agree. Joe Luter, CEO of Smithfield Foods, Inc., suggests that a solution to industry's recruitment problem may be "higher wages, which would make processing jobs more attractive to American workers."[200]

In practice, immigrants (and aliens unauthorized to work in the United States) constitute an almost "inexhaustible supply" of low-wage labor.[201] In this view, once employers become accustomed to the "flow of new immigrants,"[202] they may continue to recruit them — often at the expense of "native workers"and of less recent immigrants of whatever ethnic/racial background.[203] Bonacich concludes that "availability of a 'cheap labor' alternative" has enabled employers "to avoid improving the job and raising wages."[204] "What really needs to be addressed," argues Joe Berra of the Mexican-American Legal Defense and Education Fund, "is our immigration policy on one hand, and workers rights on the other."[205]

Meanwhile, employers have organized in order to procure more workers, "both skilled and lesser skilled." Banning together, they have created an interest group, the Essential Worker Immigration Coalition (EWIC), a body "of businesses, trade associations, and other organizations from across the industry spectrum concerned with the shortage of both skilled and lesser skilled ("essential worker") labor."[206] Among those associated with the EWIC was the American Meat Institute.[207]

199 Bonacich, Advanced Capitalism, p. 48. See also Roger Horowitz and Mark Miller, Immigrants in the Delmarva Poultry Processing Industry: The Changing Face of Georgetown, Delaware and Environs (East Lansing: Michigan State University, Julian Samora Research Institute, Jan. 1999), Occasional Paper No. 37, p. 5.
200 Stein, Son of A Chicken Man, p. 146. Some employers argue that "they can't pay more because consumers won't buy the products if they cost more." See Grimsley, "Tyson Foods Indicted in INS Probe," The Washington Post, Dec. 20, 2001, p. A13. The General Accounting Office (now Government Accountability Office) (GAO), in its report, Community Development: Changes in Nebraska's and Iowa's Counties with Large Meatpacking Plant Workforces, GAO/RCED-98-62, Feb. 1998, pp. 4-5, explains, citing local officials and company management, "sometimes, not enough local area residents are available to fill plants' openings and that at other times, not enough local area residents are willing to fill job openings at starting pay levels." GAO adds that plants "have hired increasing numbers of minority and immigrant workers" from high unemployment areas within the United States "and from Mexico, Central America, Asia, Africa, and Eastern Europe." GAO also reports, p. 2, that federal authorities have estimated "that up to 25 percent of the workers in meatpacking plants in Nebraska and Iowa were illegal aliens."
201 Otey Scruggs, Braceros, "Wetbacks," and the Farm Labor Problem: Mexican Agricultural Labor in the United States, 1942-1954 (New York: Garland Publishing, Inc., 1988), p. 68. See also Shawn Zeller, "Inside Job," The National Journal's Government Executive, Dec. 2001, p. 47 ff. Conversely, industry analyst Richard Alaniz, in "Avoiding Rehiring Costs by Retaining Good Employees," Meat and Poultry, May 1999, p. 80, states: "Recruiting and retaining employees is becoming one of the most difficult and time-consuming aspects of running a business."
202 Griffith, Hay Trabajo, p. 147.
203 Griffith, Consequences of Immigration Reform, p. 170.
204 Bonacich, Advanced Capitalism, p. 48.
205 Quoted in Leon Lazaroff, "Welcome to the Jungle," In These Times, July 8, 2002, p. 5.
206 See the website of the Essential Worker Immigration Coalition, http://www.ewic.org], visited on Nov. 28, 2003.
207 See "Essential Worker Immigration Coalition Resumes Lobbying," National Journal's CongressDaily, Mar. 15, 2002. See also the DLR, July 28, 2003, p. A6. Valdes, Barrios Nortenos, p. 249, questions the thesis that foreign workers are only taking jobs that Americans don't want. The theory, he speculates, does not "account for the late-twentieth-century trend toward dominance by Mexicans in midwestern packing plants, which European American [and, presumably, African American] workers did not want to leave."

Employers, Workers, and Immigration Authorities

With the prosperity of the 1990s, according to IBP historian Rodengen, the economy "entered one of its strongest periods on record and unemployment dropped drastically" — to below 3% in Iowa and Nebraska. For some packers, he states, this apparently "meant dealing with illegal immigrants who were seeking to fill the many open positions in company plants." Employing such workers, while attempting to secure an adequate supply of labor, he suggests, may have been inadvertent. Further, he states, IBP had been "... prohibited by law from asking too many questions about background, which meant it often couldn't get the information it needed to prevent an illegal immigrant from getting hired."[208]

During the 1990s, by estimates of a former Immigration and Naturalization Service (INS) officer,[209] about 25% of packing/processing workers may have been persons unauthorized to work in the United States and employed in violation of U.S. immigration law.[210] Some have suggested that the "largest concentration of illegally employed persons in the U.S. work in the meatpacking industry."[211] According to Stull, et al., this reflects both "targeted recruitment" and "the character and enforcement of immigration laws."[212] But, even were immigration laws enforced more strictly, compliance would be difficult. With high employee turnover rates, varying roughly from 40% and 100% per year, effective enforcement would require a continuing federal presence. Even a small measure of collusion between an employer and a worker employed illegally could, arguably, defeat such efforts.[213]

In legislating, Congress has been concerned that prevention of the illegal employment of foreign workers should not adversely impact U.S. citizens or others authorized to work in the United States.[214] Thus, some packing plants may have had "to walk a fine line during the hiring process."[215] There may be a delicate balance between laws "that protect employee rights and those that prohibit the employment of undocumented workers."[216]

---

208 Rodengen, The Legend of IBP, p. 181. Louis Jacobson, writing in the National Journal's Government Executive, Feb. 2000, p. 51 ff., reports "Several big companies have even opened recruiting offices in Mexican cities." Jacobson continues: "The companies say those offices are designed to attract the tens of thousands of Mexicans who possess legal U.S. work papers." He acknowledges that "some observers express skepticism at that explanation...," but adds: "The problem, sources say, is that immigrants have been getting increasingly clever about obtaining documents ... under false pretenses. Many employers are unable — or in some cases unwilling — to tell the difference between what is real and what is fake."

209 The Homeland Security Act of 2002 (P.L. 107-296) abolished INS and transferred its functions from the Department of Justice to the Department of Homeland Security. The transfer occurred Mar. 1, 2003.

210 See Schulz, Grappling, p.151; and Rebecca Gants, "I.N.S. Electronic Verification," Meat and Poultry, June 1996, pp. 56-58. (Hereafter cited as Gants, Electronic Verification.)

211 Ibid., p. 56, is here summarizing comments by Jerry Heinauer, district director of INS for Omaha.

212 Stull et al., Introduction: Making Meat, p. 3.

213 Hedges et al., The New Jungle, p. 38. For a discussion of recent United States immigration policy, see Douglas S. Massey, Jorge Durand, and Nolan J. Malone, Beyond Smoke and Mirrors: Mexican Immigration in an Era of Economic Integration (New York: Russell Sage Foundation, 2002), pp. 2-3, together with Vernon M. Briggs's review of that study in Industrial and Labor Relations Review, Jan. 2003, pp. 361-363.

214 Phil Olsson, "Employee Eligibility: Dealing with the Double-Edged Sword of Immigration Law," Meat and Poultry, June 1996, p. 55.

215 Rodengen, The Legend of IBP, p. 181. See Farm Bureau News, Mar. 19, 2001, p. 2.

216 Hedges, et al., The New Jungle, p. 38. Concerning the overall structure of the industry and of the labor-management relationship, see Charles Craypo, "Meatpacking: Industry Restructuring and Union Decline," in Paula B. Voos, ed., Contemporary Collective Bargaining in the Private Sector (Madison: Industrial Relations Research Association, 1994), pp. 63-96.

LABOR STANDARDS AND WORKING CONDITIONS

DOL's Bernard Anderson noted, early in 2000, that the Department had a *"long-term goal* of increasing compliance with labor laws." (Italics added.) It would focus, he affirmed, "on the low-wage industries because they have a historically high level of noncompliance and employ vulnerable workers who often won't complain about violation of their workplace rights."[217] Coping with such concerns continues to be a Department goal, although its achievement may not be easy and may involve prodding from sources outside the Department. It may also involve extended litigation. The problem is at least two-fold: defining precisely what the law provides and, thereafter, determining the character of existing industry practice.[218]

A MOVEMENT FOR CHANGE

During the fall of 1996, the National Interfaith Committee for Worker Justice (NICWJ) issued an appeal to the Department of Labor (DOL) urging action with respect to what it termed "agricultural sweatshops."[219] The Committee proposed:

- Investigation of alleged sweatshops in the poultry industry.
- That DOL "convene a 'poultry summit'" to bring together the parties at interest "to look at ways of raising wages in the industry, providing better benefits to workers, and improving working conditions."
- That DOL issue "'worker-rights guidelines' to ensure that poultry workers have the right to organize without fear of job loss or harassment" and, if voting for a union, to secure a contract within a reasonable period.

In November 1996, Secretary Robert Reich announced initiation of "a special targeted enforcement project in the poultry processing industry."[220]

A DOL survey was conducted during 1997 and 1998. It found numerous health and safety concerns: e.g., (a) workers "stationed so close together they lacerated coworkers with their knives, indicating a need for more space, more protective gear, or both;" (b) "supervisors [often] ... had trouble communicating with and providing training to workers who spoke little English"; and (c) "a number of plants were not in compliance with OSHA's process safety management standard."[221] Violations of the FLSA and of the Migrant and Seasonal Agricultural Workers Protection Act (MSPA) were found to be systemic. Some 60%

---

217 Federal News Service, Mar. 23, 2000.
218 See, for example, The [Raleigh] News and Observer, June 6, 2001, p. A17, and U.S. Newswire, Inc., May 9, 2002.
219 Chicago-based, the National Interfaith Committee for Worker Justice has special concern with low-wage workers in poultry processing who are "primarily African American and Latino, [who] often toil in unsafe and unsanitary conditions, with few benefits...." See the NICWJ website at [http://www.nicwj.org]. See also Robert Bussel, "Taking on 'Big Chicken': The Delmarva Poultry Justice Alliance," Labor Studies Journal, summer 2003, pp. 1-24; and Fink, The Maya of Morganton, pp. 121-124.
220 DLR, Nov. 27, 1996, pp. A10-A11. In November, Secretary Reich also announced his retirement, to take effect in Jan. 1997. DLR, Nov. 12, 1996, pp. AA1-AA2.
221 DLR, Sept. 18, 1998, pp. A3-4.

of surveyed plants "had violations of wage and hour and safety and health laws."[222] New inspections followed; and in October 1999, leaders of NICWJ and the AFL-CIO called for a congressional investigation of the poultry industry and "its abuse of workers."[223]

A second survey conducted by the Department in 2000 disclosed violations of the FLSA, MSPA and of the Family and Medical Leave Act.[224] It found that "none of the processing plants subject to investigation were in full compliance with all three labor statutes." NICWJ's Kim Bobo declared it "shocking there has been no improvement" since the 1997 survey. Bill Schmitz of the UFCW called poultry processing "an outlaw industry." But, the National Chicken Council termed the survey results inaccurate and misleading, according to the *Daily Labor Report*. Much of the problem, suggested Richard Lobb of the Council, stemmed from confusion about the law and DOL's questionable interpretation of it — primarily with respect to *donning* and *doffing*.[225] (See discussion below.)

FLSA COVERAGE AND RELATED ISSUES

The Fair Labor Standards Act is the primary federal statute dealing with minimum wages, overtime pay, and related matters. FLSA violations were *a central theme* in DOL's 1997 and 2000 surveys, noted above.

Donning and Doffing

Whether working with large animals (cattle, hogs, sheep) or with poultry, the slaughtering and packing process involves contact with potentially hazardous substances: blood, feces, intestinal juices, etc. Thus, workers in the industry wear protective gear varying in heft and complexity with the task to be performed. During a visit to IBP's beef plant at Finney County, Kansas, in the late 1980s, Donald Stull (with other tourists) reportedly was advised by a plant guide:

> Depending on their job, each worker may wear as much as $600 worth of safety equipment — hardhat, earplugs, cloth and steel mesh gloves, mail aprons and leggings, weight-lifting belts, or shin guards. They don't have to buy any of this equipment.[226]

Poultry processing requires less substantial equipment but what is used is, nonetheless, essential: protective hand gear, smocks, hairnets, face masks, etc.

The more complicated the equipment, the more time is consumed in preparing for work, for breaks, and in cleaning up afterward. During recent years, a question has arisen: Should the employer be required to compensate workers for time spent in pre- and post-production

---

222 DLR, Jan. 12, 2001, p. A11.
223 DLR, Oct. 13, 1999, p. C4.
224 See The Washington Times, Jan. 15, 2002, p. D3. A summary of the survey report can be found at [http://www.nicwj.org].
225 DLR, Jan. 12, 2001, p. A11.
226 Donald D. Stull, "Knock 'Em Dead: Work on the Kill Floor of a Modern Beefpacking Plant," in Lamphere, et al., Newcomers in the Workplace, p. 47.

activities such as "donning" protective garb and, at shift's end, "doffing" garments. Is time so spent included in the concept of *hours of work*? How *hours of work* is defined for implementing the FLSA would seem to fall to the Department of Labor.

Commonly, industry has not compensated workers for donning and doffing time.[227] But, through recent years, the issue has been the subject of extended compliance action by DOL — and of litigation. The courts have divided on the question, but some penalties imposed upon industry have been substantial. In 2005, the broader issue of donning and doffing was unresolved — and the time actually spent by workers in such activities similarly remained in dispute.[228] Reportedly, delegations from industry and the UFCW have met with Secretary Chao, stating their respective interpretations of the law, and DOL has commenced a review of the issue. Although it continues to enforce the FLSA's minimum wage and overtime pay requirements in the poultry industry, *DLR* reported, "it no longer is targeting the industry for special compliance scrutiny."[229]

Chicken *Catchers*

The term, *chicken catcher* might be misleading. The chicken catchers, considered here, work in teams in association with corporate processors. They may, as a team, handle as many as 30,000 to 50,000 live chickens per shift.[230] It is unpleasant work. Jacqueline Nowell of the UFCW explains: "They collect the birds by hand" for transport to a processing plant. "Chicken catchers are exposed to airborne contaminants — skin debris, broken feather barbules, insect parts, aerosolized feed ... poultry excreta ... bacteria" and "dangerous gases."[231]

The status of these workers has long been a source of contention. For example, how are such workers classified for wage/hour and labor-management relations purposes? Are they farm workers or industrial workers? The two classifications are treated differently under the FLSA and the National Labor Relations Act. Or are they *independent contractors* — and, thus, free from wage/hour requirements and collective bargaining protection?

At least since the late 1980s, the treatment of chicken catchers has been a focus of labor-management dispute and of litigation. As the century closed, the issue was still before the courts. But gradually, the status of the workers has become clearer. Judge William Nickerson (the U.S. District Court for the District of Maryland) found that the processor "... controls every significant aspect of the chicken catching operation." *DLR* summarized: "The company owns the chickens ..., it owns the trucks on which they are transported, and it determines from which farm and how many chickens are to be brought in each day."[232] Judge Nickerson

---

227 Industrial Safety and Hygiene News, July 2002, p. 14.
228 DLR, Sept. 17, 2002, p. A1. Under date of June 3,2003, the U.S. Court of Appeals for the First Circuit ruled that "[w]alking to obtain uniforms and equipment and waiting in line are not compensable time" under the FLSA (Tum v. Barber Foods Inc. d/b/a Barber Foods, 1st Cir., No. 02-1679). Then, on Aug. 5, 2003, the U.S. Court of Appeals for the Ninth Circuit ruled that "[m]eatpacking employees must be compensated" under the FLSA "from the moment they begin putting on safety gear required for their jobs until they take the gear off." (Alvarez v. IBP Inc., 9th Cir., No. 02-35042). This latter case is under appeal.
229 DLR, July 24, 2001, pp. C1-2.
230 DLR, May 5, 2000, p. A8.
231 Nowell, A Chicken in Every Pot, p. 329.
232 DLR, Mar. 1, 2000, p. A5.

found: "Although geographically their work takes them outside the processing plants, the catchers' function, in a real sense, is simply part of the production line."[233]

With time, some firms have settled disputed claims with respect to FLSA and related coverage; others continued to challenge the Department's interpretation of the law. The contests, in varying forms and jurisdictions, have moved slowly through the courts — and new issues have been raised. The question of fair labor standards for meat and poultry workers, however, has not yet been fully resolved.[234]

Line Speeds and Rest Breaks

For the past century, line speeds have been a constant worker complaint. Commons, writing of the Chicago yards in 1904, thought speed "was undoubtedly the grievance above all others."[235] With time and union pressure, some moderation was achieved; but, some suggest, things changed again with the advent of the *new breed* packers. The UFCW's Lewie Anderson, starting work at an older Armour plant, found "a pace that you could handle" to "do the work ... without killing yourself." Moving to IBP, he found the line speed "more than twice as fast" with supervisors "in there on top of the people ... screaming at them and pushing them, literally pushing them, to go faster and faster."[236]

"Worker productivity remains the key to profits — and survival — in a fiercely competitive business," states Broadway. "Worker productivity is a function of line speed; speed it up, and productivity increases."[237] Bjerklie concurs: "... the search for faster and better ways to slaughter and process meat and livestock is relentless, and has resulted in line (or 'chain') speeds of unimaginable rapidity...."[238] IBP's Peterson sew the issue a little differently. "You can't ever overwork anybody on a constant basis or they're going to quit."[239]

The issue is complex. At IBP in the 1960s, UFCW's Anderson reported "constant turnover" as a response to line speed.[240] If turnover is not regarded as entirely negative by industry, it may be a mixed blessing. Some argue that "IBP plants were accident-prone because of their accelerated line speeds and the constant pressure on workers to meet arbitrary production quotas."[241] This leads, others say,"to worker turnover" and stress-induced absenteeism.[242] A revolving workforce of sometimes "untrained, inexperienced, and often

---

233 See Heath v. Perdue Farms Inc., D. Md., No. WMN-98-3159, Feb. 24, 2000, summarized in DLR, Mar. 1, 2000, pp. A5-A6.

234 See DLR, May 5, 2000, p. A8, Aug. 20, 2001, p. A2, May 11, 2002, pp. A1-A2, Mar. 25, 2002, p. A8, June 5, 2003, pp. AA1-AA2, E1-E4, Aug. 6, 2003, pp. AA1-AA-2, E1-E11, and Sept. 10, 2003, AA1-AA2, E8-E13. Concerning yet another issue, the U.S. District court for the Northern District of Iowa, Nov. 20, 2003 (Jimenez v. Duran, N.D. Iowa, No. 01-3068-MWB), ruled that "[e]mployees of an Iowa contracting service that vaccinated and tended to chickens are exempt from the overtime requirements of the Fair Labor Standards Act." See DLR, Oct. 28, 2003, pp. AA1-AA2, E1-E7. See also Stull and Broadway, Slaughterhouse Blues, pp. 47 and 50-51.

235 Commons, Labor Conditions, p. 7.

236 Horowitz, Black and White, pp. 245-246.

237 Broadway, From City to Countryside, p. 22.

238 Bjerklie, On the Horns of a Dilemma, p. 43.

239 Kay, Bob Peterson, p. 36.

240 Kay, Bob Peterson, p. 36.

241 Craypo, Strike and Relocation, p. 193.

242 Griffith, Hay Trabajo, p. 136. See also Hackenberg, et al., Creating a Disposable Labor Force, p. 85.

young workers" may lead, some suggest, to still higher injury rates.[243] *Break time* and *rest periods* are similarly contentious issues.[244]

These questions remain unresolved. How humane can the workplace be made without unduly impacting efficiency and profitability? Though immediately of concern for OSHA purposes, the issues raised by line speeds, break time, and rest periods are not directly addressed by the FLSA.

POSSIBILITIES FOR CHANGE IN LABOR PRACTICES

It may be, after careful consideration, that workers (with their unions) and employers are satisfied with the current state of labor practices in the packing and processing industry. And, it may not be necessary to review enforcement of labor, safety and health standards, immigration law, or related issues.

The course chosen will rest, largely, with the parties at interest: labor, management, and government. How strongly does industry want a union free environment? Does it regard labor turnover, for reasons discussed above, to be a positive (or tolerable) part of the post-1960s workplace? Can industry secure an adequate workforce through domestic recruitment and employment of authorized immigrant workers?

Control of the workplace rests essentially with management — even where there is effective collective bargaining. However, even without a formal union presence, workers can be expected to demand reforms. Where such reforms are not forthcoming, workers may turn to the trade union movement for assistance and redress. At the same time, it is possible that industry will undertake changes — if only to prevent trade union initiatives and to stave off government action. If voluntary change is not forthcoming, given the results of the 1997-1998 and 2000 DOL workplace surveys, there may well be further pressure for legislative or regulatory action.[245]

LOOKING AT THE WORKPLACE

Authors, in writing of labor practices in meatpacking and poultry processing, have suggested a variety of workplace changes that could ease the strain on workers while, they argue, improving general efficiency and reducing certain labor-related costs. The utility of such proposals and the validity of projected impacts may need further study. But, they may also be worth consideration.

Reducing the line speed — sometimes associated with *cumulative trauma disorders* — has been suggested.[246] "If they slowed down the lines and rotated workers, we'd have fewer problems around here," argues Bodo Treu, workers' compensation physician for IBP at Storm

---

243 Craypo, Strike and Relocation, p. 193. See also Nowell, A Chicken in Every Pot, pp. 327-328 and 335.

244 See Stromquist, Solidarity and Survival, pp. 97-98; and Griffith, Consequences of Immigration Reform, p. 161.

245 Market power and labor/industry/community relationships are discussed in Alan Barkema, Mark Drabenstott and Nancy Novack, "The New U.S. Meat Industry," EconomicfReview, Federal Reserve Bank of Kansas City (Second Quarter, 2001), pp. 33-56.

246 Hall, The Kill Line, p. 225.

Lake.[247] "Redesign tools so they, rather than the workers' forceful motions, do the job" — "[a]utomate or restructure especially hazardous jobs."[248]

Some workers view employment in packing and processing as incompatible with age. Five years is "about the longest period a person could last on the slaughter line," some suggest.[249] If retention is desired, re-engineering of the work process could be an option. So, too, might be a seniority system that moves workers up and into work commensurate with their experience and strength. Some suggest that a firm, through such changes, could capitalize on its recruitment and training investment — while workers could look forward to a career in the industry.

Small changes may help reduce work-related injuries. Increase the number of short breaks, some have argued. Stop the line for a brief period: allowing workers time to stretch or to rotate to slightly different jobs — to do simple aerobics, or just to get away from the stress of a constantly moving line.[250] Assigning workers to a variety of jobs (mornings at one task; afternoons, another) has been proposed as a way to ease muscle strain — and relieve boredom. "But, most of all," say Stull and Broadway, "slow down the chain."[251]

"A key element of ... employee retention," affirms Mark Klein of Excel, "is to offer good wages and benefits."[252] Some restructuring of the fringe benefit package, particularly with respect to vesting (e.g., healthcare coverage) might foster workforce stability. Enhanced portability of health and pension benefits might also be an option.[253]

"Hours," Stull suggests, "vary seasonally and even weekly depending on the price and supply of fat cattle, consumer demand, and profit margins."[254] Currently, it's asserted: "Six-day weeks and mandatory overtime alternate with sudden layoffs as the packers adjust to fluctuations in meat supply and demand."[255] Might flexibility be built into such a system? Some urge a more *family-friendly* workplace: affordable daycare, flexible workhours (an option of worker choice), and fixed schedules that can be adjusted to accommodate a worker's family or other responsibilities.

IBP's Ken Kimbro suggests that a "primary reason people leave jobs is that they don't feel appreciated."[256] Low esteem for workers, some argue, is reflected in high turnover rates — and in the manner in which line workers are viewed by the communities within which they reside.[257] Increased investment in human resource management has been suggested as one potential remedy.[258] This involves "treating people with respect and dignity," Hall argues. "It

---

247 Hedges et al., The New Jungle, p. 39.
248 Hall, The Kill Line, p. 225.
249 Kay, The Nature of Turnover, p. 31.
250 Grey, Pork, Poultry, and Newcomers, p. 116.
251 Stull and Broadway, Killing Them Softly, p. 81.See also Jane Kelly, "Perdue: New Processing Plant Is Strictly for the Foodservice Market," Meat and Poultry, Dec. 1992, p. 15, for discussion of an exercise and job rotation regime at a Perdue facility in Dillon County, South Carolina.
252 Kay, The Nature of Turnover, p. 34.
253 See Stull, Of Meat and (Wo)Men, p. 115. Stull estimates gross annual earnings for line workers at between $15,000 and $22,000, depending upon the grade and seniority, may actually prevail.
254 Stull, Of Meat and (Wo)Men, p. 115.
255 Horowitz, Negro and White, p. 282. See also Benson, The Effects of Packinghouse Work, pp. 102-103, 111.
256 Quoted in Kay, The Nature of Turnover, p. 31-32.
257 Stull et al., Introduction: Making Meat, p. 4. Griffith, Consequences of Immigration Reform, p. 156, states: "...workers in industries like poultry processing are often somewhat marginal to the labor force, consisting of large proportions of unskilled workers, women, minorities, students, prisoners, and others who occupy positions in the plants seasonally or irregularly...." See also Hall, Chicken Empires, p. 15; and Campa, Immigrant Latinos, pp. 345-360.
258 Richard Alaniz, "Avoiding Rehiring Costs by Retaining Good Employees," Meat and Poultry, May 1999, p. 80.

includes training, fostering upward mobility, maintaining a complete medical program, and disciplining line supervisors who violate company policy. The payoff," he states, "includes lower-turnover, improved morale, better production, and savings on health costs...."[259]

CONSIDERATIONS OF PUBLIC POLICY

General policy and practices in meat packing and poultry processing have been debated through many years. But, there may be a number of issues that could attract attention from policy makers.

Fair Labor Standards Act

The issue of *donning* and *doffing* is rooted in the overtime pay provisions of the FLSA; but, the facts of the issue remain in dispute. How much time is actually spent putting on or taking off protective clothing and equipment? Does it vary, significantly, from one segment of the industry to another — and between employers? Enforcement and litigation depend largely upon the facts in specific cases.

The courts have divided on some of the overall (and specific) issues involved in *donning* and *doffing*. Can a solution to the current dispute be effected through regulatory reform? Through the courts? Or, should Congress define, more clearly, its intent with respect to *portal-to-portal* issues? Were Congress to modify the FLSA with respect to *donning* and *doffing* standards, would the effect be felt elsewhere: e.g., in mining, in nuclear power, or in laboratory work?[260]

Treatment of *chicken catchers* involves both the FLSA and NLRA. For labor standards and collective bargaining purposes, how are chicken catchers defined? Are they agricultural employees (exempt or afforded special treatment under the FLSA and NLRA) or are they industrial workers and protected by those statutes? Are they *independent contractors*? If *chicken catchers* are deemed to be employees (for labor standards and collective bargaining purposes), might *grow-out* farmers be similarly protected?

National Labor Relations Act

The labor-management relationship may be another area of concern. How high *is* the turnover rate in the industry? To what extent is the workforce simply migratory or casual? Such elements would likely impact the ability of workers to organize and to bargain collectively. In the context of a high turnover rate, what are the *effective* rights of short-term workers and how are they protected?

---

259 Hall, The Kill Line, pp. 228-229.
260 DLR, Jan. 9, 2003, p. A8, reported that Honda Manufacturing of Alabama "will pay $1.2 million to workers at its Lincoln, Ala., plant, after a Department of Labor investigation found that workers there were not paid for the time they spent putting on their uniforms at work." The general issue is still open, DLR reports.

How well have NLRA procedures functioned in the context of the meat packing and poultry (seafood) processing industries?[261] Employers could find themselves confronted with a continuing cycle of organizational campaigns which, whatever their outcome, could be disruptive and costly. Where a workforce may be largely transient, do organizational campaigns reflect the interest (real or perceived) of the workers? Does the transnational movement of workers suggest a need to reconsider aspects of the NLRA?

Migrant and Seasonal Agricultural Workers' Protection Act (MSPA)

The siting of industry in rural areas may have increased the necessity for recruitment of workers from outside the areas of production. In some cases, such recruitment has involved groups of workers, transported by bus or auto, and traveling long distances for work. Reportedly, by the 1990s, it had become "standard industry practice to import workers through border-state labor recruiters."[262] Given the high turnover rates, are such workers, in fact, *seasonal* or *migratory*?

Immigration issues aside, are such workers covered under the MSPA?[263] If not, should they be? What is their relationship of these workers with the agent who arranges their transportation, employment, and possible housing? If women (and potentially children) are part of this movement of workers, are special problems raised? Where they enter the country illegally, are they likely targets of extortion by labor merchants and recruiters? Are they susceptible to other forms of violence?

Administration and Enforcement Policy

Ordinarily, DOL enforcement of labor standards has been *complaint based*: that is to say, in response to a complaint from an aggrieved worker. But, complaints may not be frequent where the workforce, as in poultry processing and some aspects of meat packing, is frequently immigrant (or composed of foreign workers unauthorized to work in the United States) and where the workers may not be aware of their rights under law. At the same time, DOL and immigration authorities have sometimes adopted strategies of *targeted enforcement* of labor standards and immigration law: focusing upon a specific industry and/or geographical location.

Such initiatives (targeted enforcement) may be a response to staff and resources too limited for more uniform for more systematic policies. However, such a system, essentially intermittent and sporadic, *could* produce enforcement that is perceived to be unfair and/or

---

261 In his study, The Maya of Morganton, p. 199, Fink states: "The federal government needs to restore the 'right to organize' by strengthening penalties for infringement of the labor law...." And, he says: "Current U.S. policy attracts foreign workers but stifles them once they have arrived."

262 Cook, Hog-Tied, p. 28. See also Fink, The Maya of Morganton, pp. 17-18; and Stephanie Simon, "Latinos Take Root in Midwest," The Los Angeles Times, Oct. 24, 2002, Part 1, p. 1 ff.

263 Signed into law in Jan. 1983, MSPA (P.L. 97-470; 20 U.S.C. 1801-1872) provides basic labor protections for migrant and for seasonal agricultural workers and deals, inter alia, with transportation safety and, where appropriate, the safety and health of housing. It also provides a system of registration for persons engaged in agricultural labor contracting activities.

unequal. Are *strike forces* and *sting* operations appropriate for enforcement of labor standards?

Some have suggested a more cooperative policy between employers (and unions) and enforcement staff. But, what is the proper balance between *outreach* (or education) and enforcement, *per se*?[264]

CONCLUDING COMMENT

Change in the meatpacking and poultry processing industries impacts a wide range of public policy areas. Labor practices have been, through a number of years, a focus of Department of Labor attention. They have also been a subject of major and continuing litigation, and of a variety of enforcement campaigns.

At issue are a number of federal statutes: most notably, the Fair Labor Standards Act and the National Labor Relations Act, but of others as well. Workforce recruitment has affected (and been affected by) federal immigration policy. Implementation of existing statutes has been a continuing issue for administrative agencies.

As the industry changes, one may expect to see changes in the labor-management relationship. What their character will be may depend upon the perception of current problems and challenges.

---

264 In Slaughterhouse Blues, p. 153, Stull and Broadway review recent litigation involving the meatpacking and poultry processing industry and state the opinion that "This litany of court cases and settlements suggest that for many companies, fines are just another cost of doing business. When lawyers' fees, court costs, and fines exceed the price of improving working conditions, paying a fair wage, and preventing environmental damage, meat and poultry companies may change their ways. Until then, it will be business as usual."

In: Farm Labor: 21st Century Issues and Challenges   ISBN: 978-1-60456-005-3
Editors: A. W. Burton, I. B. Telpov, pp. 109-143   © 2007 Nova Science Publishers, Inc.

Chapter 3

IMMIGRATION: POLICY CONSIDERATIONS RELATED TO GUEST WORKER PROGRAMS[*]

Andorra Bruno

ABSTRACT

At present, the United States has two main programs for temporarily importing low-skilled workers, sometimes referred to as guest workers. Agricultural guest workers enter through the H-2A visa program, and other guest workers enter through the H-2B visa program. Employers interested in importing workers under either program must first apply to the U.S. Department of Labor for a certification that U.S. workers capable of performing the work are not available and that the employment of alien workers will not adversely affect the wages and working conditions of similarly employed U.S. workers. Other requirements of the programs differ.

The 109th Congress revised the H-2B program in the FY2005 Emergency Supplemental Appropriations Act (P.L. 109-13). Among the changes, a temporary provision was added to the Immigration and Nationality Act (INA) to exempt certain returning H-2B workers from the H-2B annual numerical cap. The FY2007 Department of Defense authorization act (P.L. 109-364) extended this exemption through FY2007. Other bills before the 109th Congress proposed to make changes to the H-2A program (S. 359/H.R. 884, H.R. 3857, S. 2087, Senate-passed S. 2611), the H-2B program (S. 278, H.R. 1587, S. 1438, S. 1918), and the "H" visa category generally (H.R. 3333), and to establish new temporary worker visas (S. 1033/H.R. 2330, S. 1438, S. 1918, H.R. 4065, Senate-passed S. 2611). S. 359/H.R. 884, S. 1033/H.R. 2330, S. 1918, and S. 2611 also would have established mechanisms for certain foreign workers to become U.S. legal permanent residents (LPRs). None of these bills were enacted. Various guest worker measures were also introduced in the 108th Congress, but they saw no action beyond committee referrals. President George W. Bush proposed a new, expanded temporary worker program in January 2004 when he announced his principles for immigration reform. In a May 2006 national address on comprehensive immigration reform, he reiterated his support for a temporary worker program.

The current discussion of guest worker programs takes place against a backdrop of historically high levels of unauthorized migration to the United States. Supporters of a

---

[*] Excerpted from CRS Report 32044, dated December 11, 2006.

large-scale temporary worker program argue that such a program would help reduce unauthorized immigration by providing a legal alternative for prospective foreign workers. Critics reject this reasoning and instead maintain that a new guest worker program would likely exacerbate the problem of illegal migration.

The consideration of any proposed guest worker program raises various issues, including the following: how new program requirements would compare with those of the H-2A and H-2B programs; how the eligible population would be defined; whether the program would include a mechanism for participants to obtain LPR status; how family members of eligible individuals would be treated; what labor market test, if any, the program would employ; whether the program would be numerically limited; how the rules and requirements of the program would be enforced; and what security-related provisions, if any, would be included.

INTRODUCTION

In 2001, the United States and Mexico began Cabinet-level talks on migration. Although the details of these discussions were not made public, two issues —legalization and a temporary worker program — dominated media coverage. The talks lost momentum after the terrorist attacks of September 11, 2001, as the Bush Administration focused its attention on security-related matters. A temporary worker program (not limited to Mexico), however, remains of interest to some Members of Congress and Administration officials. Various bills to reform existing programs for foreign temporary workers and to create new temporary worker programs have been introduced in recent Congresses. In January 2004, the Bush Administration outlined a proposal for a new temporary worker program. The President reiterated his support for a temporary worker program in a May 2006 national address. The temporary worker programs under discussion presumably would cover largely low-skilled workers.

BACKGROUND

The term *guest worker* has typically been applied to foreign temporary low-skilled laborers, often in agriculture or other seasonal employment. In the past, guest worker programs have been established in the United States to address worker shortages during times of war. During World War I, for example, tens of thousands of Mexican workers performed mainly agricultural labor as part of a temporary worker program. The Bracero program, which began during World War II and lasted until 1964, brought several million Mexican agricultural workers into the United States. At its peak in the late 1950s, the Bracero program employed more than 400,000 Mexican workers annually.[1]

The Immigration and Nationality Act (INA) of 1952, as originally enacted,[2] authorized a temporary foreign worker program known as the H-2 program. It covered both agricultural and nonagricultural workers who were coming temporarily to the United States to perform temporary services (other than services of an exceptional nature requiring distinguished merit

---

1 For additional information on these historical programs, see U.S. Congress, Senate Committee on the Judiciary, Temporary Worker Programs: Background and Issues, committee print, 96th Cong., 2nd sess., Feb. 1980.
2 Act of June 27, 1952, ch. 477, codified at 8 U.S.C.§1101 et seq. The INA is the basis of current immigration law.

and ability) or labor. Aliens who are admitted to the United States for a temporary period of time and a specific purpose are known as nonimmigrants. The 1986 Immigration Reform and Control Act (IRCA)[3] amended the INA to subdivide the H-2 program into the current H-2A and H-2B programs and to detail the admissions process for H-2A workers. The H-2A and H-2B visas are subcategories of the larger "H" nonimmigrant visa category for temporary workers.[4]

CURRENT PROGRAMS

The United States currently has two main programs for importing temporary low-skilled workers. Agricultural workers enter through the H-2A program and other temporary workers enter through the H-2B program.[5] The programs take their names from the sections of the INA that established them — Section 101(a)(15)(H)(ii)(a) and Section 101(a)(15)(H)(ii)(b), respectively. Both programs are administered by the Employment and Training Administration (ETA) of the U.S. Department of Labor (DOL) and U.S. Citizenship and Immigration Services (USCIS) of the U.S. Department of Homeland Security (DHS).[6]

H-2A PROGRAM

The H-2A program allows for the temporary admission of foreign workers to the United States to perform agricultural work of a seasonal or temporary nature, provided that U.S. workers are not available. An approved H-2A visa petition is generally valid for an initial period of up to one year. An alien's total period of stay as an H-2A worker may not exceed three consecutive years.

Employers who want to import H-2A workers must first apply to DOL for a certification that (1) there are not sufficient U.S. workers who are qualified and available to perform the work; and (2) the employment of foreign workers will not adversely affect the wages and working conditions of U.S. workers who are similarly employed. As part of this labor certification process, employers must attempt to recruit U.S. workers and must cooperate with DOL-funded state employment service agencies (also known as state workforce agencies) in local, intrastate, and interstate recruitment efforts. Employers must pay their H-2A workers and similarly employed U.S. workers the highest of the federal or applicable state minimum wage, the prevailing wage rate,[7] or the adverse effect wage rate (AEWR).[8] They also must

---

3 P.L. 99-603, Nov. 6, 1986.

4 For an overview of the INA's nonimmigrant visa categories, see CRS Report RL31381, *U.S. Immigration Policy on Temporary Admissions*, by Ruth Ellen Wasem.

5 While H-2B workers are, for the most part, low skilled, the H-2B program is not limited to workers of a particular skill level and has been used to import a variety of workers, including entertainers and athletes.

6 Prior to Mar. 1, 2003, the H-2A and H-2B programs were administered by ETA and the Immigration and Naturalization Service (INS) of the Department of Justice. The Homeland Security Act of 2002 (P.L. 107-296, Nov. 25, 2002) abolished INS and transferred most of its functions to DHS as of Mar. 1.

7 The prevailing wage rate is the average wage paid to similarly employed workers in the occupation in the area of intended employment. Additional information about prevailing wages is available at [http://www. foreignlaborcert.doleta.gov/wages.cfm].

8 The AEWR is an hourly wage rate set by DOL for each state or region, based upon data gathered by the Department of Agriculture in quarterly wage surveys. For 2006, the AEWR ranges from $7.58 for Arkansas,

provide workers with housing, transportation, and other benefits, including workers' compensation insurance.[9] No health insurance coverage is required.[10]

Both growers and labor advocates criticize the H-2A program in its current form. Growers complain that the H-2A program is overly cumbersome and does not meet their labor needs. Labor advocates argue that the program provides too few protections for U.S. workers.

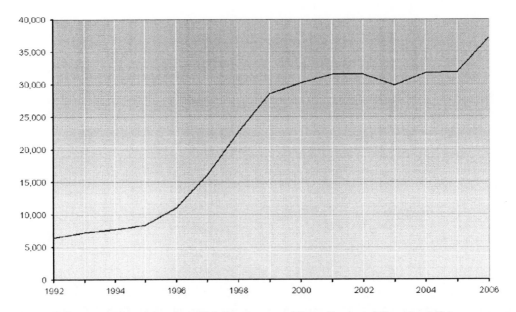

Source: CRS Presentation of data from U.S. Department of State, Bureau of Consular Affairs.

Figure 1. H-2A Visas Issued, FY1992-FY2006.

H-2A Visas Issued

The H-2A program, which is not subject to numerical limits, has grown significantly since 1992. One way to measure the program's growth is to consider changes in the number of H-2A visas issued annually by the Department of State (DOS).[11] As illustrated in Figure 1, the number of H-2A visas issued increased from 6,445 in FY1992 to 30,201 in FY2000. H-2A visa issuances remained at about 30,000 annually until FY2006, when, according to preliminary data, 37,149 H-2A visas were issued. The H-2A program, however, remains quite

Louisiana, and Mississippi to $9.99 for Hawaii. See CRS Report RL32861, Farm Labor: The Adverse Effect Wage Rate (AEWR), by William G. Whittaker.

9 Required wages and benefits under the H-2A program are set forth in 20 C.F.R. §655.102.

10 H-2A workers, like nonimmigrants generally, are not eligible for federally funded public assistance, with the exception of Medicaid emergency services. For further information on alien eligibility for federal benefits, see CRS Report RL31114, Noncitizen Eligibility for Major Federal Public Assistance Programs: Policies and Legislation, by Ruth Ellen Wasem (Hereafter cited as CRS Report RL31114); and CRS Report RL31630, Federal Funding for Unauthorized Aliens' Emergency Medical Expenses, by Alison M. Siskin.

11 There is no precise measure available of the number of the aliens granted H-2A status in any given year. While visa data provide an approximation, these data are subject to limitations, among them that not all H-2A workers are necessarily issued visas and not all aliens who are issued visas necessarily use them to enter the United States.

small relative to total hired farm employment, which stood at about 1.1 million in 2005, according to the Department of Agriculture's National Agricultural Statistics Service.[12]

H-2B PROGRAM

The H-2B program provides for the temporary admission of foreign workers to the United States to perform temporary non-agricultural work, if unemployed U.S. workers cannot be found. Foreign medical graduates coming to perform medical services are explicitly excluded from the program. An approved H-2B visa petition is valid for an initial period of up to one year. An alien's total period of stay as an H-2B worker may not exceed three consecutive years.[13]

Like prospective H-2A employers, prospective H-2B employers must first apply to DOL for a certification that U.S. workers capable of performing the work are not available and that the employment of alien workers will not adversely affect the wages and working conditions of similarly employed U.S. workers. H-2B employers must pay their workers at least the prevailing wage rate. Unlike H-2A employers, they are not subject to the AEWR and do not have to provide housing, transportation,[14] and other benefits required under the H-2A program.

In January 2005, USCIS proposed regulations to streamline the H-2B petitioning process, which would significantly alter procedures.[15] Among other changes, the proposed rule would eliminate the requirement that prospective H-2B employers file for a labor certification from DOL in most cases. Instead, employers seeking H-2B workers in areas other than logging, the entertainment industry, and professional athletics would include certain labor attestations as part of the H-2B petition they file with USCIS. According to the proposed rule, this H-2B attestation process would be similar to the process currently used for H-1B professional specialty workers.[16]

A key limitation of the H-2B visa concerns the requirement that the work be temporary. Under the applicable immigration regulations, work is considered to be temporary if the employer's need for the duties to be performed by the worker is a one-time occurrence, seasonal need, peakload need, or intermittent need.[17] According to DOL data on H-2B labor certifications, top H-2B occupations in recent years, in terms of the number of workers certified, included landscape laborer, forestry worker, maid and housekeeping cleaner, and construction worker.

---

12 For additional discussion, see CRS Report RL30395, Farm Labor Shortages and Immigration Policy, by Linda Levine.

13 For additional discussion, see CRS Report RL30395, Farm Labor Shortages and Immigration Policy, by Linda Levine.

14 While not subject to the broader transportation requirements of the H-2A program, H-2B employers are required by law to pay the reasonable costs of return transportation abroad for an H-2B worker who is dismissed prior to the end of his or her authorized period of stay.

15 The proposed USCIS rule is available at [http://a257.g.akamaitech.net/7/257/2422/ 01jan20051800/edocket.access.gpo.gov/2005/05-1240.htm]. DOL has published a companion proposal, which is available at [http://a257.g.akamaitech.net/7/257/2422/ 01jan20051800/edocket.access.gpo.gov/2005/05-1222.htm].

16 For information on the H-1B nonimmigrant classification, see CRS Report RL30498, Immigration: Legislative Issues on Nonimmigrant Professional Specialty (H-1B) Workers, by Ruth Ellen Wasem.

17 For definitions of these types of need, see 8 C.F.R. §214.2(h)(6)(ii).

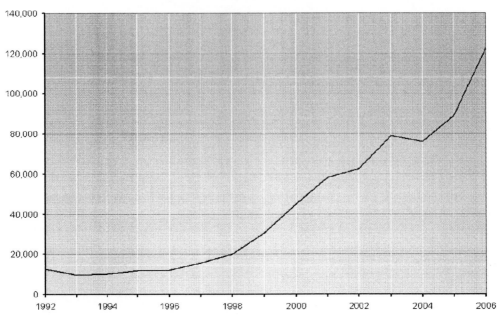

Source: CRS Presentation of data from U.S. Department of State, Bureau of Consular Affairs.

Figure 2. H-2B Visas Issued, FY1992-FY2006.

H-2B Visas Issued and the Statutory Cap

Unlike the H-2A visa, the H-2B visa is subject to a statutory numerical limit. Under the INA, the total number of aliens who may be issued H-2B visas or otherwise provided H-2B status during a fiscal year may not exceed 66,000.[18] This cap does not apply to all H-2B petitions. Petitions for current H-2B workers to extend their stay, change their terms of employment, or change or add employers do not count towards the cap. As shown in Figure 2, the number of H-2B visas issued by DOS dipped from 12,552 in FY1992 to 9,691 in FY1993 and then began to increase steadily.[19]

In FY2003, DOS issued 78,955 H-2B visas, and in FY2004, it issued 76,169 H-2B visas. While for various reasons not all visas issued during a fiscal year necessarily count against that year's cap or, in some cases, any year's cap, USCIS acknowledged that the H-2B cap was exceeded in FY2003. With respect to the FY2004 cap, USCIS announced on March 10, 2004, that it had received a sufficient number of H-2B petitions to meet that cap. On January 4, 2005, it announced that it had received a sufficient number of H-2B petitions to meet the FY2005 cap.

Following the enactment of new H-2B provisions as part of the FY2005 Emergency Supplemental Appropriations Act for Defense, the Global War on Terror, and Tsunami Relief

18 See INA §214(g)(1)(B).
19 There is no precise measure available of the number of the aliens granted H-2B status in any given year. While visa data provide an approximation, these data are subject to limitations, among them that not all H-2A workers are necessarily issued visas and not all aliens who are issued visas necessarily use them to enter the United States.

(P.L. 109-13),[20] USCIS announced that on May 25, 2005, it would start accepting additional petitions for H-2B workers for FY2005.[21] Under P.L. 109-13, for FY2005 and FY2006, returning H-2B workers counted against the annual 66,000 cap during any one of the three prior fiscal years were not to be counted again. USCIS determined that approximately 35,000 previously approved H-2B workers for FY2005 qualified as returning workers who, under P.L. 109-13, were exempt from that year's cap, opening up 35,000 slots for other H-2B workers. Employers were able to file FY2005 petitions for new H-2B workers to fill those slots, as well as for cap-exempt returning H-2B workers. According to preliminary data, 89,135 H-2B visas were issued in FY2005 and 122,541 H-2B visas were issued in FY2006. According to DOS, 50,854 of the FY2006 H-2B visas were issued to cap-exempt returning H-2B workers. The John Warner National Defense Authorization Act for FY2007 (P.L. 109-364) extends through FY2007 the provision exempting returning H-2B workers from the H-2B annual cap.

UNAUTHORIZED IMMIGRATION

The current discussion of guest worker programs has been prompted, in part, by the continued high levels of illegal, or unauthorized, immigration to the United States and related deaths along the U.S.-Mexican border. Analyses by the Pew Hispanic Center based on data from the Current Population Survey (CPS) and other sources estimate that the unauthorized resident alien population totaled 10.3 million in March 2004, 11.1 million in March 2005, and 11.5 to 12 million in March 2006, and that since 2000, this population has grown at an average annual rate of more than 500,000 per year.[22] DHS's estimates of the unauthorized alien population and its growth are somewhat lower. Based on data from the 2004 American Community Survey and other sources, DHS estimates that there were 10.5 million unauthorized aliens residing in the United States in January 2005 and that the unauthorized resident population grew at an average annual rate of 408,000 during the 2000-2004 period.[23]

Mexico remains the largest source country for unauthorized immigration. According to the Pew Hispanic Center, the unauthorized Mexican population in the United States stood at about 6.2 million in 2005, comprising 56% of the total unauthorized population. DHS estimates that there were nearly 6 million unauthorized Mexicans residing in the United States in 2005, comprising 57% of the total unauthorized population. With respect to migrant deaths, data from the United States Border Patrol indicate that more than 300 migrants died at

---

20 See discussion below of S. 352/H.R. 793 in the 109th Congress.

21 U.S. Department of Homeland Security, U.S. Citizenship and Immigration Services, "USCIS to Accept Additional H-2B Filings for FY2005 and FY2006," public notice, May 23, 2005.

22 Jeffrey S. Passel, Estimates of the Size and Characteristics of the Undocumented Population, Pew Hispanic Center, Mar. 21, 2005; Jeffrey S. Passel, Size and Characteristics of the Unauthorized Migrant Population in the U.S.; Estimates Based on the March 2005 Current Population Survey, Pew Hispanic Center, Mar. 7, 2006 (hereafter cited as Passel, Size and Characteristics of the Unauthorized Migrant Population in the U.S., Mar. 7, 2006). These reports are available at [http://pewhispanic.org/topics/index.php?TopicID=16]. Also see CRS Report RS21938, Unauthorized Aliens in the United States: Estimates Since 1986, by Ruth Ellen Wasem.

23 U.S. Department of Homeland Security, Office of Immigration Statistics, Estimates of the Unauthorized Immigrant Population Residing in the United States: January 2005, by Michael Hoefer, Nancy Rytina, and Christopher Campbell, Aug. 2006.

the U.S.-Mexican border each year from FY2000 through FY2004 and that there were 472 migrant deaths at the border in FY2005.[24]

UNAUTHORIZED WORKERS

Unauthorized workers are a subpopulation of the total unauthorized alien population. According to the March 2006 report by the Pew Hispanic Center, there were an estimated 7.2 million unauthorized workers in the U.S. civilian labor force in March 2005.[25] These workers represented about 4.9% of the labor force. In some occupations and industries, however, their share of the labor force was considerably higher. The report states:

> Unauthorized workers are employed in a variety of occupations throughout the labor force, although the distribution of the unauthorized workforce across occupations differs from that of native-born workers.
>
> Unauthorized workers are notably underrepresented in white-collar occupations.... On the other hand, unauthorized migrants are much more likely to be in major occupation groups that require little education or do not have licensing requirements.[26]

Unauthorized aliens are also overrepresented in certain industries relative to their share of the overall labor force. Table 1 presents data from the Pew Hispanic Center report on industries with high concentrations of unauthorized workers. Unauthorized aliens accounted for between 10% and 21% of workers in the industries shown.

Table 1. Estimates of Unauthorized Employment in Selected Industries, 2005

Industry Group	Unauthorized Workers (in Industry)
Private Households	21%
Food Manufacturing	14%
Agriculture	13%
Furniture Manufacturing	13%
Construction	12%
Textile, Apparel, and Leather Manufacturing	12%
Food Services	12%
Administrative and Support Services	11%
Accommodation	10%

Source: Jeffrey S. Passel, Size and Characteristics of the Unauthorized Migrant Population in the U.S., Pew Hispanic Center, March 7, 2006.

---

24 For further information on migrant deaths, see CRS Report RL32562, Border Security: The Role of the U.S. Border Patrol, by Blas Nuñez-Neto.

25 Passel, Size and Characteristics of the Unauthorized Migrant Population in the U.S., Mar. 7, 2006, at [http://pewhispanic.org/reports/report.php?ReportID=61].

26 Ibid., pp. 10-11.

Supporters of a large-scale guest worker program contend that such a program would help reduce unauthorized immigration by providing a legal alternative for prospective foreign workers. Critics reject this reasoning and instead maintain that a guest worker program would likely exacerbate the problem of illegal immigration; they argue, for example, that many guest workers would fail to leave the country at the end of their authorized period of stay.

LEGISLATION IN THE 105TH-107TH CONGRESSES

Major guest worker legislation introduced in the 105th, 106th, and 107th Congresses was limited to the H-2A program. No major nonagricultural guest worker bills were offered.[27] In the 105th Congress, for example, a Senate-approved amendment to S. 2260, an FY1999 Departments of Commerce, Justice, and State appropriations bill, would have replaced the existing labor certification process with a new set of procedures for importing H-2A workers. It would have established a system of agricultural worker registries containing the names of eligible U.S. agricultural workers. Employers interested in importing H-2A workers would first have applied to DOL for the referral of U.S. workers through a registry search. If a sufficient number of workers were not found, the employer would have been allowed to import H-2A workers to cover the shortfall. The Senate measure also would have changed wage and other requirements. The provision was not enacted.

Provisions to establish a system of worker registries and to change existing H-2A-related requirements were likewise included in two H-2A reform proposals introduced in the 106th Congress (S. 1814/H.R. 4056[28] and H.R. 4548). In addition, S. 1814/H.R. 4056 would have established a two-stage legalization program, under which farm workers satisfying specified work requirements could have obtained temporary resident status and then legal permanent resident (LPR) status. Although formal congressional consideration was limited to a Senate Immigration Subcommittee hearing, S. 1814/H.R. 4056 became the basis of a bipartisan compromise on foreign agricultural workers. That agreement, however, fell apart at the end of the 106th Congress. H.R. 4548, the other reform bill before the 106th Congress, differed from S. 1814/H.R. 4056 in that it sought to establish a pilot H-2C alien agricultural worker program to supplement, rather than replace, the H-2A program. H.R. 4548 also did not include a legalization program. H.R. 4548 was reported by the House Judiciary Committee in October 2000, but saw no further action.

Like S. 1814/H.R. 4056 in the 106th Congress, key bills before the 107th Congress coupled significant H-2A reform with legalization. S. 1161 and S. 1313/H.R. 2736 would have streamlined the process of importing H-2A workers, particularly for jobs covered by collective bargaining agreements. With respect to legalization, both proposals would have allowed foreign agricultural workers who met specified work requirements to adjust to LPR status through a two-stage process like that in S. 1814/H.R. 4056. The requirements for adjustment of status in S. 1313/H.R. 2736 differed from those in S. 1161, with the latter being more stringent. Among the other major differences between the proposals, S. 1161 would

---

27 During the 107th Congress, former Senator Phil Gramm released a preliminary proposal for a new U.S.-Mexico guest worker program that would have covered both agricultural and nonagricultural workers, but he did not introduce legislation.

28 Although S. 1814 and H.R. 4056 are not identical, they are treated as companion bills for the purposes of this discussion because they are highly similar.

have eased existing wage requirements, while S. 1313/H.R. 2736 would have mandated a study of the wage issue. No action beyond committee referral occurred on either proposal.

LEGISLATION IN THE 108TH CONGRESS

Bills to reform the H-2A program, the H-2B program, and the "H" visa category generally, as well as bills to establish new guest worker programs, were introduced in the 108th Congress. Some of these bills would have enabled certain workers to obtain LPR status. No action beyond committee referral occurred on any of the bills.

Congressional committees held related hearings during the 108th Congress. The House Agriculture Committee held a hearing on the potential impact of recent guest worker proposals on the agricultural sector, and the House Judiciary Committee's Subcommittee on Immigration, Border Security, and Claims held a hearing on the impact of guest workers on U.S. workers. In the Senate, the Judiciary Committee's Subcommittee on Immigration, Border Security, and Citizenship held hearings on evaluating a guest worker proposal and on border security under a guest worker program.

S. 1645/H.R. 3142 and S. 2823

The Agricultural Job Opportunity, Benefits, and Security Act of 2003 (AgJOBS; S. 1645/H.R. 3142) would have overhauled the H-2A agricultural worker program. It was introduced, respectively, by Senator Craig for himself and a bipartisan group of cosponsors and by Representative Cannon for himself and Representative Berman. Like the major H-2A reform bills before the 107th Congress, S. 1645/H.R. 3142 would have streamlined the process of importing H-2A workers, particularly for jobs covered by collective bargaining agreements. Under S. 1645/H.R. 3142, prospective H-2A employers would have had to file applications with DOL containing certain assurances. In the case of a job covered by a collective bargaining agreement, the employer would have had to assure, among other things, that there was an applicable union contract and that the bargaining representatives of the employer's employees had been notified of the filing of the application for H-2A workers. An employer interested in filling a job not covered by a collective bargaining agreement would have been subject to a longer list of required assurances. Among these, the employer would have had to assure that he or she would take specified steps to recruit U.S. workers and would provide workers with required benefits, wages, and working conditions. Both groups of employers would have had to assure that the job was temporary or seasonal and that the employer would offer the job to any equally qualified, available U.S. worker who applied. Unless an employer's application was incomplete or obviously inaccurate, DOL would have certified within seven days of the filing date that the employer had filed the required application.

S. 1645/H.R. 3142 further proposed to make changes to the H-2A program's requirements regarding minimum benefits, wages, and working conditions. Among these proposed changes, the adverse effect wage rate (discussed above) would have remained at the January 2003 level for three years after the date of enactment, and employers would have been permitted to provide housing allowances, in lieu of housing, to their workers if the governor of the relevant state certified that adequate housing was available.

Under S. 1645/H.R. 3142, an H-2A worker's initial period of employment could not have exceeded 10 months. The worker's stay could have been extended in increments of up to 10 months each, but the worker's total continuous period of stay, including any extensions, could not have exceeded three years.

In addition to these H-2A reform provisions, S. 1645/H.R. 3142 would have established a two-stage legalization program for agricultural workers. To obtain temporary resident status, the alien worker would have had to establish that he or she performed at least 575 hours, or 100 work days, of agricultural employment in the United States during 12 consecutive months in the 18-month period ending on August 31, 2003, and meet other requirements. To be eligible to adjust to LPR status, the alien would have had to perform at least 2,060 hours, or 360 work days, of agricultural work in the United States between September 1, 2003, and August 31, 2009, and meet other requirements. Existing numerical limits under the INA would not have applied to adjustments of status under the bill.[29]

On September 21, 2004, Senator Craig introduced a modified version of S. 1645 for himself and Senator Kennedy. The revised bill, S. 2823, was very similar to S. 1645, but there were substantive differences in the two bills' legalization provisions. Among these differences, S. 2823 contained a new provision stating that aliens acquiring temporary resident status under the bill would not be eligible for certain federal public benefits until five years after they obtained permanent resident status.[30]

H.R. 3604

Like S. 1645/H.R. 3142, the Temporary Agricultural Labor Reform Act of 2003 (H.R. 3604) proposed to overhaul the H-2A agricultural worker program. It was introduced by Representative Goodlatte for himself and more than 30 co-sponsors. H.R. 3604 would have streamlined the process of importing H-2A workers. Prospective H-2A employers would have had to file applications with DOL containing certain assurances, including that the job was temporary or seasonal; the employer would provide workers with required benefits, wages, and working conditions; the employer had made positive efforts to recruit U.S. workers; and the employer would offer the job to any equally qualified, available U.S. worker who applied. Unless an employer's application was incomplete or obviously inaccurate, DOL would have certified within seven days of the filing date that the employer had filed the required application.

H.R. 3604 would have made changes to current H-2A requirements regarding minimum benefits, wages, and working conditions. Under H.R. 3604, H-2A employers would have had to pay workers the higher of the prevailing wage rate or the applicable state minimum wage; they would not have been subject to the adverse effect wage rate (discussed above). With respect to housing, employers could have provided housing allowances, in lieu of housing, to

---

29 For a discussion of the U.S. system of permanent admissions, including numerical limits, see CRS Report RL32235, U.S. Immigration Policy on Permanent Admissions, by Ruth Ellen Wasem. (Hereafter cited as CRS Report RL32235).

30 For information on noncitizen eligibility for federal public benefits, see CRS Report RL31114.

their workers if the governor of the relevant state certified that adequate housing was available.

Under H.R. 3604, an H-2A worker's initial period of employment could not have exceeded 10 months. The worker's stay could have been extended in increments of up to 10 months each, but the worker's total continuous period of stay, including any extensions, could not have exceeded two years. H.R. 3604 would not have established a mechanism for agricultural workers to obtain LPR status.

S. 2185

Another H-2A reform bill, introduced by Senator Chambliss, was the Temporary Agricultural Work Reform Act of 2004 (S. 2185). It was similar, but not identical, to H.R. 3604. S. 2185 would have streamlined the process of importing H-2A workers. Prospective H-2A employers would have had to file applications with DOL containing certain assurances, including that the job was temporary or seasonal; the employer would provide workers with required benefits, wages, and working conditions; the employer had attempted to recruit U.S. workers using the state workforce agency; and the employer would offer the job to any equally qualified, available U.S. worker who applied. Unless an employer's application was incomplete or obviously inaccurate, DOL would have certified within 15 days of the filing date that the employer had filed the required application.

S. 2185 proposed to change current H-2A requirements concerning minimum benefits, wages, and working conditions. Under S. 2185, H-2A employers would have had to pay workers the higher of the prevailing wage rate or the applicable state minimum wage. In lieu of offering housing, they could have provided housing allowances if the governor of the relevant state certified that adequate housing was available.

S. 2185 did not contain provisions regarding the period of admission, extension of stay, or maximum period of stay of H-2A workers. It also would not have established a mechanism for agricultural workers to obtain LPR status.

S. 2010

The Immigration Reform Act of 2004: Strengthening America's National Security, Economy, and Families (S. 2010), introduced by Senator Hagel for himself and Senator Daschle, would have reformed the H-2B nonimmigrant visa. The bill would have eliminated the current restriction that H-2B workers can perform only temporary service or labor, and instead would have required that they perform "short-term service or labor, lasting not more than 9 months." S. 2010 also proposed a new H-2C visa for temporary workers coming to perform "labor or services, other than those occupation classifications" covered under the H-2A, H-2B, or specified high-skilled visa categories, if qualified U.S. workers could not be found.

Both the H-2B and H-2C categories would have been numerically limited. In each of the five fiscal years following issuance of final implementing regulations, the H-2B program would have been capped at 100,000. The cap would have then reverted back to the current 66,000 level. The H-2C program would have been capped at 250,000 in each of the five fiscal years following issuance of final implementing regulations. After these five years, the H-2C program would have terminated.

S. 2010 would have subjected both the H-2B and H-2C programs to a broad set of requirements covering recruitment, application procedures, and worker protections, among other issues. Prior to filing an application with DOL for H-2B or H-2C workers, prospective employers would have had to take specified steps to recruit U.S. workers, including posting the job on DOL's online "America's Job Bank" and with local job banks, and would have had to offer the job to any qualified, available U.S. worker who applied. In the application to DOL, the employer would have had to attest to various items, including that he or she was offering wages to H-2B or H-2C workers that were the greater of the prevailing wage rate or the actual wage paid by the employer to other similarly employed and qualified workers, and that he or she would abide by all applicable laws and regulations relating to the rights of workers to organize. DOL would have reviewed the application and required documentation for completeness and accuracy, and issued a determination not later than 21 days after the filing date.

The initial period of admission for an H-2B worker could not have exceeded nine months in a one-year period. An H-2B worker's total period of admission could not have exceeded 36 months in a four-year period. The initial period of admission for an H-2C worker could not have exceeded two years and could have been extended for an additional period of up to two years. An H-2C worker's total period of admission could not have exceeded four years.

S. 2010 would have enabled H-2B and H-2C nonimmigrants to obtain LPR status. Employment-based *immigrant* visas would have been made available to these nonimmigrants without regard to existing numerical limits under the INA. An employment-based petition could have been filed by an employer or any collective bargaining agent of the alien, or after the alien had been employed in H-2B or H-2C status for at least three years, by the alien. In addition, S. 2010 would have established a legalization program for certain unauthorized aliens in the United States.

S. 2381/H.R. 4262

The Safe, Orderly, Legal Visas and Enforcement Act of 2004 (S. 2381/H.R. 4262) was introduced, respectively, by Senator Kennedy for himself and Senators Feingold and Clinton and by Representative Gutierrez for himself and a group of cosponsors. Known as the "S.O.L.V.E. Act," the measure would have reformed the H-2B nonimmigrant visa. It would have eliminated the current restriction that H-2B workers can perform only temporary service or labor, and instead would have required that they perform "short-term service or labor, lasting not more than 9 months." S. 2381/H.R. 4262 also proposed a new H-ID visa for temporary workers coming to perform "labor or services, other than those occupation classifications" covered under the H-2A or specified high-skilled visa categories, if qualified U.S. workers could not be found.

Both the H-2B and H-1D categories would have been numerically limited. The H-2B program would have been capped at 100,000 annually, an increase from the current annual limit of 66,000. The H-1D program would have been capped at 250,000 annually.

S. 2381/H.R. 4262 would have subjected both the H-2B and H-1D programs to a broad set of requirements covering recruitment, application procedures, and worker protections, among other issues. Prior to filing an application with DOL for H-2B or H-1D workers, prospective employers would have had to take specified steps to recruit U.S. workers, including posting the job on DOL's America's Job Bank and with local job banks, and would have had to offer the job to any qualified, available U.S. worker who applied. In the application to DOL, the employer would have had to attest to various items. Among these were that the employer was offering to H-2B or H-1D workers the prevailing wage, to be determined as specified in the bill. The employer also would have had to abide by all applicable laws and regulations relating to the rights of workers to organize. DOL would have reviewed the application and required documentation for completeness and accuracy, and issued a determination not later than 10 working days after the filing date.

The initial period of admission for an H-2B worker could not have exceeded nine months in a one-year period. An H-2B worker's total period of admission could not have exceeded 40 months in the aggregate. The initial period of admission for an H-1D worker could not have exceeded two years and could have been extended for two additional periods of up to two years each. An H-1D worker's total period of admission could not have exceeded six years.

S. 2381/H.R. 4262 would have enabled H-2B and H-1D nonimmigrants to obtain LPR status. Employment-based *immigrant* visas would have been made available to these nonimmigrants without numerical limitation. An employment-based petition could have been filed by an employer, or after the alien had been employed in H-2B or H-1D status for at least two years, by the alien. In addition, S. 2381/H.R. 4262 would have established a legalization program for certain unauthorized aliens in the United States.

H.R. 3534

The Border Enforcement and Revolving Employment to Assist Laborers Act of 2003 (H.R. 3534), introduced by Representative Tancredo for himself and several cosponsors, proposed to amend the INA's "H" visa category generally. It would have eliminated the current subcategories, including the H-2A and H-2B visas, and replaced them with a single category covering aliens coming temporarily to the United States to perform skilled or unskilled work if qualified U.S. workers were not available.

An employer interested in importing "H" workers would have filed an application with DOL. Prior to doing so, the employer would have been required to post a job announcement on an Internet-based job bank that the bill would have directed DOL to create. Among other requirements of the program, the employer would have had to offer wages at least equal to the prevailing wage rate and would have had to provide "H" workers with health insurance.

H non-immigrants could only have been admitted from abroad. They would have applied to be added to a database of workers and would have had to remain in their home countries until an approved employer wanted to hire them. Their period of authorized admission could not have exceeded 365 days in a two-year period. After the two-year period, H nonimmigrant visas could have been renewed. H non-immigrants would not have been permitted to change or adjust to any other nonimmigrant or immigrant status.

Under H.R. 3534, however, the proposed guest worker program would not have been implemented until the Secretary of Homeland Security, in consultation with the Attorney General and the Secretary of State, had made certain certifications to Congress. The Secretary of Homeland Security would have had to certify, among other items, that all noncitizens legally in the United States and all aliens authorized to enter the country had been issued biometric, machine-readable travel or entry documents, and that the number of aliens who overstayed nonimmigrant visas, but were not removed from the United States, was less than 5,000.

S. 1387

The Border Security and Immigration Reform Act of 2003 (S. 1387), introduced by Senator Cornyn, would have authorized new temporary worker programs under the INA for seasonal and non-seasonal workers. S. 1387 would have established a new "W" nonimmigrant visa category for these workers, which would not have been subject to numerical limits. The W-1 visa would have covered seasonal workers, and the W-2 visa would have covered non-seasonal workers. Under the proposal, the Secretary of Homeland Security and the Secretary of State would have jointly established and administered guest worker programs with foreign countries that entered into agreements with the United States. The bill would have directed the Secretary of Homeland Security, in cooperation with the Secretary of State and the participating foreign governments, to establish a database to monitor guest workers' entry into and exit from the United States and to track employer compliance.

In order to import workers through the new programs, employers would have had to file an application with DOL. As part of the application, the employer would have had to request an attestation from DOL that there were not sufficient U.S. workers who were qualified and available to perform the work, and that the hiring of alien workers would not adversely affect the wages and working conditions of similarly employed U.S. workers. The employer also would have needed to provide various assurances in the application, including that the employer would offer the job to any equally qualified, available U.S. worker who applied; would advertise the job opening in a local publication; and would pay workers at least the higher of the federal or applicable state minimum wage. Unless an employer's application was incomplete or obviously inaccurate, DOL would have certified within 14 days of the filing date that the application had been filed. Beginning 12 months after enactment, employers would have been subject to increased penalties for knowingly employing unauthorized aliens.

The authorized period of stay for a W-1 seasonal worker could not have exceeded 270 days per year. Such a worker could have reapplied for admission to the United States each year. The initial authorized period of stay for a W-2 non-seasonal worker could not have exceeded one year, but could have been extended in increments of up to one year each; a W-2 worker's total period of stay could not have exceeded three consecutive years. Unauthorized workers in the United States would have had 12 months from enactment to apply for the program.

Among the other provisions, the bill would have created investment accounts for the guest workers, into which the Social Security taxes paid by them and by their employers on their behalf would have been deposited. The investment accounts would have been the sole property of the guest workers. In most cases, however, distributions of account funds could have been made only after the workers had permanently left the guest worker program and returned to their home countries.

Under S. 1387, guest workers could have applied for U.S. legal permanent residency only after they had returned to their home countries. Their applications would have been evaluated based on a point system to be established by the Secretary of Homeland Security. The bill did not propose a legalization mechanism for guest workers outside of existing channels, and according to Senator Cornyn's office, guest workers would have had to meet all the relevant requirements under current law.[31]

S. 1461/H.R. 2899

The Border Security and Immigration Improvement Act (S. 1461/H.R. 2899), introduced, respectively, by Senator McCain and by Representative Kolbe for himself and Representative Flake, would have established two new temporary worker visas under the INA — the H-4A and H-4B visas. S. 1461/H.R. 2899 would have placed no numerical limit on the H-4A or H-4B visas.

The H-4A visa would have covered aliens coming to the United States to perform temporary full-time employment. An employer interested in importing H-4A workers would have had to file a petition with DHS. DHS could only have approved the petition once it determined that the employer had satisfied recruitment requirements, including advertising the job opportunity to U.S. workers on an electronic job registry established by DOL and offering the job to any equally qualified U.S. worker who applied through the registry. The employer also would have had to attest in the petition that he or she: would use the employment eligibility confirmation system established by the bill to verify the alien workers' identity and employment authorization; would provide the alien workers with the same benefits, wages, and working conditions as other similarly employed workers; and did not and would not displace U.S. workers during a specified 180-day period. Aliens granted H-4A status would have been issued machine-readable, tamper-resistant visas and other documents containing biometric identifiers.

An H-4A worker's initial authorized period of stay would have been three years, and could have been extended for an additional three years. S. 1461/H.R. 2899 also would have enabled H-4A non-immigrants to adjust to LPR status. Petitions for employment-based *immigrant* visas could have been filed by an H-4A worker's employer, or by the H-4A worker, if he or she had maintained H-4A status for at least three years. Employment-based *immigrant* visas would have been made available to H-4A workers adjusting status without numerical limitation.

The H-4B visa established by the bill would have covered aliens unlawfully present and employed in the United States since before August 1, 2003. An H-4B alien's authorized period of stay would have been three years. The alien could have applied to change to H-4A status or another nonimmigrant or immigrant category, but such a change of status could not have taken place until the end of the three years. H-4B employers would have been required to use the employment eligibility confirmation system mentioned above and to comply with specified requirements applicable to H-4A employers, including providing benefits, wages,

---

31 This description of S. 1387 is based on both the bill text and clarifications provided by Sen. Cornyn's office by telephone on July 22, 2003. Some clarifying language may need to be added to the bill.

and working conditions to H-4B workers equal to those provided to other similarly employed workers.

H.R. 3651

The Alien Accountability Act (H.R. 3651), introduced by Representative Issa, would have authorized a new "W" nonimmigrant visa category under the INA for unauthorized aliens. The category would have covered aliens unlawfully present in the United States on December 8, 2003, as well as aliens residing in foreign contiguous territory who had been habitually unlawfully present in the United States during the six-month period ending on December 8, 2003. In order to be eligible for W status, the alien would first have had to register with DHS. Employment would not have been a strict requirement for W status, but the alien would have had to demonstrate an adequate means of financial support. The new category would have sunset six years after the first alien was granted W status.

The initial period of authorized admission of a W nonimmigrant would have been one year and could have been renewed up to five times in one-year increments. H.R. 3651 would not have established a special mechanism for W nonimmigrants to adjust to LPR status. It, however, would not have precluded them from doing so if they satisfied the applicable requirements under current law.

LEGISLATION IN THE 109TH CONGRESS

As in the 108th Congress, bills were introduced in the 109th Congress to reform the H-2A and H-2B programs, to reform the "H" visa category, and to establish new temporary worker visas. An amendment based on one of the H-2B bills (S. 352/H.R. 793) was enacted as part of the FY2005 Emergency Supplemental Appropriations Act for Defense, the Global War on Terror, and Tsunami Relief (P.L. 109-13). Subsequently, the John Warner National Defense Authorization Act for FY2007 (P.L. 109-364) extended one of the temporary H-2B provisions in P.L. 109-13.

As discussed below, the Comprehensive Immigration Reform Act of 2006 (S. 2611), as passed by the Senate, would have reformed the H-2A program and established a new guest worker program for nonagricultural workers. During consideration of the Border Protection, Antiterrorism, and Illegal Immigration Control Act of 2005 (H.R. 4437) by the House Judiciary Committee and on the House floor, efforts were made to add guest worker programs and language expressing support for a guest worker program, but they were unsuccessful. H.R. 4437, as passed by the House, did not contain any guest worker provisions.

The 109th Congress also held a number of hearings on immigration issues relevant to a guest worker program. The House Judiciary Committee's Subcommittee on Immigration, Border Security, and Claims held hearings on employment eligibility verification and work site enforcement. The Senate Judiciary Committee's Subcommittee on Immigration, Border Security, and Citizenship held hearings on immigration reform issues, including the establishment of a new guest worker program. The full Senate Judiciary Committee held hearings on comprehensive immigration reform, at which two major reform proposals (S. 1033/H.R. 2330 and S. 1438) were discussed.

S. 352/H.R. 793 and Related H-2b Legislation

The Save Our Small and Seasonal Businesses Act (S. 352/H.R. 793),[32] introduced respectively by Senator Mikulski and Representative Gilchrest for themselves and bipartisan groups of cosponsors, proposed to revise the H-2B program. During Senate consideration of the FY2005 Emergency Supplemental Appropriations bill (H.R. 1268) in April 2005, Senator Mikulski offered a floor amendment based on S. 352/H.R. 793. On April 19, 2005, the Senate adopted the Mikulski Amendment, as modified, by a vote of 94 to 6, and the amendment was included in the enacted measure (P.L. 109-13) as Division B, Title IV.

The H-2B title of P.L. 109-13 caps at 33,000 the number of H-2B slots available during the first six months of a fiscal year. It also requires DHS to submit specified information to Congress on the H-2B program on a regular basis, imposes a new fraud-prevention and detection fee on H-2B employers, and authorizes DHS to impose additional penalties on H-2B employers in certain circumstances. In addition, the H-2B title of P.L. 109-13 contains a temporary provision, initially scheduled to expire at the end of FY2006, that keeps aliens who have been counted toward the H-2B cap in any of the past three years from being counted again. The John Warner National Defense Authorization Act for FY2007 (P.L. 109-364; §1074) extends this returning H-2B worker exemption through FY2007. Thus, aliens who have been counted toward the H-2B cap in FY2004, FY2005, or FY2006 are not to be counted toward the FY2007 cap.

S. 2611

In March 2006, the Senate Judiciary Committee considered an immigration measure by Chairman Specter, known as the Chairman's mark. Among its many provisions, this measure, as amended and approved by the Committee, proposed to reform the H-2A program and establish a new guest worker program for nonagricultural workers. The Committee-approved measure evolved into the Comprehensive Immigration Act of 2006 (S. 2611), which the Senate passed, as amended, on May 25, 2006 on a vote of 62 to 36.

Title VI, Subtitle B of S. 2611 contained provisions on agricultural workers. These provisions were similar to those in the Agricultural Job Opportunities, Benefits, and Security Act of 2005 (AgJOBS; S. 359/H.R. 884), discussed below. Like S. 359/H.R. 884, Title VI, Subtitle B of S. 2611 would have streamlined the process of importing H-2A workers, particularly for jobs covered by collective bargaining agreements. Prospective H-2A employers would have had to file applications with DOL containing certain assurances. In the case of a job covered by a collective bargaining agreement, the employer would have had to assure, among other things, that there was an applicable union contract and that the

---

32 Although S. 352 and H.R. 793 are not identical, they are treated as companion bills here because they are nearly identical and none of their differences are substantive. The full short title of S. 352 is Save Our Small and Seasonal Businesses of 2005.

bargaining representatives of the employer's employees had been notified of the filing of the application for H-2A workers. An employer interested in filling a job not covered by a collective bargaining agreement would have been subject to a longer list of required assurances. Among these, the employer would have had to assure that he or she would take specified steps to recruit U.S. workers and would provide workers with required benefits, wages, and working conditions. Both groups of employers would have had to assure that the job was temporary or seasonal and that the employer would offer the job to any equally qualified, available U.S. worker who applied. Unless an employer's application was incomplete or obviously inaccurate, DOL would have certified within seven days of the filing date that the employer had filed the required application.

Title VI, Subtitle B of S. 2611 would have made changes to the H-2A program's requirements regarding minimum benefits, wages, and working conditions. Among these proposed changes, the adverse effect wage rate (discussed above) would have remained at the January 2003 level for three years after the date of enactment, and employers would have been permitted to provide housing allowances, in lieu of housing, to their workers if the governor of the relevant state certified that adequate housing was available. An H-2A worker's initial period of employment could not have exceeded 10 months. The worker's stay could have been extended in increments of up to 10 months each, but the worker's total continuous period of stay, including any extensions, could not have exceeded three years.

Title VI, Subtitle B of S. 2611 also proposed a legalization program for agricultural workers. This program followed the basic design of the legalization program in S. 359/H.R. 884, but included different work and other requirements and used different terminology. Under the program in S. 2611, the Secretary of DHS would have conferred "blue card status" (akin to S. 359/H.R. 884's temporary resident status)[33] on an alien worker who had performed at least 863 hours, or 150 work days, of agricultural employment in the United States during the 24-month period ending on December 31, 2005, and met other requirements. No more than 1.5 million blue cards could have been issued during the five-year period beginning on the date of enactment. To be eligible to adjust to LPR status, the alien in blue card status would have had to, among other requirements, perform either at least 575 hours of U.S. agricultural work per year for the five years after enactment, or at least 863 hours of U.S. agricultural work per year for three of the five years after enactment. Existing numerical limits under the INA would not have applied to adjustments of status under the bill.[34]

Title IV, Subtitle A of S. 2611 proposed to establish a new H-2C nonagricultural guest worker visa, which, as amended on the Senate floor, would have been capped at 325,000 annually. The H-2C visa would have covered aliens coming temporarily to the United States to perform temporary labor or services other than the labor or services covered under the H-2A visa or other specified visa categories. A prospective H-2C employer would have had to file a petition with DHS. In the petition the employer would have had to attest to various items, including that the employer was offering wages to H-2C workers that were the greater of the prevailing wage rate for the occupational classification in the area of employment or the actual wage paid by the employer to other similarly employed and qualified workers; and that there were not sufficient qualified and available U.S. workers to perform the work. Prior

---

33 The blue card status proposed under this bill is different than the blue card status proposed in S. 2087 (discussed below).
34 For information on numerical limits, see CRS Report RL32235.

to filing the petition, the prospective employer also would have been required to make efforts to recruit U.S. workers in accordance with DOL regulations. To be eligible for H-2C status, the alien would have needed to have evidence of employment and meet other requirements.

An H-2C worker's initial authorized period of stay would have been three years, and could have been extended for an additional three years. H-2C aliens could not have changed to another nonimmigrant visa category. As in S. 1438 (discussed below), an H-2C alien who failed to depart the United States when required to do so would have been ineligible for any immigration relief or benefit, except for specified forms of humanitarian relief. At the same time, H-2C non-immigrants in the United States could have applied to adjust to LPR status. Petitions for employment-based *immigrant* visas could have been filed by an H-2C worker's employer or, if the H-2C worker had maintained H-2C status for a total of four years, by the worker.

S. 359/H.R. 884

The Agricultural Job Opportunities, Benefits, and Security Act of 2005 (AgJOBS; S. 359/H.R. 884) proposed to overhaul the H-2A agricultural worker program. The bills were introduced, respectively, by Senator Craig and Representative Cannon for themselves and bipartisan groups of cosponsors. S. 359/H.R. 884 was very similar to the AgJOBs bills before the 108th Congress (S. 1645/H.R. 3142, S. 2823). Like these bills, S. 359/H.R. 884 would have streamlined the process of importing H-2A workers, particularly for jobs covered by collective bargaining agreements. Prospective H-2A employers would have had to file applications with DOL containing certain assurances. In the case of a job covered by a collective bargaining agreement, the employer would have had to assure, among other things, that there was an applicable union contract and that the bargaining representatives of the employer's employees had been notified of the filing of the application for H-2A workers. An employer interested in filling a job not covered by a collective bargaining agreement would have been subject to a longer list of required assurances. Among these, the employer would have had to assure that he or she would take specified steps to recruit U.S. workers and would provide workers with required benefits, wages, and working conditions. Both groups of employers would have had to assure that the job was temporary or seasonal and that the employer would offer the job to any equally qualified, available U.S. worker who applied. Unless an employer's application was incomplete or obviously inaccurate, DOL would have certified within seven days of the filing date that the employer had filed the required application.

S. 359/H.R. 884 would have made changes to the H-2A program's requirements regarding minimum benefits, wages, and working conditions. Among these proposed changes, the adverse effect wage rate (discussed above) would have remained at the January 2003 level for three years after the date of enactment, and employers would have been permitted to provide housing allowances, in lieu of housing, to their workers if the governor of the relevant state certified that adequate housing was available.

Under S. 359/H.R. 884, an H-2A worker would have been admitted for an initial period of employment not to exceed 10 months. The worker's stay could have been extended in increments of up to 10 months each, but the worker's total continuous period of stay, including any extensions, could not have exceeded three years.[35]

In addition to these H-2A reform provisions, S. 359/H.R. 884 would have established a two-stage legalization program for agricultural workers. To obtain temporary resident status, the alien worker would have had to establish that he or she had performed at least 575 hours, or 100 work days, of agricultural employment in the United States during 12 consecutive months in the 18-month period ending on December 31, 2004, and meet other requirements. To be eligible to adjust to LPR status, the alien would have had to perform at least 2,060 hours, or 360 work days, of agricultural work in the United States during the six years following the date of enactment, and meet other requirements. Existing numerical limits under the INA would not have applied to adjustments of status under the bills.[36]

H.R. 3857

The Temporary Agricultural Labor Reform Act of 2005 (H.R. 3857), an H-2A reform bill introduced by Representative Goodlatte on behalf of himself and a group of cosponsors, was a revision of a bill of the same name that he had introduced in the 108th Congress. H.R. 3857 would have streamlined the process of importing H-2A workers. Prospective H-2A employers would have had to file petitions with DHS containing certain attestations; they would not have filed applications with DOL as they currently do. Employers would have had to attest that the job was temporary or seasonal; that they would provide workers with required benefits, wages, and working conditions; that they had made efforts to recruit U.S. workers; and that they would offer the job to any equally qualified, available U.S. worker who applied. Unless an employer's application was incomplete or obviously inaccurate, DHS would have adjudicated the petition within seven days of the filing date.

H.R. 3857 would have changed current H-2A requirements regarding minimum benefits, wages, and working conditions. Under the bill, H-2A employers would have had to pay workers the higher of the prevailing wage rate or the applicable state minimum wage; employers would not have been subject to the adverse effect wage rate (discussed above). With respect to housing, employers could have provided allowances, in lieu of housing, to their workers if the governor of the relevant state certified that adequate housing was available.[37]

Under H.R. 3857, an H-2A worker would have been admitted for an initial period of employment not to exceed 10 months. The worker's stay could have been extended in increments of up to 10 months each, but the worker's total continuous period of stay, including any extensions, could not have exceeded 20 months.

---

35 Separate provisions in S. 359/H.R. 884 would have established a two-stage legalization program for agricultural workers.

36 For information on numerical limits, see CRS Report RL32235.

37 H.R. 3857 would not have established a mechanism for agricultural workers to obtain LPR status.

S. 2087

The Agricultural Employment and Workforce Protection Act of 2005 (S. 2087), introduced by Senator Chambliss, would have reformed the H-2A program. It would have eliminated the current limitation that H-2A nonimmigrants can perform only temporary or seasonal work and would have broadened the definition of agricultural labor or services for purposes of the H-2A visa to cover labor or services relating to such activities as dairy, forestry, landscaping, and meat processing. Like S. 359/H.R. 884 and H.R. 3857, S. 2087 proposed to streamline the process of importing H-2A workers. As under H.R. 3857, a prospective H-2A employer would have filed a petition with DHS containing certain attestations. Among them, the employer would have had to attest that he or she: would provide workers with required benefits, wages, and working conditions; had made efforts to recruit U.S. workers; and would offer the job to any equally qualified, available U.S. worker who applied. Unless the petition was incomplete or obviously inaccurate, DHS would have approved or denied it not later than seven days after the filing date.

Also like S. 359/H.R. 884 and H.R. 3857, S. 2087 would have changed current H-2A requirements regarding minimum benefits, wages, and working conditions. Under S. 2087, H-2A employers would have had to pay workers the higher of the prevailing wage rate or the applicable state minimum wage; employers would not have been subject to the adverse effect wage rate (discussed above). As under both S. 359/H.R. 884 and H.R. 3857, employers could have provided housing allowances, in lieu of housing, to their workers if the governor of the relevant state certified that adequate housing was available. Under S. 2087, an H-2A worker would have been admitted for an initial period of employment of 11 months. The worker's stay could have been extended for up to two consecutive contract periods.

Unlike S. 359/H.R. 884 and H.R. 3857, S. 2087 would have established subcategories of H-2A nonimmigrants. It would have defined a "Level II H-2A worker" as a nonimmigrant who had been employed as an H-2A worker for at least three years and worked in a supervisory capacity. The bill would have made provision for an employer of a Level II H-2A worker, who had been employed in such status for not less than five years, to file an application for an employment-based adjustment of status for that worker. Such a Level II H-2A worker could have continued working in such status until his or her application was adjudicated. Under the bill, an "H-2AA worker" would have been defined as an H-2A worker who participated in the cross-border worker program the bill would have established. These H-2AA workers would have been allowed to enter and exit the United States each work day in accordance with DHS regulations.

In addition, the bill would have established a blue card program through which the Secretary of DHS could have conferred "blue card status" upon an alien, including an unauthorized alien, who had performed at least 1,600 hours of agricultural employment for an employer in the United States in 2005 and met other requirements. An alien could have been granted blue card status for a period of up to two years, at the end of which the alien would have had to return to his or her home country. Aliens in blue card status would not have been eligible to change to a nonimmigrant status or adjust to LPR status.

S. 278

The Summer Operations and Seasonal Equity Act of 2005 (S. 278), introduced by Senator Collins, would have made changes to the numerical limits under the H-2B program. It would have required that at least 12,000 of the total number of H-2B slots available annually (currently, 66,000) be made available in each quarter of each fiscal year. It would have exempted an alien who had been counted toward the annual H-2B numerical limit within the past three years from being counted again. Both of these provisions would have expired at the end of FY2007. S. 278 also would have required DHS to submit specified information to Congress on the H-2B program on a regular basis.

H.R. 1587

H.R. 1587, introduced by Representative Tancredo for himself and several cosponsors, would have raised the H-2B cap and placed new requirements on the H-2B program. It would have increased to 131,000 the number of aliens who could be issued H-2B visas or otherwise provided H-2B status annually. Not more than half of these slots, or 65,500, would have been available during the first six months of a fiscal year. H.R. 1587 would have added new recruitment-related requirements for prospective H-2B employers, and would have mandated H-2B employer participation in the Basic Pilot program, an electronic employment eligibility verification system. H.R. 1587 also would have imposed new requirements on H-2B nonimmigrants. Among them, these aliens could no longer have been accompanied by family members.

S. 1918

The Strengthening America's Workforce Act of 2005 (S. 1918), introduced by Senator Hagel, contained guest worker provisions similar to those in the bill he introduced in the 108th Congress. S. 1918 would have revised the H-2B visa and eliminated the current restriction that H-2B workers can perform only temporary service or labor. Instead, the bill would have required workers to perform "short-term service or labor, lasting not more than nine months." S. 1918 also would have established a new H-2C visa for temporary workers coming to perform "labor or services, other than those occupation classifications" covered under the H-2A, H-2B, or specified high-skilled visa categories. The H-2B visa would have been capped at 100,000 annually, and the H-2C visa would have been capped at 250,000 annually.

S. 1918 would have subjected the H-2B and H-2C programs to a broad set of requirements concerning recruitment, application procedures, and worker protections, among other issues. Prior to filing an application with DOL for H-2B or H-2C workers, prospective employers would have had to take specified steps to recruit U.S. workers, including authorizing DOL to post the job on the online America's Job Bank and on local job banks. Employers also would have had to offer the job to any qualified, available U.S. worker who applied. In the application to DOL, the employer would have had to attest to various items. Among these were that the employer would offer wages to H-2B or H-2C workers that were the greater of the prevailing wage rate or the actual wage paid by the employer to other similarly employed and qualified workers, and that the employer would abide by all applicable laws and regulations relating to the rights of workers to organize. DOL would have reviewed the application for completeness and accuracy and issued a determination not later than 21 days after the filing date.

The initial period of admission for an H-2B worker could not have exceeded nine months in a one-year period. An H-2B worker's total period of admission could not have exceeded 36 months in a four-year period. The initial period of admission for an H-2C worker could not have exceeded two years and could have been extended for an additional period of up to two years. An H-2C worker's total period of admission could not have exceeded four years.

S. 1918 would have enabled H-2B and H-2C nonimmigrants to obtain LPR status. Employment-based *immigrant* visas would have been made available to these nonimmigrants without regard to existing numerical limits under the INA. An employment-based petition could have been filed by an alien's employer or collective bargaining agent or, after the alien had been employed in H-2B or H-2C status for at least three years, by the alien.

H.R. 3333

The Rewarding Employers that Abide by the Law and Guaranteeing Uniform Enforcement to Stop Terrorism Act of 2005 (H.R. 3333), introduced by Representative Tancredo, contained temporary worker provisions similar to those in the bill he had introduced in the 108th Congress. H.R. 3333 would have eliminated all the current "H" visa subcategories, including the H-2A and H-2B visas, and replaced them with a single "H" visa covering aliens coming temporarily to the United States to perform skilled or unskilled work. There would have been no cap on the H visa.

An employer interested in employing H nonimmigrants would have had to recruit U.S. workers by posting the job opportunity on America's Job Bank and would have had to offer the job to any equally qualified U.S. worker who applied. The employer would have had to file an application with DOL containing certain assurances, including that he or she had complied with the recruitment requirements.

Prospective H nonimmigrants, who could only have been admitted from abroad, would have had to apply to be included in a database of workers, which DOL would have been tasked with establishing and maintaining. Once an employer's application had been approved, DOL would have provided the employer with a list of possible job candidates from the database. Aliens admitted on H visas could not have changed to another nonimmigrant status or been adjusted to LPR status in the United States.

Under H.R. 3333, the new H visa program could not have been implemented until the Secretary of Homeland Security made certain certifications to Congress, including that a congressionally mandated automated entry-exit system was fully operational[38] and that at least 80% of aliens who overstayed their nonimmigrants visas were removed within one year of overstaying.

---

38 For information on the entry-exit system issue, see CRS Report RL32234, *U.S. Visitor and Immigrant Status Indicator Technology (US-VISIT) Program*, by Lisa M. Seghetti and Stephen R. Viña.

S. 1033/H.R. 2330

The Secure America and Orderly Immigration Act (S. 1033/H.R. 2330) was introduced, respectively, by Senator McCain and Representative Kolbe for themselves and bipartisan groups of cosponsors. It was discussed at the Senate Judiciary Committee hearings on comprehensive immigration reform held in July 2005 and October 2005. Its guest worker and legalization provisions were similar in some respects to provisions in bills from the 108th Congress, including S. 1461/H.R. 2899, S. 2010, and S. 2381/H.R. 4262. S. 1033/H.R. 2330 would have established two new temporary worker visas under the INA — the H-5A and H-5B visas. It would have capped the H-5A visa initially at 400,000, and established a process for adjusting the cap in subsequent fiscal years based on demand for the visas. It would have placed no cap on the H-5B visa.

The H-5A visa would have covered aliens coming temporarily to the United States *initially* to perform labor or services "other than those occupational classifications" covered under the H-2A or specified high-skilled visa categories. Prospective H-5A nonimmigrants would have filed visa applications on their own behalf. Employers would not have filed petitions with DHS for them, as they currently do to employ other nonimmigrant workers. Under S. 1033/H.R. 2330, the Secretary of State could have granted an H-5A visa to an alien who demonstrated an intent to perform work covered by the visa. To be eligible for H-5A status, an alien would have needed to have evidence of employment and to meet other requirements.

Before hiring a prospective H-5A worker, an employer would have had to post the job opportunity on a DOL electronic job registry to recruit U.S. workers. H-5A employers also would have been required to comply with all applicable federal, state, and local laws, and to use an employment eligibility confirmation system, to be established by the Social Security Administration, to verify the employment eligibility of newly hired H-5A workers.

An H-5A worker's initial authorized period of stay would have been three years, and could have been extended for an additional three years. Under S. 1033/H.R. 2330, H-5A nonimmigrants in the United States could have adjusted to LPR status. Petitions for employment-based *immigrant* visas could have been filed by an H-5A worker's employer or, if the H-5A worker had maintained H-5A status for a total of four years, by the worker.

The H-5B visa established by the bill would have covered aliens present and employed in the United States since before May 12, 2005. Aliens lawfully present in the United States as nonimmigrants on that date would not have been eligible for H-5B status. An H-5B alien's authorized period of stay would have been six years. At the end of that six-year period, the alien could have applied to adjust to LPR status, subject to various requirements. Such adjustments of status would not have been subject to numerical limitations.

S. 1438

The Comprehensive Enforcement and Immigration Reform Act of 2005 (S. 1438) was introduced by Senator Cornyn for himself and Senator Kyl. Like S. 1033/H.R. 2330, it was discussed at the Senate Judiciary Committee hearings on comprehensive immigration reform held in July 2005 and October 2005. It would have established a new "W" temporary worker visa under the INA. S. 1438 would not have placed a cap on the W visa, but would have authorized DOL to do so in the future based on the recommendations of a task force the bill would have established. In addition, S. 1438 would have amended the INA to authorize DHS to grant a new status — Deferred Mandatory Departure (DMD) status — to certain unauthorized aliens in the United States. It would have placed no limit on the number of aliens who could have received that status.

The W visa would have covered aliens coming temporarily to the United States to perform temporary labor or service other than that covered under the H-2A or specified high-skilled visa categories. S. 1438 would have repealed the H-2B visa category. Prospective W nonimmigrants would have filed applications on their own behalf. Employers would not have filed petitions with DHS on behalf of W workers, as they currently do to employ other nonimmigrant workers. Under S. 1438, the Secretary of State could have granted a W visa to an alien who demonstrated an intent to perform eligible work. To be eligible for W status, the alien would have needed to have evidence of employment, among other requirements. An employer interested in hiring a W nonimmigrant would have had to apply for authorization to do so through an Alien Employment Management System to be established by DHS. Before an employer could have been granted such authorization, he or she would have had to post the position on a DOL electronic job registry and offer the position to any equally qualified U.S. worker who applied. S. 1438 would have made it mandatory for all employers, including W employers, to verify the employment eligibility of new hires through an electronic system. Current electronic employment eligibility verification is conducted through the largely voluntary Basic Pilot program.

A W nonimmigrant's authorized period of stay would have been two years, and could *not* have been extended. After residing in his or her home country for one year, however, an alien could have been readmitted to the United States in W status. An alien's total period of admission as a W nonimmigrant could not have exceeded six years. These stay limitations would not have applied to aliens who spent less than six months a year in W status, or who commuted to the United States to work in W status but resided outside the country. S. 1438 would have made W nonimmigrants ineligible to change to another nonimmigrant status and would not have provided them with any special mechanism to obtain LPR status. Furthermore, a W nonimmigrant who did not depart the United States when required to do so would have been ineligible for any immigration benefit or relief, except for specified forms of humanitarian relief.

Aliens present in the United States since July 20, 2004, and employed since before July 20, 2005, could have applied to DHS for Deferred Mandatory Departure (DMD) status. Aliens lawfully present in the United States as nonimmigrants would not have been eligible. DHS could have granted an alien DMD status for a period of up to five years. Employers interested in employing aliens granted DMD status would have had to apply for authorization through the Alien Employment Management System mentioned above. Aliens in DMD status could not have applied to change to a nonimmigrant status or, unless otherwise eligible under INA §245(i), to adjust to LPR status.[39] Aliens who complied with the terms of DMD status and departed prior to its expiration date would not have been subject to the INA provision that bars previously unlawfully present aliens from being admitted to the United States for 3 or 10

---

39 For an explanation of INA §245(i), see CRS Report RL31373, Immigration: Adjustment to Permanent Resident Status Under Section 245(i), by Andorra Bruno.

years, depending on the length of their unlawful stay.[40] If otherwise eligible, these aliens could immediately have sought admission as nonimmigrants or immigrants. However, they would not have received any special consideration for admission. Aliens granted DMD status who failed to depart prior to the expiration of that status would have been ineligible for any immigration benefit or relief, except for specified forms of humanitarian relief, for 10 years.

H.R. 4065

The Temporary Worker Registration and Visa Act of 2005 (H.R. 4065), introduced by Representative Osborne, would have established a process for registering aliens who had been continuously unlawfully present and employed in the United States since January 1, 2005. Eligible aliens would have applied for this registration, which would have been valid for six months. Registered aliens would have been given work authorization and would have been eligible for a new "W" temporary worker visa established by the bill. To obtain a W visa, a registered alien would have had to apply at a consular office in his or her home country not later than six months after his or her registration was approved. H.R. 4065 would have placed no numerical limit on the W visa.

The initial period of authorized admission for a W nonimmigrant would have been three years and could have been extended in three year increments without limit. H.R. 4065 would have required that W nonimmigrants be continuously employed but would have placed no restriction on the type of work they could perform. W nonimmigrants would not have been prohibited from changing to another nonimmigrant classification or adjusting to LPR status. H.R. 4065, however, would have made no special provision for them to do so.

BUSH ADMINISTRATION PROPOSAL

On January 7, 2004, President Bush outlined an immigration reform proposal, at the center of which was a new temporary worker program.[41] The President featured this proposal in his 2004, 2005, and 2006 State of the Union addresses. According to a 2004 White House fact sheet on the proposal, the temporary worker program would "match willing foreign workers with willing U.S. employers when no Americans can be found to fill the jobs." The program, which would grant participants legal temporary status, would initially be open to both foreign workers abroad and unauthorized aliens within the United States. At some future date, however, it would be restricted to aliens outside the country. The temporary workers' authorized period of stay would be three years and would be renewable for an unspecified period of time. Temporary workers would be able to travel back and forth between their home

---

40 INA §212(a)(9)(B). This ground of inadmissibility, known as the "3 and 10 year bars," applies to aliens who have been unlawfully present in the United States for more than 180 days and who then depart or are removed.

41 The Administration did not offer a detailed legislative proposal. Some materials on the Administration proposal, however, are available on the White House website. The President's Jan. 7, 2004, remarks on the proposal are available at [http://www.whitehouse.gov/news/releases/2004/01/print/20040107-3.html]. A fact sheet on the proposal, entitled Fair and Secure Immigration Reform is available at [http://www. whitehouse. gov/news/releases/2004/01/print/20040107-3.html].The transc ript of a Jan. 6, 2004 background briefing for reporters is available at [http:// www.whitehouse.gov/news/releases/2004/01/print/20040106-3.html].

countries and the United States, and, as stated in the background briefing for reporters, would "enjoy the same protections that American workers have with respect to wages and employment rights." The proposal also called for increased workplace enforcement of immigration laws.

The proposal would not establish a special mechanism for participants in the temporary worker program to obtain LPR status. According to the fact sheet, the program "should not permit undocumented workers to gain an advantage over those who have followed the rules." Temporary workers would be expected to return to their home countries at the end of their authorized period of stay, and the Administration favored providing them with economic incentives to do so. As stated in the fact sheet:

> The U.S. will work with other countries to allow aliens working in the U.S. to receive credit in their nations' retirement systems and will support the creation of tax-preferred savings accounts they can collect when they return to their native countries.

Although it does not include a permanent legalization mechanism, the program would not prohibit temporary workers from applying for legal permanent residency under existing immigration law.

According to the Administration, the proposed temporary worker program should support efforts to improve homeland security by controlling the U.S. borders. The fact sheet states that "the program should link to efforts to control our border through agreements with countries whose nationals participate in the program," but does not elaborate further on this issue.

At the October 2005 Senate Judiciary Committee hearing on comprehensive immigration reform, Labor Secretary Elaine Chao reiterated the Administration's support for the immigration reform ideas that President Bush outlined in January 2004.[42] She did not offer a detailed legislative proposal and did not take a position on any of the pending immigration reform bills. Secretary Chao described the Administration's plan as having three components — border security, interior enforcement, and a temporary worker program — and not allowing "amnesty." She maintained that "an improved temporary worker program will enhance border security and interior enforcement by providing a workable and enforceable process for hiring foreign workers."

Both in her written testimony and in responses to Senators' questions, Secretary Chao made some general statements about the type of temporary worker program the Administration favors. She made reference to "streamlining the process so that willing workers can efficiently be matched with employers ... [when] there are no willing U.S. workers." Although she did not describe this streamlined process, she did state that private for-profit or nonprofit organizations could play a role in matching employers and workers. She also explained that under the President's temporary worker program, prospective employers would be subject to labor certification, as they currently are under the H-2A and H-2B programs. In describing how the President's program would overcome problems in existing guest worker programs, Secretary Chao referred generally to "a technologically advanced new system" through which "workers will have visa documentation that clearly establishes their eligibility to work" and "employers will have access to a verification system

---

42 Secretary Chao's written testimony is available at [http://judiciary.senate.gov/hearing .cfm?id=1634].

that enables them to quickly check the eligibility and verify the identity of potential employees."

On May 15, 2006, during Senate consideration of immigration reform legislation,[43] President Bush gave a national address on immigration reform. He voiced support for comprehensive immigration reform that accomplished five objectives, including creation of a temporary worker program. The President maintained that a temporary worker program was needed to secure U.S. borders, another of his five objectives. The President outlined the type of program he favors, as follows:

> I support a temporary worker program that would create a legal path for foreign workers to enter our country in an orderly way, for a limited period of time. This program would match willing foreign workers with willing American employers for jobs Americans are not doing. Every worker who applies for the program would be required to pass criminal background checks. And temporary workers must return to their home country at the conclusion of their stay.

POLICY CONSIDERATIONS

Issues raised in connection with temporary worker programs — such as U.S. economic development, Mexican economic development, law enforcement, and worker protections — coupled with the U.S. experience with the H-2A and H-2B programs, suggest policy issues likely to arise in the evaluation of guest worker proposals.

COMPARISON OF PROGRAM REQUIREMENTS

A new guest worker program could include agricultural workers or nonagricultural workers or both. It could replace or supplement one or both of the existing H-2A and H-2B programs. The assessment of any proposed program would likely include a comparison of the requirements of the proposed and existing programs, especially in the case of a new program covering both agricultural and nonagricultural workers since current H-2A and H-2B requirements vary considerably.

The area of wages provides an example. Under the H-2B program, employers must pay their workers at least the prevailing wage rate. Employers importing agricultural workers through the H-2A program are subject to potentially higher wage requirements. As explained above, they must pay their workers the highest of the minimum wage, the prevailing wage rate, or the AEWR. Therefore, a new guest worker program that covered both agricultural and nonagricultural workers and included a unified wage requirement would represent a change in existing wage requirements for employers.

---

43 See above discussion of S. 2611 in the 109th Congress.

ELIGIBLE POPULATION

A guest worker program could be limited to aliens within the country (many of whom presumably would be unauthorized aliens) or to aliens outside the country or could include both groups. The possible participation of illegal aliens in a guest worker program is controversial. Some parties would likely see their inclusion as rewarding lawbreakers and encouraging future unauthorized immigration, especially if the program enabled some participants to obtain LPR status. The option of excluding unauthorized aliens has raised another set of concerns. Some observers maintain that a large guest worker program limited to new workers could leave unauthorized aliens in the United States particularly vulnerable to exploitation by unscrupulous employers. More generally, many who view a guest worker program as a means of addressing the unauthorized alien problem see the inclusion of unauthorized aliens as integral to any proposal.

Another eligibility question is whether the program would be limited to nationals of certain countries. The Bush Administration began discussion of a guest worker program with Mexico in 2001 as part of binational migration talks, and some immigration experts maintain that "there are very good reasons for crafting a special immigration relationship with Mexico, given its propinquity, its historical ties and NAFTA."[44] Some immigrant advocacy groups, however, have argued that it would be unfair to single out Mexicans for special treatment, especially if legalization were part of the agreement.[45]

LEGALIZATION OF PROGRAM PARTICIPANTS

The issue of whether to include a legalization or *earned adjustment* program as part of a guest worker proposal is controversial. *Earned adjustment* is the term used to describe legalization programs that require prospective beneficiaries to "earn" LPR status through work and/or other contributions. Some see permanent legalization as an essential element of a guest worker proposal,[46] while others oppose the inclusion of any type of LPR adjustment program. In the current debate, reference is often made to two legalization programs established by the Immigration Reform and Control Act (IRCA) of 1986: (1) a general program for unauthorized aliens who had been continually resident in the United States since before January 1, 1982; and (2) a special agricultural worker (SAW) program for aliens who

---

44 Comment of T. Alexander Aleinikoff, Migration Policy Institute. Quoted in Eric Schmitt, "The Nation: Separate and Unequal; You Can Come In. You Stay Out," New York Times, July 29, 2001, Section 4, p. 5.

45 President Bush was asked in July 2001 whether an immigration proposal under consideration at the time to legalize the status of some unauthorized Mexicans would be expanded to cover immigrants from other countries. The President responded, "We'll consider all folks here," but did not provide further details. See Edwin Chen and Jonathan Peterson, "Bush Hints at Broader Amnesty," Los Angeles Times, July 27, 2001, Part A, part 1, p. 1.

46 For example, in an Aug. 2001 letter to President Bush and Mexican President Vicente Fox setting forth the Democrats' immigration principles, then-Senate Majority Leader Thomas Daschle and then-House Minority Leader Richard Gephardt stated that "no migration proposal can be complete without an earned adjustment program."

had worked at least 90 days in seasonal agriculture during a designated year-long period.[47] Approximately 2.7 million individuals have adjusted to LPR status under these programs.[48]

Recent H-2A reform bills suggest a willingness on the part of some policymakers to establish an earned adjustment program, at least for agricultural workers. A key set of questions about any legalization mechanism proposed as part of a guest worker program would concern the proposed legalization process and associated requirements. Major H-2A reform proposals introduced in the 107th Congress (S. 1313/H.R. 2736 and S. 1161), for example, would have established similarly structured earned adjustment programs for agricultural workers. Under both proposals, workers who had performed a requisite amount of agricultural work could have applied for temporary resident status. After satisfying additional work requirements in subsequent years, they could have applied for LPR status. The applicable requirements in the proposals, however, differed significantly. For temporary resident status, S. 1313/H.R. 2736 would have required the alien to have performed at least 540 hours, or 90 work days, of agricultural work during a 12-month period. S. 1161 would have required at least 900 hours, or 150 work days, of agricultural work during a similar period. To qualify for adjustment to LPR status, S. 1313/H.R. 2736 would have required at least 540 hours, or 90 work days, of agricultural work in each of three years during a four-year period. S. 1161 would have required at least 900 hours, or 150 work days, of agricultural work in each of four years during a specified six-year period.

Various issues and concerns raised in connection with such earned adjustment proposals for agricultural workers may be relevant in assessing other guest worker legalization programs. Among these issues is the feasibility of program participants' meeting the applicable requirements to obtain legal status. S. 1161, for example, was criticized for incorporating work requirements for legalization that, some observers said, many agricultural workers could not satisfy. It also has been argued that multi-year work requirements could lead to exploitation, if workers were loathe to complain about work-related matters for fear of being fired before they had worked the requisite number of years. A possible countervailing set of considerations involves the continued availability of workers for low-skilled industries, such as agriculture, meat packing, and services industries. Some parties have expressed a general concern that a quick legalization process with light work requirements could soon deprive employers of needed workers, if some newly legalized workers were to leave certain industries to pursue more desirable job opportunities.

TREATMENT OF FAMILY MEMBERS

The treatment of family members under a guest worker proposal is likely to be an issue. Currently, the INA allows for the admission of the spouses and minor children of alien workers on H-2A, H-2B and other "H" visas who are accompanying the worker or following to join the worker in the United States. In considering any new program, one question would

---

47 P.L. 99-603, Nov. 6, 1986. The general legalization program is at INA §245A, and the SAW program is at INA §210.

48 Certain individuals who had not legalized under the general program and were participants in specified class action lawsuits were given a new time-limited opportunity to adjust to LPR status by the Legal Immigration Family Equity Act (LIFE; P.L. 106-553, Appendix B, Title XI, Dec. 21, 2000) and the LIFE Act Amendments (P.L. 106-554, Appendix D, Title XV, Dec. 21, 2000).

be whether guest workers coming from abroad could be accompanied by their spouses and children.

If the guest worker program in question were open to unauthorized aliens in the United States, the issue of family members would become much more complicated. Relevant questions would include the following: Would the unauthorized spouse and/or minor children of the prospective guest worker be granted some type of legal temporary resident status under the program? If not, would they be expected to leave, or be removed from, the country? If the program had a legalization component, would the spouse and children be eligible for LPR status as derivatives of the guest worker?

The treatment of family members became a significant issue in the 1986 legalization programs described above. As enacted, IRCA required all aliens to qualify for legalization on their own behalf; it made no provision for granting derivative LPR status to spouses and children. Legalized aliens, thus, needed to file immigrant visa petitions on behalf of their family members. These filings were primarily in the family preference category covering spouses and children of LPRs (category 2A) and had the effect of lengthening waiting times in this category.[49] To partially address the increased demand for visa numbers, the Immigration Act of 1990[50] made a limited number of additional visa numbers available for spouses and children of IRCA-legalized aliens for FY1992 through FY1994. It also provided for temporary stays of deportation and work authorization for certain spouses and children of IRCA-legalized aliens in the United States.

As suggested by the experience of the IRCA programs, the treatment of family members in any guest worker program with a legalization component could have broad implications for the U.S. immigration system. Even in the absence of a legalization component, however, the treatment of family members in a guest worker program could have important ramifications. With respect to the program itself, for example, it could affect the willingness of aliens to apply to participate.

LABOR MARKET TEST

A key question about any guest worker program is the type of labor market conditions that would have to exist, if any, in order for an employer to import alien workers.[51] Under both the H-2A and H-2B programs, employers interested in hiring foreign workers must first go through the process of labor certification. Intended to protect job opportunities for U.S. workers, labor certification entails a determination of whether qualified U.S. workers are available to perform the needed work and whether the hiring of foreign workers will adversely affect the wages and working conditions of similarly employed U.S. workers. As described above, recruitment is the primary method used to determine U.S. worker availability. While there is widespread agreement on the goals of labor certification, the

---

49 See CRS Report RL32235.
50 P.L. 101-649, Nov. 29, 1990.
51 Questions about the existence of industry-wide labor shortages are outside the scope of this report. For a discussion of the shortage issue with respect to agriculture, see CRS Report RL30395, Farm Labor Shortages and Immigration Policy, by Linda Levine. Also see CRS Report 95-712, The Effects on U.S. Farm Workers of an Agricultural Guest Worker Program, by Linda Levine.

process itself has been criticized for being cumbersome, slow, and ineffective in protecting U.S. workers.[52]

A proposed guest worker program could retain some form of labor certification or could establish a different process for determining if employers could bring in foreign workers. As described above, past legislative proposals to reform the H-2A program sought to overhaul current labor certification requirements by, for example, establishing a system of worker registries. Another option suggested by some in H-2A reform debates is to adopt the more streamlined labor market test used in the temporary worker program for professional specialty workers (H-1B program). That test, known as labor attestation, requires employers to attest to various conditions. Some argue that labor attestation is inadequate for unskilled jobs without educational requirements. Assuming that protecting U.S. workers remained a policy priority, the labor market test incorporated in any guest worker program would need to be evaluated to determine whether it would likely serve this purpose.

NUMERICAL LIMITS

Related to the issues of labor market tests and U.S. worker protections is the question of numerical limitations on a guest worker program. A numerical cap provides a means, separate from the labor market test, of limiting the number of foreign workers. Currently, as explained above, the H-2A program is not numerically limited, while the H-2B program is capped at 66,000 annually. Like the H-2B program, other capped temporary worker programs have fixed statutory numerical limits. By contrast, a guest worker program that was outlined by former Senator Phil Gramm during the 107th Congress, but never introduced as legislation, included a different type of numerical cap — one that would have varied annually based on regional unemployment rates. According to the program prospectus released by Senator Gramm:

> Except for seasonal work, the number of guest workers permitted to enroll would be adjusted annually in response to changes in U.S. economic conditions, specifically unemployment rates, on a region-by-region basis.

Numerical limitations also are relevant in the context of unauthorized immigration. Some view a temporary worker program as a way to begin reducing the size of the current unauthorized alien population and/or future inflows. In light of the estimated current size and annual growth rate of the unauthorized population, it could be argued that a guest worker program would need to be sizeable to have any significant impact. On the other hand, critics contend that a guest worker program, especially a large one, would be a counterproductive means of controlling unauthorized immigration. In their view, temporary worker programs serve to increase, not reduce, the size of the unauthorized population.

---

52 See U.S. Department of Labor, Office of Inspector General, Consolidation of Labor's Enforcement Responsibilities for the H-2A Program Could Better Protect U.S. Agricultural Workers, Report Number 04-98-004-03-321, Mar. 31, 1998.

ENFORCEMENT

Another important consideration is how the terms of a guest worker program would be enforced. Relevant questions include what types of mechanisms would be used to ensure that employers complied with program requirements. With respect to the H-2A program, for example, the INA authorizes the Labor Secretary to —

> take such actions, including imposing appropriate penalties and seeking appropriate injunctive relief and specific performance of contractual obligations, as may be necessary to assure employer compliance with terms and conditions of employment ...[53]

A related question is whether the enforcement system would be complaint-driven or whether the appropriate entity could take action in the absence of a specific complaint.

Another enforcement-related question is what type of mechanism, if any, would be used to ensure that guest workers departed the country at the end of their authorized period of stay. Historically, the removal of aliens who have overstayed their visas and thereby lapsed into unauthorized status, but have not committed crimes, has not been a priority of the U.S. immigration system. Some have suggested that a large scale guest worker program could help address the problem of visa overstaying and unauthorized immigration generally by severely limiting job opportunities for unauthorized aliens. Others doubt, however, that large numbers of unauthorized residents would voluntarily leave the country; as explained above, they argue instead that a new guest worker program would likely increase the size of the unauthorized alien population as many guest workers opted to overstay their visas.

Other ideas have been put forth to facilitate the departure of temporary workers at the end of their authorized period of stay. One suggestion is to involve the workers' home countries in the guest worker program. Another option is to create an incentive for foreign workers to leave the United States by, for example, withholding or otherwise setting aside a sum of money for each worker that would only become available once the worker returned home. In evaluating any such financially based incentive system, it may be useful to consider, among other questions, how much money would be available to a typical worker and whether such an amount would likely provide an adequate incentive to return home.

HOMELAND SECURITY

A final consideration relates to border and homeland security, matters of heightened concern since the terrorist attacks of September 11, 2001. Supporters of new temporary worker programs argue that such programs would make the United States more secure. They cite security-related benefits of knowing the identities of currently unknown individuals in the country and of legalizing the inflow of alien workers and thereby freeing border personnel to concentrate on potential criminal and terrorist threats. Opponents reject the idea that guest worker programs improve homeland security and generally focus on the dangers of rewarding immigration law violators with temporary or permanent legal status. Security concerns may affect various aspects of a temporary worker program. Possible security-related provisions

---

53 INA §218(g)(2).

that may be considered as part of a new guest worker program include special screening of participants, monitoring while in the United States, and issuance of fraud-resistant documents.

CONCLUSION

The question of a new guest worker program is controversial. A key reason for this is the interrelationship between the recent discussion of guest worker programs and the issue of unauthorized immigration. The size of the current resident unauthorized alien population in the United States, along with continued unauthorized immigration and related deaths at the U.S.-Mexico border, are major factors cited in support of a new temporary worker program. At the same time, the importance of enforcing immigration law and not rewarding illegal aliens with any type of legalized status are primary reasons cited in opposition to such a program. It would seem that some bridging of this gap on the unauthorized alien question — perhaps in some of the areas analyzed above — would be a prerequisite to gaining broad support for a guest worker proposal.

In: Farm Labor: 21st Century Issues and Challenges
Editors: A. W. Burton, I. B. Telpov, pp. 145-171

ISBN: 978-1-60456-005-3
© 2007 Nova Science Publishers, Inc.

Chapter 4

THE COMPREHENSIVE IMMIGRATION REFORM ACT OF 2006 (S. 2611): POTENTIAL LABOR MARKET EFFECTS OF THE GUEST WORKER PROGRAM[*]

Gerald Mayer

ABSTRACT

In the 109th Congress, the Senate passed S. 2611, the Comprehensive Immigration Reform Act of 2006, which would have created a new H-2C guest worker program. The 110th Congress may consider similar legislation.

The guest worker program included in S. 2611 would allow up to 200,000 foreign workers into the United States annually. An employer would have to pay an H-2C worker the greater of the "actual" wage paid by the employer to other workers who do the same kind of work and have similar experience or the "prevailing" wage. Employers would be prevented from hiring H-2C workers if the area unemployment rate for unskilled workers averaged more than 9% for the previous six months. The language in S. 2611 would allow employers to hire skilled, semi-skilled, or unskilled workers, but not agricultural workers or certain types of skilled workers. The kinds of jobs filled under the H-2C program could be similar to the kinds of jobs filled under an existing (H-2B) program, which is used mainly to hire lower-skilled workers.

Initially, an increased supply of lower-skilled foreign workers could be expected to lower the relative wages of lower-skilled U.S. workers. If the H-2C program were enacted, an increased supply of lower-skilled foreign workers may have the greatest impact on young, native-born minority men and on foreign-born minority men in their early working years. In 2005, lower-skilled U.S. workers were mainly white, non-Hispanic males under the age of 45. But a disproportionate number of these workers were young (16 to 24), minority (black or Hispanic) men. The unemployment rate among young, native-born minority men tends to be higher than among similar nonminority men. In 2005, almost a fifth of lower-skilled workers were foreign born, and a disproportionate number of these were minority (nonwhite or Hispanic) men in their early working years (25 to 44). Foreign-born minority men in their early working years tend to earn less than similar native-born workers.

---

[*] Excerpted from CRS Report 33772, dated December 18, 2006.

In response to an initial decline in the relative wages of lower-skilled workers employers may hire more lower-skilled workers and fewer skilled workers. Thus, the initial widening of the wage gap may narrow over time. Other factors — such as technological change, trade, saving and investment, education and training, demographic changes — may also affect the wages of U.S. workers.

The H-2C program could be used by employers to meet seasonal demand, to hire foreign workers at full employment, or to fill jobs when there is a mismatch in a geographic area between the skills demanded and the skills available. In each case, U.S. workers may not be available at the wages offered. They may or may not be available at higher wages.

If employers are not able to hire qualified U.S. workers in high unemployment areas (i.e., more than 9%), there may be a mismatch between the skills available and the skills employers need.

INTRODUCTION

In the 109th Congress, the Senate passed S. 2611, the Comprehensive Immigration Reform Act of 2006.[1] The 110th Congress may consider similar legislation. S. 2611 included provisions to improve border security and the enforcement of immigration law. The bill would have also created legalization programs for unauthorized aliens, increased existing limits on legal immigration, and created a new H-2C guest worker program.

This article examines some potential labor market effects of the guest worker program included in S. 2611. The article begins with a description of the program. Next, the article describes some characteristics of lower-skilled U.S. workers with whom many H-2C guest workers may compete. The article then examines some potential labor market effects of an increased supply of lower-skilled foreign workers on competing U.S. workers (i.e., workers in the United States who have similar skills as H-2C workers). Finally, the article examines some possible effects of a provision in S. 2611 that would prevent employers from hiring H-2C workers if the area unemployment rate for unskilled workers averages more than 9% for the previous six months.

THE PROPOSED H-2C GUEST WORKER PROGRAM

S. 2611 would allow employers to hire up to 200,000 H-2C guest workers a year.[2] H-2C workers could be hired to fill skilled, semi-skilled, or unskilled jobs, but employers could not use the program to hire agricultural workers or certain skilled workers.[3] The H-2C program

---

1 S. 2611 was approved by the Senate on May 25, 2006. On Dec. 16, 2005, the House approved H.R. 4437, the Border Protection, Antiterrorism, and Illegal Immigration Control Act of 2005. H.R. 4437 would not create a new guest worker program. For more information on these bills and other immigration legislation in the 109th Congress, see CRS Report RL33125, Immigration Legislation and Issues in the 109th Congress, coordinated by Andorra Bruno; and CRS Report RL33181, Immigration Related Border Security Legislation in the 109th Congress, by Blas Nuñez-Neto and Janice Cheryl Beaver.

2 Under S. 2611, unauthorized workers who have been in the United States since Jan. 7, 2004, and meet certain conditions may be able to obtain H-2C visas. The 200,000 annual cap on H-2C visas would not apply to these workers.

3 Under an existing (H-2A) program, employers may hire foreign workers to perform temporary agricultural work. The H-2A program does not have an annual cap. For more information on the H-2A program, see CRS Report

would prohibit employers from hiring guest workers in areas with high unemployment (i.e., more than 9%) among unskilled workers. S. 2611 defines the area unemployment rate as the unemployment rate in Micropolitan Statistical Areas or Metropolitan Statistical Areas (MSAs). These areas are defined by the Office of Management and Budget (OMB).[4] S. 2611 defines unskilled workers as persons with no more than a high school education.

Under S. 2611, to get an H-2C visa an individual would have to have a job offer from a U.S. employer who meets the requirements of the act. Before hiring a foreign worker, an employer would first have to try to recruit a U.S. worker.[5] An employer would have to offer the job to any U.S. worker who applies and is qualified and available. An employer would also have to file a petition with the Secretary of Homeland Security in which the employer states that the employment of a foreign worker will not adversely affect the wages or working conditions of U.S. workers who are "similarly employed."

Once an H-2C worker is hired, an employer would have to pay the worker either (1) the actual wage paid by the employer to other workers who do the same kind of work and have similar experience or (2) the prevailing wage, whichever is greater.[6]

The H-2C visa would be effective for an initial period of three years and could be extended for another three years. The visa would be portable; that is, an H-2C worker could accept a job offer from another U.S. employer, provided the employer meets the recruitment, wage, and other requirements of the act.

Persons who receive a temporary H-2C visa could adjust to permanent status. After four years in the United States, an H-2C worker could file a petition for an employment-based

---

RL32044, Immigration: Policy Considerations Related to Guest Worker Programs, by Andorra Bruno. The H-2C program in S. 2611 would not apply to certain skilled workers who can enter the United States under existing visas. For example, the H-2C visa would not apply to persons covered by the H-1B program, which is for persons in specialty occupations (generally, occupations that require the application of specialized knowledge and a bachelor's degree or its equivalent). Nor would the H-2C program apply to persons covered by the L, O, or certain other visas. The L visa applies to intracompany transfers of executives, managers, or workers with specialized knowledge. The O visa applies to persons with "extraordinary ability" in science, business, education, the arts, or athletics or who have a record of "extraordinary achievement" in the motion picture or television industry.

4 An MSA is a geographic area that consists of at least one urban area with a population of 50,000 or more and adjacent areas that have a high degree of economic and social integration. A Micropolitan Statistical Area consists of at least one urban area with a population of 10,000 to 50,000 and adjacent areas with a high degree of economic and social integration. U.S. Office of Management and Budget, Metropolitan Statistical Areas, Metropolitan Divisions, Micropolitan Statistical Areas, Combined Statistical Areas, New England City and Town Areas, and Combined New England City and Town Areas, OMB Bulletin 06-01, available at [http://www.whitehouse.gov/omb/bulletins/fy2006/ b06-01_rev.pdf], Dec. 5, 2005, p. 2.

5 S. 2611 defines a "United States worker" as a citizen of the United States; an alien who has been admitted as a permanent resident or refugee; an alien who has been granted asylum; or an alien who has been authorized to work in the United States.

6 If a job is covered by a collective bargaining contract, the prevailing wage would be the wage covered by the agreement. If the job is not covered by a collective bargaining contract but is an occupation covered by either the Davis-Bacon Act or the Service Contract Act, the prevailing wage would be the wage that applies under those acts. If a job is not covered by a collective bargaining contract or either the Davis-Bacon or Service Contract Acts, the prevailing wage would be based on wage data for the occupation from the Bureau of Labor Statistics (BLS) or, if BLS does not have wage data that applies to the occupation, on data from another survey approved by the Secretary of Labor. For descriptions of the Davis Bacon and Service Contract Acts, see CRS Report RL32086, Federal Contract Labor Standards Statutes: An Overview, by William G. Whittaker.

visa.[7] At any time, an employer could file a petition on behalf of a worker for an employment- based visa.[8]

EFFECTS OF A NEW GUEST WORKER PROGRAM

The 110th Congress may consider a new guest worker program similar to the H-2C program approved by the Senate in the 109th Congress. If so, questions will likely arise about the potential economic effects of such a program. This section begins with a summary of estimates by the Congressional Budget Office (CBO) of the effects of the H-2C program on federal spending and the U.S. population. Next, the section describes some characteristics of lower-skilled U.S. workers with whom many H-2C workers would likely compete. The section then describes an economic framework that is useful in understanding the potential labor market effects of a new guest worker program. Finally, the section considers some possible effects of the provision in S. 2611 that would prevent employers from hiring H-2C workers if the area unemployment rate for unskilled workers averages more than 9% for the previous six months.

CBO ESTIMATES OF THE IMPACT OF THE H-2C PROGRAM

According to estimates by CBO, the H-2C program in S. 2611 would raise direct federal spending by $4.1 billion from 2007 to 2016. Most of this spending ($3.9 billion) would be for Medicaid benefits. CBO also projects that the H-2C program would increase the U.S. population by 3.3 million persons from 2007 through 2016. The projection includes both workers and their dependents (including children born to new entrants after they arrive in the United States). Of the 3.3 million increase, CBO estimates that a half million persons would have entered the United States illegally under current law.[9]

CHARACTERISTICS OF COMPETING LOWER-SKILLED U.S. WORKERS

The H-2C program in S. 2611 would allow up to 200,000 guest workers into the United States each year. These workers would compete with U.S. workers and, eventually, with previously admitted H-2C workers. The language in S. 2611 would allow employers to hire skilled, semi-skilled, or unskilled workers. However, the kinds of jobs filled under the program may be similar to the kinds of jobs filled under an existing (H-2B) program, which is used mainly to hire lower-skilled workers.[10] Also, S. 2611 includes a provision that would

---

7 For an explanation of employment-based visas, see CRS Report RL32235, U.S. Immigration Policy on Permanent Admissions, by Ruth Ellen Wasem.

8 The spouses and children of H-2C workers would be able to enter the United States under a different visa (H-4).

9 Congressional Budget Office, S. 2611: Comprehensive Immigration Reform Act of 2006, Aug. 18, 2006, pp. 4-7, 22.

10 Under the H-2B program, employers may hire temporary nonagricultural workers.Currently, the H-2B program is capped at 66,000 visas annually. The requirements for the proposed H-2C visa would not be same as the

prevent employers from hiring H-2C workers in areas with high unemployment among unskilled workers. Thus, the rest of this article focuses on the potential labor market effects of the proposed H-2C program on competing lower-skilled workers. This section of the article follows S. 2611 and defines lower-skilled workers as persons with a high school education or less. The definition of unskilled workers does not include agricultural workers (i.e., because the H-2C program in S. 2611 would not apply to agricultural workers).

This section compares three groups of U.S. workers:

-    the total civilian labor force;[11]
- all lower-skilled workers; and
- lower-skilled, foreign-born workers (a subset of all lower-skilled workers).

The description of U.S. workers is based on data from the Current Population Survey (CPS). The CPS is a monthly survey of about 55,500 households conducted by the U.S. Census Bureau for BLS.[12] In the CPS, persons with a high school education include persons with either a diploma or GED (i.e., persons who have passed General Educational Development tests). See *Appendix A* for more information on the CPS.

Table 1 shows that an increased supply of foreign-born, lower-skilled workers may have the greatest impact on young, native-born minority men and on foreign-born minority men in their early working years. The unemployment rate among young, native-born minority men tends to be higher than among similar nonminority men.[13] Foreign-born minority men in their early working years tend to earn less than similar native-born workers.[14]

All Lower-Skilled Workers Compared to the Total Civilian Labor Force

In 2005, lower-skilled U.S. workers were mainly white (81.1%), non-Hispanic (79.7%) males (56.9%) under the age of 45 (62.7%). However, compared to the total civilian labor force, a disproportionate number of lower-skilled workers were black or Hispanic (13.5% and 20.3%, respectively), between the ages of 16 and 24 (19.7%), and male (56.9%).[15]

---

requirements for the H-2B visa. For more information on the H-2B program, see CRS Report RL32044, Immigration: Policy Considerations Related to Guest Worker Programs.

11 Persons who are in the labor force are either working or actively looking for work.

12 In this report, foreign-born persons include both citizens and noncitizens of the United States. The CPS does not ask noncitizens if they are legal permanent residents, nonimmigrants who are in the United States temporarily (e.g., guest workers), or whether they are in the country without authorization. Therefore, in this report, the definition of foreign-born persons includes legal immigrants, legal nonimmigrants, and unauthorized aliens.

13 In 2005, the unemployment rate among native-born, lower-skilled minority men (either black or Hispanic) between the ages of 16 and 24 was 8.5%. Among similar nonminority men, the unemployment rate was 3.9%. Calculated by CRS from the monthly Current Population Survey (CPS).

14 In 2005, foreign-born, lower-skilled minority men (either black or Hispanic) between the ages of 25 and 44 had median weekly earnings of $440. Similar native-born men had median weekly earnings of $508. Calculated by CRS from the monthly Current Population Survey (CPS).

15 When answering the question about race in the CPS survey, respondents are allowed to choose more than one race. This report follows BLS practice and only counts blacks and whites who selected one race category. Hispanic persons may be of any race. The comparisons discussed in the text of this report are significant at the 95% confidence level. See *Appendix A* for a discussion of confidence levels.

Foreign-Born, Lower-Skilled Workers Compared to All Lower-Skilled Workers

Some research suggests that new immigrants may compete mainly with prior immigrants.[16] Therefore, this section compares foreign-born, lower-skilled workers to all lower-skilled workers. A disproportionate number of lower-skilled workers are foreign-born. In 2005, foreign-born, lower-skilled workers accounted for 18.6% of all lower-skilled workers. By comparison, foreign-born workers with more than a high school education accounted for 11.6% of all workers with more than a high school education.[17] Compared to all lower-skilled workers, foreign-born, lower-skilled workers were disproportionately nonwhite (23.0%), Hispanic (68.0%), between the ages of 25 and 44 (55.2%), and male (63.8%).

Table 1. Demographic Characteristics of the U.S. Labor Force in 2005, by Type

Characteristic	Number (in 1,000s)	Percent
Gender		
Total civilian labor force		
Male	80,033	53.6%
Female	69,288	46.4%
Total	149,320	100.0%
All lower-skilled, nonagricultural workers		
Male	35,619	56.9%
Female	26,944	43.1%
Total	62,563	100.0%
Foreign-born, lower-skilled nonagricultural workers		
Male	7,441	63.8%
Female	4,225	36.2%
Total	11,666	100.0%
Total civilian labor force		
White Only	122,291	81.9%
Black Only	17,013	11.4%
Other	10,017	6.7%
Total	149,320	100.0%
All lower-skilled nonagricultural workers		
White Only	50,745	81.1%
Black Only	8,428	13.5%
Other	3,390	5.4%
Total	62,563	100.0%
Foreign-born, lower-skilled nonagricultural workers		
White Only	8,984	77.0%
Black Only	976	8.4%
Other	1,706	14.6%
Total	11,666	100.0%

---

16 One reason why new immigrants may have a greater effect on the wages and employment of earlier immigrants is that many new immigrants move to areas where there are large concentrations of immigrants. James P. Smith and Barry Edmonston, eds., The New Americans: Economic, Demographic, and Fiscal Effects of Immigration, Washington: National Academy Press, 1997, pp. 223-224.

17 In 2005, 11.7 million of 62.6 million lower-skilled nonagricultural workers were foreign born; 10.0 million of 85.7 million nonagricultural workers with more than a high school education were foreign-born.

Table 1. Continued.

Characteristic	Number (in 1,000s)	Percent
	Gender	
Hispanic Origin		
Total civilian labor force		
Hispanic	19,824	13.3%
Non-Hispanic	129,497	86.7%
Total	149,320	100.0%
All lower-skilled nonagricultural workers		
Hispanic	12,725	20.3%
Non-Hispanic	49,839	79.7%
Total	62,563	100.0%
Foreign-born, lower-skilled nonagricultural workers		
Hispanic	7,937	68.0%
Non-Hispanic	3,728	32.0%
Total	11,666	100.0%
Total civilian labor force		
16-24	22,290	14.9%
25-34	32,341	21.7%
35-44	36,030	24.1%
45-54	34,402	23.0%
55-64	18,980	12.7%
65 and over	5,278	3.5%
Total	149,320	100.0%
All lower-skilled nonagricultural workers		
16-24	12,331	19.7%
25-34	12,466	19.9%
35-44	14,465	23.1%
45-54	13,483	21.6%
55-64	7,293	11.7%
65 and over	2,525	4.0%
Total	62,563	100.0%
Foreign-born, lower-skilled nonagricultural workers		
16-24	1,635	14.0%
25-34	3,252	27.9%
35-44	3,180	27.3%
45-54	2,222	19.1%
55-64	1,101	9.4%
65 and over	275	2.4%
Total	11,666	100.0%

Source: Calculated by the Congressional Research Service (CRS) from the monthly Current Population Survey (CPS).

Notes: Estimates are for persons age 16 and older and in the civilian labor force. Lower-skilled workers are persons with no more than a high school education. Employment estimates of lower-skilled workers are for nonagricultural persons. Estimates are monthly averages for calendar year 2005. Details may not add to totals because of rounding.

High School Dropouts Compared to All Persons with no More than a High School Education

Analysts often compare workers who have not completed high school (i.e., who do not have a diploma or GED) with workers who have no more than a high school education. Table B1 in Appendix B is similar to Table 1, except it compares the civilian labor force to nonagricultural workers without a high school education.

Compared to all lower-skilled workers (from Table 1), more persons without a high school education (from Table B1) were male (60.7% vs. 56.9%), Hispanic (37.9% vs. 20.3%), and under the age of 25 (31.7% vs. 19.7%). Over half of foreign-born nonagricultural workers with no more than a high school education had not finished high school.

Occupations

Column 4 of Table 2 shows that, in 2005, more than half (57.3%) of foreign-born, lower-skilled nonagricultural workers were employed in four major occupations: construction, production, building and grounds cleaning, and food services. In construction, the largest number of workers were employed as laborers, carpenters, painters, roofers, drywall installers, and carpet installers. In production occupations, the largest number of workers were employed as assemblers; metal and plastic workers; sewing machine operators; packaging machine operators; and meat, poultry, and fish processing workers.

Table 2. Employment of Lower-Skilled, Foreign-Born Workers in 2005, by Occupation

Occupation	Number (1,000s)		Percent	
	All Lower-Skilled Workers (1)	Foreign-Born, Lower-Skilled Workers (2)	Foreign-Born Workers as a Percent of All Lower-Skilled Workers (3)	Foreign-Born Workers by Occupation (4)
Construction and extraction	7,117	2,071	29.1%	17.8%
Production	6,963	1,750	25.1%	15.1%
Building and grounds cleaning and maintenance	4,315	1,522	35.3%	13.1%
Food preparation and serving related	5,304	1,315	24.8%	11.3%
Transportation and material moving	6,448	1,170	18.1%	10.1%
Sales and related	7,247	925	12.8%	8.0%
Office and administrative support	8,796	822	9.3%	7.1%
Personal care and service	2,511	484	19.3%	4.2%
Installation, maintenance, and repair	3,090	455	14.7%	3.9%
Management occupations	3,510	349	9.9%	3.0%
Healthcare support occupations	1,667	297	17.8%	2.6%
Education, training, and library	817	77	9.5%	0.7%
Protective service	1,087	75	6.9%	0.6%
Healthcare practitioners and technical	614	67	10.9%	0.6%
Business and financial operations	895	63	7.1%	0.5%
Arts, design, entertainment, sports, and media	537	62	11.5%	0.5%

Table 2. Continued.

Occupation	All Lower-Skilled Workers (1)	Foreign-Born, Lower-Skilled Workers (2)	Foreign-Born Workers as a Percent of All Lower-Skilled Workers (3)	Foreign-Born Workers by Occupation (4)
Community and social services	248	37	15.1%	0.3%
Architecture and engineering	318	24	7.7%	0.2%
Computer and mathematical	268	23	8.7%	0.2%
Life, physical, and social science	116	11	9.8%	0.1%
Legal	115	6	5.2%	0.1%
Total	61,985	11,605	18.7%	100.0%

Source: Calculated by the Congressional Research Service (CRS) from the monthly Current Population Survey (CPS).

Notes: Estimates are for persons age 16 and older and in the civilian labor force. Lower-skilled workers are persons with no more than a high school education. Employment estimates of lower-skilled workers are for nonagricultural persons. Total employment in *Table 2* is less than total employment in *Table 1* because some persons did not report an occupation (e.g., they may have been in the labor force but unemployed). Estimates are monthly averages for calendar year 2005. Details may not add to totals because of rounding.

Column 3 of Table 2 shows that, in the four occupations where over half of foreign-born, lower-skilled workers were employed, one-fourth or more of the lower-skilled workers were foreign-born. In building and grounds cleaning occupations, 35.3% of lower-skilled workers were foreign born. In construction, 29.1% of lower-skilled workers were foreign born; in production, 25.1% of lower-skilled workers were foreign born; and in food preparation and serving occupations, 24.8% of lower-skilled workers were foreign born. If employers used the proposed H-2C program to hire workers for these occupations, the impact on foreign-born workers may be greater than if the program were used to hire workers for other occupations. If S. 2611 were enacted, some of the workers with whom newer H-2C workers may compete could be H-2C workers admitted in previous years.

Table 3 shows that, according to BLS employment projections, from 2004 to 2014 employment will increase by 18.9 million jobs (from 145.6 million to 164.5 million, or 13.0%).[18] In those occupations that employed foreign-born, lower-skilled workers in 2005, employment is projected to increase by 17.7 million jobs (from 135.6 million to 153.4 million, or 13.1%). Employment is projected to increase in all occupations, except production (reflecting a projected decline in manufacturing employment). But the 17.7 million increase in new jobs is for all jobs, regardless of the educational attainment of the person holding the job. BLS estimates that, from 2004 to 2014, 6.9 million jobs will be filled by persons with a

---

18 Every two years BLS publishes employment projections for the next 10 years. The projections are made in a series of steps, beginning with estimates of the future size of the labor force. Projections of the size of the labor force take into account population projections by Census Bureau. The population projections include estimates of net international migration. U.S. Department of Labor, Bureau of Labor Statistics, "Employment Projections," BLS Handbook of Methods , at [http://stats.bls.gov/opub/hom/pdf/homch13.pdf], pp. 123-126; Norman C. Saunders, "A Summary of BLS Projections to 2014," Monthly Labor Review, v. 128, Nov. 2005, available at [http://stats.bls.gov/opub/mlr/2005/11/art1full.pdf], pp. 6-7. Mitra Toossi, "Labor Force Projections to 2014: Retiring Boomers," Monthly Labor Review, v. 128, Nov. 2005, available at [http://stats.bls.gov/opub/mlr/2005/11/art3full.pdf], p. 27.

high school education or less (an increase from 68.5 million to 75.4 million, or 10.1%).[19] The persons who fill these jobs may be either native-born or foreign-born.

Projections of job growth do not take into account vacancies that may occur in existing jobs. Employers may replace workers who change occupations or who leave the labor force (e.g., to return to school, raise children, or retire). Therefore, the number of *job openings* by occupation consists of the sum of the number of jobs created or lost and the number of vacancies caused by workers who change occupations or leave the labor force.[20] According to BLS projections, from 2004 to 2014, there will be 24.5 million job openings in occupations filled by persons with no more than a high school education.[21] The proposed H-2C program could allow as many as 200,000 foreign workers into the United States annually. The H-2C visa would be effective for an initial period of three years, with one three-year extension.

Within six years, there could be as many as 1.2 million H-2C guest workers in the United States. Persons who receive an H-2C visa could adjust to permanent status and become U.S. citizens.[22] If most of the annual 200,000 H-2C visas were issued to lower-skilled workers, they could fill up to 8% of the projected job openings in occupations requiring a high school education or less.

Earnings

Lower-skilled workers generally earn less than more skilled workers. In 2005, foreign-born, lower-skilled workers had median weekly earnings of $400, before taxes and other deductions. This amount compares to median weekly earnings of $576 for all workers and $438 a week for all lower-skilled workers. These estimates include both full-time and part-time workers.[23]

Research on the Effect of Immigration on Earnings

Researchers do not agree on the effect of immigration on earnings.[24] According to George Borjas, between 1979 and 1995, immigration of unskilled workers (defined as high school dropouts) reduced the wages of all high school dropouts by five percentage points relative to the wages of all other workers.[25] David Card, on the other hand, has concluded that

---

19 Daniel E. Hecker, "Occupational Employment Projections to 2014," Monthly Labor Review, vol. 128, Nov. 2005, at [http://stats.bls.gov/opub/mlr/2005/11/art5full.pdf], pp. 71, 79-80.

20 For information on "replacement needs," see chapter 5 in Bureau of Labor Statistics, U.S.Department of Labor, Occupational Projections and Training Data, available at [http://www.bls.gov/emp/optd/home.htm].

21 The 24.5 million projection accounts for 44.8% of all job openings during the 10-year period. One reason for the large number of job openings in occupations filled by persons with a high school education or less is that employee turnover in lower-skilled jobs tends to be greater than in jobs requiring more education.

22 Because S. 2611 included provisions intended to improve border security and increase enforcement of immigration law, some H-2C guest workers may be substitutes for unauthorized workers.

23 Calculated by CRS from the monthly Current Population Survey (CPS).

24 For a review of research on the labor market effects of immigration on U.S. workers, see CRS Report 95-408, Immigration: The Effects on Native-Born Workers, by Linda Levine; and Congressional Budget Office, The Role of Immigrants in the U.S. Labor Market, Nov. 2005, pp. 19-24.

25 George J. Borjas, Heaven's Door: Immigration Policy and the American Economy, Princeton: Princeton University Press, 2001, pp. 82-83.

Table 3. BLS Employment Projections, 2004-2014, by Occupation

Occupation	Projected Employment (in 1,000s)			
	2004	2014	Change 2004-2014	Job Openings[a]
Construction and extraction	7,666	8,597	931	2,439
Production	10,260	10,169	-91	2,811
Building and grounds cleaning and maintenance	5,582	6,530	948	2,062
Food preparation and serving related	10,739	12,453	1,714	5,981
Transportation and material moving	10,249	11,365	1,116	3,509
Sales and related occupations	13,803	15,082	1,279	5,890
Office and administrative support	21,149	22,454	1,304	6,803
Personal care and service	4,721	5,713	991	2,121
Installation, maintenance, and repair	5,683	6,335	652	1,963
Management	8,666	9,639	974	2,618
Healthcare support	3,092	4,149	1,057	1,540
Education, training, and library	7,992	9,589	1,596	3,242
Protective service	2,999	3,419	420	1,258
Healthcare practitioners and technical	6,015	7,562	1,548	2,706
Business and financial operations	5,736	6,831	1,095	2,105
Arts, design, entertainment, sports, and media	2,112	2,425	313	699
Community and social services	2,317	2,800	483	928
Architecture and engineering	2,360	2,649	289	809
Computer and mathematical	2,410	3,186	775	1,097
Life, physical, and social science	902	1,046	144	354
Legal	1,173	1,363	190	326
Total	135,627	153,355	17,714	51,544
Jobs filled by lower-skilled workers	68,506	75,424	6,919	24,518
Total Civilian Labor Force	145,612	164,540	18,928	54,680

Sources: U.S. Department of Labor, Bureau of Labor Statistics, *Employment by Occupation, 2004 and Projected 2014*, at [http://stats.bls.gov/emp/emptabapp.htm].

a. The number of job openings consists of the sum of the number of jobs created or lost and the number of vacancies caused by workers who change occupations or leave the labor force.

an increased supply of less skilled immigrants (also defined as high school dropouts) has had little impact on the wages of dropouts relative to the wages of high school graduates.According to Card, the main reason for this finding is that industries change their methods of production to employ the increased supply of less skilled foreign workers.[26]

---

26 According to Card, between 1979 and 2001, the wage gap between high school graduates and dropouts remained relatively steady, but the gap between college and high school graduates increased. David Card, "Is the New Immigration Really So Bad?" The Economic Journal, v. 115, Nov. 2005, pp. F307-F315, F321. Also see Ethan Lewis, Local Open Economies Within the U.S.: How Do Industries Respond to Immigration? Working Paper No. 04-1, Federal Reserve Bank of Philadelphia, available at [http://www.phil.frb.org], pp. 21-23.If an increased supply of lower-skilled workers does not affect the relative wages of workers in different skill groups, it could nevertheless change the distribution of earnings if the relative number of workers in different skill groups changes. For example, an increase in the relative number of lower paid (or higher paid) workers could increase earnings inequality.

ECONOMIC FRAMEWORK FOR UNDERSTANDING THE POTENTIAL LABOR MARKET EFFECTS OF A NEW GUEST WORKER PROGRAM

The potential labor market effects of a new guest worker program can be examined from different perspectives: (a) the *initial effect* of an increased supply of foreign workers on the wages and employment of competing U.S. workers; (b) the *long-run effect* of an increased supply of foreign workers, as U.S. workers and employers adjust to the initial change in wages and employment; and (c) the effects that take place over time as *other changes* (social, economic, and demographic) occur.

Initially, an increased supply of lower-skilled foreign workers can be expected to lower the relative wages of lower-skilled U.S workers. In response to the initial change in wages, employers may hire more lower-skilled workers (because they are relatively cheaper) and fewer skilled workers (because they are relatively more expensive). Some employers and workers may move to areas where there are better investment and employment opportunities. Other factors may also affect employment and wages; for example, changes in technology, foreign trade, saving and investment, education and training, and demographic changes.

The effects of a guest worker program may also depend on why U.S. workers are not available to meet employer demand. Thus, the effects of a guest worker program would likely differ if employer demand is for seasonal workers, for workers at full employment, or for workers with skills that are not available in local labor markets. Employers may be able to fill jobs by offering higher wages. But, at full employment, higher wages may cause inflation without increasing employment. If there is a mismatch between the skills demanded by employers and the skills available, vacancies could be filled by training workers. But worker training can take time. Qualified workers may not be available soon enough to meet employer demand.

Economic Analysis

The different perspectives for analyzing the labor market effects of a guest worker program can be described using standard economic concepts.

Short-Term and Longer-Term Effects

Economists distinguish between the short-term and the long-term effects of an increased supply of workers. For an employer, the common definition of the short-term is a period during which the quantity of at least one input is fixed and cannot be changed. It is generally assumed that the fixed input is the stock of capital goods (i.e., buildings and equipment and associated technology). If the stock of capital is fixed, in the short-term a firm can only change the quantity of variable factors, principally labor.[27] In the long-term, a firm can change the quantity of both fixed and variable inputs.

---

27 Because labor consists of both variable and fixed costs, it is sometimes called a quasi-fixed factor of production. Fixed labor costs vary with the number of workers employed, and include hiring and training costs, certain payroll taxes, and fringe benefits. Variable costs vary with the number of hours worked, and consist mainly of wages. Walter Y. Oi, "Labor as a Quasi-Fixed Factor," Journal of Political Economy, v. 70, Dec. 1962, pp. 538-539; Daniel S. Hamermesh, Labor Demand, Princeton, NJ: Princeton University Press, 1993, pp. 44-48; and Reynolds et al., Labor Economics and Labor Relations, pp. 94-95.

Scale Effect

For employers, the stock of capital goods is generally fixed in the short run. If there is a change in the price of labor relative to the price of capital or a change in the relative wages of workers with different skills, the *scale* of production may change. In the short run, an increased supply of workers can be expected to lower the wages of competing workers.[28] Therefore, if employers used the H-2C program to hire lower-skilled workers, in the short run, the wages of competing U.S. workers could be expected to fall relative to the wages of other workers.[29] At the same time, relative wages may rise for workers whose skills are complements (e.g., supervisors) to the skills of lower-skilled workers.

Substitution Effect

In the long run, employers can change the quantities of both fixed and variable inputs. In response to a change in the relative prices of inputs, employers may use relatively more of the factor that has fallen in price. Holding output constant, employers may *substitute* the lower-priced factor for other inputs. Therefore, if the H-2C program increased the supply of lower-skilled workers, employers may substitute less-skilled labor for both skilled labor and capital. Employers may hire more lower-skilled workers and fewer skilled workers. Therefore, in the short run, the wages of unskilled workers may fall relative to the wages of skilled workers (the scale effect). But, in the long run, employers may adopt more labor-intensive production methods (the substitution effect). If so, in the long run, the initial (i.e., short-run) widening of the wage gap between skilled and unskilled workers may narrow.

In the long run, both labor and capital are mobile. An increased supply of foreign workers in one geographic area may affect investment decisions and the behavior of other workers. For instance, employers may move their businesses to where there is a greater supply of labor. Workers may move to where there is a greater demand for labor. Thus, an increased supply of workers in one area of the country may affect employment and wages throughout the economy.

Social, Economic, and Demographic Changes

The scale and substitution effects of employer demand for labor are useful in explaining how an increased supply of lower-skilled workers may affect employment and relative wages in the short run and long run. But the scale effect holds the stock of capital goods constant and the substitution effect holds output constant. Over time, other changes may make it difficult to identify the effects of an increased supply of lower-skilled workers. For example, the size and composition of the domestic labor force may change. The work force may become younger or older. More U.S. workers may finish high school or go to college. Savings and investment may cause the stock of capital, employment, and output to grow. Changes in technology, consumer preferences, or trade may affect the demand for workers with different skills.[30] Some changes may be due, in part, to an increased supply of foreign workers. For example, because of an increased supply of lower-skilled foreign workers, some

---

28 The wages of competing workers may not fall in absolute terms, but they can be expected to fall relative to the wages of other workers.

29 For an explanation of how an increase in labor supply may affect wages and employment, see CRS Report 95-408, Immigration: The Effects on Native-Born Workers.

30 Technological change consists of improved equipment, the introduction of new products, and improved methods of production, transportation, and communication.

U.S. workers may get more education and training; others may leave the labor force. An increased supply of lower-skilled foreign workers may also affect the amount, kind, and location of investment as well as the kinds of technology adopted.

The Availability of U.S. Workers

The labor market effects of a new guest worker program may also depend on why U.S. workers are not available to meet employer demand.

Seasonal Demand

Employers may need workers to meet seasonal demand. An adequate supply of qualified U.S. workers may be available among unemployed workers or among persons willing to enter the labor force in response to a demand for temporary workers. Under the proposed H-2C program, an employer would have to pay a foreign worker the actual wage paid to other workers for the same kind of work and similar experience or the prevailing wage, whichever is greater. But, in local labor markets, an adequate supply of workers may not be available at these wages. Workers may be available from outside the area, but they may not be willing to travel or relocate for a temporary job. Workers with permanent jobs may not be willing to leave those jobs for a temporary job. Thus, a guest worker program may help employers meet seasonal demand by providing a temporary supply of workers. On the other hand, the availability of guest workers may discourage employers from raising wages to recruit U.S. workers. A guest worker program may also discourage employers from adopting different production methods or introducing new technologies that could reduce the demand for seasonal workers.

A Geographic Mismatch between the Skills Demanded and Skills Supplied

In some labor markets, employers may not be able to fill openings if the skills that are available locally do not match the skills that employers need.[31] Foreign workers may help meet employer demand if qualified U.S. workers are not available at the wages paid to other workers for the same kind of work or at the prevailing wage. At higher wages, employers may be able to recruit qualified workers from outside the local labor market. Alternatively, local workers could be trained to perform the available work. But training can take time, depending on the kinds of skills needed. Training may, however, be a longer-term solution to local labor shortages. Qualified U.S. workers could also be attracted to an area by higher wages.

Employers could also relocate to an area where there is an adequate supply of qualified workers.

Demand at Full Employment

At full employment (whether for seasonal or year-round work), employers may only be able to hire qualified U.S. workers by raising wages and hiring workers away from other employers.[32] But higher wages may cause inflation. Therefore, at full employment, foreign

---

31 When there is unemployment because of a mismatch in a labor market between the skills available and the skills demanded, unemployment is called structural unemployment.

32 At full employment, there are typically persons who are between jobs (e.g., because they have quit or been laid off) or persons who have entered the labor force and are looking for work. Economists call this frictional unemployment. Full employment is commonly defined as the lowest rate of unemployment that is consistent with stable prices. This rate may vary over time. CRS Report RL33734, Economic Growth, Inflation, and

workers may help meet employer demand for labor and help curb inflation. Because H-2C visas would be effective for three years (and renewable for another three years), the economy may not be at full employment when the visas expire. But without the H-2C program, some employers could potentially relocate or outsource work to a country where there is an adequate supply of labor.

EFFECTS OF THE 9% AREA UNEMPLOYMENT TRIGGER

S. 2611 included a provision that would not allow employers to hire H-2C workers if the area unemployment rate for unskilled workers averages more than 9% for the previous six months. The trigger would not affect the overall limit of 200,000 H-2C visas, which would be available to the rest of the country.

Before hiring an H-2C worker, employers would first have to try to recruit and hire U.S. workers. In high unemployment areas, the 9% trigger would restrict the supply of H-2C workers. Thus, in these areas, the potential labor market effects of the H-2C program may depend on whether U.S. workers are available to meet employer demand.

In high unemployment areas, employers may be able to hire unemployed workers, whether at the same wage paid to other workers for the same kind of work or at a higher wage. However, if employers are not able to hire qualified U.S. workers, it may be because there is a mismatch in the area between the skills some employers demand and the skills available. If there is a mismatch, employers would not be allowed to hire H-2C workers. U.S. workers could be trained to fill the demand or they could be recruited from outside the local area. Employers could also alter their method of production to reduce their need for skills that are not available or they could move to where the skills are available and the unemployment rate is 9% or lower.

Table C1 in Appendix C shows those areas of the country that may have been affected by the 9% unemployment trigger if it had been in effect in 2005. The unemployment rates shown in the table are based on the monthly CPS. If S. 2611 were enacted, BLS estimates of the unskilled unemployment rate may be more precise than those shown. Column 5 shows the confidence intervals for the unemployment rates for lower-skilled workers (in column 4). The confidence intervals show the lower and upper bounds of the estimated unemployment rates. (See *Appendix A f*or a discussion of confidence levels.) *Table C1* follows the language in S. 2611, and includes agricultural workers in the estimates of the unskilled unemployment rate.

Table C1 indicates that if the 9% trigger had been in effect in 2005, visas for H-2C guest workers would not have been issued in approximately 65 Metropolitan Statistical Area (MSAs). The labor force in these 65 MSAs accounted for an estimated 11.8% of the total labor force of 63.4 million lower-skilled workers. More than half of the MSAs were in the Midwest and West. In the Midwest, 7 of the MSAs were in Michigan, 4 in Ohio, and 3 in Illinois.[33] In the West, 11 of the MSAs were in California and 4 were in Washington. Texas had 4 MSAs where the unemployment rate among unskilled workers was more than 9%.

Unemployment: Limits to Economic Policy, by Brian Cashell; and CRS Report RL32274, A Changing Natural Rate of Unemployment: Policy Issues, by Marc Labonte.

33 Some MSAs cross state lines. One of the three MSAs in Illinois (the Davenport-Moline-Rock Island MSA) includes parts of Iowa.

As the national unemployment rate rises or falls, the number of MSAs that could be affected by the 9% trigger may also rise or fall. In 2005, the national unemployment rate was 5.1%. In 2004, unemployment was 5.5%.[34] In 2004, BLS adopted new MSA definitions issued by OMB. Therefore, the unemployment estimates for 2005 in *Table C1* can be compared with estimates for 2004. If the 9% trigger had been in effect in 2004, employers would not have been able to hire H-2C workers in approximately 63 MSAs. Compared with 2005, however, these MSAs accounted for a larger share of the lower-skilled labor force: 13.2% of an estimated labor force of 63.2 million. Eight of the MSAs were in California, 7 were in Michigan, 5 in Texas, and 4 each were in Alabama, Colorado, Illinois, and Ohio.[35]

CONCLUSIONS

If the 110th Congress were to enact a guest worker program like the H-2C program that was approved by the Senate in the 109th Congress, the initial labor market effects may be different from the long-term effects. Initially, an increased supply of foreign workers could be expected to lower the relative wages of competing U.S. workers. If the program were used mainly to hire lower-skilled foreign workers, the greatest impact may be on young, native-born minority men and on foreign-born minority men in their early working years. In response to the initial change in wages, employers may hire more lower-skilled workers and fewer skilled workers. Some employers and workers may also move to where there are better investment and employment opportunities.

An increased supply of foreign workers would likely increase total U.S. employment and output. But economists do not agree on the effect of immigration on wages. Other factors — such as technological change, trade, saving and interment, education and training, and demographic changes — may also affect wages and make it difficult to identify the effects of an increased supply of foreign workers.

The effects of a guest worker program may also depend on why U.S. workers are not available to meet employer demand. The effects would likely differ if employer demand is for seasonal workers, for more workers at full employment, or for workers with skills that are not available in the local labor market. Employers may be able to fill jobs by offering higher wages. But, at full employment, higher wages may cause inflation without increasing employment. If there is a mismatch between the skills demanded and the skills available, higher wages may not attract an adequate supply of qualified workers.

The 9% trigger in S. 2611 may encourage employers to hire U.S. workers. But, workers may not be available in local labor markets because there is a mismatch between the skills demanded and the skills available.

---

34 U.S. Department of Labor, Bureau of Labor Statistics, Labor Force Statistics from the Current Population Survey, available at [http://stats.bls.gov/cps/cpsaat1.pdf].
35 BLS adopted the new MSA definitions effective with the May 2004 CPS. Therefore, the unemployment estimates by MSA for 2004 are averages for the eight months from May to December 2004.

APPENDIX A. DATA AND METHODOLOGY

Current Population Survey

The CPS is a household survey conducted by the U.S. Bureau of the Census for the Bureau of Labor Statistics (BLS) of the U.S. Department of Labor. The monthly CPS is the main source of labor force data for the nation, including estimates of the monthly unemployment rate. The CPS collects a wide range of demographic, social, and labor market information. Approximately 55,500 households are interviewed each month, either in person or by phone.[36]

The CPS sample is representative of the civilian noninstitutional population; it does not include persons on active duty in the Armed Forces or persons in institutions such as nursing homes or correctional facilities. The survey includes civilian noninstitutional persons living in group quarters. (Group quarters are living quarters where residents share common facilities; examples include group homes, fraternities, or sororities.)[37]

The labor force includes both employed and unemployed persons. Unemployed persons are individuals who are not working but who are available and actively looking for work. Employed persons are individuals who are working for a private or public employer, are self-employed, or who work 15 hours or more per week as unpaid workers on a family farm or business. Also counted as employed are persons who are temporarily absent from work because of illness, bad weather, vacation, job training, labor-management dispute, childcare problems, maternity or paternity leave, or other family or personal reasons.[38]

Each month one-fourth of the CPS sample is asked questions about current earnings. Weekly earnings are reported for wage and salary workers. Weekly earnings consist of usual earnings before taxes and other deductions, and include tips, overtime pay, and commissions usually received (at a person's main job). The monthly CPS does not collect information on the weekly earnings of persons who are self-employed.

In this report, the data from the basic monthly CPS are annual monthly averages. The data for each month for 2005 were combined to calculate annual monthly averages.

Confidence Levels

Estimates based on survey responses from a sample of households have two kinds of error: nonsampling and sampling. Examples of nonsampling error include information that is misreported and errors made in processing collected information.

Sampling error occurs because a sample, and not the entire population, of households is surveyed. The difference between an estimate based on a sample of households and the actual population value is known as sampling error. When using sample data, researchers typically construct confidence intervals around population estimates. Confidence intervals provide information about the accuracy of estimated values. With a 95% confidence interval and

---

36 U.S. Department of Labor, Bureau of Labor Statistics, Current Population Survey: Design and Methodology, Technical Paper 63RV, Mar. 2002, p. J-8.
37 Ibid., pp. 1-1, 3-7 to 3-9, 5-4.
38 Ibid., pp. 5-3, 5-5.

repeated samples from a population, 95% of intervals will include the average estimate of a population characteristic. In *Table C1,* the estimated unemployment rate for persons with no more than a high school education is 7.4%. The confidence interval is between 7.2% and 7.6%. Because the estimate of 7.4% is based on a sample (and not the entire population) of persons with no more than a high school education, the actual unemployment rate may be higher or lower than 7.4%. With a 95% confidence interval, it can be concluded that the average unemployment rate estimated from repeated samples is between 7.2% and 7.6%.

APPENDIX B. DEMOGRAPHIC CHARACTERISTICS O PERSONS WITH LESS THAN A HIGH SCHOOL EDUCATION

Immigration analysts often distinguish between persons with a high school diploma or GED and persons who have not completed high school. Table B1 is similar to *Table 1* in the text but compares the total labor force with persons who have not finished high school.

Table B1. Demographic Characteristics of the U.S. Labor Force in 2005, by Type

Characteristic	Number (1000s)	Percent
Gender		
Total civilian labor force		
Male	80,033	53.6%
Female	69,288	46.4%
Total	149,320	100.0%
All nonagricultural persons with less than a high school education		
Male	10,933	60.7%
Female	7,064	39.3%
Total	17,997	100.0%
Foreign-born nonagricultural persons with less than a high school education		
Male	4,131	67.0%
Female	2,038	33.0%
Total	6,169	100.0%
Race		
Total civilian labor force		
White Only	122,291	81.9%
Black Only	17,013	11.4%
Other	10,017	6.7%
Total	149,320	100.0%
All nonagricultural persons with less than a high school education		
White Only	14,566	80.9%
Black Only	2,293	12.7%
Other	1,138	6.3%
Total	17,997	100.0%
Foreign-born nonagricultural persons with less than a high school education		
White Only	5,192	84.2%
Black Only	341	5.5%
Other	636	10.3%
Total	6,169	100.0%

Tabel B1. Continued.

Characteristic	Number (1000s)	Percent
Hispanic Origin		
Total civilian labor force		
Hispanic	19,824	13.3%
Non-Hispanic	129,497	86.7%
Total	149,320	100.0%
All nonagricultural persons with less than		
a high school education		
Hispanic	6,824	37.9%
Non-Hispanic	11,173	62.1%
Total	17,997	100.0%
Foreign-born nonagricultural persons with less		
than a high school education		
Hispanic	5,050	81.9%
Non-Hispanic	1,119	18.1%
Total	6,169	100.0%
Age		
Total civilian labor force		
16-24	22,290	14.9%
25-34	32,341	21.7%
35-44	36,030	24.1%
45-54	34,402	23.0%
55-64	18,980	12.7%
65 and over	5,278	3.5%
Total	149,320	100.0%
All nonagricultural persons with less than		
a high school education		
16-24	5,696	31.7%
25-34	3,514	19.5%
35-44	3,494	19.4%
45-54	2,803	15.6%
55-64	1,716	9.5%
65 and over	773	4.3%
Total	17,997	100.0%
Foreign-born nonagricultural persons with		
less than a high school education		
16-24	890	14.4%
25-34	1,788	29.0%
35-44	1,679	27.2%
45-54	1,133	18.4%
55-64	543	8.8%
65 and over	135	2.2%
Total	6,169	100.0%

Source: Calculated by the Congressional Research Service (CRS) from the monthly Current Population Survey (CPS).

Notes: Data are for persons age 16 and over. Persons with less than a high school education are nonagricultural persons who do not have a high school diploma or GED. Estimates are averages of the monthly labor force for calendar year 2005. Details may not add to totals because of rounding.

Appendix C. Areas Potentially Affected by the 9% Unemployment Trigger in S. 2611

Table C1. Labor Force Size and Unemployment Rates in 2005, by Metropolitan Statistical Area and Level of Education

Metropolitan Statistical Areas (MSAs)	Total Civilian Labor Force		Civilian Labor Force With a High School Education or Less		
	Number (1,000s) (1)	Unemployment Rate (2)	Number (1,000s) (3)	Unemploymen t Rate (4)	Confidence Intervals for Column 4 (5)
United States	149,320	5.1%	48,428	7.4%	(7.2%-7.6%)
Estimated Unemployment Rate Over 9.0%					
Lawton, OK	78	13.1%	40	22.6%	(13.3%-32.0%)
Youngstown-Warren-Boardman, OH	250	11.4%	138	17.1%	(12.6%-21.6%)
Yakima, WA	139	11.7%	76	16.2%	(10.3%-22.2%)
Visalia-Porterville, CA	180	8.9%	84	16.1%	(10.5%-21.8%)
Muskegon-Norton Shores, MI	118	11.3%	53	15.6%	(8.6%-22.7%)
Lansing-East Lansing, MI	239	8.9%	83	15.4%	(9.8%-21.0%)
Toledo, OH (Ottawa County not in sample)	325	6.9%	106	14.7%	(9.9%-19.6%)
Durham, NC	211	7.5%	78	14.0%	(8.5%-19.6%)
Waterbury, CT	105	10.2%	54	13.5%	(6.9%-20.1%)
Kalamazoo-Portage, MI	151	8.0%	56	13.4%	(7.0%-19.7%)
South Bend-Mishawaka, IN-MI (Michigan portion not identified)	167	8.4%	74	13.0%	(7.5%-18.5%)
Waco, TX	165	7.9%	76	12.9%	(7.5%-18.3%)
Albany, GA (Baker, Terrell, and Worth Counties not in sample)	81	10.8%	46	12.9%	(5.9%-19.9%)
Bakersfield, CA	357	9.1%	191	12.7%	(9.3%-16.1%)
Cedar Rapids, IA (Benton and Jones Counties not in sample)	97	7.4%	35	12.7%	(4.8%-20.6%)
Augusta-Richmond County, GA-SC	248	9.5%	117	12.6%	(8.3%-17.0%)
Tuscaloosa, AL (Greene and Hale Counties not in sample)	111	7.1%	48	12.4%	(5.7%-19.1%)
Santa Barbara-Santa Maria-Goleta, CA	182	10.1%	101	12.2%	(7.6%-16.8%)
Racine, WI	133	7.9%	66	12.1%	(6.4%-17.7%)
Bremerton-Silverdale, WA	115	7.8%	35	12.1%	(4.4%-19.9%)
Fresno, CA	404	8.5%	173	12.0%	(8.5%-15.4%)
Bellingham, WA	118	5.4%	44	11.8%	(4.9%-18.7%)
Salinas, CA	186	7.6%	85	11.7%	(6.8%-16.6%)
Jackson, MS	267	5.5%	95	11.7%	(7.0%-16.3%)
Salem, OR	184	7.8%	83	11.7%	(6.7%-16.7%)
Dayton, OH	414	7.8%	210	11.6%	(8.5%-14.7%)
Pueblo, CO	108	8.6%	42	11.6%	(4.7%-18.5%)
Leominster-Fitchburg-Gardner, MA	111	6.5%	44	11.5%	(4.8%-18.3%)
Monroe, LA	226	7.9%	122	11.5%	(7.4%-15.5%)

Table C1. Continued.

Metropolitan Statistical Areas (MSAs)	Total Civilian Labor Force		Civilian Labor Force With a High School Education or Less		
	Number (1,000s) (1)	Unemployment Rate (2)	Number (1,000s) (3)	Unemploymen t Rate (4)	Confidence Intervals for Column 4 (5)
Memphis, TN-MS-AR (Arkansas portion not identified and Tunica County, MS not in sample	611	7.6%	287	10.9%	(8.3%-13.5%)
Trenton-Ewing, NJ	160	6.2%	83	10.7%	(5.9%-15.5%)
Rochester, NY	566	6.9%	232	10.7%	(7.9%-13.6%)
Detroit-Warren-Livonia, MI	2,312	7.1%	926	10.7%	(9.2%-12.1%)
Corpus Christi, TX	200	6.8%	100	10.7%	(6.3%-15.0%)
Evansville, IN-KY (Gibson County, IN and Kentucky portion not in sample)	133	8.9%	63	10.5%	(5.0%-16.0%)
Winston-Salem, NC	152	7.4%	69	10.5%	(5.4%-15.7%)
Laredo, TX	105	7.4%	69	10.5%	(5.3%-15.8%)
Beaumont-Port Author, TX	164	6.7%	68	10.5%	(5.3%-15.7%)
Anniston-Oxford, AL	106	7.7%	58	10.5%	(4.9%-16.2%)
Oxnard-Thousand Oaks-Ventura, CA	415	6.4%	157	10.4%	(7.0%-13.9%)
Stockton, CA	266	6.9%	120	10.3%	(6.4%-14.2%)
Baton Rouge, LA	379	6.8%	184	10.3%	(7.2%-13.5%)
Vallejo-Fairfield, CA	225	5.4%	76	10.2%	(5.3%-15.1%)
Rockford, IL	197	5.9%	97	10.1%	(5.8%-14.4%)
Saginaw-Saginaw Township North, MI	97	7.4%	48	10.1%	(3.9%-16.2%)
Las Cruces, NM	104	6.3%	41	10.0%	(3.4%-16.5%)
Akron, OH	375	6.3%	180	9.9%	(6.8%-13.1%)
Lexington-Fayette, KY	246	5.1%	87	9.8%	(5.3%-14.3%)
Kansas City, MO-KS (Franklin, KS; Leavenworth, KS; Linn, KS; Bates, MO; and Caldwell, MO Counties not in sample)	1,048	6.3%	391	9.7%	(7.6%-11.8%)
Spokane, WA	239	5.6%	75	9.7%	(4.9%-14.5%)
Merced, CA	108	6.9%	49	9.6%	(3.6%-15.5%)
San Francisco-Oakland-Fremont, CA	2,370	5.6%	705	9.6%	(8.1%-11.2%)
Monroe, MI	89	6.8%	38	9.5%	(2.8%-16.2%)
Eugene-Springfield, OR	174	7.1%	66	9.5%	(4.4%-14.6%)
Davenport-Moline-Rock Island, IA-IL	183	5.2%	72	9.5%	(4.6%-14.4%)
Holland-Grand Haven, MI	120	5.1%	47	9.4%	(3.4%-15.4%)
Johnstown, PA	90	5.9%	47	9.4%	(3.4%-15.4%)
Kankakee-Bradley, IL	142	6.6%	67	9.2%	(4.2%-14.2%)
Madera, CA	95	7.3%	65	9.2%	(4.1%-14.3%)
Altoona, PA	66	6.7%	41	9.2%	(2.8%-15.6%)
Jacksonville, NC	62	7.5%	36	9.2%	(2.4%-16.0%)
Louisville, KY-IN (Washington, IN; Henry, KY; Nelson, KY; Shelby, KY; and Trimble, KY Counties not in sample)	545	6.8%	233	9.2%	(6.6%-11.9%)

Table C1. Continued.

Metropolitan Statistical Areas (MSAs)	Total Civilian Labor Force		Civilian Labor Force With a High School Education or Less		
	Number (1,000s) (1)	Unemployment Rate (2)	Number (1,000s) (3)	Unemploymen t Rate (4)	Confidence Intervals for Column 4 (5)
Topeka, KS (Jackson and Jefferson Counties not in sample)	130	5.0%	57	9.2%	(3.8%-14.6%)
Appleton,WI	104	6.6%	54	9.2%	(3.6%-14.7%)
Lake Charles, LA (Cameron Parish not in sample)	124	6.1%	60	9.1%	(3.9%-14.4%)
Estimated Unemployment Rate 9.0% or Less					
Wichita, KS	296	6.7%	129	9.0%	(5.4%-12.5%)
Huntsville, AL	185	4.1%	64	9.0%	(3.9%-14.0%)
Michigan City-La Porte, IN	91	6.9%	60	8.9%	(3.7%-14.1%)
Victoria, TX	181	6.7%	102	8.9%	(4.9%-12.9%)
Provo-Orem, UT (Juab County not in sample)	189	5.0%	55	8.9%	(3.5%-14.3%)
Greenville-Spartanburg-Anderson, SC	88	5.4%	44	8.9%	(2.9%-15.0%)
Lynchburg, VA (Appomattox and Bedford Counties and Bedford City not In sample)	104	7.6%	54	8.8%	(3.4%-14.3%)
Chicago-Naperville-Joliet, IN-IN-WI(DeKalb, IL; Jasper, IN; and Kenosha, WI Counties not in sample)	4,512	5.9%	1,631	8.8%	(7.8%-9.8%)
Greenville, SC (Laurens and Pickens Counties not in sample)	198	4.9%	75	8.8%	(4.2%-13.4%)
Springfield, MA-CT (Connecticut portion not identified)	329	6.0%	134	8.8%	(5.3%-12.2%)
New Orleans-Metairie-Kenner, LA	530	5.7%	214	8.8%	(6.0%-11.5%)
Buffalo-Niagara Falls, NY	577	6.4%	224	8.7%	(6.1%-11.4%)
Cleveland-Elyria-Mentor, OH	1,054	5.6%	439	8.7%	(6.8%-10.6%)
Baltimore-Towson, MD	1,340	4.9%	522	8.7%	(6.9%-10.4%)
Allentown-Bethlehem-Easton, PA-NJ	538	5.7%	251	8.6%	(6.1%-11.1%)
Kingston, NY	112	4.7%	48	8.6%	(2.9%-14.4%)
Spartanburg, SC	131	4.9%	57	8.5%	(3.3%-13.7%)
Anderson, IN	90	7.8%	57	8.5%	(3.3%-13.7%)
Santa Rosa-Petaluma, CA	243	5.6%	66	8.5%	(3.7%-13.4%)
Shreveport-Bossier City, LA (De Soto Parish not in sample)	203	5.7%	87	8.4%	(4.2%-12.5%)
St. Louis, MO-IL (Calhoun County, IL not in sample)	1,512	5.2%	597	8.4%	(6.8%-10.0%)
Omaha-Council Bluffs, NE-IA	437	4.7%	148	8.3%	(5.1%-11.5%)
Dallas-Fort Worth-Arlington, TX (Delta and Hunt Counties not in sample)	3,223	5.8%	1,335	8.3%	(7.2%-9.3%)
Knoxville, TN (Anderson County not in sample)	287	5.0%	111	8.2%	(4.5%-11.8%)
Mobile, AL	201	5.0%	81	8.2%	(3.9%-12.4%)

Table C1. Continued.

Metropolitan Statistical Areas (MSAs)	Total Civilian Labor Force		Civilian Labor Force With a High School Education or Less		
	Number (1,000s) (1)	Unemployment Rate (2)	Number (1,000s) (3)	Unemployment Rate (4)	Confidence Intervals for Column 4 (5)
Waterloo-Cedar Falls, IA (Grundy County not in sample)	99	5.2%	37	8.2%	(1.8%-14.6%)
San Antonio, TX	881	5.3%	408	8.0%	(6.1%-9.9%)
Tucson, AZ	400	7.4%	159	8.0%	(4.9%-11.0%)
Indianapolis, IN	881	5.3%	347	8.0%	(5.9%-10.0%)
Ann Arbor, MI	225	4.5%	52	8.0%	(2.7%-13.3%)
Scranton-Wilkes Barre, PA	288	5.5%	145	7.9%	(4.7%-11.0%)
Atlanta-Sandy Springs-Marietta, GA(Haralson, Heard, Jasper, Meriwether and Spalding Counties not in sample)	2,631	5.2%	979	7.9%	(6.7%-9.1%)
San Jose-Sunnyvale-Santa Clara, CA	1,038	5.2%	310	7.9%	(5.7%-10.0%)
Hartford-West Hartford-East Hartford, CT	622	4.8%	236	7.8%	(5.3%-10.2%)
Providence-Fall River-Warwick, MA-RI	690	5.2%	319	7.8%	(5.7%-10.0%)
Brownsville-Harlingen, TX	143	8.1%	95	7.8%	(3.9%-11.7%)
Johnson City, TN	104	5.0%	54	7.8%	(2.7%-12.9%)
Roanoke, VA (Craig and Franklin Counties not in sample)	121	5.2%	57	7.7%	(2.7%-12.7%)
Riverside-San Bernardino, CA	1,636	6.0%	818	7.7%	(6.4%-9.0%)
Pittsburgh, PA	1,199	5.2%	500	7.7%	(6.0%-9.4%)
Colorado Springs, CO	287	6.5%	96	7.7%	(3.9%-11.5%)
Worcester, MA-CT (Connecticut portion not identified)	242	6.2%	107	7.6%	(4.0%-11.2%)
Charlotte-Gastonia-Concord, NC-SC(Anson County, NC not in sample)	891	5.5%	380	7.6%	(5.7%-9.5%)
Poughkeepsie-Newburgh-Middletown, NY	348	5.3%	131	7.6%	(4.4%-10.9%)
Boulder, CO	188	5.1%	57	7.6%	(2.6%-12.5%)
Salt Lake City, UT (Toole County not in sample)	583	4.6%	225	7.6%	(5.1%-10.1%)
Olympia, WA	132	3.9%	38	7.6%	(1.6%-13.6%)
Myrtle Beach-Conway-North Myrtle Beach, SC	110	6.7%	48	7.6%	(2.2%-13.0%)
Houston-Baytown-Sugar Land, TX	2,463	5.7%	1,155	7.5%	(6.4%-8.5%)
Seattle-Tacoma-Bellevue, WA	1,771	5.0%	540	7.5%	(5.9%-9.1%)
Dover, DE	80	5.0%	43	7.5%	(1.8%-13.2%)
Portland-Vancouver-Beaverton, OR-WA(Yamhill County, OR not in sample)	1,139	5.2%	354	7.5%	(5.5%-9.4%)
Denver-Aurora, CO	1,320	4.8%	440	7.5%	(5.7%-9.3%)
Bridgeport-Stamford-Norwalk, CT	435	4.8%	143	7.5%	(4.4%-10.6%)

Table C1. Continued.

Metropolitan Statistical Areas (MSAs)	Total Civilian Labor Force		Civilian Labor Force With a High School Education or Less		
	Number (1,000s) (1)	Unemployment Rate (2)	Number (1,000s) (3)	Unemployment Rate (4)	Confidence Intervals for Column 4 (5)
Fayetteville, NC	145	5.0%	63	7.4%	(2.8%-12.1%)
Jackson, MI	152	4.9%	65	7.4%	(2.8%-12.0%)
Bloomington, IN (Owen County not in sample)	141	5.1%	59	7.4%	(2.6%-12.2%)
Milwaukee-Waukesha-West Allis, WI	820	4.6%	357	7.4%	(5.4%-9.4%)
Philadelphia-Camden-Wilmington, PA-NJ- DE	2,801	4.8%	1,162	7.4%	(6.3%-8.4%)
Green Bay, WI (Oconto County not in sample)	184	4.8%	85	7.3%	(3.3%-11.2%)
Flint, MI	173	4.8%	76	7.3%	(3.1%-11.5%)
Nashville-Davidson-Murfreesboro, TN(Cannon, Hickman and Macon Counties not in sample)	800	4.9%	342	7.3%	(5.3%-9.3%)
Boston-Cambridge-Quincy, MA-NH	2,411	4.6%	784	7.3%	(6.0%-8.6%)
Austin-Round Rock, TX	879	4.9%	290	7.2%	(5.0%-9.3%)
Norwich-New London, CT-RI (RI portion recoded to Providence NECTA)	124	6.1%	59	7.1%	(2.4%-11.9%)
Wausau, WI	89	5.0%	48	7.0%	(1.8%-12.2%)
Sacramento — Arden-Arcade Roseville, CA	1,027	5.0%	392	7.0%	(5.2%-8.9%)
New Haven, CT	308	4.6%	102	7.0%	(3.5%-10.6%)
Fort Collins-Loveland, CO	176	4.6%	54	7.0%	(2.1%-11.9%)
Canton-Massillon, OH	219	6.5%	122	6.9%	(3.7%-10.2%)
Longview, TX (Rusk and Upshur Counties not in sample)	107	6.3%	43	6.9%	(1.4%-12.4%)
Grand Rapids-Muskegon-Holland, MI	144	4.7%	64	6.8%	(2.4%-11.2%)
Modesto, CA	261	4.1%	128	6.8%	(3.7%-10.0%)
Albuquerque, NM	424	5.2%	145	6.7%	(3.8%-9.7%)
Killeen-Temple-Fort Hood, TX	162	5.0%	88	6.6%	(2.9%-10.4%)
Des Moines, IA	311	3.9%	119	6.6%	(3.4%-9.8%)
Charleston-North Charleston, SC	292	4.3%	99	6.6%	(3.1%-10.2%)
Greensboro-High Point, NC	496	5.2%	221	6.6%	(4.3%-9.0%)
Raleigh-Cary, NC	626	3.6%	217	6.6%	(4.2%-9.0%)
Niles-Benton Harbor, MI	64	6.5%	35	6.6%	(0.7%-12.5%)
Columbus, OH (Morrow County not in sample)	932	4.9%	361	6.5%	(4.7%-8.3%)
Madison, WI	346	3.3%	107	6.5%	(3.1%-9.8%)
Deltona-Daytona Beach-Ormond Beach, FL	211	4.5%	87	6.5%	(2.8%-10.2%)
Pensacola-Ferry Pass-Brent, FL	201	4.7%	88	6.5%	(2.8%-10.2%)
Tulsa, OK (Okmulgee County not in sample)	440	3.8%	170	6.5%	(3.8%-9.1%)

Table C1. Continued.

Metropolitan Statistical Areas (MSAs)	Total Civilian Labor Force		Civilian Labor Force With a High School Education or Less		
	Number (1,000s) (1)	Unemployment Rate (2)	Number (1,000s) (3)	Unemployment Rate (4)	Confidence Intervals for Column 4 (5)
New York-Northern New Jersey-Long Island, NY-NJ-PA (Pennsylvania portion not in sample. White Plains central city recoded to balance of metropolitan.)	9,171	4.7%	3,581	6.4%	(5.8%-7.0%)
Los Angeles-Long Beach-Santa Ana, CA	6,533	4.9%	2,671	6.4%	(5.7%-7.0%)
San Diego-Carlsbad-San Marcos, CA	1,449	3.5%	444	6.4%	(4.8%-8.1%)
Gulfport-Biloxi, MS	69	7.5%	37	6.4%	(0.7%-12.1%)
Minneapolis-St Paul-Bloomington, MN- WI (Wisconsin portion not identified)	1,765	3.9%	554	6.4%	(4.9%-7.8%)
Oklahoma City, OK	676	3.7%	259	6.3%	(4.2%-8.4%)
Syracuse, NY	299	5.3%	125	6.3%	(3.2%-9.3%)
Savannah, GA	288	4.4%	141	6.3%	(3.5%-9.2%)
Richmond, VA (Cumberland County not in sample)	656	4.8%	309	6.3%	(4.3%-8.2%)
Montgomery, AL	165	4.9%	77	6.2%	(2.3%-10.1%)
Orlando, FL	1,081	4.0%	457	6.2%	(4.6%-7.8%)
Champaign-Urbana, IL (Ford County not in sample)	136	2.8%	47	6.2%	(1.2%-11.2%)
El Centro, CA	74	3.5%	37	6.2%	(0.6%-11.7%)
Fort Smith, AR-OK (Oklahoma portion not in sample)	107	4.4%	54	6.2%	(1.6%-10.8%)
Grand Rapids-Wyoming, MI La Crosse, WI (Houston County not in	415	4.8%	157	6.2%	(3.5%-8.9%)
sample)	121	2.7%	44	6.2%	(1.1%-11.3%)
El Paso, TX	324	5.2%	157	6.1%	(3.4%-8.8%)
Portland-South Portland, ME	202	3.5%	68	6.0%	(1.9%-10.0%)
Fayetteville- Springdale-Rogers, AR-MO(Madison County, AR and Missouri portion not in sample)	233	3.7%	99	6.0%	(2.7%-9.4%)
Birmingham-Hoover, AL	620	4.2%	249	5.9%	(3.8%-8.0%)
Ocala, FL	125	4.7%	66	5.8%	(1.7%-9.9%)
Boise City-Nampa, ID (Owyhee County not in sample)	284	3.9%	114	5.8%	(2.7%-8.9%)
Tampa-St. Petersburg-Clearwater, FL	1,323	4.2%	536	5.7%	(4.3%-7.1%)
Fort Wayne, IN	200	5.5%	77	5.7%	(2.0%-9.5%)
Sioux Falls, SD	131	2.7%	51	5.6%	(1.1%-10.1%)
Panama City-Lynn Haven, FL	95	3.4%	46	5.6%	(0.8%-10.4%)
Chattanooga, TN-GA	254	3.5%	126	5.6%	(2.7%-8.5%)
Bend, OR	94	5.0%	45	5.5%	(0.7%-10.3%)
Phoenix-Mesa-Scottsdale, AZ	1,985	3.9%	812	5.5%	(4.4%-6.7%)

Table C1. Continued.

Metropolitan Statistical Areas (MSAs)	Total Civilian Labor Force		Civilian Labor Force With a High School Education or Less		
	Number (1,000s) (1)	Unemployment Rate (2)	Number (1,000s) (3)	Unemployment Rate (4)	Confidence Intervals for Column 4 (5)
Fort Walton Beach-Crestview-Destin, FL	126	3.3%	54	5.5%	(1.1%-9.9%)
Reno-Sparks, NV	233	3.9%	96	5.4%	(2.2%-8.7%)
Hickory-Morgantown-Lenoir, NC (Caldwell County not in sample)	139	4.8%	76	5.3%	(1.7%-8.9%)
Cincinnati-Middletown, OH-KY-IN(Franklin County , IN not in sample; Dearborn and Ohio Counties, IN not identified)	1,071	4.2%	485	5.3%	(3.8%-6.7%)
Miami-Fort Lauderdale-Miami Beach, FL	2,612	3.9%	1,116	5.3%	(4.4%-6.3%)
Las Vegas-Paradise, NM	857	4.5%	444	5.3%	(3.8%-6.8%)
Binghamton, NY	111	5.8%	50	5.3%	(0.8%-9.8%)
Vineland-Millville-Bridgeton, NJ	98	4.0%	54	5.2%	(1.0%-9.5%)
Harrisburg-Carlisle, PA	299	4.0%	147	5.2%	(2.6%-7.8%)
Virginia Beach-Norfolk-Newport News, VA-NC (North Carolina portion not identified)	738	3.8%	295	5.0%	(3.2%-6.8%)
Jacksonville, FL	659	3.5%	269	5.0%	(3.1%-6.9%)
Columbus, GA-AL (Harris County, GA not in sample)	123	3.9%	69	4.9%	(1.2%-8.5%)
Little Rock-North Little Rock, AR (Perry County not in sample)	341	3.2%	153	4.8%	(2.4%-7.3%)
Honolulu, HI	455	3.0%	164	4.8%	(2.5%-7.2%)
York-Hanover, PA	224	3.0%	125	4.7%	(2.0%-7.3%)
Washington-Arlington-Alexandria, DC- VA-MD-WV (West Virginia portion not identified. Reston central city recoded to balance of metropolitan)	3,012	2.8%	944	4.7%	(3.8%-5.7%)
Cape Coral-Fort Myers, FL	262	2.7%	122	4.7%	(2.0%-7.4%)
Charleston, WV (Clay County not in sample)	158	3.9%	74	4.7%	(1.2%-8.1%)
Joplin, MO	129	3.2%	62	4.5%	(0.8%-8.2%)
Peoria, IL	175	4.5%	64	4.5%	(0.9%-8.2%)
Springfield, IL	106	2.7%	43	4.4%	(0.0%-8.8%)
Erie, PA	112	4.1%	65	4.2%	(0.7%-7.7%)
Albany-Schenectady-Troy, NY	476	2.6%	185	4.2%	(2.2%-6.3%)
Amarillo, TX (Armstrong and Carson Counties not in sample)	123	2.6%	52	4.2%	(0.3%-8.1%)
Lafayette, LA	284	4.5%	159	4.2%	(1.9%-6.4%)
Janesville, WI	93	2.8%	51	4.2%	(0.3%-8.2%)
Port St. Lucie-Fort Pierce, FL	171	2.6%	90	4.1%	(1.1%-7.0%)
Harrisonburg, VA	112	2.4%	52	4.1%	(0.2%-8.0%)
Greeley, CO	123	3.0%	53	3.8%	(0.1%-7.4%)

Table C1. Continued.

Metropolitan Statistical Areas (MSAs)	Total Civilian Labor Force		Civilian Labor Force With a High School Education or Less		
	Number (1,000s) (1)	Unemployment Rate (2)	Number (1,000s) (3)	Unemploymen t Rate (4)	Confidence Intervals for Column 4 (5)
Asheville, NC (Haywood and Henderson Counties not in sample)	204	3.8%	80	3.7%	(0.7%-6.6%)
Midland, TX	116	2.4%	56	3.6%	(0.1%-7.1%)
Florence, AL	103	2.3%	55	3.6%	(0.0%-7.1%)
Ogden-Clearfield, UT	168	2.5%	78	3.6%	(0.6%-6.6%)
Springfield, MO (Dallas and Polk Counties not in sample)	184	2.4%	76	3.5%	(0.5%-6.5%)
Atlantic City, NJ	151	3.7%	72	3.5%	(0.5%-6.5%)
Reading, PA	222	2.4%	130	3.5%	(1.2%-5.7%)
McAllen-Edinburg-Pharr, TX	263	2.9%	172	3.4%	(1.4%-5.3%)
Lancaster, PA	228	2.8%	129	3.4%	(1.2%-5.7%)
Lakeland-Winter Haven, FL	217	3.0%	125	3.4%	(1.1%-5.7%)
Columbia, SC	330	2.9%	136	3.4%	(1.2%-5.6%)
Utica-Rome, NY	150	4.7%	65	3.0%	(0.0%-6.0%)
Naples-Marco Island, FL	156	2.1%	80	2.9%	(0.3%-5.5%)
Palm Bay-Melbourne-Titusville, FL	322	1.6%	109	2.9%	(0.6%-5.1%)
Sarasota-Bradenton-Venice, FL	317	2.2%	150	2.7%	(0.8%-4.6%)

Source: Calculated by CRS from the monthly Current Population Survey (CPS).

Notes: Data are for persons age 16 and older and in the labor force. Confidence intervals were calculated at a 90% level. See *Appendix A* for a description of confidence intervals. Following BLS practice, *Table C1* does not show estimates of the size of the labor force or the unemployment rate if the estimated size of the labor force is 35,000 persons or less. Estimates of unemployment for persons with a high school education or less are not shown if the estimate is not statistically significant (i.e., if the lower bound of the confidence interval is less than zero). Estimates are monthly averages for calendar year 2005. Details may not add to totals because of rounding.

In: Farm Labor: 21st Century Issues and Challenges
Editors: A. W. Burton, I. B. Telpov, pp. 173-188

ISBN: 978-1-60456-005-3
© 2007 Nova Science Publishers, Inc.

Chapter 5

FARM LABOR SHORTAGES AND IMMIGRATION POLICY[*]

Linda Levine

ABSTRACT

The connection between farm labor and immigration policies is a longstanding one, particularly with regard to U.S. employers' use of workers from Mexico. The Congress is revisiting the issue as it continues debate over initiation of a broad-based guest worker program, increased border enforcement, and employer sanctions to curb the flow of unauthorized workers into the United States.

Two decades ago, the Congress passed the Immigration Reform and Control Act (IRCA, P.L. 99-603) to reduce illegal entry into the United States by imposing sanctions on employers who knowingly hire individuals who lack permission to work in the country. In addition to a general legalization program, IRCA included legalization programs specific to the agricultural industry that were intended to compensate for the act's expected impact on the farm labor supply and encourage the development of a legal crop workforce. These provisions of the act, however, have not operated in the offsetting manner that was intended, as substantial numbers of unauthorized aliens have continued to join legal farmworkers in performing seasonal agricultural services (SAS).

Currently, a little more than one-half of the SAS workforce is not authorized to hold U.S. jobs. Perishable crop growers contend that their sizable presence implies a shortage of native-born workers willing to undertake seasonal farm jobs. (An increasing share of IRCA-legalized farmworkers have entered the ages of diminished participation in the SAS workforce, as well.) Grower advocates argue that farmers would rather not employ unauthorized workers because doing so puts them at risk of incurring penalties. Farmworker advocates counter that crop growers prefer unauthorized workers because they are in a weak bargaining position with regard to wages and working conditions. If the supply of unauthorized workers were curtailed, it is claimed, farmers could adjust to a smaller workforce by introducing labor-efficient technologies and management practices, and by raising wages, which, in turn, would entice more U.S. workers to seek farm employment. Farmers respond that further mechanization would be difficult for some crops, and that substantially higher wages would make the U.S. industry uncompetitive in

---

[*] Excerpted from CRS Report 30395, dated January 31, 2007.

the world marketplace — without expanding the legal farm labor force. These remain untested arguments because perishable crop growers have rarely, if ever, operated without unauthorized aliens in their workforces.

Trends in the agricultural labor market generally do not suggest the existence of a nationwide shortage of domestically available farmworkers, in part because the government's databases cover authorized *and* unauthorized employment. (This finding does not preclude the possibility of spot labor shortages, however.) Farm employment did not show the same upward trend of total U.S. employment during the 1990s expansion. The length of time hired farmworkers are employed has changed little or decreased over the years. Their unemployment rate has varied little and remains well above the U.S. average, and underemployment among farmworkers also remains substantial. These agricultural employees earn about 50 cents for every dollar paid to other employees in the private sector.

INTRODUCTION

Questions often have arisen over the years about (1) whether sufficient workers are available domestically to meet the seasonal employment demand of perishable crop producers in the U.S. agricultural industry[1] and (2) how, if at all, the Congress should change immigration policy with respect to farmworkers. Immigration policy has long been intertwined with the labor needs of crop (e.g., fruit and vegetable) growers, who rely more than most farmers on hand labor (e.g., for harvesting) and consequently "are the largest users of hired and contract workers on a per-farm basis."[2] Since World War I, the Congress has allowed the use of temporary foreign workers to perform agricultural labor of a seasonal nature as a means of augmenting the supply of domestic farmworkers.[3] In addition, a sizeable fraction of immigrants historically have found employment on the nation's farms.[4]

The intersection between farm labor and immigration has again emerged as a policy issue. The terrorist attacks of September 11, 2001 effectively quashed the discussions on this subject between the Bush and Fox Administrations that took place shortly after President Bush first came into office, but the proposal of a broad-based temporary foreign worker program that President Bush sketched in December 2003 has revived interest in the labor-immigration nexus, which continues to this day.

This article first explains the connection made over the past several years between farm labor and immigration policies. It next examines the composition of the seasonal agricultural labor force and presents the arguments of grower and farmworker advocates concerning its adequacy relative to employer demand. The article closes with an analysis of the trends in employment, unemployment, time worked and wages of authorized and unauthorized

---

1 In this report, the terms "agriculture" and "farming" will be used interchangeably as will the terms "producer," "grower," and "farmer."

2 Victor J. Oliveira, Anne B. W. Effland, Jack L. Runyan and Shannon Hamm, Hired Farm Labor on Fruit, Vegetable, and Horticultural Specialty Farms, U.S. Department of Agriculture, Economic Research Service, Agricultural Economic Report 676, Dec. 1993, p. 2. (Hereafter cited as, Oliveira, Effland, Runyan and Hamm, Hired Farm Labor on Fruit, Vegetable, and Horticultural Specialty Farms).

3 U.S. Congress, Senate Committee on the Judiciary, Temporary Worker Programs: Background and Issues, committee print, 96th Cong., 2nd sess. (Washington: GPO, 1980).

4 Philip L. Martin, "Good Intentions Gone Awry: IRCA and U.S. Agriculture," *Annals of the American Academy of Political and Social Science*, July 1994.

farmworkers to determine whether they are consistent with the existence of a nationwide shortage of domestically available farmworkers.

FARMWORKERS AND ACTIVITIES OF SSA AND DHS

During the second half of the 1990s, attention began to focus on the growing share of the domestic supply of farmworkers that is composed of aliens who are not authorized to work in the United States. The U.S. Department of Labor (DOL) estimated that foreign-born persons in the country illegally accounted for 37% of the domestic crop workforce in FY1994-FY1995. Shortly thereafter (FY1997-FY1998), unauthorized aliens' share of the estimated 1.8 million workers employed on crop farms reached 52%.[5] By FY1999-FY2000, their proportion had increased to 55% before retreating somewhat — to 53% — in FY2001-FY2002.[6]

Although a number of studies found that no nationwide shortage of domestic farm labor existed in the past decade,[7] a case has been made that the considerable presence of unauthorized aliens in the seasonal agricultural labor force implies a lack of legal farmworkers relative to employer demand. Arguably, the purported imbalance between authorized-to-work farm labor and employer demand would become more apparent were the supply of unauthorized aliens curtailed sufficiently — a fear that has plagued growers for some time.

Crop producers and their advocates have testified at congressional hearings over the last several years that they believe the latest risk of losing much of their labor force comes from certain activities of the Bureau of Citizenship and Immigration Services and the Bureau of Immigration and Customs Enforcement within the Department of Homeland Security (DHS) and the Social Security Administration (SSA). Growers have asserted that these activities have disrupted their workforces by increasing employee turnover and therefore, decreasing the stability of their labor supply. The perception that government actions might negatively impact the agricultural workforce — allegedly to the extent that crops would not be harvested, farmers would go bankrupt or produce costs to U.S. consumers would rise — has prompted a legislative response in the past.

---

5 According to U.S. Department of Labor Report to Congress: The Agricultural Labor Market — Status and Recommendations, the 1.8 million figure was developed by dividing the hourly earnings of field and livestock workers into farm labor expenditures to estimate the number of work hours on crop and livestock farms. As it was calculated that 72% of the hours were being worked on crop farms, the percentage was then applied to the Commission on Agricultural Workers' estimate for 1992 of 2.5 million persons employed for wages on U.S. farms to yield a current estimate of the hired crop workforce. The Commission had developed its earlier farm employment figure from a variety of data sources because there is no actual head count of farmworkers. For other current estimates of hired farm and crop workers see Table 1.

6 DOL, Findings from the National Agricultural Workers Survey (NAWS) 2001-2002, Research Report No. 9, Mar. 2005. (Hereafter cited as DOL, Findings from the NAWS 2001-2002).

7 Commission on Agricultural Workers (CAW), Report of the Commission on Agricultural Workers, (Washington: GPO, Nov. 1992). (Hereafter cited as CAW, Report of the Commission on Agricultural Workers.). U.S. General Accounting Office (GAO), H-2A Agricultural Guestworker Program: Changes Could Improve Services to Employers and Better Protect Workers, GAO/HEHES-98-20, Dec. 1997. (Hereafter cited as GAO, H-2A Agricultural Guestworker Program). DOL, A Profile of U.S. Farmworkers: Demographics, Household Composition, Income and Use of Services, Research Report No. 6, Apr. 1997. (Hereafter cited as DOL, A Profile of U.S. Farmworkers.) And, annual calculations in the early 1990s by the U.S. Departments of Labor and Agriculture.

The SSA and DHS activities are briefly described below:

(1) The SSA sends "no-match letters" to employers who submit a substantial number of W-2 forms for which the agency cannot find corresponding earnings records in its database.[8] The purpose of the letters is to make wage reports more accurate so that the agency can properly credit earnings to employees' records for future benefit payments. As part of this effort, the SSA has encouraged employers not to wait until the annual submission of W-2 forms and instead, to use its Enumeration Verification Service (EVS) to match the names/social security numbers of employees with those in the agency's database.[9]

Growers have told the SSA that their concern with using the EVS is that when they discuss any discrepancies with employees, the employees do not return to work. The National Council of Agricultural Employers testified in 2000 about the large and growing numbers of employers receiving no-match letters.[10] The American Farm Bureau Federation said at the time that growers are apprehensive about being liable for penalties (commonly referred to as employer sanctions[11]) due to "constructive knowledge" of illegal workers on their payrolls if they do not act on the SSA letters.[12] The agency's correspondence clearly states, however, that there are many reasons why discrepancies can occur and that the letter, by itself, should not form the basis for taking any adverse actions against employees.

SSA responded to the growers' concerns in a variety of ways in the past few years. For example, the agency translated into Spanish portions of the letter so that if growers show it to farmworkers they can see they have nothing to fear from it. In addition, based upon a change in selection criteria that went into effect in January 2003, SSA sends far fewer no-match letters to employers. In 2005, just 127,652 no-match letters were sent to employers.[13]

(2) The Illegal Immigration Reform and Immigrant Responsibility Act of 1996 (IIRIRA, P.L. 104-288) provided for increased border enforcement efforts and for an employment verification pilot.[14] Employer participation in the program, which was set to last no more than four years, has been voluntary, and the program has involved a limited number of areas. Nonetheless, organizations of growers testified that inclusion of the pilot in P.L. 104-288 merely delayed the creation of a mandatory nationwide verification system.[15] Although Congress extended the program for five years through 2008 and expanded it through the Basic Pilot Program Extension and Expansion Act of 2003 (P.L. 108-156) to include all states, employer participation remains optional. The Basic Pilot continues to be little-used: as

---

8 For additional information on no-match letters, see CRS Report RL32004, Social Security Benefits for Noncitizens: Current Policy and Legislation, by Dawn Nuschler and Alison Siskin.

9 Conversations with SSA staff.

10 Testimony of James S. Holt on behalf of the National Council of Agricultural Employers before the Senate Judiciary Subcommittee on Immigration, May 4, 2000.

11 For additional information on employer sanctions, see CRS Report RS22180,Unauthorized Employment of Aliens: Basics of Employer Sanctions, by Alison M. Smith.

12 Testimony of Josh Wunsch on behalf of the American Farm Bureau Federation before the Senate Judiciary Subcommittee on Immigration, May 4, 2000; and Alexander T. Aleinikoff, "The Green Card Solution," The American Prospect, December 1999.

13 Testimony of James B. Lockhart III, Deputy Commissioner of Social Security, before the Subcommittee on Oversight of the House Committee on Ways and Means, Feb. 16, 2006.

14 Work eligibility verification demonstrations in addition to the IIRIRA pilots are authorized under Section 274A(d)(4) of the Immigration and Nationality Act and Presidential Executive Order 12781 of Nov. 20, 1991. For more information see Karen I. Miksch, INS Pilot Programs for Employment Eligibility Confirmation, Carnegie Endowment for International Peace, International Migration Policy Program, Nov. 1998.

15 Testimony of Bob L. Vice on behalf of the National Council of Agricultural Employers and the American Farm Bureau Federation before the House Judiciary Subcommittee on Immigration and Claims, Sept. 24, 1997.

of early 2006, after the pilot was expanded nationwide, only about 5,500 employers (representing some 22,500 employer sites) had signed agreements with DHS and SSA.[16]

Currently, employers fulfill the legal requirement to not knowingly hire illegal workers by viewing documents that show the new-hire's identity and eligibility to work in the United States, and by completing an I-9 (employment eligibility verification) form. Under an initiative referred to as the Basic Pilot, employers can access the DHS system to validate a newly hired citizen's or non-citizen's eligibility to work.[17] If employers receive a final nonconfirmation of employment eligibility, they must either fire the new-hire or be subject to financial penalties.[18]

(3) The Bureau of Immigration and Customs Enforcement (another former part of the Immigration and Naturalization Service, INS) reportedly increased its audits of I-9 forms even before September 11, 2001, but the incidence was and remains relatively low according to the agency. In the audits, the bureau checks the authenticity of employees' work authorization documents against government records. At the audits' completion, employers are given a list of employees whose documents were deemed to be invalid. According to a representative of the growers, "Frequently, INS audits of agricultural employers reveal that 60 to 70 percent of seasonal agricultural workers have provided fraudulent documents. The employer is then required to dismiss each employee on the list who cannot provide a valid employment authorization document, something few workers can do."[19] This estimate of hired farmworkers who have secured their jobs through presentation of fraudulent documents is at the high end of figures reported elsewhere, however.[20]

While a grower representative testified that "agriculture has historically not been a major target" of immigration enforcement activities, he pointed to some experiences involving Vermont dairy farmers and Georgia onion growers in the last few years. The increased attention that has been paid to homeland security since September 11, 2001 and the better integration of agencies within DHS led the American Farm Bureau Federation to speculate during a 2004 hearing that more raids could be forthcoming.[21] A representative of the

---

16 Testimony of James B. Lockhart III, Deputy Commissioner of Social Security, and Barbara D. Bovbjerg, Government Accountability Office, before the Subcommittee on Oversight of the House Committee on Ways and Means, Feb. 16, 2006.

17 Under the Basic Pilot, employers electronically send worker information to DHS, which forwards it to SSA. SSA compares the information provided against its database, and in the case of non-citizens, additionally refers the employer request to DHS. If DHS is unable to verify the employee's work authorization against its automated records, the request is forwarded to a DHS field office where further research is conducted. If SSA is unable to confirm the worker's SSN, name, and date of birth or the DHS records search cannot verify worth authorization, the employer is sent a tentative nonconfirmation response. The employer then is to check the accuracy of the information with the worker, inform him or her of the government's finding, and refer the worker to either SSA or DHS to clear up the matter. If the worker does not contest the finding, a final nonconfirmation is issued to the employer.

18 In addition to potential fines under immigration law, the Internal Revenue Service (IRS) may charge employers $50 for each W-2 form that omits or includes an incorrect Social Security number, up to $250,000 per employer in a calendar year. The IRS is unaware of any employer having to pay a penalty for submitting an erroneous wage report, according to testimony of Mark W. Everson, IRS Commissioner, before the Subcommittee on Oversight of the House Committee on Ways and Means, Feb. 16, 2006.

19 Testimony of James S. Holt on behalf of the National Council of Agricultural Employers before the Senate Judiciary Subcommittee on Immigration, May 12, 1999.

20 Perhaps one-fourth to three-fourths of the hired farm labor force may have relied on fraudulent documents to gain employment, according to U.S. Department of Agriculture, "Status Report: Hired Farm Labor in U.S. Agriculture," Agricultural Outlook, Oct. 1998.

21 Testimony of Larry Wooten on behalf of the American Farm Bureau Federation before the House Committee on Agriculture, Jan. 28, 2004.

National Foundation for American Policy testified, however, that DHS "does not have the resources to enforce those [immigration] laws in a manner that would stop employers from using illegal workers."[22]

THE COMPOSITION OF THE SEASONAL FARM LABOR FORCE

Immigration legislation sometimes has been crafted to take into account the purported labor requirements of U.S. crop growers. In 1986, for example, Congress passed the Immigration Reform and Control Act (IRCA, P.L. 99-603) to curb the presence of unauthorized aliens in the United States by imposing sanctions on employers who knowingly hire individuals who lack permission to work in the country. In addition to a general legalization program, P.L. 99-603 included two industry-specific legalization programs — the Special Agricultural Worker (SAW) program and the Replenishment Agricultural Worker (RAW) program[23] — that were intended to compensate for the act's expected impact on the farm labor supply and encourage the development of a legal crop workforce. These provisions of the act have not operated in the offsetting manner that was intended, however, as substantial numbers of unauthorized aliens have continued to join legal farmworkers in performing seasonal agricultural services (SAS).[24]

On the basis of case studies that it sponsored, the Commission on Agricultural Workers concluded in its 1992 report that individuals legalized under the SAW program (i.e., SAWs) and other farmworkers planned to remain in the agricultural labor force "indefinitely, or for as long as they are physically able."[25] According to the DOL's National Agricultural Workers Survey, two-thirds of SAWs stated that they intended to engage in field work until the end of their working lives.[26]

For many SAWs, the end of their worklives — at least their worklives in farming — may now be near at hand. The diminished physical ability generally associated with aging in combination with the taxing nature of crop tasks could well be prompting greater numbers of SAWs to leave the fields. Relatively few farmworkers are involved in crop production beyond the age of 44 and even fewer beyond the age of 54 (19% and 7%, respectively, in FY2001-FY2002).[27] The Commission on Agricultural Workers noted that the typical SAW in 1990 was a 30-year-old male who "is likely to remain in farm work well into the 21st century."[28] As the average age of an authorized foreign-born cropworker in FY2001-FY2002 was 40,[29] he is

---

22 Fawn H. Johnson, "Immigration: Goodlatte Calls for Prevailing Wage in H-2A Program, Condemns Amnesty," Daily Labor Report, Jan. 29, 2004, p. A-3.
23 The INS approved more than 1 million of the applications that individuals filed under the SAW program to become legal permanent residents. Anticipating that SAWs would leave farming because IRCA did not require them to remain in order to adjust their status, P.L. 99-603 included the RAW program as a back-up measure to ensure growers of an adequate labor supply. The RAW program was never used because the annual calculations of farm labor supply and demand that were made by the U.S. Departments of Labor and Agriculture during the FY1990-FY1993 period found no national shortages of farmworkers.
24 Seasonal agricultural services (SAS) were defined broadly in IRCA as field work related to planting, cultivating, growing and harvesting of fruits and vegetables of every kind and other perishable commodities. The terms "SAS," "seasonal farm work," "field work" and "crop work" are used interchangeably in this report.
25 CAW, Report of the Commission on Agricultural Workers, p. 75.
26 CAW, Report of the Commission on Agricultural Workers, p. 75.
27 DOL, Findings from the NAWS 2001-2002.
28 CAW, Report of the Commission on Agricultural Workers, p. 80.
29 DOL, Findings from the NAWS 2001-2002.

now at the age of diminished participation in SAS labor. It thus appears that the 1986 legalization program has become less useful over time in fulfilling the labor requirements of crop producers.

A combination of factors likely has contributed to the decrease in SAWs' share of agricultural employment.[30] While the share of IRCA-legalized farmworkers has been falling over time due to aging and the availability of nonfarm jobs,[31] the leading factor probably is the substantially increased presence of illegal aliens.[32] In the first half of the 1990s, unauthorized workers rose from 7% to 37% of the SAS labor force.[33] Their share climbed to 52% by FY1997-FY1998;[34] then, rose further to 55% by FY1999-FY2000, before it dropped somewhat to 53% in FY2001-FY2002.[35] Moreover, the number of SAS workdays performed by unauthorized aliens more than tripled between FY1989 and FY2002.[36] In addition, of the many foreign-born newcomers to the sector in FY2000-FY2002, 99% were employed without authorization.

Unauthorized aliens, arguably, have been displacing legal workers from jobs in the agricultural industry. Farmworker advocates assert that crop producers prefer unauthorized employees because they have less bargaining power with regard to wages and working conditions than other employees. Growers counter that they would rather not employ unauthorized workers because doing so puts them at risk of incurring penalties. They argue that the considerable presence of unauthorized aliens in the U.S. farm labor force implies a shortage of legal workers.

Farmworker groups and some policy analysts contend that even if the previously described DHS and SSA activities were to deprive farmers of many of their unauthorized workers, the industry could adjust to a smaller supply of legal workers by (1) introducing labor-efficient technologies and management practices, and (2) raising wages which, in turn,

---

30 Alternatively, there are a number of reasons why SAWs would remain in farm employment (e.g., limited English-language fluency and little formal education). In light of these competing factors, the Commission on Agricultural Workers concluded that it would be difficult to estimate the attrition rate of SAWs from the fields. The existence of fraud in the SAW program further complicates such a calculation because the stock of SAWs who genuinely were farmworkers is unknown: when Congress was debating immigration proposals in the mid-1980s, the U.S. Department of Agriculture estimated that there were 300,000 to 500,000 unauthorized farmworkers, but more than twice the upper-end estimate were legalized under the SAW program; this large discrepancy, as well as additional research, led to the widely held conclusion that fraud was extensive.

31 DOL, Findings from the National Agricultural Workers Survey: 1997-1998, Research Report No. 8, Mar. 2000. (Hereafter cited as DOL, Findings from the National Agricultural Workers Survey: 1997-1998.). Note: In addition to the more than 1 million workers legalized through the SAW program, about 7% (119,000) of the 1.7 million aliens granted legal permanent resident status under IRCA's general amnesty program were employed in agriculture when they filed their applications. Oliveira, Effland, Runyan and Hamm, Hired Farm Labor in Fruit, Vegetable, and Horticultural Specialty Farms.

32 The Commission on Agricultural Workers determined that the design of the SAW program was, at least in part, responsible for the increase in unauthorized immigration because if dependents of SAWs did not similarly have their status adjusted, they might have illegally entered the United States to join family members. In addition, the network or kinship recruitment process for SAS work continued to flourish and to facilitate not only job placement, but also migration by assisting in border-crossing and in acquiring fraudulent work authorization documents. These findings led the Commission to conclude that "the concept of a worker-specific and industry-specific legalization program was fundamentally flawed. It invited fraud, posed difficult definitional problems regarding who should or should not be eligible, and ignored the longstanding priority of U.S. immigration policy favoring the unification of families." CAW, Report of the Commission on Agricultural Workers, p. 67.

33 DOL, A Profile of U.S. Farmworkers.

34 DOL, Findings from the National Agricultural Workers Survey: 1997-1998.

35 DOL, Findings from the NAWS 2001-2002.

36 DOL, Farmworkers in the Post-IRCA Period and Findings from the NAWS 2001-2002.

would entice more authorized workers into the farm labor force. Grower advocates respond that further mechanization would be difficult to develop for many crops and that, even at higher wages, not many U.S. workers would want to perform physically demanding, seasonal farm labor under variable climactic conditions. Moreover, employer representatives and some policy analysts maintain that growers cannot raise wages substantially without making the U.S. industry uncompetitive in world markets which, in turn, would reduce farm employment. In response, farmworker supporters note that wages are a small part of the price consumers pay for fresh fruits and vegetables and accordingly, higher wages would result in only a slight rise in retail prices. These remain untested arguments as perishable crop growers have rarely, if ever, had to operate without unauthorized aliens in their workforces.

A FARM LABOR SHORTAGE?

Trends in the farm labor market generally do not suggest the existence of a nationwide shortage of domestically available farmworkers, in part because the government's statistical series cover authorized *and* unauthorized workers. This overall finding does not preclude the possibility of farm labor shortages in certain areas of the country at various times of the year (i.e., spot labor shortages).

Caution should be exercised when reviewing the statistics on farmworkers' employment, unemployment, time worked and wages that follow. The surveys from which the data are derived cover somewhat different groups within the farm labor force (e.g., all hired farmworkers as opposed to those engaged only in crop production or workers employed directly by growers as opposed to those supplied to growers by farm labor contractors), and they have different sample sizes. A household survey such as the Current Population Survey (CPS) could well understate the presence of farmworkers because they are more likely to live in less traditional quarters (e.g., labor camps) and of unauthorized workers generally because they may be reluctant to respond to government enumerators. And, some of the surveys have individuals as respondents (e.g., the CPS and DOL's National Agricultural Workers Survey) while others have employers as respondents (e.g., the U.S. Department of Agriculture's National Agricultural Statistics Service Farm Labor Survey). Surveys that query employers are more likely to pickup unauthorized employment than are surveys that query individuals.

Employment

The demand for and supply of labor typically cannot be measured directly. Instead, proxies are used such as the trend in employment. Decreases in an occupation's employment or small gains compared to those recorded for other occupations might signal that labor demand is not approaching a supply constraint.

Table 1. Hired Farm Employment

		Economic Research Service (ERS) [b]		National Agricultural Statistics Service (NASS) [c]		
Year	Total nonfarm wage and salary employment[a]	Hired farm workers[d]	Hired crop workers[e]	Hired farm workers[f]	Agricultural service workers[g]	Total
1990	105,705	886	419	892	250	1,142
1991	104,520	884	449	910	259	1,169
1992	105,540	848	409	866	252	1,118
1993	107,011	803	436	857	256	1,113
1994	110,517	793	411	840	250	1,090
1995	112,448	849	433	869	251	1,120
1996	114,171	906	451	832	236	1,068
1997	116,983	889	432	876	240	1,116
1998	119,019	875	458	880	246	1,126
1999	121,323	840	440	929	233	1,162
2000	125,114	878	468	890	243	1,133
2001	125,407	745	392	881	244	1,125
2002	125,156	793	370	886	225	1,111
2003	126,015	777	372	836	236	1,072
2004	127,463	712	368	825	277	1,102
2005	129,931	730	393	780	282	1,062
2006	132,449	748	351	752	255	1,007

(numbers in thousands)

Source: Created by the Congressional Research Service (CRS) from sources cited below.

Note: n.a. = not available.

a. Data are from the monthly CPS, a survey of households, as reported by the DOL's Bureau of Labor Statistics (BLS) for individuals age 16 or older. b. Data are from the monthly CPS as reported by the U.S. Department of Agriculture's ERS for individuals age 15 or older. c. Data are from the Farm Labor Survey (FLS), a quarterly survey of farm operators, as reported by the U.S. Department of Agriculture's NASS. The statistics reflect individuals on employers' payrolls during the survey week in January, April, July, and October. Data for Alaska are not included. 1990-1994 annual averages for all hired farmworkers and all annual averages for agricultural service workers were calculated by CRS. d. In the CPS, an individual's occupation is based on the activity in which he spent the most hours during the survey week. Hired farmworkers are those whose primary job is farmwork and for which they receive wages, as opposed to unpaid family workers or self-employed farmers.

Hired farmworkers include individuals engaged in planting, cultivating, and harvesting crops or tending livestock whom growers employ directly or through agricultural service providers (e.g., farm labor contractors and crew leaders), as well as farm managers, supervisors of farmworkers, and nursery and other workers. e. The ERS disaggregates hired farmworkers by the kind of establishment employing them (i.e., establishments primarily engaged in crop production, livestock production or other). As "other" includes agricultural service providers, the figures for crop workers are limited to farmworkers whom growers employ directly.

f. The FLS counts as hired farmworkers only those persons paid directly by farmers. Hired farmworkers include field workers (i.e., those who plant, cultivate and harvest crops), livestock workers (i.e., those who tend livestock, milk cows or care for poultry) and supervisory workers (e.g., managers or range foremen) as well as other workers on farmers' payrolls (e.g., bookkeepers, secretaries or pilots). g. Includes contract, custom, or other workers supplied to farmers but paid by agricultural service firms (e.g., farm labor contractors or crew leaders).

Although the employment of hired workers engaged in crop or livestock production (including contract workers) has fluctuated erratically over time, the trend overall has been downward (see columns 3 and 7 in Table 1). The employment pattern among crop workers hired directly by growers (i.e., excluding those supplied by farm labor contractors and crew leaders) has regularly risen and then fallen back, but to a higher level through 2000 (column 4). This ratcheting upward of employment produced a 12% gain over the 1990-2000 period. In contrast, other wage and salary workers have experienced steady and robust job growth over almost the entire period: from 1990 to 2000, wage and salary employment in nonfarm industries advanced by 18%. These divergent employment patterns suggest that hired farmworkers did not share equally in the nation's long economic expansion, and appear to be inconsistent with the presence of a nationwide farm labor shortage.

The labor market continued to contract in 2002, despite the 2001 recession's end in November 2001. Nonfarm wage and salary employment showed signs of revival in 2003 that have since continued. In contrast, employment of hired farmworkers has not followed a consistently upward trend. (See columns 3 and 7 of *Table 1*).

Farm employment is subject to considerable seasonal variation during the course of a year, which annual average data masks. Demand for hired farm labor typically peaks in July when many crops are ready to be harvested. The July employment data from the NASS Farm Labor Survey has ranged from less than 1.1 million to less than 1.5 million between 1990 and 2005. In July 2005, employment was a little more than 1.3 million.

Unemployment

Employment data paint an incomplete picture of the state of the labor market. At the same time that employment in a given occupation is decreasing or increasing relatively slowly, unemployment in the occupation might be falling. Employers would then be faced with a shrinking supply of untapped labor from which to draw. A falling unemployment rate or level would offer some basis for this possibility.

As shown in *Table 2*, the unemployment rate of hired farmworkers engaged in crop or livestock production (including contract labor) is quite high. Even the economic boom that characterized most of the 1990s did not reduce the group's unemployment rate below double-digit levels, or about twice the average unemployment rate in the nation at a minimum. Discouragement over their employment prospects in agriculture or better opportunities elsewhere may have prompted some unemployed farmworkers to leave the sector as evidenced by their reduced number after 1998 (see column 4 of the table).

Other observers have examined the unemployment rates in counties that are heavily dependent on the crop farming industry. The GAO, for example, found that many of these agricultural areas chronically experienced double-digit unemployment rates that were well above those reported for much of the rest of the United States. Even when looking at monthly unemployment rates for these areas in order to take into account the seasonality of farm work, the agency found that the agricultural counties exhibited comparatively high rates of joblessness.[37] These kinds of findings imply a surplus rather than a shortage of farmworkers.[38]

Table 2. The Rate and Level of Unemployment

Year	All occupations	Unemployment rate Hired farmworkers	Number of unemployed hired farmworkers (in thousands)
1994	6.1	12.1	109
1995	5.6	12.5	121
1996	5.4	11.5	118
1997	4.9	10.6	106
1998	4.5	11.8	117
1999	4.2	10.6	100
2000	4.0	10.6	104
2001	4.7	12.1	103
2002	5.8	11.4	102
2003	6.0	12.9	100
2004	5.5	11.4	92
2005	5.1	9.0	72
2006	4.6	9.4	78

Source: CPS data tabulated by the BLS (column 2) and the ERS (columns 3 and 4).

Note: In the CPS, an individual's occupation is based on the activity in which he or she spent the most hours during the survey week. The ERS defines hired farmworkers as individuals aged 15 or older whose primary job is farmwork and for which they receive wages. Hired farmworkers include individuals engaged in crop or livestock production whom growers employ directly or through agricultural service providers (e.g., farm labor contractors), as well as farm managers, supervisors of farmworkers, and nursery and other workers.

n.a. = not available.

Another perspective on the availability of untapped farm labor comes from the DOL's National Agricultural Worker Survey (NAWS).[39] During FY2001-FY2002, the typical crop worker spent 66% of the year performing farm jobs. The remainder of the year, these farmworkers either were engaged in nonfarm work (10% of the year) or not working (16%) while in the United States, or they were out of the country (7%).[40] This pattern also suggests an excess supply of labor, assuming that the workers wanted more farm employment. Grower advocates contend that the pattern is a manifestation of working in a seasonal industry. Even in a month of peak industry demand, however, only a small majority of farmworkers hold farm jobs.[41]

---

37 GAO, H-2A Agricultural Guestworker Program.
38 See also testimony of Cecilia Munoz, on behalf of the National Council of La Raza before the Senate Judiciary Subcommittee on Immigration, May 12, 1999.
39 See "Note" in Table 5 for information about the survey.
40 DOL, Findings from the NAWS 2001-2002.
41 DOL, Findings from the National Agricultural Workers Survey: 1997-1998.

Time Worked

Another indicator of supply-demand conditions is the amount of time worked (e.g., hours or days). If employers are faced with a labor shortage, they might be expected to increase the amount of time worked by their employees.

The Seasonality of Demand: Hours Versus Employment

Recent data reveal no discernible year-to-year variation in the average number of weekly hours that hired farmworkers are employed in crop or livestock production. According to the NASS Farm Labor Survey (FLS), the average workweek of hired farmworkers has ranged narrowly around 40.0 hours since the mid-1990s. Thus, neither the trend in employment nor in work hours imply the existence of a farm labor shortage.

There also is not much variability in demand over the course of a year based on hours worked. In 2006, for example, the average week of hired farmworkers was 33.2 hours in mid-January, 40.8 hours in mid-April, 41.0 hours in mid-July and 41.6 hours in mid-October.

The instability of the demand for farm labor within a year (i.e., seasonality) is reflected in employment levels more than in work hours per week. The FLS data show that in 2006, for example, farmers had 614,000 workers on their payrolls in mid-January; 720,000 in mid-April; 876,000 in mid-July; and 797,000 in mid-October.

The Number of Days Worked

Another measure of time worked available from the FLS is "expected days of employment" (i.e., farm operators are asked the number of days they intend to utilize their hired farmworkers over the course of a year). As shown in *Table 3*, they anticipated a low of 579,000 farmworkers on their payrolls for at least 150 days in 2006 and a high of 679,000 (un)authorized workers in 2002. These "year-round" workers typically have accounted for at least three-fourths of hired farmworkers in the current decade.[42]

According to the NAWS, the number of actual farm workdays varies by legal status.[43] Unauthorized workers averaged 197 days in crop production, compared to 185 days for authorized workers in FY2001-FY2002. More unauthorized than authorized workers were likely to spend at least 200 days in farm jobs (58% and 50%, respectively). Within the authorized population, citizens averaged 175 days and permanent residents, 195 days of employment in farming during the year.

---

42 These figures potentially are relevant to legislation that would link eligibility for legalization to time spent in farm work. While some might wish to use the above-described data to roughly estimate the number of unauthorized farmworkers who would be eligible to adjust status, they describe the expectations of farmers and they do not distinguish between legal and illegal workers. In addition, the data could produce an underestimate because they omit the more than 200,000 contract workers on the payrolls of agricultural service providers. Alternatively, the data could produce an overestimate because they include employees not normally thought of as farmworkers (e.g., bookkeepers, secretaries or pilots).

43 DOL, Findings from the NAWS 2001-2002.

Table 3. Hired Farmworkers by Expected Days of Employment

	(numbers in thousands)		
	150 Days or more of expected employment		
Year	Number of hired workers	Percent of all hired farmworkers	149 Days or less of expected employment
1994	597	71	243
1995	598	69	271
1996	593	71	239
1997	629	72	247
1998	639	73	241
1999	666	72	263
2000	640	72	251
2001	658	75	224
2002	679	77	207
2003	635	76	201
2004	611	74	246
2005	594	76	185
2006	579	77	173

Source: Annual averages calculated by CRS from quarterly releases of the FLS.

Note: The NASS FLS counts as hired farmworkers only those persons paid directly by farmers (i.e., contract, custom or other workers paid directly by agricultural service providers are excluded). Hired farmworkers include field workers (i.e., those who plant, cultivate and harvest crops), livestock workers (i.e., those who tend livestock, milk cows or care for poultry) and supervisory workers (e.g., crew leaders or range foremen) as well as other workers on farmers' payrolls (e.g., bookkeepers, secretaries or pilots).

Wages

Economic theory suggests that if the demand for labor is nearing or has outstripped the supply of labor, firms will in the short-run bid up wages to compete for workers. As a result, earnings in the short-supply field would be expected to increase more rapidly than earnings across all industries or occupations. The ratio of, in this instance, farm to nonfarm wages also would be expected to rise if the former's labor supply were especially constrained.

As shown below in *Table 4*, the average hourly earnings of field workers (excluding contract workers) rose to a greater extent than those of other employees in the private sector between 1990 and 2006, at 73.2% and 64.2%, respectively. Nonetheless, field workers' pay has hardly increased compared to other workers' pay: at $9.06 per hour in 2006, field workers still earn little more than 50 cents for every dollar earned by other private sector workers.

NAWS data reveal much slower growth in wages compared to the FLS, which cannot be explained by the different periods covered in *Table 4* and *Table 5*. Between 1990 and 2002, the most recent year for which NAWS data are available, the average hourly earnings of crop workers rose to a lesser extent based on the NAWS (39.6%) than on the FLS (55.3%). The NAWS also produces lower wage estimates than those from the FLS. In 2002, the average hourly earnings of crop workers were $7.30, according to the NAWS, while they were $8.12

according, to the FLS. These disparities likely are related to differences between the two surveys.[44]

Table 4. Average Hourly Earnings of Field Workers and Other Workers in the Private Sector

	(in nominal dollars)		
Year	**Average hourly wages of field workers**	**Average hourly wages of production or nonsupervisory workers in the private nonfarm sector**	**Ratio of hourly field worker wages to private nonfarm worker wages**
1990	$5.23	$10.19	0.51
1991	5.49	10.50	0.52
1992	5.69	10.76	0.53
1993	5.90	11.03	0.53
1994	6.02	11.32	0.53
1995	6.13	11.64	0.53
1996	6.34	12.03	0.53
1997	6.66	12.49	0.53
1998	6.97	13.00	0.54
1999	7.19	13.47	0.53
2000	7.50	14.00	0.54
2001	7.78	14.53	0.54
2002	8.12	14.95	0.54
2003	8.31	15.35	0.54
2004	8.45	15.67	0.54
2005	8.70	16.11	0.54
2006	9.06	16.73p	0.54
1990-2006 change	66.2%	58.1%	—

Source: Created by CRS from FLS (column 2) and BLS (column 3) employer survey data.

Note: Field workers are a subset of hired farmworkers who engage in planting, tending and harvesting crops. The data relate to all field workers regardless of method of payment (i.e., those paid an hourly rate, by the piece or a combination of the two). Contract, custom, or other workers paid directly by agricultural service providers are excluded.

The wages of crop workers, as shown in *Table 5*, rose to a lesser extent in the 1990-2002 period than those of other workers in the private sector (39.6% and 46.7%, respectively) — just the opposite of the relationship between the FLS and BLS data (55.3% and 46.7%, respectively). As a result of the relatively lower wage estimates and the relatively slower

---

44 Although the populations covered by the NAWS and the FLS are similar, the NAWS's wage figures include contract labor while those from the FLS do not. As workers supplied to growers by farm labor contractors generally are paid less than direct-hires, this difference could have contributed to the lower hourly earnings of the NAWS. In addition, the NAWS questions workers; the FLS, employers. Figures supplied by employers usually are thought to be more accurate than those recalled by workers. And, while both surveys are designed to reflect seasonal variations during the course of a year, they do not cover identical reference periods.

wage growth derived from the NAWS, the typical crop worker was estimated to have dropped below 50 cents for every dollar paid to other private sector workers since the mid-1990s.

Table 5. Average Hourly Earnings of Crop Workers and Other Workers in the Private Sector

Year	Average hourly wages of crop workers	Average hourly wages of production or nonsupervisory workers in the private nonfarm sector	Ratio of hourly crop worker wages to private nonfarm worker wages
	(in nominal dollars)		
1990	$5.23	$10.19	0.51
1991	5.57	10.50	0.53
1992	5.33	10.76	0.50
1993	5.46	11.03	0.50
1994	5.54	11.32	0.50
1995	5.72	11.64	0.49
1996	5.69	12.03	0.47
1997	5.81	12.49	0.47
1998	6.40	13.00	0.48
1999	6.54	13.47	0.48
2000	7.00	14.00	0.48
2001	7.11	14.53	0.49
2002[a]	7.30	14.95	0.49
1990-2002 change	39.6%	46.7%	—

Source: Created by CRS from NAWS worker (column 2) and BLS employer survey data (column 3).

Note: Crop workers include field packers, supervisors and other field workers who engage in such activities as planting, tending and harvesting crops. Initially, the survey included only field workers on perishable crop farms to comply with IRCA: NAWS was developed to enable the DOL to calculate changes in the supply of SAS labor, which was then used in the shortage calculation conducted by the U.S. Departments of Labor and Agriculture for triggering the RAW program. In the mid-1990s, the survey was expanded to include field workers in non-perishable crops (e.g., silage or other crops intended solely for animal fodder). The data relate to the farm earnings of field workers age 14 or older, regardless of method of payment (i.e., those paid an hourly rate, by the piece or a combination of the two). The sample includes direct-hires and contract labor. The survey is conducted at different times over the course of a year to capture seasonal variations.

a. Calendar year data, except for 2002 which covers January to September.

CONCLUSION

In summary, indicators of supply-demand conditions generally are inconsistent with the existence of a nationwide shortage of domestically available farmworkers in part because the measures include both authorized and unauthorized employment. This finding does not preclude the possibility of farmworker shortages in certain parts of the country at various times during the year. The analysis does not address the adequacy of authorized workers in the seasonal farm labor supply relative to grower demand.

Whether there would be an adequate supply of authorized U.S. farmworkers if new technologies were developed or different labor-management practices were implemented continues to be an unanswered question. Whether more U.S. workers would be willing to become farmworkers if wages were raised and whether the size of the increase would make the industry uncompetitive in the world marketplace also remain open issues. These matters remain unresolved because perishable crop growers have rarely, if ever, had to operate without unauthorized aliens being present in the domestic farm workforce.[45]

---

45 In the conference report for the DOL's FY2000 appropriation (H.Rept. 106-479), the Congress charged the DOL with reporting on ways to promote a legal domestic workforce in the farm sector and on options for such things as improving farmworker compensation, developing a more stable workforce, and enhancing living conditions. The report (U.S. Department of Labor Report to Congress: The Agricultural Labor Market — Status and Recommendations), issued in December 2000, recommended that the federal minimum wage be raised, agency funding for labor law enforcement increased, appropriations for AgWork (i.e., an internet-based, on-line job matching system specifically for agricultural employees and employers) continued, growers' greater use of automated employee verification systems encouraged, H-2A program streamlining further pursued while maintaining protections for U.S. and foreign farmworkers, and discussions held with countries from which farmworkers come to "explore ways in which their legal rights can be better protected." The DOL concluded that IRCA's farm legalization program failed to turn an unauthorized into an authorized workforce. It asserted that congressional proposals to ease growers' access to temporary farmworkers outside the existing H-2A program "would not create a legal domestic agricultural workforce" and instead "would lower wages and working and living conditions in agricultural jobs resulting in fewer domestic workers continuing employment in agriculture and perpetuating the industry's dependence on a foreign labor force." The DOL pointed out that another approach to creating an authorized supply of crop workers has never been tried — increasing wages and improving working conditions "by normalizing legal protections for farm workers and increasing mechanization," which has the potential to attract more U.S. workers to agriculture and raise the productivity of a possibly smaller farm labor force. In recognition that there might be short-run increases in growers' labor costs were its recommendations implemented, the DOL urged the Congress to consider ways to temporarily assist them.raise the productivity of a possibly smaller farm labor force. In recognition that there might be short-run increases in growers' labor costs were its recommendations implemented, the DOL urged the Congress to consider ways to temporarily assist them.

In: Farm Labor: 21ˢᵗ Century Issues and Challenges ISBN: 978-1-60456-005-3
Editors: A. W. Burton, I. B. Telpov, pp. 189-194 © 2007 Nova Science Publishers, Inc.

Chapter 6

THE EFFECTS ON U.S. FARM WORKERS OF AN AGRICULTURAL GUEST WORKER PROGRAM[*]

Linda Levine

ABSTRACT

Guest worker programs are meant to assure employers (e.g., fruit, vegetable, and horticultural specialty growers) of an adequate supply of labor when and where it is needed while not adding permanent residents to the U.S. population. They include mechanisms, such as the H-2A program's labor certification process, intended to avoid adversely affecting the wages and working conditions of similarly employed U.S. workers. If amendment of the H-2A program or initiation of a new agricultural guest worker program led growers to employ many more aliens than is now the case, the effects of the Bracero program might be instructive: although the 1942-1964 Bracero program succeeded in expanding the farm labor supply, studies estimate that it also harmed domestic farm workers as measured by their reduced wages and employment. The magnitudes of these adverse effects might differ today depending upon how much the U.S. farm labor and product markets have changed over time, but their direction likely would be the same.

The nation has had a long history of guest worker programs targeted at the agricultural industry, which have enabled farmers to temporarily import foreign workers to perform seasonal jobs without adding permanent residents to the U.S. population. Unsuccessful attempts were made during the past few Congresses to amend the H-2A program, the only means currently available to employers who want to legally utilize aliens in temporary farm jobs. Recent interest among some Members of Congress in a broad-based guest worker program has renewed efforts to enact legislation that relates specifically to the agricultural sector (e.g., S. 359/H.R. 884, the Agricultural Job Opportunity, Benefits, and Security Act; H.R. 3857, the Temporary Agricultural Labor Reform Act; and S. 2087 (Agricultural Employment and Workforce Protection Act).[1]

---

[*] Excerpted from CRS Report 95-712, dated March 9, 2006.
1 For information on guest worker legislation see CRS Report RL32044, *Immigration: Policy Considerations Related to Guest Worker Programs*, by Andorra Bruno.

ARGUMENTS FOR AND AGAINST AN AGRICULTURAL GUEST WORKER PROGRAM

The elements of the debate concerning an agricultural guest worker program have changed very little over the years. Its principal points are twofold:

- whether there is an adequate supply of workers in the United States to fulfill the widely fluctuating labor requirements of some farmers; and
- whether the temporary admission of aliens to perform seasonal farm jobs adversely affects the labor market prospects of domestic workers.[2]

Growers of perishable, labor-intensive crops (e.g., fruit, vegetable, and horticultural specialty products) whose demand for directly hired and contract workers typically peaks during the harvest season argue that they need access to foreign labor because insufficient U.S. workers are available at that time. They assert that importing workers to perform seasonal farm tasks does not harm U.S. workers because the two groups do not compete. In other words, they contend that domestic workers are largely unwilling to perform the farm work in question — even if higher wages were offered them. Domestic workers, it is claimed, have more attractive alternatives to seasonal farm employment (e.g., nonfarm jobs arguably are less strenuous and dirty as well as more stable and prestigious). Without access to foreign labor, grower advocates maintain that crops could not be harvested; consumer prices would rise due to the reduced supply of U.S.-grown produce; and the nation would become more dependent on low-wage foreign competitors for a portion of its food supply.

Farm worker advocates contend that if growers raised wages and improved working conditions, more domestic workers would be willing to accept seasonal farm employment. They assert that the employment and wage prospects of domestic workers are depressed by additions to the U.S. labor supply through guest worker programs. It is argued that these programs also harm similarly employed U.S. workers by weakening incentives to develop and adopt innovations that improve their working conditions and labor-saving technologies that increase their productivity (and hence, the wages of a smaller workforce). Opponents of temporary alien worker programs further declare that growers prefer foreign over domestic workers because the former are not covered by the same laws as domestic workers (e.g., Migrant and Seasonal Agricultural Worker Protection Act, Unemployment Insurance, and Social Security); are less demanding due to lower wages and poorer working conditions in their home countries; and are easier to control because they cannot easily work for another U.S. employer if the grower terminates them.

The remainder of this article focuses on the impact an agricultural guest worker program might have on U.S. workers. The adequacy of the domestic supply of farm workers is addressed in another CRS Report.[3]

---

2 In this report, workers referred to as "U.S." or "domestic" include native-born and foreign-born individuals authorized to work, as well as unauthorized aliens, in the United States.

3 CRS Report RL30395, Farm Labor Shortages and Immigration Policy, by Linda Levine.(Hereafter cited as CRS Report RL30395, Farm Labor Shortages and Immigration Policy.)

THE LABOR MARKET EFFECTS: ECONOMIC THEORY

Fundamentally, the debate over the effect on U.S. workers of temporarily admitting foreign workers centers on whether an increase in the supply of labor reduces the wages and employment of domestic workers. Economic theory can help clarify this debate.

Before the entrance of foreign workers to the U.S. labor market, the amount of labor that domestic workers are willing to supply to employers is represented by the curve labeled S in **Figure 1**. It is upward sloping because workers are willing to supply more labor services in response to higher wages. Employers' demand for labor is represented by the curve labeled D, which slopes downward because employers are willing to employ more workers at lower wages. Equilibrium in this labor market occurs at point A, where those willing to work for wage W 1 equals employer willingness to hire at that wage. In the absence of foreign labor, then U.S. farm employment is equal to E_1 and U.S. farm workers' wage rate is equal to W1.

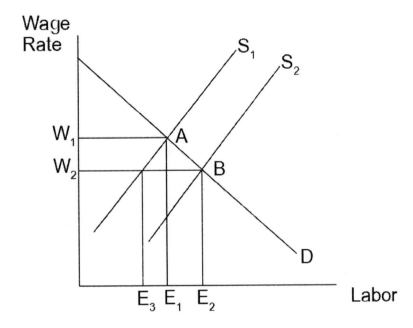

Figure 1. The Effects on Domestic Workers of an Increase in the Supply of Foreign Workers

The addition of foreign workers expands the total quantity of labor at any given wage rate. This is represented by the rightward shift of the supply curve to S_2 with the additional labor represented by the difference between S1 and S2. This increase in the labor force will only find employment if the wage falls, for only at a lower wage will employers be willing to hire more workers. Thus, equilibrium after the importation of labor occurs at point B, where the wage rate of domestic and alien farm workers drops to W2 and employment of domestic and alien farm workers expands to E2.

In summary, the theory of supply and demand predicts that *the wage rate for all workers falls* from W1 to W2 after the entrance of foreign workers to the U.S. labor market. As a result of the drop in wages, *total employment expands* from E1 to E2 *domestic employment contracts* from E1 to E3; and alien worker employment is equal to E2 minus E3.

Because the lower wage (W2) makes farm work less rewarding, some domesticworkers likely will look for jobs outside the agricultural sector. Employment of domestic farm workers accordingly will decline (from E2 to E3). While the total employment of foreign workers (E2 minus E3) expands, a portion is at the expense of the farm jobs formerly held by domestic workers (E1 minus E2). This is called the *displacement effect*. The size of the displacement effect depends on the shape of the labor demand and domestic labor supply curves.

Along with lower domestic employment in agriculture, the presence of foreign farm workers reduces the amount of wages that accrues to domestic farm workers. Because the addition of foreign workers also expands output, agricultural prices are expected to fall and thereby benefit U.S. consumers including domestic farm workers.

The H-2A Program

Authorized under the Immigration and Nationality Act at Section 101(a)(15)(H)(ii)(A) as modified by the Immigration Reform and Control Act of 1986 (IRCA, P.L. 99-603), the H-2A program was begun in 1952. It allows an unlimited number of foreign workers to temporarily enter the United States to fill seasonal farm jobs at employers who demonstrate the existence of labor shortages by undertaking recruitment requirements prescribed by the U.S. Department of Labor (DOL). As part of the DOL's *labor certification* process, farmers applying for admission of H-2A workers must offer to pay them and domestic workers the higher of the (federal or state) minimum wage, prevailing wage, or adverse effect wage rate and to provide free government-approved housing to out-of-area domestic as well as H-2A workers.[4]

Principally East Coast growers of perishable labor-intensive crops, who largely did not utilize the Bracero program, were the original applicants for H-2A workers. The H-2A program "was able to escape the heavy criticism levelled against the bracero program primarily by keeping a low profile."[5] In other words, there were a great many more braceros than H-2A workers when both the Bracero program (1942-1964) and H-2A program (1952-present) were in effect. (The Bracero program is discussed shortly.)

More recently, program data show that DOL certification of foreign workers for employment at grower applicants generally has been on the rise since FY1999. From 41,827 in that year, the number of H-2A job certifications reached 48,366 in FY2005.[6]

Despite the increase in DOL certifications, the number of H-2A workers remains quite small compared to the 1.1 million hired farm and agricultural service workers employed in 2005.[7] Thus, even if the labor certification process has not operated as intended — to protect similarly employed U.S. workers — the H-2A program's low utilization suggests that its overall impact on the domestic farm labor force has been minimal. However, the reliance on

---

4 For additional H-2A program information see CRS Report RL30852, Immigration of Agricultural Guest Workers: Policy, Trends, and Related Issues, by Ruth Ellen Wasem and Geoffrey K. Collver; and CRS Report RL32861, Farm Labor: The Adverse Effect Wage Rate (AEWR), by William Whittaker.
5 Monica L. Heppel and Sandra L. Amendola, Immigration Reform and Perishable Crop Agriculture (Lanham, MD: University Press of America, Inc., 1992), p. 30.
6 In FY2000, DOL issued 44,017 H-2A job certifications; in FY2001, 44,824; in FY2002, 41,894; in FY2003, 44,033; in FY2004, 44,619; and in FY2005, 48,366.
7 CRS Report RL30395, Farm Labor Shortages and Immigration Policy.

the H-2A program of tobacco, fruit (e.g., apple, peach, and tomato), vegetable (e.g., onion and squash), and grain growers in some states (e.g., North Carolina, Virginia, Kentucky, Idaho, California, and Texas) might have had a more substantial effect on domestic farm workers in certain local labor markets.

Proposals to modify the H-2A program (e.g., changing labor certification) seemingly would make it easier for growers to temporarily employ foreign workers. Farmers, as a consequence, would likely import more H-2A workers than they had previously. Given authorized aliens' potentially greater share of the hired and contract farm labor force as a result of changes to guest worker policy, it appears that the effects of the Bracero program on domestic farm workers are more relevant than the (unquantified) effects of the H-2A program.

The Bracero Program

At its peak in 1956, the Bracero program allowed some 445,000 Mexican workers to take temporary jobs in the U.S. agricultural industry.[8] The few studies that tried to empirically estimate the labor market impact of the Bracero program are examined below.

Morgan and Gardner examined a seven-state area, in which more than 90% of braceros had been employed, to estimate the impact of the program on the wage and employment levels of hired farm labor. Its effect was found to be consistent with economic theory: the Bracero program increased total farm employment, reduced employment of domestic farm workers, and lowered the farm wage rate. Morgan and Gardner concluded that the wage loss to all nonbracero farm workers was 6% to 7% of total wages paid to farm workers in the bracero-using states between 1953 and 1964, or some $139 million per year (in 1977 dollars). U.S. farmers were found to have gained from the program by being able to hire about 120,000 more workers at 15-20 cents less per hour than they would have in the program's absence. Such a large employment response (about 26%) to a much smaller decrease in wages (less than 9%)is consistent with the informal observation that braceros were a substitute for mechanization, notably in High Plains cotton, and that the end of the program substantially accelerated the mechanization of Texas cotton. This is also the period in which the tomato harvester came into widespread use in California.[9]

Wise examined the experience in California for two heavily bracero-dependent crops to determine whether U.S. workers would accept farm jobs if wages were raised. He estimated that a small increase in wages would bring about a larger increase in the supply of domestic farm workers: in winter melon production, a 1% increase in wages was associated with a 2.7% increase in the domestic supply of labor; in strawberry production, a 1% increase in wages was related to a 3.4% increase in the domestic labor supply.[10] Similarly, Mason found that a small increase in wages paid by the formerly bracero-dominated pickle industry in

8 For information on the Bracero program see U.S. Congress, Senate, Committee on the Judiciary,Temporary Worker Programs: Background and Issues, committee print, 96th Cong., 2d sess. (Washington: GPO, 1980).

9 Larry C. Morgan and Bruce L. Gardner, "Potential for a U.S. Guest-Worker Program in Agriculture: Lessons from the Braceros," in Barry Chiswick, ed., The Gateway: U.S. Immigration Issues and Policies, (Washington: American Enterprise Institute, 1982). Note: The wage loss associated with the Bracero program was incurred by authorized and unauthorized farm workers since both groups were included in the labor supply estimate.

Michigan induced a larger increase in U.S. workers willing to pick the crop.[11] *At least for the mid-to-late 1960s, then, these findings appear to refute the notion that increased agricultural wages would not have prompted many more domestic workers to accept farm employment.*

Wise additionally found that termination of the Bracero program led to a decrease in total employment, an increase in U.S. farm worker employment, and an increase in wages on strawberry and melon farms in California. More precisely, he estimated that without bracero labor from the mid-1950s to mid-1960s, domestic farm worker employment in California would have been between 51% (in strawberry production) and 261% (in melon production) higher, and wages would have been between 12% (in strawberry production) and 67% (in melon production) higher.[12]

While Mason estimated that shortly after the Bracero program's demise farm wages rose significantly in Michigan, he was unable to determine how much the absence of bracero labor or other variables contributed to the increase.[13] In contrast, Jones and Rice found that the trend in farm wages did not change significantly in four southwestern states between the 1954-1964 bracero period and the 1965-1977 post-bracero period.[1414] Although the latter study would imply that the Bracero program's end did not have an impact on farm wages, *the lack of a discernible wage effect might be explained by the replacement of braceros with unauthorized aliens — which effectively would have left the supply of labor little changed.*

In summary, the limited empirical research on the impact of the Bracero program on U.S. workers suggests that while the program successfully expanded the supply of temporary farm labor, it did so at the expense of domestic farm workers as measured by their reduced wages and employment. Although the magnitudes of these adverse effects might differ today depending on the extent to which U.S. farm labor and product markets have changed over time, their direction likely would be the same.

10 Donald E. Wise, "The Effect of the Bracero on Agricultural Production in California," Economic Inquiry, v. XII,
    no.4, Dec. 1974. (Hereafter cited as Wise, The Effect of the Bracero on Agricultural Production in California.)
11 John D. Mason, The Aftermath of the Bracero: A Study of the Economic Impact of the Agricultural Hired Labor
    Market of Michigan from the Termination of Public Law 78, (Ph.D. diss., Michigan State University, 1969).
    (Hereafter cited as Mason, The Aftermath of the Bracero.)
12 Wise, The Effect of the Bracero on Agricultural Production in California.
13 Mason, The Aftermath of the Bracero.
14 Lamar B. Jones and G. Randolph Rice, "Agricultural Labor in the Southwest: The Post Bracero Years," Social
    Science Quarterly, v. 61, no. 1, June 1980.

In: Farm Labor: 21st Century Issues and Challenges
Editors: A. W. Burton, I. B. Telpov, pp. 195-200

ISBN: 978-1-60456-005-3
© 2007 Nova Science Publishers, Inc.

Chapter 7

FARM LABOR: THE ADVERSE EFFECT WAGE RATE (AEWR)*

William G. Whittaker

ABSTRACT

American agricultural employers have long utilized foreign workers on a temporary basis, regarding them as an important labor resource. At the same time, the relatively low wages and adverse working conditions of such workers have caused them to be viewed as a threat to domestic American workers.

Some have argued that foreign *guest workers* compete unfairly with U.S. workers in at least two respects. First, they are alleged to compete unfairly in terms of the compensation that they are willing to accept. Second, their presence is alleged to render it more difficult for domestic workers to organize and to bargain collectively with management.

To mitigate any "adverse effect"for the domestic workforce, a system of wage floors was developed that applies, variously, both to alien and citizen workers —i.e., the *adverse effect wage rate* (AEWR).

This article deals with one element of the immigration issue: the question of the use of H-2A workers. It introduces the *adverse effect wage rate*, it examines the concerns out of which it grew, and it explains at least some of the problems that have been encountered in giving it effect.

The article is based, statistically, upon the AEWR issued each spring by the Employment and Training Administration, U.S. Department of Labor. It will be updated periodically as new information becomes available.

The article is written *from the perspective of labor policy, not of immigration policy*. For discussion of immigration policy, see the Current Legislative Issues (CLIs) on the Congressional Research Service webpage.

American agricultural employers have long utilized foreign workers on a temporary basis, regarding them as an important labor resource. At the same time, the relatively low

---

* Excerpted from CRS Report 32861, dated March 17, 2006.

wages and adverse working conditions of such workers have caused them to be viewed as a threat to domestic American workers.

To mitigate any "adverse effect" for the domestic workforce, a system of wage floors has been developed that applies, variously, both to alien and to citizen workers — the *adverse effect wage rate*.

The AEWR deals specifically with agricultural workers (i.e., H-2A workers). It involves persons "having a residence in a foreign country which he has no intention of abandoning" and "who is coming temporarily to the United States to perform agricultural labor" of "a temporary or seasonal nature" "...if unemployed persons capable of performing such service or labor cannot be found" in the host country.[1] An AEWR has been developed for each state (see table below) and is announced early each year prior to the growing/production season.

AN INTRODUCTION TO THE AEWR

Where countries with widely different economies exist side-by-side, the more prosperous is likely to draw to itself workers from its lower-wage neighbors. Though wages of American agricultural workers are low in comparison with wage rates in the general economy, they are relatively high by the standards of neighboring less developed countries. Thus, a continuing supply of workers has been available for employment in the United States at wage rates and under conditions that American workers, arguably, neither would accept nor, for economic reasons, could accept.

MEXICAN GUEST WORKER UTILIZATION: A BRIEF HISTORICAL OVERVIEW

Low-wage labor has entered the United States from a variety of countries and under diverse circumstances. Indeed, importation of low-wage labor has been a longstanding tradition.[2] Here, our concern is with workers from Mexico — a primary focus of U.S. agricultural labor policy. We are dealing with two migratory thrusts. On the one hand, there are workers who, attracted by relatively higher wages in the United States (or by other aspects of American society), have come north as immigrants seeking permanent employment. Conversely, there has been a body of workers who, responding to public policy, have been encouraged to come north —not to seek citizenship but to provide employers with a

---

1 8 U.S.C. §§ 1101(a)(15)(H)(ii)(a) and (b). See also CRS Report RL32044, Immigration: Policy Considerations Related to Guest Worker Programs, by Andorra Bruno.

2 There is an extensive literature on the continuing quest of certain American employers for low-wage workers. See, for example, Roger Daniels, Asian America: Chinese and Japanese in the United States Since 1850 (Seattle: University of Washington Press, 1988); Michael L. Conniff, Black Labor on a White Canal: Panama, 1904-1981 (Pittsburgh: University of Pittsburgh Press, 1984); and Edward D. Beechert, Working in Hawaii: A Labor History (Honolulu: University of Hawaii Press, 1985). For more recent experience, see Peter Kwong, Forbidden Workers: Illegal Chinese Immigrants and American Labor, (New York: The New Press, 1997); and Edna Bonachich, and Richard P. Appelbaum,Behind the Label: Inequality in the Los Angeles Apparel Industry (Berkeley: University of California Press, 2000).

continuing source of low-wage labor and, at the end of a work period, to return to their country of origin. These latter are the "guest workers" or "braceros."[3]

In the late 19th and early 20th centuries, movement across the U.S.-Mexican frontier was relatively unrestricted. Mexican nationals joined a resident Mexican-American population in the fields and mines of the Southwest. With World War I, workers from Mexico were recruited to offset the loss of American workers drafted into military service. After the war, a secondary problem arose: how to get the Mexican workers to go back to Mexico — an issue aggravated by the Great Depression. Then, World War II broke out and America turned once more to Mexico for low-skilled/low-wage labor. The result, in various forms, was the *bracero* program.

By war's end in 1945, agricultural employers had become accustomed to employing Mexican labor that was characterized at the time as docile, non-union, temporary, and payable at low rates while, at the same time, being able and highly motivated. Through the process, a large body of Mexican workers had become acculturated to the American world of work. Having learned at least fragmentary English, they were able to function within the American system without the institutional support of the formal *bracero* program. In short, some might argue, the *bracero* program had been a training school for foreign workers operating outside the normal immigration structure. The *bracero*/guest worker programs, however, were also a source of contention, raising a number of socio-economic questions. Opposition continued to grow until, in 1964, the program was terminated.

Even with termination, however, a body of foreign workers remained in the United States — a force that was augmented by Mexican workers who crossed the border without proper authorization. As American agricultural workers (many of Mexican heritage) sought to improve their economic status through organization, they were confronted by this alien workforce. Several dilemmas were posed. How might the demand of agribusiness (and of certain other employers) for low-wage workers be satisfied within the context of American labor-management policy and without imperiling the economic livelihood of resident/domestic American labor? And, as the ex-*bracero* community became a political force within the United States, how might these sometimes conflicting objectives be achieved without offending this new body of Americans?[4]

---

3 U.S. agricultural workers can be divided into two groups: American workers and foreign workers. Herein, American workers are either U.S. citizens or permanent residents, and are distinguishable from foreign (alien, non-immigrant) workers who are in the country on a temporary basis. Further, some foreign workers may be here "legally" — others, "illegally."

4 Joseph F. Park, in his study, The History of Mexican Labor in Arizona during the Territorial Period (M.A. Thesis, University of Arizona, 1961), deals with early cross-frontier labor migration and its impacts. More generally, see Mark Reisler, By The Sweat of Their Brow: Mexican Immigrant Labor in the United States, 1900-1940 (Westport: Greenwood Press, 1976); Otey M. Scruggs, Braceros, "Wetbacks," and the Farm Labor Problem: Mexican Agricultural Labor in the United States, 1942-1954 (New York: Garland Publishing, 1988); Abraham Hoffman, Unwanted Mexican Americans in the Great Depression: Repatriation Pressures, 1929-1939 (Tucson: The University of Arizona Press, 1974); Francisco E. Balderrama and Raymond Rodriguez, Decade of Betrayal: Mexican Repatriation in the 1930s (Albuquerque: The University of New Mexico Press, 1995); and Richard B. Craig, The Bracero Program: Interest Groups and Foreign Policy (Austin: University of Texas Press, 1971).

COPING WITH "ADVERSE EFFECT"

By mid-century, these concerns came to be addressed in immigration law. The Immigration and Nationality Act of 1952, as amended, provides for admission to the United States of a person "having a residence in a foreign country which he has no intention of abandoning" and "who is coming temporarily to the United States to perform agricultural labor" of "a temporary or seasonal nature" "... if unemployed persons capable of performing such service or labor cannot be found in this country."[5] Later, the act directs that a petition for admission of such persons (H-2A workers) "may not be approved by the Attorney General unless the petitioner [the prospective employer] has applied to the Secretary of Labor" for certification that:

A) there are not sufficient workers who are able, willing, and qualified, and who will be available at the time and place needed, to perform the labor or services involved in the petition, and

B) the employment of the alien in such labor or services *will not* adversely affect the wages and working conditions of workers in the United States similarly employed.[6]

If the requirements of paragraphs (A) and (B) are to be effective, they impose a heavy policy burden and responsibility upon the Secretary of Labor.[7]

Paragraph (A) focuses upon availability. Are there domestic American workers who are "able" and "qualified" to satisfy the normally low or semi-skilled requirements of temporary agricultural labor? Did Congress mean to have the Secretary assess the skill and ability of each potential domestic agricultural laborer? If not, then these qualifications are reduced largely to a single standard: willingness to be employed. Even that measure can be complex. Must the potential worker be "willing" to work at whatever wage an employer may be willing to offer and under whatever conditions may exist — even if adverse?

Almost by definition, the H-2A worker is willing to accept a lower wage and conditions more adverse than would be acceptable to most American workers. Thus (following documentable recruitment efforts), a prospective employer can affirm that American workers are unavailable and that he is only offering the H-2A worker employment that American workers "don't want and won't accept." In other labor markets, however, some may argue, movement toward higher wages and improved conditions could be expected to attract American workers.[8]

As part of his responsibility under paragraph (A), the Secretary of Labor has developed a three-tiered wage rate requirement. The regulations state:

---

5 8 U.S.C. §§ 1101(a)(15)(H)(ii)(a) and (b).

6 8 U.S.C. §§ 1188(a)(1)(A) and (B). Italics added.

7 The conditions under which H-2A workers may be employed are set forth in detail in 20 C.F.R. Part 655. The AEWR is only one small aspect of the H-2A program. For a discussion of the program and of current issues, see CRS Report RL30852, Immigration of Agricultural Guest Workers: Policy, Trends, and Legislative Issues, by Ruth Wasem and Geoffrey Collver.

8 Questions persist about possible farm labor shortages and the impact of foreign workers.See CRS Report RL30395, Farm Labor Shortages and Immigration Policy, by Linda Levine.

If the worker will be paid by the hour, the employer shall pay the worker at least the adverse effect wage rate in effect at the time the work is performed, the prevailing hourly wage rate, or the legal federal or State minimum wage rate, whichever is highest...[9]

Table 1. Adverse Effect Wage Rate by State, 1990-2005 (in current dollars and cents)

State[a]	1990	1991	1992	1993	1994	1995	1996	1997	1998	1999	2000	2001	2002	2003	2004	2005	2006
Alabama	4.29	4.46	4.91	5.04	5.43	5.66	5.40	5.92	6.30	6.30	6.72	6.83	7.28	7.49	7.88	8.07	8.37
Arizona	4.61	4.87	5.17	5.37	5.52	5.80	5.87	5.82	6.08	6.42	6.74	6.71	7.12	7.61	7.54	7.63	8.00
Arkansas	4.04	4.40	4.73	4.87	5.26	5.19	5.27	5.70	5.98	6.21	6.50	6.69	6.77	7.13	7.38	7.80	7.58
California	5.90	5.81	5.90	6.11	6.03	6.24	6.26	6.53	6.87	7.23	7.27	7.56	8.02	8.44	8.50	8.56	9.00
Colorado	4.51	5.00	5.29	5.44	5.57	5.62	5.64	6.09	6.39	6.73	7.04	7.43	7.62	8.07	8.36	8.93	8.37
Connecticut	4.98	5.21	5.61	5.82	5.97	6.21	6.36	6.71	6.84	7.18	7.68	8.17	7.94	8.53	9.01	9.05	9.16
Delaware	4.89	4.93	5.39	5.81	5.92	5.81	5.97	6.26	6.33	6.84	7.04	7.37	7.46	7.97	8.52	8.48	8.95
Florida	5.16	5.38	5.68	5.91	6.02	6.33	6.54	6.36	6.77	7.13	7.25	7.66	7.69	7.78	8.18	8.07	8.56
Georgia	4.29	4.46	4.91	5.04	5.43	5.66	5.40	5.92	6.30	6.30	6.72	6.83	7.28	7.49	7.88	8.07	8.37
Hawaii	7.70	7.85	7.95	8.11	8.36	8.73	8.60	8.62	8.83	8.97	9.38	9.05	9.25	9.42	9.60	9.75	9.99
Idaho	4.49	4.79	4.94	5.25	5.59	5.57	5.76	6.01	6.54	6.48	6.79	7.26	7.43	7.70	7.69	8.20	8.47
Illinois	4.88	5.05	5.59	5.85	6.02	6.18	6.23	6.66	7.18	7.53	7.62	8.09	8.38	8.65	9.00	9.20	9.21
Indiana	4.88	5.05	5.59	5.85	6.02	6.18	6.23	6.66	7.18	7.53	7.62	8.09	8.38	8.65	9.00	9.20	9.21
Iowa	5.03	4.85	5.15	5.65	5.76	5.72	5.90	6.22	6.86	7.17	7.76	7.84	8.33	8.91	9.28	8.95	9.49
Kansas	5.17	5.20	5.36	5.78	6.03	5.99	6.29	6.55	7.01	7.12	7.49	7.81	8.24	8.53	8.83	9.00	9.23
Kentucky	4.45	4.56	5.04	5.09	5.29	5.47	5.54	5.68	5.92	6.28	6.39	6.60	7.07	7.20	7.63	8.17	8.24
Louisiana	4.04	4.40	4.73	4.87	5.26	5.19	5.27	5.70	5.98	6.21	6.50	6.69	6.77	7.13	7.38	7.80	7.58
Maine	4.98	5.21	5.61	5.82	5.97	6.21	6.36	6.71	6.84	7.18	7.68	8.17	7.94	8.53	9.01	9.05	9.16
Maryland	4.89	4.93	5.39	5.81	5.92	5.81	5.97	6.26	6.33	6.84	7.04	7.37	7.46	7.97	8.52	8.48	8.95
Massachusetts	4.98	5.21	5.61	5.82	5.97	6.21	6.36	6.71	6.84	7.18	7.68	8.17	7.94	8.53	9.01	9.05	9.16
Michigan	4.45	4.90	5.16	5.38	5.64	5.65	6.19	6.56	6.85	7.34	7.65	8.07	8.57	8.70	9.11	9.18	9.43
Minnesota	4.45	4.90	5.16	5.38	5.64	5.65	6.19	6.56	6.85	7.34	7.65	8.07	8.57	8.70	9.11	9.18	9.43
Mississippi	4.04	4.40	4.73	4.87	5.26	5.19	5.27	5.70	5.98	6.21	6.50	6.69	6.77	7.13	7.38	7.80	7.58
Missouri	5.03	4.85	5.15	5.85	5.76	5.72	5.90	6.22	6.86	7.17	7.76	7.84	8.33	8.91	9.28	8.95	9.49
Montana	4.49	4.79	4.94	5.25	5.59	5.57	5.76	6.01	6.54	6.48	6.79	7.26	7.43	7.70	7.69	8.20	8.47
Nebraska	5.17	5.20	5.36	5.78	6.03	5.99	6.29	6.55	7.01	7.12	7.49	7.81	8.24	8.53	8.83	9.00	9.23
Nevada	4.51	5.00	5.29	5.44	5.57	5.62	5.64	6.09	6.39	6.73	7.04	7.43	7.62	8.07	8.36	8.93	8.37
New Hampshire	4.98	5.21	5.61	5.82	5.97	6.21	6.36	6.71	6.84	7.18	7.68	8.17	7.94	8.53	9.01	9.05	9.16
New Jersey	4.89	4.93	5.39	5.81	5.92	5.81	5.97	6.26	6.33	6.84	7.04	7.37	7.46	7.97	8.52	8.48	8.95
New Mexico	4.61	4.87	5.17	5.37	5.52	5.80	5.87	5.82	6.08	6.42	6.74	6.71	7.12	7.61	7.54	7.63	8.00
New York	4.98	5.21	5.61	5.82	5.97	6.21	6.36	6.71	6.84	7.18	7.68	8.17	7.94	8.53	9.01	9.05	9.16
North Carolina	4.33	4.50	4.97	5.07	5.38	5.50	5.80	5.79	6.16	6.54	6.98	7.06	7.53	7.75	8.06	8.24	8.51
North Dakota	5.17	5.20	5.36	5.78	6.03	5.99	6.29	6.55	7.01	7.12	7/49	7.81	8.24	8.53	8.83	9.00	9.23
Ohio	4.88	5.05	5.59	5.85	6.02	6.18	6.23	6.66	7.18	7.53	7.62	8.09	8.38	8.65	9.00	9.20	9.21
Oklahoma	4.65	4.61	4.87	5.01	4.98	5.32	5.50	5.48	5.92	6.25	6.49	6.98	7.28	7.29	7.73	7.89	8.32
Oregon	5.42	5.69	5.94	6.31	6.51	6.41	6.82	6.87	7.08	7.34	7.64	8.14	8.60	8.71	8.73	9.03	9.01
Pennsylvania	4.89	4.93	5.39	5.81	5.92	5.81	5.97	6.26	6.33	6.84	7.04	7.37	7.46	7.97	8.52	8.48	8.95
Rhode Island	4.98	5.21	5.61	5.82	5.97	6.21	6.36	6.71	6.84	7.18	7.68	8.17	7.94	8.53	9.01	9.05	9.16
South Carolina	4.29	4.46	4.91	5.04	5.43	5.66	5.40	5.92	6.30	6.30	6.72	6.83	7.28	7.49	7.88	8.07	8.37
South Dakota	5.17	5.20	5.36	5.78	6.03	5.99	6.29	6.55	7.01	7.12	7.49	7.81	8.24	8.53	8.83	9.00	9.23
Tennessee	4.45	4.56	5.04	5.09	5.29	5.47	5.54	5.68	5.92	6.28	6.39	6.60	7.07	7.20	7.63	8.17	8.24
Texas	4.65	4.61	4.87	5.01	4.98	5.32	5.50	5.48	5.92	6.25	6.49	6.98	7.28	7.29	7.73	7.89	8.32
Utah	4.51	5.00	5.29	5.44	5.57	5.62	5.64	6.09	6.39	6.73	7.04	7.43	7.62	8.07	8.36	8.93	8.37
Vermont	4.98	5.21	5.61	5.82	5.97	6.21	6.36	6.71	6.84	7.18	7.68	8.17	7.94	8.53	9.01	9.05	9.16
Virginia	4.33	4.50	4.97	5.07	5.38	5.50	5.80	5.79	6.16	6.54	6.98	7.06	7.53	7.75	8.06	8.24	8.51
Washington	5.42	5.69	5.94	6.31	6.51	6.41	6.82	6.87	7.08	7.34	7.64	8.14	8.60	8.71	8.73	9.03	9.01
West Virginia	4.45	4.56	5.04	5.09	5.29	5.47	5.54	5.68	5.92	6.28	6.39	6.60	7.07	7.20	7.63	8.17	8.24
Wisconsin	4.45	4.90	5.16	5.38	5.64	5.65	6.19	6.56	6.85	7.34	7.65	8.07	8.57	8.70	9.11	9.18	9.43
Wyoming	4.49	4.79	4.94	5.25	5.59	5.57	5.76	6.01	6.54	6.48	6.79	7.26	7.43	7.70	7.69	8.20	8.47

Source: Compiled from data provided by the U.S. Department of Labor, Employment and Training Administration. See *Federal Register*, Feb. 26, 2003, pp. 8929-8930; Mar. 19, 2003, p. 13331; Mar. 3, 2004, pp. 10063-10065; Mar. 2, 2005, pp. 10152-10153; and Mar 16, 2006, pp. 13633-13635.

a. The U.S. Department of Agriculture does not calculate an AEWR for Alaska.

---

[9] 20 C.F.R. § 655.102(b)(9)(i). The regulations set out separate requirements if the worker is paid on a piece rate basis. See 20 C.F.R. § 655.102(b)(9)(ii).

The AEWR is set forth by the Department of Labor (DOL), based upon data gathered by the Department of Agriculture (DOA). DOA conducts a quarterly survey of the wages of field and livestock workers throughout the United States. The AEWR, then, is a weighted average of the DOA findings, calculated on a regional basis. It is adjusted, each year, taking into account prior experience with the change of the "average hourly wage rates for field and livestock workers (combined) based on the USDA Quarterly Wage Survey."[10] The rate (see *Table 1*) is set for each state (except Alaska for which no rate has been fixed). The AEWR has no *direct* effect where an employer does not seek to engage H-2A workers. However, if he does engage H-2A workers and subsequently locates and hires American workers, then he is required to pay each group not less than the AEWR.

Paragraph (B) presents a more complex issue: i.e., demonstrating that employment of H-2A workers "will not adversely affect the wages and working conditions of workers in the United States similarly employed." Many view the AEWR structure as effectively setting *a cap* on the earnings of certain agricultural workers. If domestic workers are not available at the specified rate, the employer is allowed to employ foreign workers who, given the disparity in wage rates between Mexico and the United States, will almost always be available at the AEWR.

The H-2A option provides agricultural employers with an alternative source of labor and, in effect, expands the pool of available workers — enhancing competition for available jobs. With that option open to them, agribusiness employers may have no need to revise their recruitment and employment policies to make such employment more attractive to American workers. Further, some may view the availability of foreign agricultural workers as a device through which to deter trade unionization of domestic agricultural workers and to preclude the necessity of bargaining with domestic U.S. workers with respect to wages and conditions of employment.

---

10 20 C.F.R. § 655.207(a), (b) and (c). Concerning the methodology for calculation of the AEWR, see Federal Register, June 1, 1987, pp. 20496-20533, and Federal Register, July 5, 1989, pp. 28037-28051.

INDEX

A

access, 12, 67, 83, 113, 136, 177, 188, 190
accommodation, 72
accounting, 96
accuracy, 121, 122, 132, 161, 177
achievement, 100, 147
activism, 77
adequate housing, 119, 120, 127, 129, 130
adjustment, 117, 130, 138, 139
administration, ix, 11, 17, 33, 34, 37, 43, 49, 50, 51, 64
advertising, 76, 124
advocacy, 138
Africa, 98
African American(s), 73, 98, 100
age, xi, 10, 24, 38, 45, 67, 105, 145, 149, 151, 152, 153, 163, 171, 178, 181, 187
agent, 32, 36, 107, 121, 132
aging, 178, 179
Agricultural Job Opportunity, Benefits, and Security Act, xiii, 118, 189
agricultural sector, xiii, 93, 118, 189, 192
agriculture, vii, 1, 10, 14, 23, 27, 32, 36, 49, 110, 139, 140, 174, 177, 179, 182, 188, 192
Alaska, 85, 88, 181, 199, 200
alternative(s), x, 57, 58, 98, 109, 117, 190, 200
amendments, viii, 2, 24, 26, 28, 31, 32, 33, 36, 42, 43, 45, 48, 50, 53, 55, 61
anger, 48
animals, viii, 63, 65, 67, 101
annual rate, 115
Arizona, 37, 197
Asia, 98
assessment, 17, 78, 137
assets, 47
asylum, 147
Athens, 70

athletes, 111
attachment, 70, 92
attacks, 73
attention, vii, 1, 28, 34, 106, 108, 110, 175, 177
attitudes, 75
Attorney General, 29, 32, 39, 55, 123, 198
authenticity, 177
authority, 6, 8, 12, 17, 20, 43, 44, 49, 50
automation, 89
availability, 5, 73, 98, 139, 140, 158, 179, 183, 198, 200
avoidance, 94
awareness, 27, 94

B

bacteria, 102
Balkans, 90
banks, 121, 122, 131
bargaining, ix, xii, 63, 69, 78, 81, 82, 87, 106, 118, 127, 128, 147, 173, 179, 200
base rate, 84, 87
beef, 65, 66, 67, 69, 86, 87, 88, 93, 96, 101
behavior, 97, 157
benefits, 33, 34, 58, 60, 69, 72, 90, 93, 94, 100, 105, 112, 113, 118, 119, 120, 124, 125, 127, 128, 129, 130, 142, 148
beverages, 3
bias, 79
birds, 68, 69, 102
birth, 41, 177
black women, 92
Blacks, 72, 73, 91
blame, 45
blood, 97, 101
boilers, 68
bonding, 9
Border Patrol, 27, 39, 40, 115, 116

border security, 118, 136, 146, 154
boredom, 105
bounds, 159
boys, 90
Bracero program, xii, 110, 189, 192, 193, 194
breeding, 43, 55
Bureau of the Census, 161
bureaucracy, 38, 49
Bush Administration, 110, 135, 138
by-products, 65

C

California, 23, 24, 33, 35, 37, 39, 46, 52, 59, 60, 74,
    159, 160, 193, 194, 196
Cambodia, 95
campaigns, 81, 107, 108
Canada, 87, 88
candidates, 132
capital accumulation, 94
capital goods, 156, 157
capital intensive, 66
carrier, 55
case study, 70
catfish, 92
cattle, 66, 101, 105
CBO, 148
Census, 149, 153
Census Bureau, 149, 153
Central America, 89, 96, 98
certainty, 53
certificate, 7, 8, 14, 15, 17, 18, 27, 29, 32, 39, 41, 55,
    57
certification, x, xii, 7, 8, 15, 78, 87, 109, 111, 113,
    117, 136, 140, 141, 189, 192, 193, 198
channels, 124
chaos, 81
charitable organizations, 47
Chicago, 65, 67, 71, 72, 73, 74, 75, 77, 88, 100, 103,
    166
chicken, 68, 69, 89, 102, 106
chickens, 68, 69, 102, 103
child labor, 3
childcare, 161
children, 38, 107, 139, 140, 147, 148, 154
China, 88
Chinese, 196
Cincinnati, 170
citizenship, 57, 196
civil rights, 59, 77
Civil War, 83, 84
classification, 113, 128, 135
cleaning, 101, 152, 153, 155

clients, 34, 53
closure, 86
collateral, 90
collective bargaining, ix, 63, 78, 90, 102, 104, 106,
    117, 118, 121, 127, 128, 132, 147
College Station, 67
collusion, 99
commerce, 8, 13, 31, 38, 66
Committee on the Judiciary, 28, 110, 174, 193
commodities, 27, 178
commodity, 32, 37, 56
common carriers, 38
communication, 79, 157
Communist Party, 78
community, 5, 48, 65, 74, 77, 91, 94, 104, 197
community relations, 104
compensation, xiii, 27, 46, 58, 59, 60, 104, 112, 188,
    195
competence, 21
competition, 67, 78, 82, 84, 90, 200
complexity, 101
compliance, 19, 33, 34, 57, 60, 78, 99, 100, 101, 102,
    123, 142
components, 136
composition, 157, 174
Comprehensive Immigration Reform Act, xi, 125,
    145, 146, 148
concentration, 99
conception, 69
conditioning, 56
confidence, 149, 159, 161, 171
confidence interval, 159, 161, 171
conflict, x, 20, 64, 83
confrontation, 84
confusion, 101
Congress, vii, viii, x, xi, xiii, 1, 2, 3, 4, 5, 9, 13, 17,
    21, 26, 28, 31, 32, 33, 37, 40, 41, 43, 44, 45, 46,
    48, 49, 51, 52, 58, 59, 60, 61, 65, 76, 78, 99, 106,
    109, 110, 115, 117, 118, 123, 125, 126, 128, 129,
    131, 132, 133, 137, 139, 141, 145, 146, 148, 160,
    173, 174, 175, 176, 178, 179, 188, 189, 193, 198
Congressional Budget Office (CBO), 148, 154
Congressional Research Service (CRS), ix, 10, 64,
    111, 112, 113, 114, 115, 116, 119, 127, 129, 132,
    134, 140, 146, 147, 149, 151, 153, 154, 157, 158,
    163, 171, 174, 176, 181, 185, 186, 187, 189, 190,
    192, 195, 196, 198
Connecticut, 166, 167
consciousness, 79
consensus, 52, 58, 59, 60
consent, 61
consolidation, 67, 81, 83, 86
Constitution, 39

constraints, 39, 69
construction, 113, 152, 153
consultants, 90
consumers, 98, 176, 180, 192
consumption, 65, 69
contaminants, 102
control, 6, 8, 25, 32, 37, 45, 59, 68, 69, 72, 76, 80,
    82, 83, 84, 97, 136, 190
control condition, 77
corn, 41, 44, 45, 55, 88
corporations, 36
correlation, 10, 94
costs, ix, 5, 8, 20, 22, 55, 56, 63, 67, 68, 69, 84, 90,
    93, 97, 104, 106, 108, 113, 156, 176, 188
cotton, 7, 193
counsel, 22, 37, 77
counseling, 37
country of origin, 96, 196
Court of Appeals, 102
coverage, 24, 25, 31, 34, 41, 45, 46, 47, 48, 51, 58,
    60, 103, 105, 110, 112
covering, 30, 68, 81, 121, 122, 132, 137, 140
credit, 4, 136, 176
crime, 14
criticism, 16, 19, 25, 192
crop production, 178, 180, 181, 184
crops, xii, 15, 30, 35, 36, 39, 41, 55, 56, 173, 175,
    180, 181, 182, 185, 186, 187, 190, 192, 193
cultural differences, ix, 63
culture, 67, 90
current limit, 130

D

daily living, 5
dairy, 130, 177
danger, 78
database, 122, 123, 132, 176, 177
dating, 79
death, 60
deaths, 115, 116, 143
debt, 5, 68, 88, 89
decisions, 22, 157
defects, 51
definition, 7, 8, 16, 29, 42, 45, 46, 49, 52, 96, 130,
    148, 149, 156, 198
Delaware, 98
delivery, 32
demand, xi, 67, 69, 73, 92, 97, 104, 105, 133, 140,
    146, 156, 157, 158, 159, 160, 174, 175, 178, 180,
    183, 184, 185, 187, 190, 191, 192, 197
democracy, 76, 79
Democrat, 43

Democrats, 46, 138
demographic change, xi, 146, 156, 160
demographics, ix, x, 63, 64, 70, 91
Department of Agriculture, 43, 64, 69, 111, 113,
    174, 177, 179, 180, 181, 199
Department of Defense, x, 109
Department of Homeland Security, 99, 111, 115, 175
Department of Justice, 99, 111
depression, 86
derivatives, 140
desire, 8, 40
detection, 126
developed countries, 196
dignity, 105
direct action, 76
directives, 16
disability, 24, 94
discipline, 72
disclosure, 60
discrimination, 77
disenchantment, 29
displacement, 192
dissatisfaction, 50
distribution, 116, 155
District of Columbia, 14
diversity, 74, 77
division, 20, 53
dollar costs, 93
domestic labor, 11, 157, 192, 193
dominance, viii, ix, 63, 64, 66, 71, 98
draft, 26, 33, 73
drinking water, 23
drying, 32
due process, 18
duties, 31, 33, 35, 36, 113

E

earnings, 11, 24, 66, 105, 149, 154, 155, 161, 175,
    176, 185, 186, 187, 200
Eastern Europe, 98
economic boom, 75, 182
economic development, 66, 137
economic incentives, 136
Economic Research Service, 64, 69, 174
economic status, 197
economic theory, 193
education, xi, 4, 5, 17, 30, 32, 40, 43, 44, 46, 50, 51,
    52, 53, 59, 61, 68, 98, 108, 116, 146, 147, 148,
    149, 150, 151, 152, 153, 154, 155, 156, 158, 160,
    162, 163, 164, 165, 166, 167, 168, 169, 170, 171,
educational attainment, 153
egg, 68

elders, 32
election, 51, 78
Emergency Supplemental Appropriations Act, x,
    109, 114, 125
employees, vii, ix, xii, 1, 7, 11, 30, 31, 32, 35, 36,
    37, 42, 43, 45, 46, 47, 48, 49, 51, 53, 55, 64, 85,
    89, 91, 93, 94, 98, 102, 106, 118, 127, 128, 137,
    174, 176, 177, 179, 184, 185, 188
England, 147
English language proficiency, 96
environment, viii, ix, 2, 42, 63, 69, 87, 90, 104
equilibrium, 191
equipment, 56, 66, 101, 102, 106, 156, 157
equity, viii, 2, 53
ETA, 111
Europe, 71, 75
evening, viii, 2, 45
evidence, 7, 10, 41, 57, 128, 133, 134
evolution, viii, x, 2, 64
excess supply, 183
exclusion, 24
excuse, 57, 94
Executive Order, 176
exercise, 44, 105
expenditures, 89, 175
exploitation, 5, 17, 51, 53, 91, 138, 139
Exposure, 64, 68, 69, 86, 92
extraction, 152, 155
eyes, 47

F

failure, 4, 18, 33, 49, 53, 60, 77
Fair Labor Standards Act, ix, 28, 30, 61, 64, 65, 101,
    103, 106, 108
fairness, 53
faith, 55
family, x, 11, 47, 54, 55, 56, 69, 82, 105, 110, 131,
    139, 140, 161, 179, 181
family members, x, 110, 131, 139, 140, 179
Farm Labor Contractor Registration Act (FLCRA),
    vii, viii, 1, 2, 13, 16, 17, 18, 20, 21, 26, 27, 28, 29,
    31, 32, 33, 34, 35, 36, 37, 38, 41, 42, 43, 44, 45,
    46, 47, 48, 49, 50, 51, 52, 53, 54, 61
farmers, xii, 5, 7, 9, 10, 12, 23, 27, 30, 35, 40, 42, 44,
    45, 46, 47, 48, 49, 50, 51, 53, 58, 61, 66, 68, 69,
    106, 173, 174, 176, 177, 179, 181, 184, 185, 189,
    190, 192, 193
farms, 27, 54, 69, 174, 175, 187, 194
fat, 105
fear, 94, 100, 139, 175, 176
feces, 101
federal government, 6, 23, 107

federal law, 58
Federal Register, 16, 17, 34, 41, 199, 200
federalism, 5
feet, 68
females, 92
film, viii, 2
financial resources, 47
financial support, 125
firms, viii, ix, 35, 36, 37, 63, 64, 66, 67, 79, 82, 84,
    85, 89, 90, 91, 93, 96, 103, 181, 185
first aid, 24
fish, 80, 152
fixed costs, 156
flexibility, 91, 105
floating, 11
fluctuations, 69, 105
focusing, viii, 2, 38, 107
food, 3, 45, 80, 84, 85, 88, 152, 153, 190
Ford, 17, 19, 20, 25, 28, 30, 31, 33, 34, 35, 36, 37,
    38, 39, 40, 42, 43, 51, 169
foreign language, 96
formal education, 92, 179
Fort Worth, 77, 166
Fox Administration, 174
fragmentation, 87
fraud, 28, 126, 143, 179
freedom, 44, 79
freezing, 32
frictional unemployment, 158
fringe benefits, 94, 156
fruits, 178, 180
frustration, 60
full employment, xi, 146, 156, 158, 160
funding, 188
funds, 22, 124

G

gambling, 3, 5
GAO, 98, 175, 182, 183
gases, 102
gender, ix, 63, 72, 92
General Accounting Office, 98, 175
generation, 73
Georgia, 70, 177
girls, 90
Globalization, 70
goals, 140
government, xii, 13, 27, 44, 45, 78, 104, 123, 174,
    175, 177, 180, 192
Government Accountability Office, 98, 177
grading, 32
grassroots, 21

Great Depression, 197

groups, 7, 39, 43, 49, 53, 68, 71, 73, 74, 75, 79, 90, 107, 116, 118, 126, 127, 128, 133, 138, 149, 155, 179, 180, 190, 193, 196

growth, 68, 90, 112, 115, 141, 154, 182, 185, 187

growth rate, 141

guest worker, x, xi, xii, 9, 109, 110, 115, 117, 118, 123, 124, 125, 126, 127, 131, 133, 136, 137, 138, 139, 140, 141, 142, 143, 145, 146, 148, 156, 158, 160, 173, 189, 190, 193, 197

guidance, 37

guidelines, 100

H

H-2A program, x, xii, 9, 109, 112, 113, 117, 137, 141, 142, 146, 188, 189, 192, 193

hands, 23, 35, 36

harassment, 46, 50, 51, 53, 100

harm, 190

Harvard, 66, 76, 82

harvesting, 36, 39, 41, 43, 55, 56, 174, 178, 181, 186, 187

Hawaii, 90, 112, 196

hazardous substances, 101

hazards, viii, 2

health, 17, 24, 32, 42, 43, 47, 69, 100, 104, 105, 106, 107, 112, 122

health insurance, 69, 112, 122

high school, 44, 81, 147, 148, 149, 150, 151, 152, 153, 154, 155, 157, 162, 163, 171

hiring, xi, 37, 48, 51, 55, 82, 85, 91, 95, 96, 99, 123, 133, 134, 136, 140, 145, 146, 147, 148, 156, 158, 159

Hispanic(s), xi, 70, 89, 90, 91, 97, 115, 116, 145, 149, 150, 151, 152, 163

Hmong, 69

hog, 83

hogs, 66, 88, 101

homeland security, 136, 142, 177

Honda, 106

host, 36, 196

hostility, 71, 83

House, 3, 4, 5, 6, 7, 8, 9, 10, 11, 12, 13, 17, 18, 19, 20, 21, 22, 24, 25, 26, 27, 28, 30, 31, 32, 33, 34, 35, 36, 37, 38, 39, 40, 41, 43, 44, 45, 46, 47, 50, 52, 53, 54, 59, 60, 61, 72, 80, 117, 118, 125, 138, 146, 176, 177, 178

households, 149, 161, 181

housing, 3, 8, 11, 15, 22, 32, 35, 37, 42, 51, 55, 57, 107, 112, 113, 119, 120, 127, 129, 130, 192

hybrid, 44

I

identification, 14, 27

identity, 82, 124, 137, 177

illegal aliens, 28, 30, 38, 39, 40, 41, 98, 138, 143, 179

imagination, 46

immigrants, ix, 63, 71, 74, 89, 91, 95, 96, 97, 98, 99, 122, 124, 128, 135, 138, 149, 150, 155, 174, 196

immigration, vii, viii, ix, x, xi, xiii, 1, 2, 12, 14, 27, 28, 29, 40, 64, 75, 90, 98, 99, 104, 107, 108, 109, 110, 113, 115, 117, 125, 126, 128, 133, 134, 135, 136, 137, 138, 140, 141, 142, 143, 146, 154, 160, 173, 174, 177, 179, 195, 197

Immigration Act, 126, 133, 140

Immigration and Nationality Act, x, 55, 109, 110, 176, 192, 197

implementation, 17, 33, 43

incentives, 66, 86, 190

incidence, 177

inclusion, 24, 138, 176

income, 44, 69

indication, 58

indicators, 187

industrial relations, 87

industry, viii, ix, x, xi, xii, 5, 6, 33, 34, 40, 45, 53, 59, 60, 63, 64, 66, 67, 68, 69, 71, 72, 73, 74, 75, 76, 79, 81, 82, 83, 86, 87, 88, 89, 90, 91, 92, 93, 95, 96, 97, 98, 99, 100, 101, 102, 103, 104, 105, 106, 107, 108, 113, 140, 147, 173, 174, 178, 179, 180, 182, 183, 188, 189, 193

inequality, 155

infant mortality, 58

infant mortality rate, 58

inflation, 77, 156, 158, 160

initiation, xi, xii, 100, 173, 189

injuries, 9, 58, 59, 105

injury, 59, 60, 94, 104

innocence, 27

INS, 39, 41, 97, 98, 99, 111, 176, 177, 178

insecurity, 20

inspections, 48, 101

inspectors, 21, 24

instability, 93, 184

institutions, 47, 161

insurance, 7, 8, 14, 15, 16, 20, 24, 38, 41, 42, 46, 56, 57, 94, 112

integration, 69, 70, 147, 177

intentions, 46

Internal Revenue Service, 177

international migration, 153

internet, 188

Internet, 122

interpretation, 16, 17, 36, 37, 48, 49, 50, 101, 103
interval, 161, 171
intervention, 5
investment, xi, 22, 105, 124, 146, 156, 157, 160

J

job matching, 188
job training, 161
jobs, xi, xii, 10, 28, 30, 69, 71, 73, 75, 85, 86, 87, 89,
    90, 94, 96, 97, 98, 102, 105, 117, 118, 127, 128,
    135, 137, 141, 145, 146, 148, 153, 154, 155, 156,
    158, 160, 173, 177, 179, 183, 184, 188, 189, 190,
    192, 193, 200
judiciary, 136
Judiciary, 117, 118, 125, 126, 133, 136, 176, 177,
    183
Judiciary Committee, 117, 118, 125, 126, 133, 136
jurisdiction, 23, 32, 50, 57, 59
justification, 6, 14

K

killing, 103

L

labor force, xii, 71, 73, 74, 96, 105, 116, 149, 150,
    151, 152, 153, 154, 155, 158, 159, 160, 161, 162,
    163, 171, 173, 174, 175, 177, 178, 179, 180, 188,
    191, 192, 193
labor markets, 90, 158, 198
labor relations, 94
labour, 74, 96
land, 66, 69
language, xi, 20, 21, 28, 29, 35, 36, 40, 42, 51, 55,
    56, 58, 96, 124, 125, 145, 148, 159, 179
Latin America, 96
Latinos, 94, 105, 107
law enforcement, 137, 188
laws, 5, 12, 14, 17, 19, 21, 23, 24, 26, 27, 28, 33, 40,
    46, 60, 69, 99, 100, 101, 121, 122, 132, 133, 136,
    178, 190
lawyers, 39, 41, 43, 108
layoffs, 105
leadership, 6, 21, 30, 74, 76, 78, 80, 81, 84
learning, 93
legal protection, 188
legislation, vii, viii, ix, xi, xiii, 1, 2, 3, 4, 6, 8, 9, 12,
    13, 16, 18, 21, 22, 25, 26, 33, 41, 42, 43, 45, 46,
    47, 49, 50, 51, 53, 59, 60, 61, 64, 77, 117, 137,
    141, 145, 146, 178, 184, 189

legislative proposals, 141
LIFE, 139
limitation, 113, 122, 124
literacy, 12
literature, 64, 67, 83, 91, 196
litigation, ix, x, 33, 35, 38, 53, 64, 100, 102, 106, 108
livestock, 56, 67, 103, 175, 181, 182, 183, 184, 185,
    199
living conditions, 58, 188
local community, 85
local government, 5, 67
local labor markets, 156, 158, 160, 193
location, 9, 35, 70, 107, 158
logging, 113
long distance, 107
Los Angeles, 74, 107, 138, 169, 196
Louisiana, 112

M

machinery, 22, 56
males, xi, 70, 92, 145, 149
management, vii, ix, x, xii, xiii, 1, 3, 11, 22, 23, 37,
    40, 48, 63, 64, 67, 70, 71, 72, 73, 75, 77, 78, 82,
    83, 84, 85, 86, 87, 90, 93, 98, 99, 100, 102, 104,
    106, 108, 161, 173, 180, 187, 195, 197
management practices, ix, xii, 64, 173, 180, 187
mandates, 13
manpower, 19, 25, 73
manufacturing, 153
market(s), ix, x, xii, 6, 37, 63, 65, 66, 67, 68, 69, 70,
    79, 80, 87, 88, 92, 93, 110, 140, 141, 146, 148,
    154, 156, 158, 159, 160, 161, 174, 180, 182, 190,
    191, 193
market share, 67
marketing, 69
Marshall Islands, 96
Maryland, 102
meals, 37, 91
meanings, 37, 49
measures, x, 12, 109, 187
meat, viii, ix, x, 63, 64, 65, 66, 67, 69, 73, 74, 76, 80,
    81, 86, 87, 88, 89, 90, 92, 93, 95, 97, 103, 105,
    106, 107, 108, 130, 139, 152
media, 34, 110, 152, 155
median, 149, 154
Medicaid, 112, 148
medical care, 94
medication, 68
membership, 73, 78, 79, 80
men, xi, 3, 11, 20, 23, 72, 76, 78, 145, 149, 160
Mexican Americans, 94, 197

Mexico, xi, 11, 27, 40, 74, 89, 93, 94, 96, 97, 98,
    110, 115, 117, 138, 143, 173, 196, 197, 200
Miami, 170
Migrant and Seasonal Agricultural Workers'
    Protection Act (MSPA), vii, viii, 1, 2, 54, 55, 57,
    58, 59, 60, 61, 100, 101, 107
migrants, 2, 3, 9, 11, 32, 45, 115, 116
migration, viii, ix, x, 63, 64, 66, 67, 73, 109, 110,
    138, 179, 197
military, 197
milk, 181, 185
minimum wage, 24, 101, 102, 111, 119, 120, 123,
    129, 130, 137, 188, 192, 198
mining, 106
Minnesota, 75, 84
minorities, 54, 77, 90, 105
minority, xi, 53, 81, 98, 145, 149, 160
Missouri, 85, 89
mobility, 5
momentum, 53, 110
money, 3, 11, 22, 24, 26, 44, 142
morale, 106
morning, 39
mothers, 93
motion, 16, 147
motivation, 69
movement, ix, x, 6, 63, 64, 72, 73, 75, 76, 77, 79, 81,
    90, 104, 107, 197, 198
muscle strain, 105

N

NAFTA, 87, 138
narcotics, 5
nation, viii, xii, 2, 13, 73, 88, 161, 174, 182, 189, 190
National Labor Relations Act, ix, 23, 64, 65, 102,
    106, 108
nationality, 12, 14, 27, 74, 90
Native Americans, 47
Nebraska, 42, 70, 73, 87, 91, 93, 94, 96, 98, 99
negotiating, 72
network, 75, 179
New England, 147
New Jersey, 9, 24, 169
New Mexico, 197
New Orleans, 166
New York, 64, 65, 70, 71, 75, 77, 78, 80, 81, 84, 90,
    98, 99, 138, 169, 196, 197
non-citizens, 177
nonenforcement, 18
nonwhite, xi, 145, 150
North America, 6, 11, 68, 71
North Carolina, 39, 46, 70, 71, 88, 170, 193

nursing, 161
nursing home, 161

O

obligation, 30, 94
Occupational Safety and Health Act, ix, 64
Office of Management and Budget, 147
Oklahoma, 88, 169
OMB, 147, 160
operator, 2, 11, 13, 26
organization(s), viii, ix, 2, 7, 13, 47, 49, 53, 54, 63,
    71, 72, 75, 76, 77, 78, 79, 82, 86, 91, 98, 136,
    176, 197
orientation, 92
oversight, 61
overtime, 101, 102, 103, 105, 106, 161
ownership, 32, 36, 57

P

Pacific, 30
packaging, 32, 152
Panama, 169, 196
parents, 30
partnerships, 36
payroll, 4, 20, 156
penalties, xii, 18, 28, 29, 40, 49, 102, 107, 123, 126,
    142, 173, 176, 177, 179
perception, 74, 108, 175
perceptions, vii, 1
performance, 142
permit, 8, 136
personal, 9, 14, 21, 45, 79, 91, 161
pesticides, 24
plants, ix, 45, 63, 65, 66, 67, 69, 70, 73, 74, 75, 78,
    82, 83, 84, 85, 86, 87, 89, 90, 92, 98, 99, 100,
    101, 103, 105
policy makers, 106
policymakers, 139
poor, 59
population, x, xii, 91, 96, 110, 115, 116, 141, 142,
    143, 147, 148, 153, 161, 184, 189, 197
pork, 86, 87, 88
port of entry, 41
portability, 105
poultry, viii, ix, x, 41, 43, 55, 56, 63, 64, 67, 68, 69,
    80, 88, 89, 90, 91, 93, 95, 96, 100, 101, 102, 103,
    104, 105, 106, 107, 108, 152, 181, 185
poverty, 42
power, 6, 25, 69, 80, 86, 104, 106, 179
preference, 140

premiums, 60
president, 22, 69, 71, 77, 79, 81, 87, 97
President Bush, 135, 136, 137, 138, 174
pressure, 78, 82, 103, 104
prevention, 99, 126
prices, 44, 158, 180, 190, 192
prisoners, 105
private education, 13, 47
private sector, xii, 174, 185, 186
producers, 174, 175, 179
product market, xii, 189, 194
production, ix, 45, 57, 63, 64, 68, 82, 84, 85, 86, 87,
    88, 89, 91, 96, 102, 103, 106, 107, 152, 153, 155,
    156, 157, 158, 159, 181, 182, 183, 184, 186, 187,
    193, 194, 196
production quota, 103
productivity, 103, 188, 190
profit, 3, 37, 47, 69, 89, 105, 136
profit margin, 105
profitability, 66, 83, 85, 92, 94, 104
profiteering, 3
profits, 103
program, viii, x, xi, xii, 2, 9, 10, 11, 21, 39, 52, 57,
    77, 87, 92, 106, 109, 110, 111, 112, 113, 117,
    118, 119, 120, 121, 122, 123, 124, 125, 126, 127,
    128, 129, 130, 131, 132, 134, 135, 136, 137, 138,
    139, 140, 141, 142, 143, 145, 146, 148, 153, 154,
    156, 157, 158, 159, 160, 173, 174, 176, 178, 179,
    187, 188, 189, 190, 192, 193, 194, 197, 198
promote, 76, 188
propaganda, viii, 2
prosperity, 99
public education, 30
public policy, x, 32, 57, 59, 64, 89, 108, 196
public service, 19
Puerto Rico, 14

Q

qualifications, 198
quality control, 69
query, 180

R

race, 72, 73, 91, 149
radio, 19
radius, 32, 45, 46, 55
rain, 24
range, 26, 87, 93, 108, 161, 181, 185
reality, 97
reasoning, x, 110, 117

recall, 21, 28, 35
recession, 182
recognition, 13, 188
recreation, 37
recruiting, 3, 6, 11, 27, 29, 32, 35, 37, 96, 99
reduction, 86
reforms, 104
refugees, 90
regional, 19, 67, 141, 199
regional unemployment, 141
regulation, viii, 2, 5, 8, 21, 41, 42, 51, 57, 73
regulations, 5, 6, 9, 13, 14, 15, 16, 17, 18, 33, 34, 37,
    39, 40, 41, 44, 49, 57, 113, 120, 121, 122, 128,
    130, 132, 198
relationship(s), vii, ix, x, 1, 17, 35, 36, 60, 63, 64, 67,
    69, 80, 84, 93, 99, 106, 107, 108, 138, 186
relative prices, 157
religion, 90
repair, 152, 155
reputation, 84
resistance, 97
resolution, 17, 51
resource management, 105
resources, 25, 47, 48, 91, 107, 178
restructuring, 17, 48, 55, 67, 79, 83, 85, 86, 88, 89,
    105
retail, 65, 67, 70, 71, 73, 76, 80, 180
retention, 93, 96, 105
retirement, 69, 100, 136
retribution, 73
rhetoric, 78
risk, xii, 173, 175, 179
rural areas, 66, 90, 93, 107
rural communities, ix, 64, 96
rural population, 68

S

safety, 32, 42, 47, 56, 100, 101, 102, 104, 107
sales, 5, 36, 80, 87
sample, 161, 164, 169, 170, 180, 187
sampling error, 161
sanctions, xi, 173, 176, 178
SAS, xii, 173, 178, 179, 187
savings, 89, 106, 136
savings account, 136
scarcity, 96
scattering, 74
school, 30, 150, 152, 154, 155, 162, 163, 197
science, 147, 153, 155
seafood, 91, 107
search, 44, 74, 103, 117, 177
seasonal variations, 186, 187

seasonality, 182, 184

second generation, 74

Secretary of Homeland Security, 123, 124, 132, 147

security, x, 4, 30, 97, 110, 136, 142

seed, 44, 45, 56

self-employed, 65, 161, 181

senate, 136

Senate, x, xi, 3, 4, 5, 6, 7, 8, 9, 10, 12, 13, 17, 18, 19, 20, 21, 22, 23, 24, 25, 26, 27, 28, 29, 30, 31, 43, 44, 48, 50, 53, 54, 61, 109, 110, 117, 118, 125, 126, 127, 133, 136, 137, 138, 145, 146, 148, 160, 174, 176, 177, 183, 193

September 11, 110, 142, 174, 177

series, 5, 16, 35, 37, 41, 51, 73, 153, 180

service provider, 181, 183, 184, 185, 186

settlements, 108

shape, 23, 192

sharing, 3

sheep, 42, 43, 55, 66, 101

shellfish, 64

short run, 157

shortage, xii, 98, 140, 173, 174, 175, 179, 180, 182, 183, 184, 187

shrimp, 85

sign, 27

signs, 17, 94, 182

similarity, 42

single market, 68

sites, 86, 177

skills, xi, 66, 69, 71, 92, 93, 95, 96, 97, 146, 156, 157, 158, 159, 160

skin, 102

social integration, 147

social justice, 77

social security, 4, 17, 24, 40, 176

Social Security, 20, 22, 24, 124, 133, 175, 176, 177, 190

social services, 153, 155

society, 4, 95, 196

sole proprietor, 36

solidarity, 72, 76, 77

South Carolina, 105

South Dakota, 86

Southeast Asia, 70, 89, 91, 93, 96

spectrum, 78, 79, 98

speculation, 34

speed, 72, 103, 104

spelling, vii, 1

spin, 83

sports, 152, 155

St. Louis, 166

St. Petersburg, 169

stability, 91, 96, 105, 175

stages, 22, 87

standards, vii, ix, 1, 16, 17, 32, 42, 48, 54, 56, 64, 82, 84, 103, 104, 106, 107, 196

State of the Union address, 135

statistics, 180, 181

statute of limitations, 60

statutes, vii, viii, ix, 1, 2, 64, 101, 106, 108

steel, 74, 101

stock, viii, 36, 63, 66, 72, 156, 157, 179

storage, 32

strain, 104

strategies, 67, 96, 107

strength, 73, 75, 81, 82, 87, 91, 105

stress, 103, 105

strikes, 47, 70, 71, 73, 81, 82, 87

stroke, 72

structural unemployment, 158

structuring, 66

students, 30, 32, 44, 55, 105

substitutes, 154

substitution, 157

substitution effect, 157

sugar, 7, 11

summer, 44, 45, 60, 68, 69, 86, 91, 92, 94, 100

supervision, 30, 49

supervisors, 40, 100, 103, 106, 157, 181, 183, 187

supply, viii, ix, xi, xii, 2, 3, 6, 57, 63, 66, 69, 70, 71, 89, 91, 95, 98, 99, 105, 145, 146, 149, 155, 156, 157, 158, 159, 160, 173, 174, 175, 178, 180, 182, 184, 185, 187, 188, 189, 190, 191, 192, 193, 194, 196

supply curve, 191, 192

Supreme Court, 58

surplus, 11, 183

survival, 94, 103

sweat, 100

systems, 136, 188

T

tactics, 53

targets, 107

teachers, 30

technological change, xi, 146, 160

technology, 79, 91, 156, 157

telephone, 124

television, viii, 2, 37, 147

temporary jobs, 193

Tennessee, 77

tension, x, 64

territory, 7, 125

terrorist attack, 110, 142, 174

Texas, 26, 35, 38, 40, 42, 53, 67, 75, 87, 96, 159, 160, 193, 197
Thailand, 95
The Homeland Security Act, 99, 111
theory, 3, 98, 185, 191
thinking, 35
threat, xiii, 8, 11, 32, 86, 195
threats, 142
tobacco, 193
trade, ix, x, xi, 63, 64, 70, 72, 76, 77, 78, 79, 90, 91, 94, 96, 98, 104, 146, 156, 157, 160, 200
trade union, ix, x, 63, 64, 70, 72, 77, 78, 79, 90, 91, 94, 96, 104, 200
tradition, viii, 63, 76, 83, 196
traffic, 82
training, vii, xi, 1, 71, 93, 100, 105, 106, 146, 152, 155, 156, 158, 160, 197
transactions, 15
transformation, 67
transition, 68, 79
transport, 7, 8, 9, 37, 38, 46, 57, 102
transportation, 3, 4, 10, 15, 22, 24, 25, 27, 35, 40, 42, 46, 51, 55, 56, 107, 112, 113, 157
trauma, 104
trend, xii, 98, 174, 180, 182, 184, 194
turnover, ix, 7, 64, 70, 79, 86, 89, 92, 93, 94, 95, 99, 103, 104, 105, 106, 107, 154, 175

U

unemployment, xi, xii, 30, 98, 99, 141, 145, 146, 147, 148, 149, 158, 159, 160, 161, 162, 171, 174, 175, 180, 182
unemployment rate, xi, xii, 141, 145, 146, 147, 148, 149, 159, 160, 161, 162, 171, 174, 182
uniform, 11, 34, 107
unionism, 75, 76, 77, 79, 80
unions, ix, 63, 64, 71, 73, 75, 76, 77, 78, 79, 80, 81, 82, 91, 95, 104, 108
upward mobility, 106
urban centers, viii, ix, 63, 64
USDA, 200
users, 33, 174

V

vacancies, 154, 155, 156
vacuum, 67, 80
validity, 104
values, 161
variability, 184
variable, 156, 157, 180

variable factor, 156
variables, 194
variation, 55, 182, 184
vegetables, 23, 178, 180
vehicles, 14, 57
Vermont, 177
Vietnam, 95
violence, 72, 78, 107
Virginia, 4, 6, 8, 42, 44, 170, 193
visa program, x, 109
visas, x, 109, 111, 112, 114, 115, 121, 122, 123, 124, 125, 128, 131, 132, 133, 139, 142, 146, 147, 148, 154, 159
vision, 90
voice, 12, 13, 29, 30, 31, 32, 54
voting, 12, 100

W

wage level, 97
wage rate, xiii, 3, 8, 10, 11, 15, 55, 56, 77, 82, 83, 97, 111, 113, 118, 119, 120, 121, 122, 127, 128, 129, 130, 132, 137, 191, 192, 193, 195, 196, 198, 199, 200
wages, x, xi, xii, xiii, 10, 11, 22, 23, 28, 30, 66, 67, 70, 77, 81, 82, 83, 85, 86, 87, 89, 90, 91, 92, 93, 95, 96, 97, 98, 100, 105, 109, 111, 112, 113, 118, 119, 120, 121, 122, 123, 124, 125, 127, 128, 129, 130, 131, 136, 137, 140, 145, 146, 147, 150, 154, 155, 156, 157, 158, 160, 173, 175, 179, 180, 181, 183, 185, 186, 187, 188, 189, 190, 191, 192, 193, 194, 195, 196, 198, 199, 200
Wall Street Journal, 69, 89
war, 73, 77, 78, 110, 197
War on Terror, 114, 125
war years, 73, 78
weakness, 72
wear, 27, 101
welfare, 17
wheat, 42
White House, 44, 135
wine, 23
winter, 73, 79, 92, 94, 193
Wisconsin, 19, 26, 169
witnesses, 11, 19, 34, 37, 53, 57
women, 23, 66, 76, 105, 107
work environment, 67
work ethic, 97
working conditions, x, xii, xiii, 8, 10, 11, 28, 70, 77, 87, 95, 96, 100, 108, 109, 111, 113, 118, 119, 120, 123, 124, 125, 127, 128, 129, 130, 140, 147, 173, 179, 188, 189, 190, 195, 198, 200
working hours, 43

working women, 91
workplace, 70, 74, 93, 97, 100, 104, 105, 136
World War, viii, ix, 63, 64, 74, 76, 77, 81, 88, 89, 95,
    110, 174, 197
writing, 9, 56, 68, 99, 103, 104

Y

yield, 175